Village Politics and the Mafia in Sicily

Village Politics and the Mafia in Sicily

Filippo Sabetti

McGill-Queen's University Press
Montreal & Kingston · London · Ithaca

© McGill-Queen's University Press 2002
ISBN 0-7735-2475-4
Legal deposit fourth quarter 2002
Bibliothèque nationale du Québec

First published in 1984 by Rutgers, the State University,
under the title *Political Authority in a Sicilian Village*.
Reprinted in paperback, with a new introduction, in 2002.

Printed in Canada on acid-free paper.

McGill-Queen's University Press acknowledges the support of the Canada
Council for the Arts for our publishing program. We also acknowledge the
financial support of the Government of Canada through the Book Publishing
Industry Development Program (BPIDP) for our publishing activities.

National Library of Canada Cataloguing in Publication

Sabetti, Filippo
Village politics and the Mafia in Sicily/Filippo. – 2nd ed.

First ed. published New Brunswick, N.J.: Rutgers University Press, 1984
under title: Political authority in a Sicilian village.

Includes bibliographical references and index.

ISBN 0-7735-2475-4

1. Local government – Italy – Sicily. 2. Political participation – Italy – Sicily.
3. Mafia – Italy – Sicily. 4. Power (Social sciences) 5. Sicily (Italy) –
Social conditions. I. Title.

JS5796.S55S22 2003   320.8'0945'8   C2002-904525-8

For Judy

Contents

Preface to the Second Edition

This new edition of work originally published in 1984 under the title *Political Authority in a Sicilian Village* makes it available to the public once again. While much has changed in Sicily, as in the rest of Italy, in the past twenty years, I hope this introduction will make clear how I came to study what I did, anticipate some of my principal findings, and, by incorporating research done since the book was first published, show that it still has something to offer today.

The narrative is presented as a form of what can be called contextual explanation. It may be worth emphasizing that to explain why some particular condition or phenomenon exists is not, and should not be taken as, another way of justifying its existence. Even revolutionaries who want to change the world for the better need to understand the status quo. By exploring the question of whether the structure of basic social institutions has been the primary instrument for advancing human welfare or an essential source of human adversity, the book helped refocus studies of village politics, the mafia, and Sicily.

As I read over the text, I realized that the description of the village as it stood in 1978, sketched in chapters 2 and 9 (at 207–8, and 217–19), needed some updating. Also, I should have clearly stated that the description of the local mafia leader as a "profitable altruist" (96) came not from a mafia sympathizer but from a peasant turned merchant who was opposed to the mafia and had fought it as a young land worker. I do, however, explain how that villager, like most other villagers, came to see that an evil phenomenon may have, in some cases, positive aspects.

In further preparation for this edition, I returned to Sicily in March 2002[1] and revisited the village where I had done fieldwork over the course of the 1970s. I was saddened to learn that most of the people who had cooperated with me or instructed me in their ways had died.

1. Thanks to a related project funded by the Social Sciences and Humanities Research Council of Canada (# 410-01-0624), which I wish to acknowledge.

In my visit to the cemetery I recalled their faces and voices from the pictures on family tombs and in the community mausoleum. Villagers I had first met as young people were now middle-aged artisans, farmers, and professionals. Some had chosen to remain in the village; others had moved to neighboring towns or to provincial and regional capitals. (I managed to see some of the latter in their new surroundings.) Still others moved back and forth between the village and the outside world. A boy who had been described to me by his peasant father as "a rambunctious teenager" has now become a respected member of the community and something of a celebrity as a self-taught sculptor, with an established record of expositions and workshops in Sicily and as far away as South Korea. The local girl (described on p. 20) from a family with strong American roots, who attended an American university and married someone from Egypt in the summer of 1977, returned to the village with her family, after several years abroad, to run a general store. Her Egyptian husband has dabbled in local politics, serving a four-year term as an elected official and presiding over the communal council. She is seriously thinking of setting up a bed-and-breakfast, since the village still lacks an inn.

As news spread that I had arrived in the village, ten people rushed home to get their copies of the Italian edition of the book[2] to have it autographed. One villager had taken the trouble to draw up a list of the people discussed in the book, matching actual names with the pseudonyms I had used; his guesses turned out to be correct. Most of the villagers are not "bookish," but the few who are enjoy combing newspapers and books for inaccuracies about local events and people. They were, however, either too polite or too kind to disclose whatever errors of fact they may have found in my book. Now that they were finally convinced that I was not some kind of spy, the men and women I met in and around the village were most anxious to bring me up to date on people and events. A three-time mayor graciously put at my disposal his files of newspaper clippings and communal deliberations about local events between 1976 and 2000. In the first edition, to protect the anonymity of the people discussed, I had given the town of Villalba the pseudonym of Camporano. Most local people, however, no longer see

---

2. Filippo Sabetti, *Politica e Potere in un Comune Siciliano* ed. Saverio DiBella (Cosenza: Pellegrini Editore, 1993).

any reason for me to disguise the real name of their town and they all urged me to reveal it in this edition.

Villalba is notorious for having at one point been a capital of the mafia. In 1954 even The *New York Times* printed news of the death of the local mafia chief, Calogero Vizzini, widely known as "Don Calò."[3] But "Don Calò" is not the only villager known to the outside world: two other villalbesi well-known outside the town have fought the mafia and written about Villalba's contentious events. They are Luigi Lumia and Michele Pantaleone. Though I could not reveal their identity originally, their points of view were taken into account in the narrative; both, in fact, speak out on many subjects, especially in chapters 8 and 9. I met with each of them several times in Villalba and Palermo. I remain especially grateful to Michele Pantaleone for his help in finding lodging for me in 1971–72, when I first stayed in the village, and for allowing his most trusted and closest aide to instruct me about the ways of the town and its people for at least two hours almost every day for about a year. Of course, I could not automatically accept what I heard as truth, even from such gracious sources. One problem was that Lumia and Pantaleone had a history of disagreements, to the point that judicial authorities were required to settle their disputes. One such disagreement was finally settled (in Lumia's favor) as late as 2002. I was compelled to treat their accounts, including interviews and conversations, as I treated all other primary evidence—as in need of confirmation.[4] The

---

3. *The New York Times*, "Mafia Leader C. Vizzini Dies," July 13, 1954, sect.1, 2. He died on July 11.

4. Pantaleone was the local Socialist leader; Lumia belonged to the Communist party (PCI). Over time Lumia occupied different positions of leadership in the PCI and in 1978 was mayor of Villalba. I generally found Lumia's accounts more reliable than Pantaleone's and this also applies to Lumia's two-volume history entitled *Villalba: Storia e Memoria*. (Caltanissetta: Edizioni Lussografica, 1990). As a villager, Lumia has an incomparable grasp of local history as well as access to people, papers, and the PCI archives that no outside researcher can match. But his accounts and interpretations are more political than scholarly, so need sifting. One example should suffice: Lumia is perhaps the only (former) Communist analyst to recognize publicly that the collapse of the regional association of Left cooperatives (USCA) by 1949 was due to corrupt practices internal to USCA itself. Despite this, he cannot resist insinuating that somehow such practices may have been due to the mafia: see Lumia, *Villalba*, 2:484. There is no evidence of mafia involvement in the internal affairs of the Communist-run USCA in 1949; I report what I found on 172.

purpose of my work was, after all, to trace and explain local developments in which Lumia and Pantaleone, and members of their families, had been central protagonists, often acting as estate managers, rentiers, private guards (*campieri*), and professional people as well as politicians, mafiosi, and antimafia fighters. I discuss the procedures used to weigh all the evidence collected, theirs included, in chapter 1 and in the note at the end of the book.

My interest in Sicily was originally stimulated by a concern with theories of collective action and inaction and the reading of Dolci. When I began working on the topic in 1970, there was an overwhelmingly dominant paradigm in the approach to the study of Sicily and Southern Italy—an approach that is still predominant in some quarters. According to this reading, attempts to create a united Italy had been unsuccessful because the middle class had failed in its mission to usher in an effective system of centralized government and administration *à la* both Max Weber and democratic (i.e. Jacobin or Socialist) reforms. It is this interpretation that is behind Gramsci's description of the South as "a general social disintegration"—a view accepted by subsequent Gramscian and non-Gramscian analysts. The Gramscian understanding is given additional refinements for Sicily, culminating in the generalization, deemed to be self-evident, that the rise and presence of mafia groups were the result of arrangements, usually made by landlords and estate managers, to manipulate peasant labor. From this vantage point, it becomes easier to project the themes of ungovernability, backwardness, and violence—grouped together as "the Sicilian problem"—back in time and portray them as almost immemorial features of Sicilian history. The Sicilian problem thus becomes the history of Sicily itself.[5]

My own view of the grave inadequacies of the dominant paradigm, and of the characterization of the Sicilian problem itself, was greatly influenced by two factors. The first was the work of an American political scientist, Vincent Ostrom, whose unparalleled inquiry into the study and practice of the American compound republic and public administration, and, more generally, the foundations of self-governing societies and theories of constitutional choice opened new theoretical

---

5. Subsequent to the publication of this work, I have explored different dimensions of these issues at greater depth in, among others, *The Search for Good Government: Understanding the Paradox of Italian Democracy* (Montreal: McGill-Queen's University Press, 2000), esp. chapters 2, 3, 8, and 9.

vistas and challenged me to extend them to the study of comparative politics. Second, public choice theory led me to appreciate anew the nineteenth-century Italian school of public finance and to discover the intellectually invigorating work on constitutional political economy of the great Sicilian political economist Francesco Ferrara (1810–1900).[6] Second, as someone originally trained in both history and political science, I was uneasy with the huge generalizations that characterized the dominant approach in social science to the cut-and-thrust of history itself, as well as the lack of attention to ongoing contests of ideas and movements as people sought to influence one another. I set out to confront the historical puzzle of what went wrong with Sicilian development by refocusing the way in which we in social science have looked at its history, doing so with a tool kit fashioned in the American Midwest and amplified with elements of the Sicilian intellectual tradition[7]—without, however, the Sicilian sensitivity about speaking badly of Sicily.

As noted earlier, my inquiry was driven by the attempt to determine whether the structure of basic institutions has been the primary instrument for advancing human welfare or the essential source of human adversity among Sicilian villagers. The reasons for examining the Sicilian problem within the microcosm of a single Sicilian community are made clear in chapter 1 (esp. 13–15). I hoped that, although the book deals with a single village, the argument could be applied to other villages in and beyond Sicily—and even wherever there are communities of people struggling to realize their self-governing capabilities. If the issues explored here were specific *only* to the Sicilian problem, this study would be of only marginal interest to such important topics as collective-action dilemmas in constitutional political economy, the provision and production of goods and services in the public sector, the sustainability of rural infrastructures, and, more generally, the problem-solving potential of individuals in an interdependent situation. But they are not: the

---

6. In addition to 226–7, 231, and 237 in the present work, I have dealt more specifically with his ideas in "Un precursore siciliano di 'Public Choice'? Francesco Ferrara e lo sviluppo delle scienze sociali in Nord America," *Francesco Ferrara e il suo tempo*, ed.Piero Barucci and Massimo Ganci (Rome: Editrice Bancaria, 1990), 259–74, and *The Search for Good Government*, esp. chap. 2.
7. A recent compendium of some aspects of this tradition can be found in *Federalisti siciliani* ed. Assemblea regionale siciliana. Quaderno no.3 (Palermo: Renna, 2000).

problematics explored here lie at the very core of comparative politics. In fact, since the book first appeared a rich literature has become available that suggests that what I set out to explore was neither outlandish nor misplaced and that we can think more theoretically and comparatively about the topic. Hence the results of my research, revolutionary and extremely upsetting for some when the book was first published, now find greater support and have contributed to ongoing inquiries in several fields of study, such as the political economy of crime and punishment in Sicily and as far away as Russia and Japan; the challenge of understanding modernity as "seeing like a State" or "seeing like citizens"; the dynamics of contentious politics; the conditions under which citizens give, refuse, and withdraw their consent to government; and investigation of what makes government ineffective and leads people to work outside the law.[8] The history of Sicily constitutes a rich laboratory for examining different political experiments and exploring several theoretical puzzles in the social sciences.

I set out to trace approximately two hundred years of political-economic experience concerned with the development of structures to sustain village life—that is, both before and after the so-called abolition of feudalism in 1812. Initially I had only an intuitive sense of what

---

8. Diego Gambetta, *The Sicilian Mafia: The Business of Private Protection* Cambridge: Harvard University Press, 1993); Federico Varese, "Is Sicily the Future of Russia? Private Protection and the Rise of the Russian Mafia." *Archives of European Sociology* 35 (1994): 224–58, and his most recent study, *The Russian Mafia: Private Protection in a New Market Economy* (Oxford: Oxford University Press, 2001); Oriana Bandiera, "Land Reform, the Market for Protection and the Origins of the Sicilian Mafia: Theory and Evidence." London School of Economics and CEPR paper, 8 April 2002; Curtis Milhaupt and Mark West, "The Dark Side of Private Ordering: An Institutional and Empirical Analysis of Organized Crime," *University of Chicago Law Review* 67 (2000): 41–99; James C. Scott, *Seeing like a State: How Certain Schemes to Improve the Human Condition Have Failed* (New Haven: Yale University Press,1998); Vincent Ostrom, "The Challenge of Modernity: Seeing like Citizens," *The Good Society* 10, no.2 (2001): 40–1; Doug McAdam, Sidney Tarrow, Charles Tilly, *Dynamics of Contention* (New York: Cambridge University Press, 2001); Margaret Levi, *Consent, Dissent and Patriotism* (New York: Cambridge University Press, 1997); Frank Anechiarico and James B. Jacobs, *The Pursuit of Absolute Integrity: How Corruption Control Makes Government Ineffective* (Chicago: University of Chicago Press, 1996); Hernando de Soto, *The Other Path: The Invisible Revolution in the Third World* (New York: Harper and Row, 1989).

Stephan R. Epstein, an economic historian, has more recently set on solid empirical foundations: "despite the use of seemingly 'archaic' tools [oxen and scratch ploughs], both yield ratios and production per hectare in Sicily up to the eighteenth century were equivalent to, or higher than, that in most advanced northern European countries (England, Flanders, the Netherlands), and substantially better than in northern Italy or the Baltic regions."[9] In other words, feudalism and capitalism (and markets) coexisted with varying degrees of success in Sicilian development before the eighteenth century. Moreover, the North European model of agricultural work is not in itself an indicator of progress: had it actually been adopted in Sicily, it would have caused an economic disaster. Epstein warns us not to project failings in Sicilian agriculture during the eighteenth-century onto previous centuries.[10]

For reasons explained in chapter 1, I do not have robust data to permit a careful "before-after" evaluative study of the impact of the 1812–16 changes in the structure of property rights and governmental arrangements on Villalba. My evidence about the community before 1812 is impressionistic. This problem, in my view, does not weaken the discussion in chapter 4 of the Caracciolo reform in the 1780s, which occurred just about the time Villalba was being settled. Nor does it weaken my unpacking of the meaning of the abolition of feudalism and the accompanying constitutional reforms of 1812 and 1816. I clarify what went wrong in the eighteenth century, show why Caracciolo's attempt to get rid of existing Sicilian political institutions and start over met with stiff opposition from the very people he thought needed to be delivered from bondage, and explain why by the time Tocqueville visited the island in 1827 evocation of the word Sicily already conjured up the picture of an island and a people plagued by governmental failures and general social disintegration.

I found that the chief problem for Sicily was not the "Anglo-Sicilian" constitution of 1812 but rather its suppression and the extension of absolutist rule in 1816. In chapter 4 I describe why "the creation of a legal-rational order *à la* Weber in 1816 represents a breakdown and *not* the beginning of modernization in Sicily" (224). I argue that this is not

---

9. Stephan R. Epstein, *An Island for Itself: Economic Development and Social Change in Late Medieval Sicily* (Cambridge: Cambridge University Press, 1992), 164.
10. Ibid., 163.

because the legal-rational order *à la* Weber was imposed from the outside (a *fuorviante* or misleading issue), but because

> rather than facilitat[ing] individual and collective efforts on behalf of common interests shared by islanders, [centralized government and administration] created an antithesis of interests between rulers and ruled, and between landowners and landless. The antithesis evolved into successive revolts, culminating in the very collapse of the Kingdom of Two Sicilies and the creation of the Kingdom of Italy in 1860–61. But the iron law of oligarchy inherent in the forced creation of unity through centralized government and administration remained, just as the proprietary claims of great landowners continued to be determinants of the human condition in the countryside. (224)

I am not suggesting that the creators of Italian unification deliberately set out to victimize people. Instead, I suggest that Italian leaders assumed or took for granted that reconstruction of agricultural and communal activities, undertaken as part of their state making—what in other contexts James C. Scott has more recently characterized as "seeing and thinking like a State"[11]—would have primarily beneficial effects. I set out to explore the relationship between expectations and results and what ordinary citizens—mostly peasants in this case—can do to cope with the exigencies of life under such circumstances.

Recent historical works by Lucy Riall[12] and James Fentress[13] do not use the theoretical distinctions or language of social scientists but in their own fashion they address critical issues raised by my work and related inquiries. Riall and Fentress find it useful to go back to the problem of governability under the post-1816 Bourbons. They emphasize the challenges that centralized government and administration faced before and after 1860 with respect to public order and local-central government relations and correctly suggest that many of the difficulties in government performance can be attributed to institutional problems,

---

11. James C. Scott, *Seeing like a State.*
12. Lucy Riall, *Sicily and the Unification of Italy: Liberal Policy and Local Power 1859–1866.* Oxford: Clarendon Press, 1998.
13. James Fentress, *Rebels and Mafiosi: Death in a Sicilian Landscape.* Ithaca: Cornell University Press, 2000.

including the issue of how to create an administrative class and secure coordination and compliance through bureaucratic means. Their work can be viewed as complementing my own. On three points, however, my analysis differs from Riall's and is much closer to Fentress's.

First, I find untenable Riall's belief that unification *à la* Gramsci could have taken place if Cavour had somehow stopped being Cavour and instead acted like a French Revolutionary; such if/then propositions ignore the actual people and facts. Second, as Fentress and I discuss, what might more realistically have occurred—and, if it had, would have given Cavour and his government greater support, legitimacy, and consensus—would have been a decision to act on the political decentralization experiment suggested by Ferrara in his 1860 memorandum to Cavour, and, at the same time, cease confiscation of church property in Sicily, where a majority of people were strongly attached to the church. These possibilities are based on what we know about the people and facts, but the rush of events militated against them.[14] Third, if Riall had looked more closely at the beliefs and aspirations of Sicilian democrats from the 1840s to the revolt of 1866, she would have found what Fentress presents better than I do: that most Sicilian democrats were not Jacobins, or "Gramscian" *ante litteram*. Most, if not all, wanted self-government, with independence or autonomy for Sicily based on a revised version of the 1812 constitution.[15] They anticipated that a free labor market together with communal government and parliament recast on the principles of self-government would seriously diminish the ability of large landowners to determine living conditions for those in the countryside. But, as I try to show in the text, they did not have sufficient time to put such self-government in place.

---

14. I treat these issues at greater length in *The Search for Good Government: Understanding the Paradox of Italian Democracy*, esp. 47–9.

15. They also wanted to resurrect the symbols of the Sicilian nation, including its flag, coat of arms, and parliament, suppressed in 1816. The issue of the Sicilian language, a written language since the twelfth century, with its own dictionary since the sixteenth, is more complicated. Suffice it to say that Sicilian dictionaries continue to be published and sold to this very day. The last volume of a projected five-volume comprehensive dictionary, started in the 1970s, is scheduled to appear by 2004.

In spite of the regime change in 1860, Sicilian peasants found themselves locked into what in 1876 Sidney Sonnino[16] called an "iron circle"—in effect, a many-person analogue to the prisoner's dilemma of modern game theory. On the one hand, labor contracts were imposed on them by a monopoly of large landowners or their agents, supported by the arms of the state; on the other, they bore the cost of government, without any voice in its decisions and little benefit from its actions. Most Sicilians were thus left without legal responses while the central government would not tolerate any kind of illegal remedy. In chapter 4 I cite directly from Sonnino's study. A logic of mutually destructive relationships came to dominate work and community life. How did people cope with, or extricate themselves from, this situation?

I begin to answer this question in chapter 5. They did so in at least three ways: through armed revolts, by pursuing individualistic action in communal and agricultural activities and in matters of peace and security (which in the end made everything worse), and through various voluntary collective efforts—a wheat bank, an agrarian association, chain migration, and church confraternities used as mutual aid societies. More recent studies suggest that I did not sufficiently emphasize the commitment of the Villalba clergy in the second half of the nineteenth century to promoting such undertakings as local civic assets.[17] Still, my findings about local concerted action are important for two reasons.

---

16. Sidney Sonnino was the traveling companion of two other young social scientists, Leopoldo Franchetti and Enea Cavalieri. They set out to study Sicilian conditions both before, and then in response to, the 1875 parliamentary commission better known as the Bondadini Report. Cavalieri interrupted his sojourn in Sicily to travel to Canada and the United States to study the prospects of liberal democracy there. Franchetti and Sonnino were both Tuscan noblemen and members of parliament. Sonnino later served as prime minister and foreign minister of Italy.

17. See the information contained in, among others: Giuseppe Caramma, *Monsignor Giuseppe Vizzini da Villalba a Roma. Contesto Sociale e Carriera Ecclesiastica di un Vescovo 'Romano'" (1874–1913)*. Unpublished thesis. Catania: Università di Catania, Facoltà di Scienze Politiche, 1994–95; Francesco Lomanto, *Popolazione, vita cristiana e cura pastorale a Villalba attraverso i libri parrocchiali* (San Cataldo: Centro Studi sulla Cooperazione "A. Cammarata", 1994); Cataldo Naro, "Dal prefetto Mori al secondo dopoguerra: 1924–1956," *Il Vangelo e la lupara*, ed. Augusto Cavadi (Bologna: Edizioni Dehoniane, 1994), 1:29–57. The Archangelo Cammarata Center for the Study of Cooperation in San Cataldo and the research by Cataldo Naro have done much to bring out the positive role that church-sponsored associations have played in local development and in the creation of human and social capital. .

The first is that the existence of such civic assets suggests that most generalizations about the South are untenable. Any serious difficulties experienced by local undertakings were due more to the constraints imposed by the structure of the central government and the systemic power of large landowners or rentiers than to what Mancur Olson in his classic study characterized as the logic of collective inaction. The second reason my findings are important contradicts my own expectations at the outset of the study: it was membership in church-sponsored associations that generated considerable social capital and by the 1890s led some people, including the then-young Calogero Vizzini, to consider doing something collectively about the absence of peace and security in the countryside. (The state police, at this point, were as much a danger as the brigands.) The Villalba mafia thus emerged as an alternative social regime.

Thus, contrary to what much of the literature of the 1960s and the 1970s would have us believe, the mafia in Villalba is of relatively recent origin; it does not go back to the 1860s. And, more importantly, it started as a form of private protection and had little or nothing to do with large estates. Fentress's archival research on the Sicilian interior and coastal towns has added a new, historical, twist to my findings. It suggests that the story of the mafia must be understood against the background of the uprisings of 1820, 1848, 1860, and 1866 and, more generally, Sicily's struggle for freedom in the first half of the nineteenth century. Fentress found, as I did, that many of the social and political modes of behavior that have evolved, and often become ways of life, in Sicily must be understood as responses to strictly political phenomena. We both place in sharp relief the political basis of agrarian problems. Our respective studies also stress the importance of the institutional context to understanding the emergence of the mafia, recognizing that variations in the historical and institutional context matter. So just as I found that the mafia of Villalba developed out of a civic, self-help tradition, Fentress has found that the mafia of Misilmeri and other coastal towns without large estates developed out of a revolutionary tradition. Our findings are not contradictory but complementary. Our respective research transforms into a variable what is often viewed as a constant: the emergence of mafia groups as illicit, criminal enterprises. Our findings do not challenge the empirical validity of the received wisdom where it is relevant but rather its generalizability to the entire of Western Sicily since the 1860s.

As noted in the text, what I found does not in any way deny the possibility that some mafia groups may have originated as exploitative counter-governments developed by estate managers and their armed bands under the protection of large landowners. Nothing in my theoretical perspective or presumptive knowledge precludes this possibility. Indeed, the potential for the Villalba mafia to become a protection racket and a criminal organization, victimizing villagers and landowners alike through violence, intimidation, and silence (*omertà*), was there from the very beginning: an outlaw regime can gain legitimacy through the protection services it offers and then exploit the position it has acquired, recreating the problems of political organization that plague the lawful regime.

The chief problem with some of the best anthropological research is that it presumes what must be shown empirically. For instance, contrary to what it claims, the anthropological work of Anton Blok[18] does not give us an account of the mafia of a Sicilian village between 1860 and 1960; it focuses on the period between 1912 and 1922, and even for that period the evidence is hardly robust. Blok also fails to recognize what Gambetta clearly notes: "violence is a means, not an end; a resource, not the final product."[19] There is a serious gap between the model of the mafia presented by Blok and the evidence adduced in its support.[20] Equally, one would hardly know from Blok's narrative that the village he studied, Contessa Entellina, is an Albanian town with a long history rich in revolutionary and Socialist tradition, at times combined with intense ethnic conflict, very different from the Weberian perspective of order and power that informs Blok's analysis.[21] Equally problematic is the study by Jane Schneider and Peter Schneider. After choosing the town of Sambuca di Sicilia "as the focal point of [their] research,"[22] they provide little or no evidence about that town, or about the local mafia, its origins, and its operation. One suspects that their attempt to place

18. Anton Blok, *The Mafia of a Sicilian Village 1860–1960: A Study of Violent Peasant Entrepreneurs* (New York: Harper, 1974).

19. Gambetta, *The Sicilian Mafia*, 2.

20. This point has also been noted by Rosario Mangiameli, "Dalle bande alle cosche. La rappresentazione della criminalità in provincia di Caltanissetta." In *Economia e società nell'area dello zolfo secoli XIX-XX* ed. Giuseppe Barone and Claudio Torrisi (Caltanissetta: Salvatore Sciascia Editore, 1989), 193.

21. It is doubtful that states have ever possessed an actual monopoly on the use of force, as Michael Taylor notes in *Community, Anarchy and Liberty* (New York: Cambridge University Press, 1982), 4–6.

22. Jane Schneider and Peter Schneider, *Culture and Political Economy in Western Sicily* (New York: Academic Press, 1976), 9.

the course of Sicilian development within the framework of the world system laid out by Immanuel Wallerstein precluded them from examining the rich archival sources of the actual town.

By contrast, chapters 6 to 9 in the present book cover the entire life span of the Villalba mafia: the rise of the mafia, 1890s–1908; the mafia in action, 1909–26; the re-emergence of the mafia, 1943; the mafia in action, 1944–52; the collapse of the mafia, 1953–56. Conclusions can be drawn about each phase or block of time.

Conclusions about the Villalba mafia are far from settled, for five complicating reasons. 1) Given the empiricist epistemology prevalent in the social sciences, we have increasingly adopted a positivist, unproblematic view of the monopoly of state powers and neglected to appreciate what Sonnino emphasized and other studies beyond Sicily have found[23] —that is, we have tended to ignore the fact that people, in some basic sense, build their own social and political realities and opportunities and that what officialdom may do in the formal regime is only part of the story. If some concepts or institutions do not work, or work against them, people will create their own adaptations, which may develop into extreme forms of illegal problem-solving if officialdom continues to think it can govern while people are actually going their own way. 2) The crimes that the Villalba mafia is usually associated with are older than the mafia itself, going as far back as biblical times—a point also made by Fentress for the area he studied[24]—and it is not always easy to distinguish which crimes are the mafia's and which are not. 3) While there was some opposition, the Villalba outlaw regime enjoyed the support of many, if not most, villagers, who stood to profit from it and did not regard state laws as the final determinant of what was criminal or illegal. 4) Short of leaving the village, other alternatives available to local people after 1918 and after 1944 were, if not worse than what was done by the mafia, not always desirable. 5) The polemical use of the term "mafia" in public discourse and the dynamics of contention have often clouded points one, two, three, and four.

The mafia as an octopus (*piovra*) has a long and rueful history in polemical writings about Sicilian criminality. The world of Sicilian criminals and that of the myths and half-truths that surround their activities overlap, making the task of distinguishing fact from fantasy exceedingly

---

23. See the works cited in footnote 8, especially de Soto, *The Other Path.*
24. Fentress, *Rebels and Mafiosi,* 45–6.

difficult.[25] As noted in chapter 1, at the time Sicily became a province of a united Italy, the term "mafia" was used to label antigovernment opposition, including republicans and Bourbon loyalists. Christopher Duggan's work on Fascism and the mafia[26] suggests the extent to which the idea of the mafia held by Fascists obscured rather than advanced knowledge about Sicily's problems. Duggan's analysis complements what I found for the post-1944 period, up to the 1960s.

At the very least, the history of the Villalba mafia sketched here serves to answer the question that Giovanni Falcone, the Sicilian antimafia magistrate, raised before he was killed in 1992: "Why is it that men, even some endowed with real intellectual abilities, are compelled to create criminal careers for themselves in order to survive with dignity?"[27]

There are other important points not always explicit in the text that should be pointed out. For instance, it is important to recognize that support for the mafia among local people cannot be understood without reference to the actions of those who oppose it—the antimafia forces. In the post–World War I period the antimafia were from the nationalist Right; post–World War II they were from the Left. I found that ideological choices following World War II made the Left insensitive to the needs of its strongest potential allies (the peasants) in a fashion reminiscent of developments in the North of Italy following War World I. A doctrinaire definition of land reform also did a great deal to drive peasants to the Right—and the equally doctrinaire behavior of the local Leftists ruled out any early possibility of capturing the protest vote that was there for the taking. A patron who alienates potential clients by being too ideologically intransigent is not going to succeed, and this mistake occurred often in Villalba. Recent research has revealed that the regional Communist leader Girolamo Li Causi was aware of this problem, to the point of having a more nuanced, less Manichean, view of the mafia, even though he had been fired upon in the Villalba square

25. This problem is more widespread, as T. R. Naylor makes clear in *The Wages of Crime: Black Markets, Illegal Finance, and the Underworld Economy* (Montreal: McGill-Queen's University Press, 2001).

26. Christopher Duggan, *Fascism and the Mafia* (New Haven: Yale University Press, 1989).

27. Giovanni Falcone, *Cose di Cosa Nostra*. In collaborazione con Marcelle Padovani (Milan: Rizzoli, 1991), 72.

in 1944.[28] But whatever he discussed behind closed doors did not succeed in improving the fortunes of the Left.[29]

Also in contrast to prevailing interpretations, the argument advanced in the book is not that the Christian Democratic Party (DC) was 'captured" by the mafia, but rather the reverse. With access to immense resources through its control of the regionalist state, the DC undermined the mafia and ensured its rapid demise. By the middle of the 1950s, the DC had displaced the Villalba mafia, at about the same time that the Left coalition destroyed itself. Any reader searching my text for evidence of movement of the mafia from the countryside to the big cities and for the presumed change in the nature of the mafia from an agrarian phenomenon to a "mafia business," one principally involved in living off development, construction contracts, and the drug trade, will be disappointed. Villagers who left the town in the post-war period to go elsewhere—to places like Albenga in North Italy, or Trenton, New Jersey—did not bring the local mafia with them. The Villalba mafia did not move on to greater opportunities elsewhere; it ended in Villalba. This occurred because, as I try to show, the mafia phenomenon is not a constant but varies in terms of partners in crime, demand for illegal products, criminal opportunities, and the laws and regulations of government as well as contingencies of time and place. The mafia of Calogero Vizzini does not fit the 1980s model of Cosa Nostra,[30] but even in this later manifestation it is an exaggeration to view mafia groups as some sort of privatized Leviathan.

As I note in the Epilogue, the depopulated and calm look of Villalba in the 1970s gave no hint of its contentious two-hundred years history. To what extent, then, does the general conclusion of the study—that the Sicilian problem is ultimately grounded in a structure of authority

---

28. See in particular, Rosario Mangiameli, *La mafia tra stereotipo e storia* (Caltanissetta: Salvatore Sciascia Editore, 2000), passim, esp.15–16.

29. See the revealing recollections found in Michele Perriera, *Marcello Cimino. Vita e morte di un comunista soave* (Palermo: Sellerio Editore, 1990); and Giuliana Saladino, *Romanzo civile* (Palermo: Sellerio Editore, 2000).

30. I have pursued this examination in *The Search for Good Government: Understanding the Paradox of Italian Democracy,* chaps. 6–7. For what we can learn from North American studies on organized crime, see, among others, the collection of essays in *Il Crimine in America*, ed. Saverio DiBella, Filippo Sabetti, Pierre Tremblay (Cosenza: Pellegrini Editore, 2000).

relationships that impinges on the pursuit of individual and joint or collective opportunities—still hold in the new millennium?

Villalba over the past twenty years suggests that, contrary to the Prince of Lampedusa's famous saying, things do not change to remain the same. They can change for the better, without overhauling the entire political system and with only some modifications in the rules that structure opportunities and constraints on individuals from the state. Small changes in the macro structure of authority relationships, helped by the collapse of the post-war party system in the early 1990s, have made the national and regional governments and bureaucracies less hostile to local concerns and more open to communal self-government. At the same time, the insecurity about claims over rural property rights that followed the 1950s land reform was resolved by the 1970s—whether this was done formally, informally, or by some combination of the two is not entirely clear. What is clear is that secure property rights have encouraged villagers to pursue opportunities in the market economy and to achieve a level of physical and economic well-being unimaginable thirty years ago.

Unlike most other Sicilian and Southern villages, the population of Villalba has remained at about 2,000; in the past twenty years there have been on average an equal number of births and deaths annually (about 28). What helps explain the relatively stable population is not just a widespread preference for living there (recorded on 25), better roads, which have increasingly made it more attractive to those who work outside, and a slow but steady growth in public employment (noted on 219), but renewed confidence in the local economy. The rediscovery of agriculture as a source of income was already noticeable in the late 1970s (207–8). Until then there were only two grain merchants. There are now four, each with new and expanded storage facilities for durum wheat. These changes can be used as proxy measures for increased production by local farmers. Agricultural activities have continued to grow, in part because of increasing outside demands for local specialties, supported by communal policies that, since the middle of the 1970s, have encouraged brand-name recognition of local delicacies (the "lentils of Villalba" and the *siccagnu* tomato) and in part because they give local people a sense of self-reliance and personal satisfaction. Local people have shown themselves quite capable of devising ingenious ways of relating constructively with one another and of building mutually productive social relationships. Every summer, in fact, there are local produce festivals held in conjunction with festivities in honour of the village's patron saint; these generate publicity beyond

Sicily and attract people from outside, not just expatriates. Two brothers who left many years ago to work as blacksmiths in Piedmont have returned to Villalba as electrical-mechanical entrepreneurs to set up what local people call "our little Fiat." By 1998 they employed twenty full-time workers to make aluminum products and produce automobile parts for a Fiat plant elsewhere in Sicily; they are now trying to diversify their production by building, among other things, special ovens for drying tomatoes and other vegetables for export. But all these wealth-producing activities are not easily translatable into official statistics, largely because most of the people who generate this wealth do not consider themselves fully employed—they still see themselves as looking for secure employment or as aspiring to work at something better. Not surprisingly, but most erroneously, in 1995 official statistics ranked Villalba as the commune with the highest rate of unemployment (70%) in Italy.[31]

There are also reasons to be optimistic when we look at Villalba's politics. The unused capacity for lawful communal self-government noted in the text is now being released as a result of several factors that have come together in the past twenty years. By 1978 village politics had culminated in the breakdown of the Demochristian hegemony, leaving a Left coalition in charge of communal politics. This coalition managed to stay in power for a few years and then gave way to a new Demochristian administration. Providing communal services continued to take precedence over party control and internal party squabbles. There have been four other communal governments since the early 1980s, but the different administrations have remained committed to acting on behalf of community interests and concerns, albeit in different ways and with different emphases. These changes in local political life are due partly to a new generation of community leaders anxious not to repeat the mistakes of their fathers and committed to providing good government, but they are also due to other factors: the collapse of the post-war party system (which did not occur in the way predicted in the text, 240) and the renewed efforts of national and regional governments, following the Bassanini decentralization laws, to return some of their authority over communal affairs to local elected officials at the very time policies of the European Union are reaching citizens more and more directly. Like most other contemporary communes, the Villalba commune has its own charter of

---

31. Cited in Luigi Ronsisvalle, "A Villalba: mafia, chiesa e rivoluzione operaia in piazza." *La Sicilia* (Catania), 18 April 1998, 12.

self-rule, brought in in the mid-1990s in consultation with the entire population. This charter, which some villalbesi grandiously see as "our own chapters of the land," recalling those of pre-1812 times, can be found, with other information, on the web (www.comune.villalba.cl.it). The present mayor is a cardiologist, who lists politics as his hobby on the commune's web page. As a general rule, the delivery of public services from the field offices of the national and regional bureaucracy—such as health services over which the Villalba commune has managed to have some say and control—has increased and improved considerably in the past twenty years—making Villalba part of the productive and smaller private and public enclaves of a Sicily that works.[32] Some problems, such as the availability of water, remain, but these are not within the grasp of the local government and the community. They are part of the structure of authority relationships that still does not work well.

The positive changes suggest that vigorous local government and many types of voluntary efforts are part of the answer to tackling the Sicilian problem but are not sufficient in and of themselves to overcome that problem. Productive, small-scale self-organization is difficult to sustain over time in a larger political system that continues to privilege control rather than service and to impose uniform rules without regard to contingencies of time and place. For these reasons, the positive changes that have taken place in Villalba in the past twenty years are not stable and may not last. Solving the Sicilian problem and maintaining what has been achieved in Villalba recently involve the design of a delicately balanced system with effective organizations ranging from the very small to the very large—in short, self-governance on a continental, European scale. The possibility of "democracy in Europe"[33] offers the only secure basis for people in Sicily to solve their own problems and share in the making of a European compound republic.

Now that I have anticipated so much of what follows, readers should turn to the text and reach their own conclusions about village politics and the mafia in Sicily.

Filippo Sabetti
Montreal, May 26, 2002

---

32. See *Il Mezzogiorno che funziona*. Ed. Dolores Deidda (Rome: Formez/Donzelli Editore, 2001).
33. Larry Siedentop, *Democracy in Europe* (London: Penguin Books, 2000).

Acknowledgments

This study was begun as a paper for a public policy seminar at Indiana University with Vincent Ostrom in the spring of 1970. A concern with theories of collective action stimulated my interest in Sicily. Danilo Dolci's work there provided a first exposure. Ezio Cappadocia, Alfred Diamant, and Vincent Ostrom helped me plan this book and bore with me cheerfully through the years of its creation. During the long accouchement many other people helped with counsel, encouragement, and funding, and in some cases a combination of all three.

The writing and counsel of Anton Blok, Jeremy Boissevain, and Jane and Peter Schneider introduced me to the study and people of Sicily; the work of Denis Mack Smith provided guidance at different stages of the project, and his encouragement at a low point in this long process helped to sustain interest. I have learned so much from their efforts that I am now in a position to offer an alternate assessment of political economy in Western Sicily. Participation in the 1971 Workshop on Peasants in Europe, sponsored by the Council for European Studies and organized by Suzanne Berger at M.I.T.'s Endicott House, provided opportunities to become better acquainted with interdisciplinary and comparative projects on rural societies and to enrich the preparatory work for research in the field. Anton Blok, James M. Buchanan, Mattei Dogan, Jerre Mangione, and Leonard G. Sbrocchi graciously consented to my use of their names for establishing important contacts in the initial phase of field research. The intellectual exchange I have shared with colleagues associated with the Workshop in Political Theory and Policy Analysis, codirected by Elinor and Vincent Ostrom at Indiana University, and with colleagues associated with the Workshop on Covenant and Politics, organized by Daniel J. Elazar and John Kincaid at the Center for the Study of Federalism, Temple University, emphasized the importance of pressing beyond traditional modes of political reasoning and prevented "premature closure" of my ideas. I should like sometime to meet the standards of collegiality that James M. Buchanan, Giuseppe

Di Palma, Richard F. Hamilton, H. G. Koenigsberger, Humbert S. Nelli, and Charles Tilly showed in responding to my calls for help at different junctures of the project.

In Sicily, no matter where I turned, I usually found people willing to help. Of course, the greatest help came from "Camporanesi" of all social, economic, and political conditions. This book would have been even more difficult to research without their willingness to put up with many curious and impertinent questions and to share their profound and subtle understanding of Sicilian and Camporano life and events. In the course of writing it, I have had to state some hard truths; this has been done with regret, but without malice and without any design other than to unravel and explain the Sicilian problem.

Several people, none of whom is to be held responsible for the outcome, have offered comments. Ezio Cappadocia, James B. Christoph, Alfred Diamant, Robert H. Evans, Vincent Ostrom, Richard Stryker, and Alan S. Zuckerman read preliminary drafts of each chapter. Their insightful criticisms and suggestions have been immensely helpful in my preparation of the final product. Giuseppe Di Palma, Richard F. Hamilton, H. G. Koenigsberger, Anthony C. Masi, Mark Sproule-Jones, Sidney Tarrow, Charles Tilly, and Charles A. Weeks have each read selected chapters; I deeply appreciate their suggestions, many of which have found their way into the final draft. Robert E. Brown was especially thoughtful in his extended comments on chapter 1.

Joseph Brugnano, Thomas C. and Celia Bruneau, Paul Casavina, Jr., Charles S. Hyneman, Brian Nelson Jones, Stephen Krizmanich, Robert Leonardi, Brian Loveman, Michael A. Maggiotto, Raffaella Nanetti, Leroy N. Rieselbach, James T. Thomson, Stephen L. Vaughn, Eric M. Uslaner, and Dina A. Zinnes taught me things in and out of books. Of the librarians who have rendered me assistance over the past years, I express particular gratitude to the staffs of the Italian State Archives in "Mozarra," Palermo, and Rome, of the Biblioteca Nazionale and the Società Siciliana per la Storia Patria in Palermo, of the Communal Library of Mozarra and Palermo, and of the Interlibrary Loan Office at Indiana University.

For the first opportunity to visit, study, and live in Sicily, I would like to thank the Canada Council. A small but essential budget from the Faculty of Graduate Studies and Research of McGill University, a leave fellowship from the Social Sciences and Humanities Research Council of Canada, and a travel grant from the Ministère des Affaires intergouvernementales,

Gouvernement du Québec, provided opportunities to do additional research in Sicily over several years. The Canada Council, the Workshop in Political Theory and Policy Analysis at Indiana University, and the Faculty of Graduate Studies and Research of McGill University supported part of the writing stage of the project. My appreciation must also encompass the Woodrow Wilson Foundation and Indiana University for providing financial assistance during my graduate education.

Members of my family, now deceased and living, in North America and elsewhere, reserved so much understanding, encouragement, and material assistance for my academic activities that it is impossible to acknowledge them fully. Mario, Rosanna, and Pia Pietrangeli went from elementary school to university as they helped to organize, expand, and maintain order in my Sicilian files.

Finally, I have nothing but praise for the combination of firmness and support shown by Marlie Wasserman of Rutgers University Press. Her help too has been invaluable. Also at the Press, Leslie Mitchner has been unfailingly helpful and courteous in seeing the book through the publication process. What I owe Ezio Cappadocia, Alfred Diamant, and Vincent Ostrom the dedication of the first edition tried to say.

Notre-Dame-de-Grâce, Québec
May 26, 1983

Village Politics and the Mafia in Sicily

1

Introduction:
The Sicilian Problem

Tocqueville, writing about his travels in Sicily in 1827, used an imaginary discussion between a Sicilian and a Neapolitan to present contradictory assessments of political authority in Sicily. The Sicilian complained that Bourbon rule was bringing ruin and misery to his island. The Neapolitan answered that complaint by voicing what has since then become the predominant explanation of governmental weakness and failure in Sicily:

> Are you not your own worst oppressors? Granted that tyranny exists in Sicily, but where has it held in its grasp such base instruments? Is it Neapolitans who occupy your public offices? No, one encounters only Sicilians. It is Sicilians—Sicilians alone—who bear the yoke of Naples; who bless their burden as long as they are in turn permitted to impose it upon the unfortunate Sicily. It is Sicilians who sit in your tribunals and make of justice a public auction. If we wanted to corrupt you, you certainly have more than met our expectations. (Tocqueville, 1827: 52–53; this and subsequent translations are mine unless otherwise indicated.)

Against the stark backdrop of governmental failures and general social disintegration, local outlaw societies or mafia groups stand out as the

3

most successful long-term efforts at collective action in Sicily. These mafia groups have, however, been viewed, especially from outside of Sicily, as gangs of malefactors, as expressions of the fundamental asociality of islanders (e.g., Titone, 1964: 155–308), as outlaw protective agencies of large landowners or urban capitalists, and, more generally, as impediments to human development (e.g., *Ulisse*, 1969). The study of mafia groups and how they actually work in Sicily has, in fact, become impenetrable on any premise except that of killing or murder.

The multitude of problems inherent in governmental failures, general social disintegration and outlaw societies has often been characterized as the Sicilian problem or in Italian as *sicilitudine*. The present study is an effort to provide a more satisfactory explanation of *sicilitudine* within the microcosm of a single Sicilian community. Although the book deals with a single village, the argument applies to other villages in and beyond Sicily and Southern Italy—in brief, wherever there are communities of people struggling to realize their self-governing capabilities.

The Problem of Social Organization

The inadequacy of public service systems, the frustration of public officials, and a substantial measure of citizen alienation have remained normal features of Sicilian life, despite Sicily's regional autonomy since 1947. The 1950 regional agrarian reform was expected to improve the working and living conditions of a large part of the Sicilian population and to increase agricultural productivity. The reform did away with large landholding and, correlatively, rural classes as critical elements of the Sicilian problem, but it also had other effects. Land reform areas that were the site of "land-to-the-tillers" struggles are now almost lifeless and deserted. Food shortages follow almost every harvest year. Acute lack of water for domestic and agricultural uses is still accompanied by millions of cubic meters of water running to waste into the sea. Central government programs ranging from "green plans" to "forced industrial growth," undertaken by the Fund for Southern Development (*Cassa per il Mezzogiorno*), have failed to yield the expected results. Thus governmental failures refer not only to the production and delivery of essential public services but also to the maintenance of appropriate institutional arrangements for the pursuit of individual and joint opportunities in the market

4

economy and to reform efforts aimed at improving performance in both the public and private sectors.

Governmental Failure and Development

The contemporary structure of Sicilian governmental arrangements dates back to the abolition of feudalism in 1812 and to the extension of centralized administration by the Neapolitan government in 1816. These changes meant a wholesale remodeling of the structure of basic social institutions—from property law and farm tenancy in agricultural activities to communal and intendancy law in community life and services and the governmental institutions for determining, enforcing, and altering the legal basis of those institutions. By the 1820s the new structure of basic social institutions, including center-periphery relations, proved to be inadequate in providing essential public services and in improving the quality of human life, especially in the countryside.

Against this backdrop, it becomes easy to see why many analyses of Sicilian history and politics have echoed the diagnostic assessment voiced by Tocqueville's Neapolitan. But simply because islanders occupy public offices in Sicily it does not necessarily follow that institutional weakness and failure are related to basic faults in Sicilian character. By drawing upon the distinction between individuals engaged in constitutional choice and individuals pursuing their relative advantage within governmental structures, modern public choice scholars have been able to resolve several paradoxes inherent in collective or social choices and to provide a better understanding of the strategic opportunities afforded to individuals by different types of decision-making arrangements—from constitutional "contracts" to property rights (see, e.g., Buchanan and Tullock, 1962; Mueller, 1979; North, 1981; V. Ostrom, 1974; Sproule-Jones, 1972, 1983). Thus, if one translates that Neapolitan's questions into modern political economy terms, one is confronted *not* with cultural or personality problems, but with institutional ones, such as: What were the terms and conditions under which Sicilians acted in public offices? Could they be held accountable for their authoritative actions and by whom? At the same time, the condition of sole proprietorship over large tracts of land means that landowners or landlords can also be powerful "governors" in practical control of the daily lives and living conditions of the masses of peasants and rural workers. What

5

were the legal prerogatives of Sicilians as citizens and workers and could they be sustained? To what extent were Sicilians in public offices required to impose the yoke of Naples on other Sicilians? Were islanders allowed to solve their own problems?

These institutional problems are, in turn, part of a larger constitutional or state-making problem. Amid name changes from the Bourbon to the Savoy monarchy and from Fascist to Republican Italy, central government officials have retained ultimate authority over Sicilian developmental opportunities. Under these conditions, choices about basic policies and the availability of different organizational arrangements for pursuing new developmental opportunities have continued to reside only with members of the ruling class—in essence, "development by administration" (Loveman, 1975 and 1976a). But can development be administered? Is it possible, then, that the persistence of institutional weakness and failure in Sicily is directly related to the process of state making?

Social Disorganization and Voluntary Collective Action

Sicily belongs to a part of Italy usually characterized as an area of general social disintegration, to suggest the persistence of social disorganization, associational incapacity, and entrepreneurial weakness. If one is willing to go beyond the parameters interposed by the prevailing treatments of general social disintegration and to translate interests into the appropriate Sicilian terms, one will find a rich variety of local ventures at concerted action in Sicily. Voluntary joint or collective efforts range from agricultural "institutes" and rural and artisanal workers' solidarity leagues (*fasci*) to wheat banks and mutual-aid confraternities in the nineteenth century and from knitted bedspread "schools" to wine-producing consortia in more contemporary times. Even before the land reform law in 1950, Sicilian peasants came together to seize land and to establish common ventures for its cultivation; some of these undertakings competed with other peasant groups organized as local mafia groups. Since the 1950s, individuals like Lorenzo Barbera, Danilo Dolci, and Tullio Vinay have engaged in attempts to help organize cooperative efforts among Sicilian peasants and artisans in the same countryside that until Fascist rule had the highest number of operating farmer cooperatives in Italy (Briggs, 1978; Bruccoleri, 1913: 106–164; La Loggia, 1955: 506; Prestianni, 1956; Schifani, 1950, 1954).

6

The existence of such voluntary collective action, thus, challenges the image of Sicilians as "men who play alone" (Dolci, 1966) and live in a state of general social disintegration. It also raises questions about collective action and entrepreneurship seldom considered when dealing with Southern Italian political development.

If, as the predominant wisdom about governmental failure suggests, Sicilians are incapable of properly exercising public or governmental responsibilities, one should not expect them to be capable of the much more difficult task of voluntarily organizing collective undertakings. The analysis of the theory of collective action by Mancur Olson (1965) suggests that individuals sharing a common interest cannot automatically be expected to undertake collective action to advance that interest. Olson details, in fact, how calculations associated with individual choice and voluntary agreement give rise to collective *inaction*. Hence, Olson's analysis would lead one to believe that common undertakings to realize common benefits are difficult to organize and maintain by voluntary efforts. At the same time, analyses of organizations in action since Michels's study of political parties in 1912 suggest that the pattern of political inequality inherent in collective decision-making arrangements is apt to create serious splits of interests between the leaders and the led and radical disjunctions between organizational goals and organizational actions. Positions of leadership and appeals to organizational goals can become, in the words of Philip Selznick, "protective covers behind which uncontrolled discretion can occur" (1966: ix). Yet, the various voluntary efforts presented above suggest that Sicilian peasants and artisans do possess the skills and knowledge necessary to realize self-governing capabilities. How, then, have succeeding generations of Sicilians overcome the problem of collective inaction? How have Sicilians taking part in voluntary concerted efforts managed to cope or deal with the oligarchical tendencies inherent in organizational life?

Mancur Olson assumed the existence of a legal order that does not hinder voluntary joint efforts and of instrumentalities of government that do not foreclose the development of alternative sources of supply of public services implied by voluntary collective undertakings. Yet such an assumption is problematic in the case of Sicily. In spite of constitutional changes from the Bourbon to the Savoy monarchy and from Fascist to Republican Italy, the legal order has allowed public and party officials to disregard, in Vincent Ostrom's words, "citizens as essential co-producers of many public goods and services" (1977: 35–36; see also

7

Barbera, 1980; Whitaker, 1978). In fact, the degree to which state regulations and government and party officials have hindered, if not openly combated, autonomous voluntary undertakings and entrepreneurship points to another facet of the Sicilian problem that is seldom considered: to what extent Sicilian peasants and artisans have been foreclosed by government authorities from an opportunity to organize and maintain joint or collective enterprises. It is possible, then, that general social disintegration is not a lack of community concern or an inability to act, but the presence of institutional arrangements that create impediments to voluntary collective actions rather than facilitating those actions.

Criminal Association and Self-Help

Some North American analysts are wont to trace the origins of the Mafia as a Sicilian secret organization to the Palermitan revolt against their French rulers in 1282, the Sicilian Vespers. Somehow during the nineteenth century the Mafia ceased to be a protective society for poor Sicilians and became, first, an instrument of big landowners to keep peasants down and then an overarching criminal association extorting money and goods from peasants. It was this Mafia that reached North American shores to become "an enemy within" (e.g., Gage, 1971; Reid, 1964). There is, however, no evidence about either the origin of mafia groups dating as far back as 1282 or the existence of a single, unified, clandestine protection or criminal organization known as the Mafia.

One of the earliest references to local protective societies is the Trapani procurator's report to the Neapolitan minister of justice in 1838. In that report, the Trapani procurator warned the minister of the propensity of central government officials to victimize peasants and artisans for personal profit and the villagers' "recourse to somewhat strange and dangerous remedies" (quoted in Colajanni, 1900: 36). These "strange and dangerous remedies" were local friendship and defensive societies that villagers had established to deal with public officials.

Moreover, until the annexation of Sicily into the new Italian kingdom in 1860–1861, the West Sicilian word *maffia* or *mafia* stood only for such individual qualities as self-dignity, self-respect, self-reliance, courage, and excellence. "A man of mafia" or "mafiusu," for example, described an individual who had "the consciousness of being a man" or true courage as distinguished from boldness, arrogance, or truculence. As adjectives, the words *mafiusu* or *mafiusa* also stood for "pretty,"

8

"handsome," or "good" as in the case of a pretty girl (*'na picciotta mafiusa*), a handsome boy (*'nu picciuttu mafiusu*), or a good broom (*'na scopa mafiusa*) (see, e.g., Albini, 1971: 103).

The Sicilian term *mafiusu* became known throughout the new Italian kingdom with somewhat different connotations as a result of successive productions of the Sicilian-language play *I Mafiusi di la Vicaria*. Written by two Palermitans in 1862 and subsequently enlarged and retitled simply *I Mafiusi*, the popular drama portrayed the language and actions of several prisoners of the Palermo penitentiary who had succeeded in organizing prison life among fellow prisoners—in short, by displaying the attributes typified by the word *mafia*. Their effort represented an attempt to maintain some self-esteem and personal dignity among inmates of an authoritarian institution dominated only by security considerations. An English-language observer, in fact, noted that the title of the drama should be translated *The Heroes of the Penitentiary* (Paton, 1898: 360). But the pejorative or negative connotations inherent in the very setting and characters of the play were transferred by implication to the words *mafia* and *mafiusi*.

It is likely that the absorption of the Sicilian words *mafia* and *mafiusu* with negative connotations into the daily language of Italian-speaking public officials and journalists was aided by the existence in the official Italian language of similar-sounding words already loaded with bad connotations. Among users of the Tuscan or Florentine language, the official Italian language, *maffia* or *mafia* signified misery, poverty, or wretched existence. As late as 1885, the Fanfani dictionary of the Italian language still defined *mafia* only as "misery" (1885: 330). Modern dictionaries of the Italian language still define *mafia* in part as misery (see the Zingarelli dictionary of the Italian language, 1962: 912). Thus when in 1865 *mafia* first appeared in a police and prefectoral report to the minister of the interior about "a crime of mafia" committed in the Sicilian countryside, it is not entirely clear what that criminal act was and how the word *mafia* was used (Novacco, 1964: 201).

Following the suppression of the Palermitan uprising against Piedmontese rule in 1866 and the confiscation of church property in 1867, central government officials stationed in Sicily began to use *mafia* as a summary term to describe Sicilian events and activities that threatened the central government's monopoly of authority. As a summary term, *mafia* stood for activities ranging from expressions of Bourbon and clerical loyalties to republican, anarchist, and socialist opposition to the

9

Savoy monarchy, from local resistance to, or evasion of, conscription to local mutual-aid or self-help societies, from the erosion of public standards of conduct, or corruption, to *any* kind of criminal act (see Novacco, 1964: 202). Sicilians pursuing, or involved in, these activities were usually prosecuted for belonging to "a criminal association," a legal concept originally borrowed from the French penal code and amplified to refer to five or more persons bound by an intent (*pactum sceleris*) to commit acts against persons, private property, and the state (see Scarlata, 1904). Thus by the 1870s, the word *mafia* became a synonym for criminal association. Yet, when the terms *mafia* and *mafiosi* were used by Sicilians and Italians to orient each other to a topic of discourse like local outlaw societies, the load of unexamined presumptions in those terms was so great as to cause grave misunderstandings and to foreclose intelligent communications.

In preparation for "a war on the mafia," prefects in Western Sicily were asked in 1874 to compile lists of all the mafiosi in their provinces. A police official suggested to the Girgenti prefect in September of that year that, in order to comply with the central government request, he would have to send "Your Excellency the list of all the male population of (his town) between the age of seventeen and seventy" (quoted in Candida, 1956: 118). Those villagers were all mafiosi—they had all engaged in some form of behavior that ultimately threatened or diminished the authority of the state. Thus it was difficult to wage a successful "war on the mafia." Moreover, antistate behavior did not seem to be just a Sicilian phenomenon. In 1878, for example, there were almost as many criminal associations or mafias prosecuted in Lombardy as there were in Westen Sicily (*Rivista Penale*, 1878, cited in Lombroso, 1879: 102, note 1; see also De Viti De Marco, 1898).

In turn, the history of how successive central governments—whether of the left or the right—struggled to maintain a monopoly over the supply of public services and to foreclose possibilities for Sicilian peasants and artisans becoming coproducers of many public services led Sicilian proponents of an Italian federal republic like Napoleone Colajanni to aver that it was state officials who were the members of a Grand Criminal Association (Colajanni, 1885, 1895, 1900, and 1905). Colajanni, in fact, anticipated that in order "to combat and destroy the kingdom of the mafia it was necessary that the Italian government cease to be the king of the mafia" (1900: 111; see also Ganci, 1964). At the same time, ordinary Sicilians also continued to use the words *mafia* and *mafiusi* in their original meanings. As an English-language travelogue published at the turn of the century reported, "(o)ften in Palermo today one hears the street-cry '*arancie mafiuse*'—(to mean) 'fine oranges' " (Paton, 1898: 360; see also Pitrè, 1870–1913: xv, 290).

Students of Sicilian or South Italian political development have rarely shown an awareness of the implications that the contradictory usages and meanings of the terms *mafia* and *mafiosi* have for an understanding of outlaw societies. For the most part, and at best, they have simplistically talked about the existence of widespread criminal and vendetta organizations.

A recent attempt by Henner Hess to elucidate the basis of modern accounts of mafia groups indicates how the images evoked by the words *mafia* and *mafiosi* have served as a myth about contemporary outlaw societies:

> The post-war situation . . . gave rise to a crop of books by authors on the Left, inspired by the hardships of the peasants and written as indictments. Naturally there was a temptation to present the conservative forces as a bloodthirsty Moloch. 'The mafia' was more easily comprehended and more easily attacked as a counter-type. Yet it seems that most of these authors—Sicilians—realized that this was just a polemical device: their information on the structures of 'the mafia' is vague and no concrete analysis is offered. They know what reality looks like, but the social and political clash calls for slogans. And these then acquire their own historical legitimacy. (Hess, 1970: 92–93; see also Longo, 1957)

Practically all the English-language scholarly and popular references to mafia activities in Sicily are based upon these postwar accounts of outlaw societies (e.g., Hobsbawm, 1959; Lewis, 1964; Mack Smith, 1968b: passim; Tarrow, 1967: 68–69, and 1977a: 62–63). In fairness, it must be added that independent and scholarly research on mafia groups has occurred more recently (e.g., Blok, 1974; Hess, 1970: esp. 124, note 63). Some Left analysts have begun to question or take issue with postwar Left analyses as well (see, e.g., Macaluso, 1971; Marino, 1976).

The historical legitimacy of the slogans acquired a more general legitimacy with the Opening to the Left by Demochristian party and government officials in the early 1960s. Thus slogans and *not* empirical investigation provided the basis for waging another war on the mafia in 1965.

The same governmental agencies that were experiencing serious institutional weakness and failure were now expected somehow to wage a successful struggle against an enemy whose existence derived more from political slogans than critical analysis (see also Blok, 1974: 227–228). The failure of this new antimafia campaign to achieve a decisive victory has served to strengthen belief in the existence of a hydralike criminal association reaching on and beyond the Italian peninsula, and to thicken the veil of ignorance about outlaw societies and how they actually work in Sicily.

The inadequacy of standard explanations of mafia groups, coupled with a knowledge of the poor performance of governmental arrangements and of the institutional impediments to voluntary undertakings, leads to outlandish conjectures about outlaw societies. Given the costliness of state solutions to the problem of social organization, what alternative social regimes could Sicilians develop that would enable them to cope with the contingencies of life and survive in that struggle?

These alternative social regimes require their own system of entrepreneurship for preserving enforcement capabilities outside the established law and for maintaining an appeal to constituencies of potential supporters. Such outlaw societies are confronted with all the problems of political organization, including the possibility that their rule-making and rule-enforcing mechanisms can become mechanisms for tyranny and shakedown rackets. Thus, whether Sicilian outlaw societies were or are gangs of malefactors, expressions of the fundamental asociality of islanders, outlaw protective agencies of rural or urban capitalists, and, more generally, impediments to human development is still a question for empirical study—not for political mythology. I am not saying that *the* mafia as a set of criminal organizations has never existed; I am saying that the rise and operation of Sicilian mafia groups should be more carefully investigated.

In sum, the Sicilian problem is ultimately grounded in the structure of authority relationships that impinges upon the pursuit of individual opportunities and upon the pursuit of joint or collective opportunities—in essence, the problem of social organization itself. The fundamental question about the Sicilian problem is not, Is there a "legal-rational" structure of government? (as students of political development or development administration ask); nor, What kind of center-periphery system does Sicily belong to? (as some other analysts ask); nor, Do Sicilians have amoral values or civic vices? (as still other analysts ask). Rather, the fundamental question is one of whether the structure of government is so constituted as to facilitate individual and collective efforts on behalf of common interests shared by islanders or whether it is a mechanism of exploitation by "foreigners" who come as members of ruling parties and ruling bureaucracies or as members of an international *imperium.*

A Village as Microcosm of the Sicilian Problem

One way of dealing with these puzzles is to examine the Sicilian problem within the microcosm of a single Sicilian community. City people in Sicily usually refer to their villages as "the footprints that God left on his way to better things." Yet these communities have made as well as suffered history. All the major Sicilian events as well as the major national and international events—whether from Madrid, Naples, Rome, or Washington—have had repercussions at the local level. Villagers have dealt with those events as well as coped with the problems in their daily life. If one can disaggregate the elements in a set of problems where it seems easiest, if one can diagnose situations that demonstrate more clearly the conditions that impinge upon the pursuit of individual opportunities and upon the pursuit of joint or collective opportunities, then one can better understand the Sicilian problem. At the same time, one may identify the conditions that affect the choice of institutional arrangements for agricultural development and village life which might enhance the long-term welfare potential of villagers.

The Sicilian community taken as a microcosm in order to explain or unravel the Sicilian problem is "Camporano," a fictitious name for a village in Western Sicily. The choice of Camporano was partly by a conscious selection and partly by a fortuitous circumstance.

The search for a village was based upon the following criteria: (1) that it has not more than five thousand inhabitants, this being the criterion used in the Italian administrative system to denote the smallest unit of communal government and, at the same time, affording the possibility of using participant observation; (2) that it was in existence before the abolition of feudalism and the introduction of central government jurisdiction; (3) that it was affected by the 1950 land reform law; (4) that it is known as "a mafia town"; and (5) that the particular language used by villagers should not be too difficult to learn in a short time, hence excluding Albanian or Greek settlements. There are at least 45 out of

13

some 160 villages in Western Sicily that meet all these criteria. The number of communes with not more than five thousand inhabitants has decreased since 1860 to represent less than 20 percent of the entire Sicilian population in 1951 (Saba and Solano, 1966: 15). But such small towns are still prototypical of the larger societal and historical problem (cf. Peattie, 1968: chapter 1).

In consultation with several social scientists, community development organizers, rural Left leaders, and Jesuit educators, who had worked or were working in Sicily, the preliminary number of Sicilian villages was reduced to five: two in the largest Western province and one from each of the other three Western provinces. I traveled to all the five villages and spent roughly two days in each. One village was the only community that did not have an inn and I became the guest of an unemployed agricultural worker I met on the bus from Palermo. His warm hospitality failed, however, to allay my more than usual concern for physical danger there (see also Cavalieri, 1925: xvi–xvii; Guarino, 1949; Villari, 1878: 325). Earlier I had learned that a carabiniere assigned to that village had resigned from the police force rather than serve in "a dangerous zone" and that two anthropologists, who had intended to study that community in the 1960s, had eventually chosen another village. I could not verify the story about the carabiniere. But, before I could receive assurances from those anthropologists that an interest in studying a larger community and not a concern for great physical danger had led them to drop that community, a chain of events associated with a fortuitous encounter in the streets of Palermo led me to settle in precisely that village—Camporano.

After a tour of the five villages, I returned to Palermo still undecided about which community to study. They all seemed to have similar general characteristics—but, because of what I had learned, Camporano appeared to be a more dangerous and more difficult community to study. One morning, as I was walking toward the Palermo branch of the National Library (*Biblioteca Nazionale*), I met the mayor of Camporano. He had come to Palermo to persuade regional officials to act quickly on some communal matters. After a few preliminary remarks, he asked me if I wanted to join him in his errands. As a result, I was able to meet two former villagers, now high administrative officials in Palermo. They, in turn, introduced me to a regional official, a "prefectoral" commissioner, who in the late 1960s had been in charge of Camporano communal affairs. All these officials had been accused by a former Camporano Left leader of belonging to the mafia. Criminal libel suits and countersuits

14

had followed and by 1971 were still pending. Yet, they encouraged me to contact that former Left leader, whom I had already met, to get the other side of the story. I was thus introduced, and without reticence, to some critical aspects of Camporano life and problems. Hence, a fortuitous encounter in the streets of Palermo ended my search for a microcosm of the Sicilian problem (cf. Pitt-Rivers, 1954: 2).

The Scope of this Inquiry

To search out and sketch the structures for ordering relationships in public endeavors represents the starting point of this study. Yet the structure of basic social institutions establishing the basis for the pursuit of both individual and joint or collective opportunities provides only a first order of approximation in creating organized relationships (see also Blok, 1974: xxix; Vile, 1967: 314). A knowledge of changes over time in rural property rights, tenancy arrangements, communal rules, and governmental institutions for determining, enforcing, and altering the legal basis of those social institutions needs to be combined with a knowledge of changes over time in agricultural and governmental activities and community life, more generally. The confluence of these two streams of knowledge is exemplified by what Llewellyn and Hoebel, in their study of the law ways of the Cheyenne people, called "trouble cases"—"instances of hitch, dispute, grievance, trouble" (1941: 21; see also Kjellberg, 1975; Selznick, 1966). Trying to discover how and why communities like Camporano have become what they are is not easy (Bates, 1978; Blok, 1974: xxx; Brogger, 1971: 18). But, by seeking out and examining trouble cases over the course of approximately two hundred years of Camporano political economy, one might begin to unravel the Sicilian problem (cf. Binder et al., 1971; Schneider and Schneider, 1976a; Tilly, 1964: 339–342).

Trouble cases come from two sources: documents in the public archives and accounts from villagers. The state archives in the provincial and regional capitals were consulted for evidence about the organization of village life under baronial jurisdiction, communal activities monitored by provincial authorities before and after Italian unification, and intergovernmental relations in bureaucratic administration. Documents about public administration accessible in state archives in Sicily were those deposited at least fifty years ago. Matters related to criminal court

15

decisions are less accessible—only judicial documents deposited at least seventy years ago, before 1900, can be consulted, and these I found of use. By contrast, no such impediments existed in the consultation of communal deliberations and transactions at the Camporano commune, of Camporano land dispute and civil law proceedings before the district judge (*pretura*), and of statutes and annual reports of Camporano cooperatives, wheat banks, and church-sponsored mutual-aid societies submitted to the provincial court (*tribunale*), and of these I consulted all. Difficulties in making full use of all other papers and documents deposited before 1890 at communal, *pretura*, and *tribunale* archives were owing to the way these papers and documents had been moved to new archival locations. The central state archive in Rome was consulted especially for minutes of nineteenth-century parliamentary commissions on Sicilian agricultural problems and prefectoral and private reports to the minister of the interior on land seizure in the Camporano area after World War I; there I was also given an opportunity to consult police and prefectoral reports of the 1920s and 1930s, but the available information shed little light on Camporano political economy during the Fascist period. Accounts from villagers of all social, economic, and political standings represent a rich and overlapping source of data for some seventy years of village life, from the turn of the century to the late 1970s. These include disputes whose recollection was in most cases like, in villagers' words, "putting salt on the wound."

These principal sources of information were augmented and complemented by accounts of various epochs and events gleaned from published and unpublished material such as historical works, regional and national parliamentary reports, and church and private documents of the time. A monograph on Camporano public health written by a local physician in 1886 and a history of the town written by an expatriate villager turned journalist in 1900 not only conveyed useful information about people and events but also illuminated some of the most elementary characteristics of nineteenth-century village life that are often wrapped in obscurity (see Grew, 1974: 255). The periodical sections of the Palermo branch of the National Library and of the communal library in the provincial capital have a vast holding of regional and provincial newspapers, especially after 1880. I combed most of the regional newspapers and all the provincial newspapers for reports on Camporano political economy and found innumerable accounts of Camporano events written by village correspondents especially between 1871 and 1922 and

16

between 1944 and 1967 (see also Galasso, 1977: 504). In part as a result of the United States Freedom of Information Act, classified documents about American government involvement in Sicilian affairs during and after World War II have become accessible. I have relied upon the documentation already available, among others, in *Gli americani in Italia* by Roberto Faenza and Marco Fini (1976).

The first fieldwork in Sicily took place between the fall of 1971 and the summer of 1972. Further data collection there took place in the winter of 1976 and in the summer of 1977 and 1978. The modern Camporano setting described in chapter 2 is as it appeared in 1978, the last time I undertook research in the village itself. A short stay in Palermo in December 1980 and two trips to continental Italy in 1981—all for other projects—allowed me to augment material gathered earlier. An opportunity to extend field research over several years eased access to people and papers in and outside of Camporano, reduced the uncertainties in written and oral accounts, and fortified the present analysis. For obvious reasons and following other village studies (cf. Davis, 1978; Evans, 1976: xviii; Pitt-Rivers, 1978), archival and other material bearing directly on Camporano political history and economy will not be fully cited or identified. For the same reasons I have used pseudonyms for villagers and outsiders connected with Camporano that have no relation to their real names, and I hope to no one else's. I believe that these changes do not affect the validity of the political dynamics portrayed. They affect only the richness and vividness of details of some Camporano events. Yet, at least two problems remain in the evidentiary base of this work.

The reason for selecting a village in existence prior to the 1812–1816 changes in the structure of property rights and governmental arrangements was to determine the effects of the changes on the conduct of agricultural and communal activities. At the time of the search, however, the importance of the change from baronial jurisdiction to national jurisdiction was not fully appreciated. Moreover, a preliminary inquiry about the origins of Camporano indicated that it "dated back to 1751." Only after I had already settled in Camporano did I discover I had drawn inappropriate conclusions from this phrase. I had understood it to mean the establishment of the village. It referred, instead, to the purchase of the fief on which Camporano was founded in the 1770s. This incident provided an early and salutary warning about the need to examine the load of assumptions inherent in words. In addition, I later discovered that baronial records bearing upon the conduct of village life before 1812–1816 were, in part, destroyed by villagers during the 1820 revolt. As a result, existing records of pre-1812 times furnish sketchy and inadequate accounts of early village political economy; they do not permit a careful "before-after" evaluative study of the impact of those changes on agricultural and communal activities. My "before-after" generalizations are inferences derived from impressionistic evidence. A more careful search for the research site would have obviated this shortcoming.

Efforts to piece together individual accounts of instances of hitch, dispute, grievance, and trouble recalled events that engaged the passions and interests of most villagers and revealed who did what wrong. The recent government war on the mafia increased the discomfiture and prudence of Camporanesi who witnessed, fought against, or took part in mafia activities. Villagers—mafiosi and nonmafiosi alike—had an incentive to conceal what they did or what they remember. Some, in fact, agreed to discuss matters and volunteered to furnish "incontrovertible documentation," but during my entire stay in Camporano they somehow never found time to do so. The redundancy in villagers' recollections facilitated efforts to insure the reliability of trouble cases—old and new wounds. Yet it is also likely that possible twists of selective observation and of selective memory may have crept in—or critical trouble cases may have been left completely uncovered (cf. Wylie, 1964: ix).

The data presented in the study represent but a glimpse of approximately two hundred years of political economy experience concerned with the development of structures to sustain village life. This history can be used, however, to examine the terms and conditions of political economy in the Sicilian countryside and thus to provide an initial and tentative assessment of whether the structure of basic institutions has been the primary instrument for advancing human welfare or has been the essential source of human adversity among Sicilian villagers.

2

The Setting

Camporano, a village of twenty-four hundred persons, sits like an amphitheater on a steep slope in a range of mountains in Western Sicily. No major highway passes through its territory and the nearest railroad station is a few kilometers away in the valley below. In order to go to Camporano one must either take the road that connects it with Mozarra—the provincial town some fifty kilometers away—or wait for the bus at the railroad station for one of its four daily rounds to and from the village. Communications with Mozarra and the rest of Sicily have improved since 1875, when in a parliamentary inquiry a carabiniere captain pointed out how heavy rains during autumn and winter made the only road connecting Camporano with Mozarra practically impassable, thus isolating the village for days (minutes of the *Relazione della Giunta per l'inchiesta sulle condizioni della Sicilia*, Romualdo Bonfadini, Rapporteur, 1876; hereafter cited as Bonfadini). But today Camporanesi still find it easier to reach the cities than some of the neighboring towns with which their village is linked administratively.

The settlement dates back to 1751 when a merchant, Antonio Udo, bought the uncultivated estate (*feudo*) and its baronial title from a Spanish prince and attracted peasants from as far away as Caltagirone in Eastern Sicily. At that time an increasing demand for grain in Sicily and in Europe made it profitable to reclaim large tracts of land. The crisscross of straight, wide streets attests to its relatively recent origins. Unlike the neighboring town of Terrano, Camporano has no historic monuments—no Arab fortress, no Norman or Aragonese castle—even though peasant villagers still refer to themselves as Mogatesi, from the Arab name of the Mogata fief on which Camporano was built. All villagers speak a Sicilian rich in Arab, Norman, and Aragonese words. In part because of the American roots in the village, several English words have become part of the local language. When in the summer of 1977 a Camporano girl, who had earlier attended an American university, and her spouse from Egypt were married in the local church, several villagers could follow the entire English-language service without difficulty. In spite of the popularity of national television and radio programs and the return of emigrants from the Italian continent, the Italian language remains essentially a school language like French and a church language like Latin used to be. University students and professional people—villagers with the greatest facility in the official language—speak it only when dealing with strangers and, even then, do not hesitate to drop Sicilian words and expressions into their conversation, like village women use salt and pepper and a touch of lemon in cooking.

A plaque on the main entrance of the now dilapidated manor commemorates the fiftieth anniversary of Garibaldi's overnight stay in 1862. There is not even a monument to the World War I dead, a usual sight in any village on the Italian mainland; a small marble tablet with a list of those fallen in the two world wars sits too high for anyone to read on the wall of a three-story building that houses in part the five-room offices of the commune. At the bottom of the bell tower of the main church in the piazza, the *chiesa madrice*, a stone tablet commemorates the day when the bell tower was completed in the late 1950s. The other village church, a smaller one, built by Baron Udo around 1770, has been so remodeled as to be indistinguishable from the other. What was once the manor chapel is now a chicken coop.

Tourists seldom visit Camporano. After the death of the local mafia leader, "Don" Mariano Ardena, many journalists made brief trips to the village cemetery to see where "Don Mariano" was buried. His family mausoleum sits across from that of a senator and high magistrate of the realm. According to the cemetery custodian, very few journalists have visited it in the past ten years. The secretary of the commune, the manager, and the teller of the local branch of the Banco di Sicilia, the veterinarian, the tax inspectors (*guardie di finanza*), the labor inspectors, and eighteen of some twenty teachers—outsiders who *have to* work in the

20

village—long to return to their towns after their duties. Some of them are required by law to reside in the village but, unlike the four carabinieri who are there to maintain law and order, they have found means to evade the law. All of them dislike living in Camporano. Life in Camporano is dreary and offers few amenities to them. To emphasize this point, they refer to the many villagers who have left for Frankfurt, Montreal, Trenton, and Turin in search of a better life.

The territory of Camporano extends over approximately two thousand hectares of land, bounded to the southeast by small tributaries that are part of the southwest drainage system. The area consists mainly of irregular chains of hills and mountains with altitudes varying between 560, 778, and 891 meters above sea level. Sixty-five percent of all the Sicilian communes are 300 meters above sea level, as opposed to 47 percent of the mainland communes (La Loggia, 1955: 500). Eighty percent of the Mozarra area is between 300 and 600 meters above sea level, 9 percent below 300 meters, and 11 percent above 600 meters (Ente di Sviluppo Agricolo [ESA], Regione Siciliana, 1969: II, 8; hereafter cited as ESA).

Although the climate of Sicily can generally be described as Mediterranean, the relatively high inland region in which Camporano is located lacks some of the characteristic features. The summer is long, hot, and dry, but winter is less mild with frost and even snow in February. Precipitation on the island increases with elevation. Today in Camporano rainfall averages about 630 millimeters per year (ESA, 1969: II, 28). Rainfall has increased since 1880 when it was reported as 449 millimeters (*Atti della Giunta per la Inchiesta Agraria sulle condizioni della Classe agricola, La Sicilia*, Abele Damiani, Rapporteur, 1884 and 1885: vol. XIII, book II, part iv; hereafter cited as Damiani). But it is still insufficient to support intensive agriculture. Eighty percent of rainfall occurs between October and March, 13 percent between April and June and only 7 percent during the summer months.

The limestone region in which the village is located has a thin, clayey sand soil rich in lime but poor in humus. Down in the valley soil is usually deep and fertile as it consists of coarse alluvium washed down by streams and torrential rain. The natural forest was finally cleared between 1845 and 1890. Deforestation, plowing fields unsuitable for cultivation and overgrazing have accelerated the process that produces a rapid runoff and soil erosion.

The average lot size in Camporano is three hectares, well below that of the province (six hectares) which, in turn, is one of the lowest in Sicily.

21

There are about seven hundred lots or "farms." The 1950 land reform divided some eight hundred hectares of the Mogata fief into four hundred tracts of land. The smallest tracts are one-quarter hectares; the average tracts are about two hectares. The transfer of property did not radically affect land use patterns in the village. Camporanesi have continued to engage in extensive cultivation of cereals. Land is divided into two fields that are alternatively cultivated between hard wheat and legumes. The yield per hectare varies between twelve and fifteen *quintali* (a quintale = 100 kg., 268 lbs.), and much of the wheat is sold on the national market through local and regional intermediaries. Since about 1975, as a result of an increasing demand for tomatoes in Sicily and Italy, the tomato plant has for the most part replaced the fava bean as the alternating crop to wheat. Crops of olives, grapes, and other fruits are also important but cover a small area. By and large, plowing, harvesting, threshing, and even collecting of crops, are now done with modern farm machinery. Animal husbandry is practiced on a small scale.

The commune functions both as the local office for the vast bureaucracy of the central and regional governments and as an expression of local government. The secretary of the commune, with the assistance of eight clerks and typists, is responsible for the collection, maintenance, and transmission of vital statistics and other records, for the application of certain national plans, for issuing identity cards for men, and mules until recently, and for keeping a list of all the pension applicants. As a state representative the secretary is also initially responsible for the drafting of measures taken by the communal council or by the mayor's executive junta (the *assessori*). Five communal clerks work full time on issuing certificates, revising the electoral lists, and complying with monthly requests for vital statistics from Palermo and Rome.

Much like the local streets that bear national names, so village politics is characterized by national party labels. Since the 1978 local elections, communal government is controlled by a Left-led "civic list" or coalition made up of Communists (PCI), Socialists (PSI), Social Democrats (PSDI), and former Demochristian (DC) sympathizers. The mayor is Salvatore Albano, a fifty-two-year-old teacher and Communist who lives elsewhere in Sicily. The vice-mayor is a young Socialist land surveyor who works in Palermo. The other councilors of the twelve-member majority Left group include an unemployed university graduate, a grain merchant, a butcher, two agricultural laborers, a peasant, an artisan, and a war veteran on pension who is also the PCI secretary. The four

22

Demochristian opposition councilors are a former DC mayor and cooperative organizer, a lawyer who lives elsewhere in Sicily, a regional government employee who commutes to his place of work in Mozarra, and a peasant turned café owner.

As recently as twenty-five years ago Camporano used to export priests and nuns, but today no young villager is in the seminary or the novitiate. There are only two priests in the village now. The establishment of a Catholic youth recreation center and the organization of neighborhood prayer groups have not generated new religious vocations among young Camporanesi. Sunday masses are, however, well attended and there is a price for a seat—roughly ten cents—which goes to the sacristan. It is common to have the seat paid by someone else in the church as a sign of friendship and respect. With the exception of a few official nonbelievers like the PCI secretary, all villagers strolling in the village square follow the tradition of coming to a full stop when the main church bells strike the Vesper every afternoon.

Unlike other towns, the church in Camporano has no property. The villagers living on and beyond the Italian continent help in part to maintain the orphanage run by three nuns and to celebrate the feast of the patron saint, Saint Joseph. The archpriest, Pietro Valle, would not ask the peasants and artisans to contribute to the upkeep of the orphanage; he knows that they have little money to spare. The other priest, Giacomo Nicosia, is an old, kind, simple man, "a priest's priest" the villagers say. Both are greeted as "Father." Unlike in other parts of Italy, the appellative "don" in Sicily is reserved to priests who have achieved distinction. The last one so addressed was Father Gaetano Ardena, brother of the mafia leader.

Like other villages and towns in Sicily and the mainland South, in Camporano there has been a constant exodus of population to the city. As recently as 1951, Camporano had five thousand inhabitants; today it has half that number. The local midwife, who has been in the village since 1938, prophesied in 1971 that when she retired in 1973, there would be no need to replace her. Of those who remained, only a few had their babies delivered in the village, preferring to go to a hospital fifty kilometers away. Today the midwife's post is in fact still vacant. No one else has yet been sent by the regional government to replace the retired midwife, who now informally counsels expectant mothers. The pharmacist, who followed his father's profession and likes to live in the village, keeps the pharmacy open thanks to an annual subvention from the state.

23

Today over 45 percent of the population of Camporano is over forty-five years old, as opposed to 20 percent in 1951. The only doctor, himself sixty-six, laments the fact that he had no training in pediatrics or gerontology. His son, a physician, has moved to the city, as did two other recent graduates of medical school. Camporano no longer has a harness maker; repairs to old harnesses are done in a nearby town. Mules, donkeys, oxen, or carts have also ceased to be the major means of transportation. Most of the families, including peasant families, have some kind of motorized transportation such as a Fiat 500, a motorcycle, or a small three-wheeled *furgoncino* or *motozappa* used as a kind of pickup truck. The two blacksmiths still shoe a few mules and horses, but most of their business is constructing iron frames for doors, windows, and gates. There are two automobile repair shops, which also fix farm machinery. There is but one tailor; his one apprentice left recently to become a part-time mailman in and around Camporano. The two remaining cobblers also sell factory-made shoes.

For those who reside in the village, life is not dreary. The three cafés and the newly established snack bar on the main streets, "the circle of culture," the DC, PSI, and PCI headquarters, the Catholic workers' circle (ACLI), as well as the three barbershops provide the context in which men meet to play cards, to sip their *Averna*, and to comment on events. The circle of culture now temporarily shares its building with "the circle of Mogata," a club of artisans and peasants left without a location since the building it occupied in the piazza is being transformed by the new proprietor into a modern house. Of the ten copies of the Palermo daily *Giornale di Sicilia* and of the twelve copies of the Catania daily *La Sicilia* that are sold every morning by two of the three tobacco stores, one copy each goes to the circle of culture. Both are avidly read and commented on. The copies of the Communist-leaning newspaper from Palermo, *L'Ora*, generally remain unsold.

The piazza provides the meeting place for most villagers. There information is sought and exchanged. It is also a strategic spot to catch the mayor whenever he comes to Camporano. Knowing the individuals pacing up and down the village square, one can have a good understanding of what they are talking about. Girls no longer take their weekend strolls there. For several years now Camporano teenagers have been using a street away from the village square, near the outskirts of town, as their own piazza.

Women stroll in both piazze. In their daily visits to one of the six meat markets, one of the twelve grocery or general stores, they learn of new happenings, renew old friendships, and bargain for better prices. Schoolchildren complain that there is little for them to do in the village, but most of them like to live "among people of their own kind." When 106 of them were asked whether or not they liked to live among people of their own kind, 65 percent answered yes, 25 percent answered no, and 12 percent were undecided.

Those Camporanesi who have left like to go back at least for the feast of the patron saint, celebrated during the third week of every August. The feast of Saint Joseph is normally on March 19; the villagers moved the date to August for their convenience. A national, regional, or local election, when the State pays most of the train fare from and to the place of work almost anywhere in Western Europe, is also a good time to visit Camporano. Many are reported to take advantage of such opportunities. For the May 1972 general election, at least ten Camporanesi living in Northern Italy and West Germany came back to the village to vote. They all said that they would prefer to return to live in the village if there were work for them. By 1978, however, three of the expatriate villagers interviewed in 1972 had, perhaps permanently, returned to Camporano because they could no longer find work outside the village.

Camporano does indeed offer few amenities, but these are features of village life not uncommon elsewhere. In 1880 most houses in Camporano were single rooms with beaten earth floors, where families with ten or fifteen children lived with their pigs, goats, chickens and, if wealthy enough, a mule or a donkey (see Damiani, 1885: vol. XIII, book II, part iv). In 1951 the situation had changed little.

By 1978 most of the single-room houses had added at least another floor on top. In spite of the decrease in population and the construction of three public housing projects accommodating at least twenty-five families, most families still live in crowded but, by local standards, comfortable quarters. Of thirty-four agricultural workers asked, just three had their own two-room house. The others were renting at an average of a hundred dollars a year, in most cases equal to about 20 percent of their annual income. The commune is also short of rooms; council meetings are held in another government office. Until the middle of the 1970s, four elementary-school classes were held in an old building that lacked adequate sanitary facilities. A new elementary-school building, built near the remains of another never completed twenty years ago, is still not sufficient to house all the classrooms. Children have to take turns going to school.

Most houses are cold in winter and hot in summer. The carabiniere barracks, the bank, the post office, the orphanage, and the private houses of the doctor, the tax collector, a construction supplier, and a regional employee are the only buildings with electrical central heating. The new school building has no central heating and the small electric heaters are usually reserved for the teachers. Only since the 1950s has electric power reached the village on a regular basis. People in winter still sit around small braziers of charcoal and, those who can afford them, electric and butane gas heaters. Wood for fuel is lacking. Telephones in private houses are now almost as widespread as TV sets.

Until the end of the 1960s, discarded oil drums were used as water tanks in the front of most houses. By 1978, not more than ten such water tanks could be observed on village streets. They have been replaced by appropriate water tanks generally located on roofs. Practically all houses now have modern kitchen appliances and indoor plumbing. In the 1971 census the number of houses with a bath had risen to 189 from only 9 in 1961; most houses had a bath by 1978. Water is still scarce, however. Even in winter it is not unusual to get water from the tap just four or five times a week and only for a few hours each time. Those who can afford to, prefer to drink bottled mineral water, home-delivered gratis by two of the three cafés. Lack of water however, is not just a Camporano problem—it is a problem in most towns of a semiarid region like Sicily.

The local food stores carry most of the national and regional products. In addition, there are local products that provide a staple and fresh diet. Two bakeries bake and distribute bread every day; the six meat markets provide fresh lamb, pork and veal at least twice a week; fresh and preserved artichokes, and broad beans are, among others, local delicacies; goat and cow milk is available daily; a local farmer produces a variety of cheese at reasonable prices. Judging by the daily stops that outsiders who work in Camporano make to the local grocery stores, they seem to prefer local products to those they can purchase in Mozarra.

An observer of the local scene may easily unravel questions about what amenities the village offers. He may not so easily unravel questions about whether the structure of basic social institutions in Camporano has been the primary instrument for advancing human welfare or has been the essential source of human adversity among villagers. It is against this setting of Camporano that we now turn to an examination of this question over the course of village life since the establishment of a settlement on the Mogata fief in the eighteenth century.

3

Village Life under
Baronial Jurisdiction

The Norman landing near Messina in 1060 signaled the end of two hundred years of Moslem rule in Sicily. The new and independent kingdom of Sicily that emerged combined Moslem and Norman institutions of government to insure both the authority of the royal government over the interests common to all parts of the island and the realization of self-governing capabilities by diverse ethnic and local communities (see Genuardi, 1921; La Lumia, 1881–1883: I; Waern, 1910). Centralized government was thus accompanied by "decentralized administration" (Tocqueville, 1835: I, 89–101) appropriate to a polyglot nation and civilization. By the end of the twelfth century, however, the vicissitudes of Norman dynastic succession exposed Sicily to the competing claims of European princes and swept away its independence. The Sicilian realm became a province of successive European empires. Yet below the power of alternating viceregal administrations, certain vestiges of Sicilian independence, although half-destroyed, were still distinguishable. Parliament, baronial jurisdiction, and local laws and privileges, commonly described as feudal, kept alive a spirit of independence and self-reliance as well as a sense of the Sicilian nation. At the same time, viceregal administration and baronial jurisdiction emerged as critical agencies for both state making and capitalization.

Until the eighteenth century, the rule by different monarchs of different royal houses had little effect upon the territorial jurisdiction of Sicilian barons. By 1770, two-thirds of the Sicilian population, residing in 282 of the 367 villages and towns, lived under baronial control. Camporano was one of the last villages established under baronial jurisdiction. In 1765, thirty-seven families settled on the Mogata fief. In the 1798 census the settlement had a population of eleven hundred and a name, Camporano. A hundred years later, the village had a population of five thousand. Since the 1890s emigration has tended to keep the village population below five thousand.

This chapter examines the constitution of village life under baronial jurisdiction. Baronial records bearing upon the local political economy until 1812 were, in part, destroyed by villagers during the 1820 revolt. Existing archival and baronial records, together with information gleaned from a history of Camporano written in 1900 that utilized baronial documents apparently no longer available, provide but a glimpse of that early village life. To give contextual mapping to the Camporano experience, I first sketch the essential characteristics of Sicilian government in the eighteenth century and suggest reasons why and how they were so.

Sicily in the Eighteenth Century

The succession of Spanish Bourbon, Hapsburg, French Bourbon, and Savoy monarchs ended in 1759 with the proclamation of Ferdinand IV of Naples, the third son of the Spanish king, as the new ruler of Sicily. The change from the Spanish Bourbons to the Neapolitan Bourbons attached Sicily to the South Italian peninsula for the first time in more than three centuries. The proximity between the two parts of King Ferdinand's domain threw into sharp relief the institutions of Sicilian government.

Whereas Naples was an absolute monarchy, Sicily was a limited or constitutional monarchy without, however, Sicilians being entirely free citizens. Whereas the Neapolitan parliament, tamed to servility and silence, had fallen into desuetude by 1642, the Sicilian parliament, though weakened in its organization and powers, stubbornly clung to its last vestiges of authority in matters of taxation and to its claim of representing the Sicilian nation before the monarch. The parliament of Sicily consisted of three branches: the baronial, the ecclesiastical, and the do-

29

manial. By that time Sicily was the only part of Italy with a parliamentary and representative tradition going back to medieval times (see Koenigsberger, 1978). Koenigsberger's analysis of that tradition under Spanish rule suggests some of its passive features:

> The parliament of Sicily fought no major battles; yet its very existence (like that of a "fleet in being" that never fires its guns but yet preserves its country from defeat) safeguarded the privileges of the island. And if these privileges, like all similar privileges during the *ancien régime*, benefited only a comparatively small section of the population, every Sicilian benefited from relatively low taxes. In the end it remained true that in Sicily the Spaniards nibbled, but that elsewhere in Italy they ate and devoured. (Koenigsberger, 1971: 93)

Koenigsberger found that the Spaniards got much less money out of Sicily than out of their other Italian dominions in part because of the strength and effectiveness of the Sicilian parliament.

The vicissitudes of viceregal administration and baronial jurisdiction joined to give parliamentary lords hegemonic control of parliament and considerable standing vis-à-vis successive viceroys (Calisse, 1887; di Castro, 1601; Genuardi, 1924; Koenigsberger, 1951: 52). Hence, whereas the Neapolitan aristocracy had become a court nobility, the Sicilian aristocracy still retained some of the functions inherent in the prerogatives of rule. Whereas Naples was becoming a highly centralized system of government with growing distinction between statemaking and capitalization, Sicily was still a highly fragmented system of viceregal administration and baronial jurisdiction functioning as economic and political enterprises.

Viceregal Administration

The principal features of eighteenth-century viceregal administration dated back to the sixteenth century when Spanish Hapsburg rulers brought to a successful end the efforts of the previous rulers, the Aragonese, to exclude Sicilian barons from royal councils. This was achieved by obtaining the consent of the Sicilian parliament to a reform, among others, of the Court of the Royal Patrimony. Too late, parliamentary barons realized the implications of their consent. While holders of the great feudal offices of state were allowed to keep their ranks and titles, all effective authority was withdrawn from them and transferred to the viceroy and senior viceregal officials. The extension of viceregal authority was designed to harness Sicilian economic resources for the Hapsburg empire and to insure sole imperial control over Sicilian defense. At that time the empire stretched from North Africa to the Baltic, and Sicily was a critically important outpost in the defense of Christendom against the Turks and the Barbary states (see Crivella, 1593; Koenigsberger, 1951).

The Court of the Royal Patrimony, while retaining some judicial functions, took over the grand chamberlain's supervision of public finance to become the viceroy's principal administrative agency for bringing under imperial direction, supervision, and control all other central administrative agencies. The reach of the Patrimony over the whole field of political economy ran, however, against several constraints interposed by other more or less independent institutions, such as parliament, baronial jurisdiction, and local laws and privileges.

In order to mitigate these constraints and to cope with the difficulties inherent in controlling the details of the entire central administration, successive viceroys resorted to several strategies. They concentrated all possible authority in the few offices, like that of the auditor general of the Patrimony, which could be legally held by Spaniards. They came to rely increasingly upon selected Sicilian civil servants who toured the island as viceregal commissioners or inspectors. The viceroy's deputy and the auditor general of the Patrimony became, as one viceroy suggested, "the pivots" on which hinged the entire central administration (quoted in Koenigsberger, 1951: 101). These developments led to a transformation of the viceregal household into a viceregal secretariat—in effect, a duplicate chain of command to make the administrative agencies of the Patrimony work "as they should." Thus, by the second half of the sixteenth century centralized administration was established among a crowd of autonomous, uncoordinated, and lesser powers.

The protracted imperial wars in Europe during the seventeenth century exposed Sicily to extraordinary financial demands. Soon it became increasingly apparent that the two principal sources of imperial revenues in Sicily, parliamentary donatives or grants and export taxes on wheat imposed without the consent of parliament, were inadequate in meeting increasing military expenditures (Koenigsberger, 1951: 126–127; Mack Smith, 1968a: 201, 203–204, 208; Petino, 1946; Titone, 1955: 321–331, and 1961: 98–100). As a result, viceroys in Sicily were ordered "to sell everything which can be sold and even which cannot be sold" (quoted in Mack Smith, 1968a: 220)—in brief, government offices and even domanial towns. In 1621, the occasional sale of criminal and civil jurisdiction (the *merum et mistum imperium*) to individual barons became an established legal practice, further strengthening the local independence of the aristocracy and the seigneurial courts. If the financial and military demands of the Spanish empire stimulated the centralization of viceregal administration, the changing nature of those demands undermined that state-making process.

This chain of events did not exhaust Sicilian economic resources. Indeed the seventeenth century was the period when not only new palaces and churches were built by private individuals but also vast public works projects were carried out by local officials, and scores of new villages were established by old and new barons. But the secure investment of commercial profits in regalian rights or government offices served to reduce the availability of capital for the transformation of Sicilian technological inventions and patents into an industrial revolution (see Baviera Albanese, 1974). Political simony or "rent seeking" (Krueger, 1974; Tullock, 1967) also created additional economic difficulties for the viceregal administration as holders of new government posts and titles claimed exemptions from taxation or other privileges. The succession of different monarchs of different royal houses that followed the disintegration of the Spanish Hapsburg rule of Sicily did not put a stop to the sale of government posts—it simply increased their prices or made them into inheritable property.

By the second half of the eighteenth century, the administrative machinery of the Patrimony was still that fashioned by sixteenth-century viceroys. But the practice of rent seeking had built up year by year so many nonviceregal "pivots" within the Patrimony that viceregal administration, while keeping its earlier form, had been drained of its substance (see Arnolfini, 1768; Brancato, 1946–1947: 245–265; Pontieri, 1943: 87). Hence, though the viceroy of Sicily continued to represent and claim the power of sovereign, he enjoyed but a small portion of it. The parliamentary barons could still flatter themselves, in the words of contemporary jurists, as being "associates of the sovereign" in governing Sicily (quoted in Pontieri, 1943: 267; see also Santamaria, 1881: 123). In 1770 their territorial jurisdiction extended to about seven hundred and eighty thousand of the approximately one million one hundred seventy-six thousand people living in villages and towns.

Baronial Jurisdiction

The claim of baronial jurisdiction was based on the argument that the original Norman barons had strictly been, not feudatories of Count Roger, but his comrades-in-arms (*commilitones*) who, by helping him to conquer Sicily, had won for themselves a share of sovereignty in the land (Mack Smith, 1968b: 291). But, at least since the fourteenth century, the opportunity to become a parliamentary baron was opened to anyone (cf. Ferrigno, 1915–16: 133) with sufficient capital to purchase a fief, to pay for a royal license to people it (*licentia populandi*), and to organize the land under baronial jurisdiction as an economic enterprise. Possession of land, and not feudal title or ancient lineage as such, carried with it the right to govern people living on it.

At the same time, the internal organization of each fief, at least since the twelfth century, was subject to an agreement (*concordia* or *pactum*) between the baron and the settlers, specifying the rights and duties of each. The agreement, which became known as the Pact of the Land or the Chapters of the Land, was stipulated with minor exceptions in the language common to the contracting parties "for precaution, certitude, and firmness" (from a 1482 agreement, quoted in Garufi, 1947: 25). It represented the constitution of individual lands or settlements. A baron could sell the fief to someone else but the charter of the village remained in force and the basic rights of villagers could not be changed without the consent of all the townsfolk, meeting as "the regular parliament" or "general assembly." Civil disputes between barons and villagers were adjudicated by the judicial branch of the Patrimony, as chapters of the land were generally endorsed by the viceroy. Thus, the meaning of baronial jurisdiction had reference to the rights and duties that each baron enjoyed under the constitution of each fief. Territorial jurisdiction of a baron was constrained, at least in theory, by the constitution of each fief (see Garufi, 1908; Genuardi, 1911; Sorge, 1910–1916; Starrabba, 1879; Testa, 1973: 91–172; Verdirame, 1904a, 1904b, 1905a, 1905b, 1906; cf. Fenoaltea, 1975; North, 1981: chapter 10).

The practice of grounding the constitution of settlements upon the consent of the barons and the settlers and, correlatively, the practice of assigning the conduct of communal affairs to local residents often acted not only as a constraint to baronial despotism but also as an incentive for barons and settlers alike to sustain mutually productive relationships

(Diecidue, 1966; Genuardi, 1911: 43, and 1921; La Colla, 1883; Salvioli, 1902; Santacroce, 1907; Verdirame, 1905a, 1906). It became not uncommon for barons and local residents to come to the aid of each other in times of distress (Cancila, 1974: 15–16). In other instances, barons came to the rescue of their tenants by shouldering or canceling payment of their taxes during bad harvest or drought years (Titone, 1961: 35–36, 38–40). Moreover, whenever communal officials were involved in renegotiating the terms and conditions of the Chapters of the Land on behalf of the villagers and whenever villagers revolted en masse against their barons for levying what seemed intolerable increases in imposts, the protestors justified their acts of resistance or civil disobedience, and appealed for the resolution of conflict, on the necessity to realize their joint advantages *with* the lord (see Battaglia, 1895; Ferrigno, 1915–16; Genuardi, 1911: 80; Guarnieri, 1889; Pupillo-Barrese, 1903: 38, 64; cf. Scott, 1976).

These aspects of the manorial system suggest covenantal rather than contractual arrangements (see Elazar, 1978; Fenoaltea, 1975; North and Thomas, 1971). They entered in many ways into the pattern of Sicilian life to become important features of the Sicilian political tradition (Gallo, 1969). But the manorial system also had less positive aspects.

Though by the sixteenth century, master-servant relationships had given way to relationships between large landlords on one hand, and tenant sharecroppers, wage earners, and small independent farmers or copyholders (*burgisi*) on the other, many features of villenage remained (Peri, 1965 and 1978). The need to have the consent of both contracting parties in order to alter the decision-making capabilities assigned under a village charter set limits upon the development of a new charter to meet the changing economic situation. In turn, settlers faced the critical problem of trying both to insure the integrity of the mutually agreed terms and conditions and to prevent unilateral changes in the constitution of fiefs at the same time when, given the particular division of labor and the inequalities of conditions, they were in a markedly asymmetrical system of interdependence with the lord. As a result, the history of baronial jurisdiction is also the history of exploitative relationships of rulers to ruled, ruinous lordships, and antiquated agrarian economies (Li Vecchi, 1975; Salvioli, 1902: 390; Tricoli, 1966; cf. Blum, 1978; North, 1981: chapter 10; Popkin, 1979: chapter 2).

The availability of capital resulting in part from the growth of market

34

economy, the increasing demands for Sicilian wheat in Europe, the rise in population stimulated by the influx of Greek and Albanian refugees from the Turkish empire, and the relatively open entry rule for becoming a parliamentary baron joined to make the seventeenth century "the golden age of baronial jurisdiction." Old and new barons risked enormous sums of money to reorganize bankrupt fiefs and to establish new ones—in effect, to colonize the Sicilian interior. The critical part played by old and new lords in the colonization of the Sicilian interior has led different historians of different ideological persuasions to refer to these Sicilians as "bold and courageous agrarian capitalists" (Titone, 1955: 54; see also Pontieri, 1943: 52–55; Renda, 1963: 24–25, and 1974: 54–56). But barons were not the only agrarian capitalists. Though we know less about the settlers, in part because the assumption of self-sufficiency has led many researchers to neglect the capital requirements of frontier settlements, they were also engaged in the task of creating capital. Scattered evidence in several works suggests that many settlers were able to outfit themselves with their own resources, literally taking their capital equipment with them (see Di Giovanni, 1876; Garufi, 1922, 1946, 1947; Gattuso, 1976; Testa, 1973). In turn, this "frontier movement" had the effect of renewing and strengthening the number and position of parliamentary barons in the state-making process. The colonization of the Sicilian interior also led barons and settlers to covenant or contract consciously with one another to create new communities.

By the eighteenth century, the basic rights and duties of villagers and barons and the facilities to determine, enforce, and alter them had become so widespread and recognized that some fiefs were peopled without written agreements. Also by that time, some inherent weaknesses in the constitution of established fiefs had reached staggering proportions.

The extent to which baronial jurisdiction functioned according to its design and performance criteria depended, in part, upon the willingness or interest of each baron to exercise his (or her) residual authority and control over the management of the fief so as to constrain those who found it to their advantage to shirk their efforts and function as free riders in the production process. Yet there were at least three reasons why barons had incentives to shirk these very responsibilities and to turn over the management of their estates to rentiers (*gabelloti*), in exchange for a constant share of the estate earnings. First, while the primogeniture law of succession and the law of entails assured the transmission of baronies over time, they could not necessarily assure the transmission of a

35

willingness or interest to manage or direct estates to successive barons. It was difficult to expect the entrepreneurial skills possessed by the first lord to be continued by inheritance (cf. Bagehot, 1867: 63). Second, while the first-born sons stood to inherit baronies, they did not have sole claims to baronial earnings. Their brothers and sisters were entitled to receive at least one-third of those earnings without, however, shouldering any responsibility or risk for the economic productivity of the estate. Third, some barons found it difficult to resist the attraction provided by the tax-free position of Palermo and, thus, tended to abandon their fiefs to establish themselves in the capital city.

There developed a situation whereby many barons could not, in the words of the Sicilian economist Abbé Balsamo, "be persuaded that without the necessary attention, labor bestowed, and prudence, their forefathers could neither have acquired, nor bequeathed that to their descendants which secures them from the chilling hand of poverty" (Balsamo, 1809: 13). In turn, leasing estates for a very short period helped barons to keep abreast of inflation but also discouraged rentiers from managing the estates as if they were their own (cf. Greenfield, 1934: 19–26; Romeo, 1950: 28–32). In such circumstances, shirking and free riding became widespread and, in certain cases, assumed major proportions.

Some barons unilaterally canceled long leasehold or copyhold contracts (the *enfiteusi* or emphyteusis) when they found their fixed incomes sharply reduced by inflation, even though under emphyteusis land could not be taken away from the cultivator as long as he, his family, or his heirs cultivated it. Baronial agents left to themselves were prone to do the same. In order to make quick returns, both rentiers and cultivators often underinvested in the factors of production (Sergio, 1777: 7–9). Some boards of local officials became self-perpetuating local oligarchies operating with immunity from barons and villagers alike (Li Vecchi, 1975). Villagers found that recourse to the viceregal administration so as to command the services of impartial officials or to sustain existing agreements against new demands and unilateral cancellations of contracts was neither always readily available nor always impartial (Guarnieri, 1892: 145). In 1752, the Spanish Bourbon monarch ratified the arbitrary abrogation of *enfiteusi* by barons without any compensation to dispossessed cultivators in exchange for baronial support—further eroding the integrity of the Patrimony.

Thus the extent to which baronial jurisdiction did not function "as it should" was due to a lack of baronial willingness or interest to exercise residual authority and control over the management of fiefs, but also to the failure of viceregal administration to provide the supporting structures for the formulation and maintenance of Chapters of the Land. Only exposure to the competitive pressures existing in the "frontier movement" and in the wheat market served as effective means to bias or rig the structure of individual and family incentives toward a consideration of a wider community of interests and a longer time horizon. This exposure also accounts, in part, for the establishment of settlements like Camporano in the eighteenth century.

The Mogata Fief and the Constitution of Camporano

The site on which Camporano was established had been an Arab settlement known as Mogattah. The vicissitudes of the Norman conquest apparently forced most of the Arab population to desert the settlement. Between 1197 and 1750 the fief retained its geographic boundary but remained most of the time uncultivated. By the second half of the eighteenth century, an increasing demand for grain in Sicily and Europe made it profitable to reclaim uncultivated fiefs. In 1751, Antonio Udo, an enterprising merchant from a Mozarra rentier family, purchased the fief and its title of nobility. He died in 1780 and it was left to his son Filadelfio, the second baron of Mogata, to insure the realization of Mogata as an economic and political enterprise.

Between 1765 and 1790, at least 250 families settled on the fief. The provenience of Mogata cultivators tends to support Titone's observation that the establishment of new baronial communities "became for (the settlers) that which the American colonies came to mean for rebels and refugees of so many European countries" (Titone, 1955: 81). At least half of the total number of settlers originated from baronial towns where the management of agricultural activities was in the hands of rentiers and where boards of local officials had become self-perpetuating oligarchies. At least twenty-two settlers came from "places unknown," a traditional euphemism that described people fleeing from creditors or jails, or both.

By the time Mogata was populated, the basic rights and duties of the

37

baron and the villagers had become so established that no separate pact or chapters of the land were drawn up. The second baron of Mogata became a member of the Sicilian parliament when the fief reached the required entry rule of eighty tax-paying families. This event took place before 1798. In the 1798 *riveli* or census, the settlement, now called Camporano, had a population of eleven hundred.

By the turn of the eighteenth century, the essential structure of basic social institutions was at work in Camporano. Baron Udo differed from the rest of the villagers by certain exemptions and privileges. In spite of diverse social conditions, villagers were, however, connected among each other and with the Udo family through common interests arising from the conduct of agricultural and village affairs.

The Organization of Agricultural Activities

The fief consisted of about eleven hundred salms (*salme*), about twenty-five hundred hectares. The discrepancy between this figure and that cited in chapter 2 is attributable to several factors, including differences between old and new measures of the salm and the hectare and inaccuracies in the original cadastral survey. The Sicilian salm refers to both a unit of land surface and a unit of cubic measure. In the Camporano area, a salm of land is slightly more than two hectares; a salm of wheat is roughly two hundred and twenty kilograms. Both types of salms are subdivided into sixteen *tumoli*; one *tumolo* equals one bushel.

Each settler was given a salm of land in return for two salms of wheat to be paid to the baron each year. The baron anticipated the first seed. This agricultural contract was the emphyteusis lease. By 1810, ninety-six new tracts of land of a salm each were given to additional settlers, bringing to at least 350 salms the land cultivated through copyhold contract. At the time, half a salm of land yielded from five to eight salms of wheat a year. The settler used the other half salm of land to cultivate legumes. Thus, the early settlers could produce sufficient products to insure their subsistence and to sell their surplus. At the same time, the baron was assured of a fixed annual income. This long-term land contract provided the basis for the development of the burgisi, the small landowning class of Camporano.

All the villagers enjoyed the usufruct rights (*usi civici*) of common property resources like grass, water and, apparently, gypsum. Usufruct rights were inherent in the *jura civitatis* and for this reason villagers were known as communists. The protection and maintenance of a safe yield of common property resources was assigned to local officials known as *bagli*.

Unlike many other nobles of his time, the second baron of Mogata took an active part in the direction and supervision of agricultural activities. He was aided by a number of paid employees who made up the administration of baronial jurisdiction as an economic enterprise. The number of paid servants changed over the years, but the number of important employees remained fairly constant. The most important employee was the overseer or steward who was in charge of the day-to-day management of the agricultural enterprise. In his task he was assisted by private guards on horseback, the *campieri*, who scouted the fields, animals, and crops. The other permanent employees of some importance were the accountant or bookkeeper, the storekeeper, and the oxen and horse drivers. Their salaries were paid partly in money and partly in kind.

The estate administration served not only to supervise the copyhold leases but also to direct the cultivation of the rest of Mogata. About seven hundred salms of land were farmed by the baron, using the cereal-based rotation pattern, wheat, pasture, and fallow, that had become characteristic of Sicilian latifundia. The usual contract between the baron and each cultivator was the *metateria* (half) system of sharecropping. The original settlers farmed their own lots as well as the baron's land. By 1812, the agricultural labor force was divided between the *enfiteuti* and sharecroppers known as the burgisi, and the casual laborers known as the *annalori* and *jurnatari*. A sharecropper possessed at least a mule or a plow; a casual laborer tended to have neither.

The Organization of Village Life

The organization of village life took place according to the familiar principles of baronial jurisdiction. The baron designated the area for establishing the village (cf. Gattuso, 1976: 15). A church was completed by 1785. Apparently, the feudal claims that the baron could make on villagers dealt only with services for remuneration (*perangarie*), such as bringing a load of wood and hay and a chicken to the manor. The board of local officials included a captain, a judge, four jurors, a prison jailer, a secretary, and a treasurer. The baron appointed these officials after

39

consulting all the male family heads. Their terms of office lasted one year, in keeping with the local maxim that public officials, like pigs, should not last more than one year.

Camporano jurors decided, in consultation with Baron Udo, what local taxes to levy and at the same time collected taxes for the royal government. Local taxes were levied on all villagers. At least until 1812, Baron Udo was exempt from paying local taxes. He bore, however, almost all the cost of village government, including the maintenance and upkeep of the church, and other expenses for the care of souls. The baron retained the right to name the vicar. He was not, however, exempt from paying land tax. If the 1811 *riveli* records are correct, Udo paid almost all the land tax that jurors collected for the viceregal administration. The village budget for 1812 shows that the major proportion of local revenues was for the care of orphans and for the salaries of the doctor, the midwife, and the elementary schoolteacher.

Community life was characterized by specialization and jointness of efforts between the lord and settlers, including the sharing, in varying degrees, of the residual claims of the earnings of baronial jurisdiction as an economic enterprise. Thus it would seem that, unlike the case of other villages and towns, the essential structure of baronial jurisdiction provided those early Camporanesi with the rudiments of local self— government.

Conclusion

The transformation of the realm of Sicily into a province or dominion of successive empires served not only to combine and fuse together state making and capitalization but also to channel them into two different processes. These processes were centralized viceregal administration and baronial jurisdiction. While the vestiges of Sicilian independence constrained the reach of centralized administration, the changing "practice of empire" (Koenigsberger, 1951) undermined the very principles of centralized administration. In turn, the growth of feudal settlements threw into sharp relief basic flaws inherent in baronial jurisdiction as a political and economic enterprise. This Sicilian past hardly fits the model histories of sovereign states. But it does not give full support to center-periphery concepts of dependency-marginality theory either. Parliament, baronial jurisdiction, and local laws and privileges were by no means expressions of self-rule and autonomy. But they did work to limit the capacity of metropolitan centers of successive economic world systems to extract and exploit Sicilian resources with immunity. The *Capitula regni Siciliae* or liberties of Sicily outlasted several empires and economic world systems; islanders continued to trade their grain with the rest of Europe until the eighteenth century. This Sicilian past does not entirely bear out the moral economy notion, nor does it destroy it.

The establishment of Camporano took place within the context of baronial state making and capitalization. By the early 1810s, the very efforts to repair the failings of Sicilian government stood to pry Sicily loose from her political tradition and to sweep away the fragile Camporano beginnings.

4

National Jurisdiction and Village Relationships

In the course of the latter part of the eighteenth century, as Camporanesi were fashioning the rudiments of local self-government, viceregal officials sought to repair the failings of Sicilian government by attempting to attach to themselves and weld into a whole all the elements of authority that were dispersed among an array of autonomous, uncoordinated, and lesser powers. By confounding the need to reform the fragmented but not overlapping system of Sicilian government with the desire to bring the island closer to the level of Neapolitan political development, viceregal reform became synonymous with Neapolitan oppression. Baronial opposition to viceregal reform became, instead, synonymous with the defense of the liberties of Sicily.

In a calculated move, the barons introduced in 1812 their own political reform. They relinquished their claims to territorial jurisdiction but also forced the Neapolitan Bourbon king to recognize a fully independent parliamentary monarchy for Sicily. Thus the 1812 constitutional monarchy was set alongside that of "Sicily's sister island," Britain. But, unlike the British case, the events that made the 1812 Sicilian constitutional experiment possible also helped to bring it down. In 1816 the Neapolitan government extended its jurisdiction to all the Sicilian communities. In 1860 the annexation of Sicily to the nascent kingdom of

Italy reiterated central government jurisdiction over Sicilian affairs and finalized the end of the Sicilian nation.

This chapter examines how the shift from baronial to central jurisdiction affected the organization and conduct of village life in Camporano. I shall first focus upon the events associated with the transition from baronial to central jurisdiction. I shall then turn to the reconstitution of village relationships after 1816 by examining the organization and conduct of agricultural and communal affairs and the position of Camporanesi in the nation-state. The villagers' efforts to minimize their exposure to the consequences deriving from the reconstituted political economy will provide the essential focus for subsequent chapters. The Camporano archival data for this and the next chapter come primarily from the records of the Camporano commune and the state administrative agencies.

From Baronial to Central Jurisdiction

By the 1770s a concern for the failings of the Sicilian political economy and the consequences that these were having upon Sicilian life was becoming widespread among members of the baronial class. This concern was stimulated by the writings of publicists who, as ecclesiastics, noblemen, or jurists, had already special interests in economics, education, and law. The study of Sicilian history, coupled with the discovery of Blackstone, Hume, and Adam Smith, led the great majority of Sicilian publicists to conclude that governmental reforms advantageous to all could be introduced in accordance with the Sicilian political tradition.

A concern for the failings of the Sicilian political economy, filtered through the Neapolitan political tradition, led Bourbon officials to antithetical conclusions. In order to repair those failings, they reasoned, it was necessary to bring down the entire edifice of Sicilian government— in effect, to extend absolutist rule over the island. As was shown in chapter 3, previous such attempts had been incidental to royal or imperial financial policies. Monarchs had been less concerned with the suppression of parliament, baronial jurisdiction, and local laws and privileges than in making money out of them. Now, royal reforms intended to sweep away the very *Capitula regni Siciliae* (Pontieri, 1943, 1961). Neapolitan remedial policy was thus unprecedented in both intent and scope.

43

The marquis Domenico Caracciolo of Villamaina appeared to the Bourbon court as the best Neapolitan official to possess the skills and knowledge necessary to effect basic changes in Sicily. As the Neapolitan envoy in Paris for more than a decade, the sixty-six-year-old former magistrate had developed an admiration for the ability with which successive French monarchs had curtailed seigneurial jurisdiction and centralized the organization of the French state. The study of French political practices and ideas led the marquis of Villamaina to conclude that in order to repair Sicilian government, it was necessary "to liquidate the heredity of the past" (quoted in Pontieri, 1943: 164). No intermediate power, secondary organizations, or deliberative assemblies should stand in between the monarch and the Sicilian people.

Caracciolo became viceroy in 1781. As soon as he reached Sicily, the new viceroy confounded in indiscriminate hatred (see Renda, 1974: 91–93) all things Sicilian—both the worst and what was best in Sicilian political tradition. He attempted to check baronial abuses but also to undermine the political covenant between the monarch and the barons. He sought to reduce the gross inequalities in parliamentary taxation and the accumulated immunities of local corporations but also to erase representative and secondary institutions. He tried to break down class distinctions but also to suppress the political rights and liberties of both the aristocracy and the lowest classes. Like the French he admired and the Neapolitans he served, the marquis of Villamaina could envisage political equality and free trade but could not envisage political liberty and free institutions. By declaring himself the enemy at once of Sicilian barons and Sicilian institutions, Caracciolo transformed baronial opposition to tax reforms into a defense of the Sicilian nation. As a result, baronial pressures on Sicilian officials in Naples to have the Bourbon court recall the viceroy received the support of the very same people Caracciolo thought needed to be delivered from bondage.

If the marquis of Villamaina failed "to liquidate the heredity of the past," he did, however, introduce several reforms that, among others, strengthened the reach of viceregal administration and brought baronial jurisdiction back to better performance levels. At the same time, before leaving Sicily in 1786, Caracciolo prevailed upon King Ferdinand to force the royal courts to reinterpret the legal basis of baronial jurisdiction. In 1788, the Bourbon monarch issued a pragmatic sanction or royal decree stating that fiefs were held in return for duties performed and could not be bequeathed or alienated like alodial property. Barons were not associates of the king in governing Sicily.

Events associated with the French Revolution introduced critical variations in the conflict between the Bourbon crown and the Sicilian aristocracy. First, war compelled the royal family to seek refuge in Sicily and to depend upon money voted by the Sicilian parliament. Second, the Bourbons' flight to Sicily occurred at a time when, in part as a result of Caracciolo's reforms, most barons had acquired a new awareness of their constitutional rights. Third, the British occupation of Sicily in 1806 not only strengthened Sicilian defense against French invasion from the Calabrian coast and furnished the Bourbon king with much-needed subsidies from the British government, but also gave Sicilian noblemen and publicists like the prince of Castelnuovo and Abbé Balsamo an opportunity to renew their ties with "Sicily's sister island" (see De Mattei, 1927: 51–52; Giarrizzo, 1966). Another circumstance associated with the French Revolution was the spread of Jacobin ideas among members of the Sicilian professional class, but this had not yet become a determining factor in Sicilian public life.

In 1810, the one-hundred and twenty-fifth parliament met to hear a speech from the throne extolling the *Capitula regni Siciliae*—"institutions lost by other nations for lack of public spirit and national energy and preserved only in the two most famous islands in the world, Great Britain and Sicily" (quoted in Rosselli, 1956: 14). This doffing of the hat to Sicilian political tradition was accompanied by a call for an extraordinary donative of 360,000 Sicilian *onze* a year (about £235,000) and a new distribution of taxes. The barons, led by the prince of Belmonte, the prince of Castelnuovo and the prince of Cassaro and supported by the ecclesiastical lords, reduced the royal request to half and presented a counterplan for taxation that went beyond the very tax reforms they or previous barons had bitterly opposed during Caracciolo's viceroyalty. Their counterplan called, among others, for a single tax of 5 percent on the income of all the real estate outside of Palermo, including the barons' as well as the king's.

Rather than face the baronial challenge or seek more British subsidies, the Bourbon monarch tried to increase his revenues without parliamentary consent. A majority of peers, including the second baron of Mogata, requested the king to withdraw the nonparliamentary taxation and to trust to the bounty of parliament for the supply of his wants. King

Ferdinand responded by ordering the arrest and exile of the leaders of the protesting lords. At this point the British minister plenipotentiary and commander of the seventeen thousand British soldiers in Sicily, the Whig nobleman William Bentinck, intervened in the conflict between the crown and the parliament.

Bentinck successfully pressured King Ferdinand to set free the imprisoned barons, to withdraw the extraparliamentary taxes, and to replace the Neapolitan ministry with a Sicilian ministry. While Lord Bentinck became, in effect, the viceroy of Sicily, the new ministry, now made up of three of the five imprisoned barons, called parliament together in June 1812. The barons, led by Belmonte and Castelnuovo and aided by Balsamo, turned to the British constitution and the very terminology of British politics to deal once and for all with Neapolitan designs over Sicily and to adapt the medieval Sicilian constitution to modern conditions. In part because of the common origin of both nations in the Norman conquest, Sicilians as early as the sixteenth century tended to call up the English constitution when defending Sicilian liberties. Therefore, it is easy to understand why in 1812 the English constitution still "seemed an attractive model to those who wished to mend rather than end their ancient institutions" (Rosselli, 1956: 5).

"The Anglo-Sicilian constitution" swept away baronial jurisdiction and feudal dues and privileges. Fiefs would now be alodial or private properties. The three houses of parliament were replaced by a House of Commons and a House of Lords. Money bills were to originate only in the Commons. The administration of justice was entrusted to a body of independent judges; everyone was equal before the law and no one could be imprisoned without due process. While Sicily was divided into twenty-three districts, municipal institutions were recast upon principles of local self-government. The realm of Sicily was declared independent of the realm of Naples and of every other country or dominion.

Before the new constitution took effect, critical policy differences emerged between Belmonte, who could be compared to "a great Whig nobleman," and Castelnuovo, who drew inspiration from Republican Rome and America (Rosselli, 1956: 7). Soon after the election of the first reform parliament in 1813, both Belmonte and Castelnuovo faced *at once* all the problems that had accompanied the British parliament between the seventeenth and the nineteenth centuries. As a result, they experienced serious difficulties in checking King Ferdinand's efforts to wreck the constitution, in establishing and following the principle of cabinet responsibility, and in maintaining parliamentary support for their ministry in the face of an emerging "Jacobin party" in the Commons and a resurgent "*statu-quo-ante* Caracciolo party" in the Lords. The range of factors that impinged on the ability of Sicilian leaders to govern was far greater than that experienced by their British counterparts (see Balsamo, 1848; La Lumia, 1881–1884: IV, 393–458; Romeo, 1950: 145–146; Rosselli, 1956; cf. Binder et al., 1971).

By 1814, the constitutional barons could neither make use of parliament nor manage public affairs without it. What they needed was a long time span in order to work out or solve the accumulation of governmental issues and problems generated by the constitutional reform experiment; but time they did not have.

Lord Bentinck's intervention in Sicilian affairs had given Sicilian leaders hope that British support would serve to maintain conditions favorable to the long-term survival of the new Sicilian constitution. It was, however, an ill-founded hope. British policy in Italy, anchored as it was to Austria, ran precisely against the very survival of the Sicilian constitutional experiment. By 1814, with the specter of Napoleonic domination of Europe receding in the background, the British foreign minister Castlereagh replaced Bentinck with a minister who had the same regard for the 1812 constitution as King Ferdinand had. Thus Sicily's constitutional experiment was ultimately decided not at Palermo but at the Congress of Vienna (Rosselli, 1956: 155). While the very abolition of feudalism served to pry Sicily loose from her political tradition, it took the Congress of Vienna to make of Sicily, in the famous words of a contemporary Neapolitan historian, "a posthumous conquest of Napoleon" (Luigi Blanch, quoted in Rosselli, 1956: 153).

In December 1816 the Bourbon king became Ferdinand I of the new Kingdom of the Two Sicilies. The Sicilian parliament was abolished; so were the Sicilian flag and freedom of the press. The Napoleonic code and the system of French administration imposed on the Neapolitan provinces during the French occupation, were now found to be useful instruments to extend absolutist rule over Sicily. Seven Sicilian provinces were created and administered by provincial intendants and nonelected communal officials. The enforcement of regulations issued from Naples became, however, subject to serious institutional weakness and failure. At the same time, control over agricultural resources now gave Sicilian barons and their agents a political power they never had before. By the 1870s, the situation had changed little. As Sidney Sonnino (1847–

47

1924), a future prime minister of Italy, observed in his now classic study of Sicilian rural conditions in 1876:

> The situation we found in 1860 persists today. . . . We have legalized the existing oppression and are assuring the impunity of the oppressors. In modern societies, tyranny of the law is restrained by fears of remedies outside of the law. In Sicily, with our institutions patterned on liberal formalism rather than informed by a true spirit of liberty, we have furnished the oppressing classes the legal means to defend their oppression and to take over all the public positions by the use and abuse of brute power [*forza*] that was and continues to be in their hands. We are now strengthening the oppressors' hands by reassuring them that, no matter how far they push their oppression, we will not tolerate any kind of illegal remedy, while there can be no legal remedy, for they have legality on their side. (Sonnino, 1877: 339)

As a result, Sicilian peasants found themselves locked in what Sonnino called an "iron circle" (see also La Loggia, 1894: 221–226; Romano, 1958: chapter 18). On one hand, they suffered labor contracts imposed by the monopoly of large landowners or their agents and supported by the arms of the state; on the other, they bore the cost of government, without voice and with little benefit. Most Sicilians continued to face conditions of life devoid of opportunities and remedies for enhancing their long-term welfare potential well after they became Italians. It is important to anticipate what will become apparent in this and the next chapter. I am not suggesting or implying that the fathers of Italian unification deliberately set out to victimize people. Even Bourbon leaders showed genuine interest in improving conditions of life in the South. I am suggesting that both Bourbon and Italian leaders assumed or took for granted that the reconstitution of agricultural and communal activities as a function of their statemaking would have primarily beneficial effects (cf. Cammett, 1963; Davis, 1979; Landi, 1977; Romeo, 1980; Sabetti, 1982).

The Reconstitution of Agricultural Activities

The 1812 parliament redefined the meaning of fiefs from a bundle of rights enjoyed by barons and villagers alike to a private property enjoyed by the barons alone. While the abolition of common property rights gave barons extensive proprietary authority over natural resources, the abolition of remaining feudal dues and privileges gave barons very limited scope and domain of authority over the local population. Private property in land was now joined by a free labor market. But the way local government and parliament were reconstituted in 1812 represented a serious devaluation of rural proprietorship as determinant of authority and power among Sicilians (see also Loveman, 1976b: 3–21). The creation of the Kingdom of the Two Sicilies changed all this. The destruction of representative institutions annuled the devaluation of rural proprietorship—in effect placing the labor force in a subject position vis-à-vis large landowners without the limitations that large landowners had faced under feudalism. By the end of the nineteenth century, the land workers themselves began to place some limitations on the rights of rural proprietors. Chapter 5 will deal with some of the initial efforts. The rest of this section examines the legal position of Mogata, the fate of the civic usufructs, and the internal organization of the former fief as determinants of authority and power among villagers. The development of different social classes resulting from the organization of agricultural activities will be presented in chapter 5.

The Legal Position of the Ex-Fief of Mogata

The Neapolitan government attempted to divide the former fiefs by abolishing the system of entails and primogeniture and by permitting creditors to take land in settlement of debts incurred by the aristocracy. These efforts, together with the succession laws of the Napoleonic Code favoring younger sons, gradually broke up some large estates only to have new large landowners emerge. The change from the Bourbon to the Savoy monarchy in 1860, accompanied as it was by the requirements of electoral and parliamentary politics, gave old and new "barons" additional means to maintain and, in some cases, to extend the territorial integrity of their lands. Whatever limitations occurred in rural proprietorship in the course of the nineteenth century, they took place more as a

49

result of market pressures and accidental circumstances than as a result of governmental policies. By the end of the nineteenth century the *latifondi* or large estates still covered half the Sicilian territory (see Ganci, 1973; Mack Smith, 1965).

In Camporano the first-born son of the baron continued to own the Mogata estate. When the direct line of the Udo family became extinct in 1850, the fief passed to a member of the cadet line, Liborio Udo. When he died in 1889, his heirs sold the estate, now some thirteen hundred hectares, to an industrialist who, in turn, gave it to his daughter upon her marriage to a Sicilian prince. The transfer of property did not affect, however, the conduct of agricultural activities. Nor did it affect some six hundred hectares held under emphyteusis lease, whose rent continued to be collected by heirs of the original lords (see also Barbera, 1964).

Common Property Rights

Between 1825 and 1827 the Bourbon government recognized the enclosure of feudal land by barons but, at the same time, decreed that the local population should be compensated for the loss of immemorial communal rights. In Camporano a local commission, headed by the mayor, surveyed and reported to the intendant the common property rights enjoyed by "Camporano communists" but, like the work of similar commissions elsewhere, nothing seems to have come out of this.

Perhaps one reason why the 1825–1827 laws had little or no effect was that, in spite of the 1812 abolition, Camporanesi had continued to obtain water for themselves and their animals, to glean in the stubble, to pasture animals, and to quarry gypsum and rock for building on Mogata as they had done in the past. The situation in Camporano was not exceptional for, as a student of public economy found in 1825, throughout Sicily there were still "vast extensions of territory where one person owns the land, another the trees, a third has the right to cut down trees, and a fourth can pasture his animals" (Palmeri, 1826: 57). Why this state of affairs persisted in Camporano may also be attributable to the absence of Epifanio Udo, the third baron of Mogata, who for his participation in the "separatist revolt" of 1820, had to leave Sicily for a few years.

As soon as he was able to return to Camporano, Udo took charge of his estate. In the late 1820s he carried out so many improvements and innovations on his land that he won a government prize for dedication to rural economy. Although it is clear that these activities gave work to several

50

hundred villagers, it is not clear how they affected the civic usufruct rights that villagers enjoyed. There must have been some friction or conflict between baron Udo and villagers, but these events must not have been of a sufficient magnitude to break the commonality of interests that united them. When, for example, in 1837 the cholera epidemic reached Camporano, Udo did not hesitate to transform his manor into a free dispensary of medicine and foodstuffs. A few years later, however, common property rights on Mogata did become an issue between the baron and Camporanesi.

Following his tour of Sicilian provinces in 1838, King Ferdinand II instructed intendants to resolve the common-property-rights question. These instructions, amalgamated in an 1841 law (texts in Battaglia, 1895; 85–92, 298–314), divided civic usufruct rights into two groups: essential rights such as water, grazing, and quarrying, which were eligible for compensation; and non-essential rights such as gleaning in the stubble and gathering wild herbs, which were not eligible for compensation. In an attempt to maintain some support among the Sicilian barons, the Neapolitan government stipulated that the common property rights subject to compensation were either those in use before 1735 or those usurped by barons before and after that date and that, in either case, the burden of proof lay with the local population. As a result, this law proved difficult to enforce and open to innumerable abuses (see Damiani, 1884: vol. XIII, book I, 103; *Inchiesta parlamentare sulle condizioni dei contadini nelle provincie meridionali e nella Sicilia, Sicilia*, Giovanni Lorenzoni, Rapporteur, 1910: vol. VI, book I, 258–342; hereafter cited as Lorenzoni, 1910). Camporano is one of the cases where the compensation laws themselves undermined the civic usufruct rights of local residents.

Acting on behalf of villagers, Camporano officials attempted to have these compensatory laws apply to Mogata. But they could not demonstrate either that members of the Camporano community had enjoyed essential civic usufruct rights before 1735 or that successive barons had usurped those rights, as the fief was settled without written agreement. Attorneys for Udo contended that whatever common property rights settlers had enjoyed on Mogata before and after 1812 were not legal or lawful, but expressions of the benevolence of successive Mogata proprietors. They were able to show that after 1812 at least thirteen villagers quarrying gypsum and rock on Mogata had done so with baronial permission and after paying a small fee; and that as late as August 1838 the

51

Camporano mayor had appealed to baronial philanthropy for the communal use of Mogata water springs.

In 1843 the Mozarra intendant ruled that villagers could not be compensated for the loss of civic usufruct rights when they had not lawfully enjoyed them in the first place. The decision by the intendant disposed of the common property claims of villagers. Yet, according to a report to the intendant prepared by an intendancy official sent to Camporano in 1840, Baron Udo had not been insensitive to the villagers' claims. According to this report, Baron Udo had been prepared "to give up (some land) with the liberality of a donor and not with the servility of a debtor." So it seems that the very attempt by Camporano communal officials to have him give up land "with the servility of a debtor" produced the greatest social cost for villagers.

Mogata as Private Property

The 1843 intendancy decision clarified the position of Mogata as private property. But what helped to maintain the proprietary rights of succeeding barons over the natural resources and control over the labor force was the internal administration of the former fief.

The day-to-day management of the estate continued to be in the hands of the overseer, who became known as the steward. He was assisted by at least two private guards, the *campieri*; the noticeable change after 1843 was the increased importance of *campieri* in monitoring trespasses and in enforcing agricultural "contracts." From the 1840s until the 1880s, the overseers came from the Vallera family.

When Antonio Udo inherited the estate from Epifanio in the middle of the 1840s, he showed very little interest in continuing the agricultural innovations and experimentations of his predecessors. He preferred extensive cultivation of wheat, as it assured him of relatively quick and safe returns. He took part in the 1848 revolt against Naples, and when this revolt collapsed he was forced to go into exile. In need of money, he went so far as to order the sale of strips of land from Mogata. He died in 1850, leaving Mogata and the baronial title to a member of the Palermitan cadet line of his family, Liborio Udo.

For the fifth baron of Mogata, the wheat economy also meant relatively high and quick profit, with little or no investment in the factors of production. After 1860, as the Udo family maintained its business interests outside of Camporano, Liborio Udo found it useful to lease at least 300 hectares from Mogata to local gabelloti or rentiers, in return for a fixed annual amount of money paid one year in advance and renewable every six years. The local rentiers came either from the peasant class of burgisi who, by being the descendants of the first settlers, had accumulated sufficient means to rent large tracts of land, or from the professional class, who liked to derive quick profit from their investment. Each rentier would, in turn, sublease the land into numerous lots to peasant workers, the so-called *paraspolari*, according to the cereal-based rotation pattern of Mogata as a whole. In this way each rentier became, in effect, a surrogate baron. By 1860 the overseer of Mogata, Vincenzo Vallera, had also become a "baron." The sale of Mogata in 1890 did not radically change the administration and cultivation of the estate.

The fixed natural resources capable of producing agricultural products together with an increasing labor population, legally deprived of both common property rights and countervailing political authority, allowed the Mogata baron and rentiers to dictate the labor contracts regulating work on the land. Already by the 1830s, Camporano workers were farming neighboring estates. But at least by the middle of the 1840s, what was similar in the Mogata and neighboring estates was the form of share tenancy.

Share Tenancy

Share tenancy continued to be called metateria (half), but the terms of the "contract" underwent critical changes by the 1840s. The contract lasted not more than two years for each lot of land. The number of salms received for cultivation varied from year to year. Generally each of some four hundred burgisi received a salm. From available records of share tenancy, including those gathered by successive parliamentary commissions (Bonfadini, 1876; Damiani, 1885; Lorenzoni, 1910), I can reconstruct how metateria worked in the case of a burgise family.

In the first year, the peasant tilled the land at his expense. He could manure it with the prescribed two quintals of stable dung. He generally sowed it with beans, a nitrogenous crop and staple food. If he had the seed or obtained it from the wheat bank (to be discussed in chapter 5), the crop was all his. If the baron or the rentier had provided the seed, he reclaimed it with at least 25 percent premium. The yield for a salm so cultivated varied from seven to ten salms of either beans or lentils. But the cost of production left very little surplus.

53

In the second year, the land was sown with wheat. The crop was first equally divided between the sharecropper and the landowner or the rentier. The average yield for a salm of land was about sixteen salms of wheat. Then from the sharecropper's part, several deductions were made in favor of the baron (or the rentier), amounting to about three salms of wheat. A sharecropper would be left with no more than five salms of wheat—barely the estimated subsistence for a sharecropper's family of five (Battaglia, 1895: 132).

As a means of softening opposition to national conscription among the Sicilian population, the Italian government in September 1861 issued a decree mitigating the provisions of rural labor contracts for the labor population. In Camporano both the baron and the local public officials had little or no incentive to comply with it. As several communal deliberations between 1851 and 1880 make clear, for them the land question was not the terms and conditions of agricultural activities but the relatively small size of the Camporano territory. Moreover, as we shall see in the next chapter, when in 1875 Camporano sharecroppers abstained en masse from farming the land so as to pressure Baron Udo to alter the metateria arrangements, the central government intervened to quell that attempt. In 1876, a parliamentary commission went so far as to conclude its study of Sicilian conditions with the observation that "in Sicily, there exist(ed) neither a political nor a social (landholding) question" (Bonfadini, 1876: 1077)—a view shared by the Camporano public officials and rentiers who testified before it. By 1885, following the collapse of the wheat bank as a successful going concern, the conditions of life for the majority of Camporano peasants had not improved; most likely, they had worsened, as a more reliable parliamentary inquiry suggested (Damiani, 1884: vol. XIII, book I). The other side of the local political economy, communal activities, did little to alleviate this state of affairs.

The Reconstitution of Communal Activities

Until 1816, a serious shortcoming in the organization of villages like Camporano had been how to deal with problems that affected the welfare of a number of neighboring communes. There had been no mechanisms for different local officials to come together on matters of common concern (but see Verdirame, 1905b: 129–132, and 1906). The changes that

54

took place after 1816 sought to overcome this shortcoming by introducing coordination through an overarching system of bureaucratic administration reaching from the center of government in Naples to each Sicilian village and town. Coordination through this hierarchy of public functionaries was, in turn, accompanied by changes in governmental arrangements at the local level that lawfully gave most residents little or no say in the conduct of public affairs.

After 1816, Camporano communal officials—a mayor and ten councilors forming the *decurionato*—were appointed by and responsible to the intendant. The simplicity of the structure of communal government went hand in hand with the clearly defined and concentrated authority and responsibility of communal and intendancy officials to support absolutist rule. As the British consul for Sicily, John Goodwin, described the new structure of government,

> The civil administration is so constituted, that a chain of correspondence is kept up between the mayor of every commune and the minister of the interior through the (intendant) and the sub-(intendant). *This theoretical advantage is accompanied by a practical inconvenience.* Communal and district magistrates, who, if left to themselves, would act promptly and vigorously on occasions of danger, often do nothing at all, from being obliged to consult their superiors before they take a decisive step. (1842: 186; emphasis added)

The annexation of Sicily to the new Italian state in 1860 did not radically alter the system of public administration described by the British consul.

Amid name changes from the Bourbon to the Savoy monarchy, the underlying principles affecting the organization and operation of communes like Camporano remained invariant. Local government institutions were designed to be responsive to the preferences or directives of central government authority and not to the preferences of diverse communities of people—since most of these preferences ran contrary to the very foundations of either monarchy. State making, or the forced creation of unity through administrative measures, in both 1816 and 1860–1865 required no less. At the same time, the fathers of Italian unification were not unaware of the institutional weakness and failure that had characterized the Bourbon forced creation of unity. But, in their view, the critical difference after 1860 was that the ideological forces and political preferences that would work through and upon administrative structures were liberal-parliamentary and not absolutist. For these reasons, the institutional arrangements of centralized government and administration in Sicily were still presumed to be *neutral* devices and not fundamental determinants of behavior in themselves (see Colajanni, 1883; De Stefano and Oddo, 1963: 77–84; Fried, 1963: 313–314; Ghisalberti, 1963; Pavone, 1964; Sabetti, 1977: 115–121, and 1982).

The Conduct of the Camporano Commune

The selection of Camporano public officials—whether by appointment by the intendant or the prefect or selection by diverse electoral laws—made no difference in what services the commune provided. Different public officials did affect how specified communal tasks were carried out. By being responsible to and controlled by distant intendancy or prefectoral functionaries, Camporano officials had considerable incentives to evade their responsibilities and to exploit the positions of authority for private gain. By controlling agricultural resources and in the process gaining skills in the language of officialdom, local persons acquired public positions that allowed them, in turn, to strengthen their hold on community life. Moreover, when some Camporano officials attempted to deal with local questions outside of the assigned tasks, they had to defer decisions on those questions to intendancy or prefectoral officials, if not to the ministry of the interior in Naples or in Rome. The union of centralized public administration with government elected by democratic vote in 1860 served to magnify goal displacement and risk avoidance as the characteristic features of center-periphery relations in Camporano. In sum, the conduct of communal government produced consequences that radically deviated from those anticipated by the artificers of both the Kingdom of the Two Sicilies and the Kingdom of Italy.

The collection of revenues and the application of national legislation suggest why and how the structure of political authority allowed local public officials to utilize lawful instruments to pursue their individual opportunities and to impose the costs of these opportunities on other villagers. Given the local political economy conditions, the provision of public instruction simply turned to the benefit of the sons and daughters of the professional and landowning individuals, thus continuing to deprive a majority of villagers of necessary skills in the language of officialdom.

The Selection of Camporano Officials

From 1818 to 1860, the intendant selected local officials on a staggered basis every three years from a list of "eligibles" prepared by the communal clerk, under the supervision of the incumbent mayor, the parish priest, and the Camporano district judge. The Mogata overseer was twice appointed mayor and his mayorship is the only instance of this period when there was a full correspondence between dominance over Camporano agricultural resources and dominance over Camporano communal affairs. On the whole, mayors and councilors came from and represented diverse social classes. This may in part explain why, in the case of the civic usufruct rights question discussed earlier, local officials did not hesitate to act on behalf of villagers against Baron Udo, albeit with unfavorable results. The selection of Camporano public officials until 1860 tends to support Alberto Asor Rosa's observation that intendants tried to act as "ethical observers" or as agents of the "ethical state" vis-à-vis local interests and classes (Asor Rosa, 1975: 915–916; see also Landi, 1977).

From 1861 to almost the turn of the century, the prefect as the provincial representative of the central government continued to appoint Camporano mayors, if only out of the fifteen-member communal council elected on a very limited franchise. The tenure of mayor varied from two to four years. But, as we shall see in chapter 5, access to the exercise of governmental prerogatives through elections served to transform the prefect from an "ethical observer" into an electoral agent of the national ruling coalition and to increase the correspondence between dominance over agricultural resources and dominance over communal affairs in Camporano. For most of the second half of the nineteenth century, the mayor was either a member of the Udo family or a relative of the Mogata overseer Vincenzo Vallera.

Taxation and Communal Revenues

From 1818 onward, both local and national taxes were levied by the central government. Communal officials, now state officials, were entrusted with the collection of revenues. By appropriating to itself the choice of local fiscal policy, the central government resorted to a general food impost and animal tax which fell mostly on the peasant population. By 1820, practically all of the Camporano communal revenues (some 1,315 ducats) came from the excise tax on wheat and wine, and from mule and donkey tax. Abolished by Garibaldi in 1860 in order to attract the support of the Sicilian peasantry, the grist tax was introduced again in 1863 as it was the easiest tax to collect at the local level. The grist tax was abolished by 1885, but several sorts of consumption tax and tax on draft animals remained the major sorts of consumption and national revenues in Camporano. By 1880 the annual communal revenues amounted to some 51,800 lire. While the Camporano peasant population contributed a disproportionate share of total government revenues, it received very little in return (see also Aliberti, 1967; La Loggia, 1894; Pantaleoni, 1891).

In the absence of reliable cadastral data, land tax was based on the number of hectares reported by communal officials, but there was confusion between various land measures still in use. The old salm, the legal salm, and the hectare continued to be used at the discretion of landowners and public officials (cf. Lupori, 1960). As a result, not only could large landowners obscure how much land they owned, but they could also adjust the land tax at their discretion. This became evident during the parliamentary inquiry of 1884–1885. While the Mozarra cadastral data showed the territory of Camporano to be over twenty-two hundred hectares, Camporano officials reported no more than thirteen hundred hectares (Damiani, 1885: vol. XIII, book II). At the same time it was difficult for owners of small tracts of land both to obscure how much they possessed and to escape paying land tax.

Local Issues and Bureaucratic Preemption

In the discussion of agricultural activities, I have already alluded to the difficulties generated by the application of national laws dealing with common property rights. There are two related local issues that highlight difficulties in center-periphery relations. These are the usurpation of the *trazzere regie* or "royal roads," and the expropriation of water springs.

Usually not less than seventeen meters wide, *trazzere* or "sheep tracks" became increasingly used as the main roads to connect villages and towns in Sicily. The Mogata fief was established on three such roads that, since the Arab period, connected the Sicilian hinterland from Agrigento to Trapani and from Palermo to Catania. In the list of *trazzere regie*, published in Palermo in 1895, there appear, however, none by the Mogata fief. Yet there is evidence to suggest at least one such public road was a source of dispute between the Udo family and communal officials.

In a directive issued by the Ministry for Sicilian Affairs to Camporano officials on September 8, 1841, the mayor was instructed "under the strictest accountability, to proceed with the reintegration of a *trazzera* going down the valley and other usurped *trazzere*." The matter was taken up again by the Council of State in 1868, confirming the legal prerogatives of the commune to reintegrate the sheep tracks usurped by members or rentiers of the Udo family. An instruction issued by the Mozarra prefect in a circular of April 1879, reaffirmed the earlier decision of the Council of State. But the 1895 list of *trazzere* suggests that neither the 1868 nor the 1879 central government directive was enforced.

There is no additional documentation. It is not clear why the 1841 central government instruction, coming as it did when the baron and communal officials were involved in litigation over civic usufruct rights, was not enforced. However, in the 1868 and 1879 cases, central government directives reached Camporano when the mayor who was to apply them was a member of the Udo family. It was difficult to expect that official to act against his own interest when the structure of communal government provided him with incentives to disregard the instruction.

The December 1841 law about compensation for lost common property rights also dealt with the question of public water supplies. Article 36 affirmed that villagers had usufruct rights of the available water supplies. However, it was unclear how these rights could be enjoyed on the ex-fiefs now private property (text in Battaglia, 1895: 308; cf. Ghisalberti, 1963: 126–127). Landowners contended that the abolition of common property rights also put an end to public rights over water. They went on exercising monopoly over water springs and streams. By the end of the nineteenth century, private and public rights over water springs in Sicily and elsewhere were still unclear, and subject to considerable uncontrolled private discretion (see Bruccoleri, 1913: 58–61; *Corriere di Girgenti*, 1913; Riccobono, 1918: 51–58). What followed in Camporano was thus part of a larger problem.

Of the ten water springs in the village territory, four were for drinking water. Prior to 1841, two of these had been channeled to serve several public fountains and water troughs in the village. As long as the two water springs serving the village provided sufficient water supplies for the population, the Udo family's control over the other sources of water supply remained unchallenged. By 1860, however, the volume of water serving the village had gradually decreased while the population increased. The need for more water became imperative. Rivalry between two local notables finally brought the matter of public water supply into the open in 1865 to confirm what probably everyone knew.

Sometime in the 1850s Francesco Vallera, a close relative of the Mogata overseer, built a cistern for irrigation purposes, tapping the water supply of one of the springs serving the village. Successive mayors had apparently tolerated this illegal appropriation. But from 1864 to 1868, the mayor was Antonio Fuxa, an agronomist and a prosperous burgise, who did not approve of Vallera's action. In November 1865, he notified council members of his resolution to forbid Vallera from tapping more water from the spring and to press for an expropriation of the cistern. A communal deliberation seeking permission to do so was sent to the prefect. Almost two years later, in February 1867, the Mozarra prefect authorized the mayor of Camporano to proceed with legal action against Vallera. Sometime early in May 1868, expropriation was carried out.

The delay with which the prefect answered the mayor's request gave rise to questions about additional sources of water supply. On March 2, 1866, the communal council deliberated, for the prefect's "knowledge, assent, and action," that the other two springs of drinking water held by Udo should be expropriated for public use. Permission was also sought to initiate proceedings (*pratiche*) to obtain a loan for the estimated expenses of expropriation and construction of water mains (some sixteen thousand lire). While prefectoral officials were considering the matter, there was a serious water shortage in 1868. The two original water sources serving the village were drying out. At the same time, in April 1868, the prefect appointed Udo as the new mayor, to last until 1872. Now the baron found himself in a position to pursue a course of action that stood to affect his economic opportunities. The position of relative immunity he occupied permitted him to avoid having his water rights challenged.

Water shortage continued to pose a problem for most villagers. By 1877, lack of water had become so critical that neither local officials nor the prefect could ignore or deny it without danger. There could no longer be delays in tapping the Mogata water springs.

The deed drawn up between the baron and the commune, subsequently approved by the prefect, stipulated that the baron cede his water rights to the Funa spring in return for five hundred lire rent to be paid by the commune annually. At the same time, water was conducted at communal expense into the Udo drinking trough near the manor. The mayor, Ciro Vallera, also agreed to erect an inscribed stone tablet on the trough to commemorate the baron's generosity. This measure did not solve the water shortage in the village but it suggests how the baron could influence local public officials to extract a good return for "expropriation."

Public Instruction

Until 1886, when the Italian state began to contribute to the financing of public instruction at the local level, revenues for the five elementary classes (three for male, two for female students) in Camporano came mostly from the collection of local consumption and animal taxes. But the peasant population from whom these revenues derived could not afford to send its children to elementary school. Children were needed to augment the meager income of their parents. By 1881, not more than one-third of school-age children—102 males and 89 females—attended elementary school, and of these only a few completed the five-year program. The literacy rate in the village at that time was 10 percent, about 500 individuals. This was also the situation existing throughout the Mozarra province (Damiani, 1885: vol. XIII, book II).

Villagers possessed at most only the rudiments of a language in which public matters were transacted, rights asserted, and grievances aired. The difficulties in acquiring knowledge and use of "the" Italian language compounded the plight of the peasant population. At the same time, knowledge and use of that language continued to enhance the privileged position of the landed and professional class in Camporano (see also Colajanni, 1883: 145–148). An old peasant saying, well known in slightly different versions in and beyond Camporano, suggests that most parents must not have been unaware of the value and importance of education for their children: "a slash of a pen, like a slash of a sword, is enough to right a wrong or defeat injustice and exploitation" (Sciascia, 1969: 4; cf. Pinna, 1971: 141–152).

Camporanesi in the Nation-State

The shift from baronial to national jurisdiction also meant additional changes. Public security in the countryside became the responsibility of the central government. Until 1859, the Mozarra area was policed from dawn to dusk by a small brigade of mounted police (*compagnia d'armi*) of not more than fifteen men. Reinforcements by the carabinieri after 1860 did not improve public security. The success of this police work depended in large measure on gaining adequate information about the occurrence of crimes or the whereabouts of suspected and actual offenders. Yet the need to gain information and cooperation ran against the professional nature of carabiniere work. Somehow these police officers were expected to remedy their ignorance of territories and language and to generate cooperation without having contacts with or being exposed to villagers. As a result, they became increasingly isolated from the community they were supposed to serve. As carabinieri found it easier to concentrate their efforts on enforcing petty regulations against villagers, their own presence came to generate a hostile environment that was counterproductive for obtaining peace and security throughout the Camporano countryside. By the 1870s, these police officers had taken on the characteristics of soldiers of an occupying army, but the problem of peace and security in the countryside remained (cf. D'Alessandro, 1959; Franchetti, 1877: 14–19; Mosca, 1884: 195–200).

A special permit was needed to carry arms, but such permits were issued at the discretion of provincial and local officials, who tended to favor some and exclude others. Most Camporano peasants ignored the law and armed themselves. In 1862 there was a general requisition of unregistered firearms throughout Sicily, and some eighty hunting rifles and six pistols were confiscated by the Camporano carabinieri. As we shall see in the next chapter, individualistic efforts at self-protection also failed to ensure lasting peace and security in the Camporano area.

Perhaps no single manifestation of membership in the nation-state directly affected the lives of Camporanesi as much as that of conscription. National conscription was first introduced in Sicily by the Bourbon government in 1818. The problems of enforcement were so great that, after the 1820 revolt, the Bourbon government was forced to withdraw it. In 1861 the Italian government simply extended the Piedmontese seven-year army duties to Sicily. Strong opposition to conscription ensued and it has been estimated that by 1862 at least twenty-five thousand young Sicilians took to the hills to evade the law (De Stefano and Oddo, 1963: 219–232; Restifo, 1976: 140; Seton-Watson, 1967: 26). Many of these draft dodgers became, in Eric Hobsbawm's words, "social bandits" (Hobsbawn, 1959; see also Blok, 1972)—further complicating the work of police officials. In 1873 army duties were reduced to three years but still posed considerable hardship to most Sicilian villagers.

From 1863 to 1914, an average of at least 100 Camporanesi per year were eligible for army duty. Of some 120 eligible men in 1863, apparently only 20 went voluntarily. While some were captured around the village by the army, a few became social bandits. During the latter part of the nineteenth century, resistance to army duty among Camporanesi did not differ from that of inhabitants of other Sicilian villages (see Battaglia, 1895: 209–211, 296).

Conclusion

The conflict between the Neapolitan Bourbons and the Sicilian barons over the failings of Sicilian government served to diminish and annul the institutional means that Camporano villagers were fashioning for the realization of their self-governing capabilities. What under Caracciolo's viceroyalty had first appeared as another passing phase in the perennial conflict among "princes" emerged by the 1840s as a radically new set of institutional arrangements for the conduct of public and private endeavors. These arrangements were centralized government and administration, private property in land, and a free labor market. The creation of the Kingdom of the Two Sicilies made the island part of the model histories of European sovereign states.

While the central government dominated the structure of legal relationships without, however, any effective legal remedies for governmental failures, the large landowners and their agents, secure in their prerogatives as private entrepreneurs, extended their control over people. For a majority of Camporanesi, the new political economy came to mean private authority of some local persons, without the limitations in the exercise of that authority existing prior to 1812. Whatever limitations occurred in the private authority of persons resulted more out of humanitarianism or conflict among those persons than out of the reconstitution of village relationships. With the annexation of Sicily to the nascent Kingdom of Italy, the features of this new social order emerged in all their magnitude to lock rulers and ruled, landowners and landless, in a more lasting iron circle. At the same time, the liberation and unification of Italy in 1860–1865 could not be achieved in any other way.

Two more general conclusions or hypotheses can be drawn from this chapter. First, without an appropriate political base, private property in land and a free labor market can neither assure nor sustain what North and Thomas call *The Rise of the Western World* (1973). The political base of Sicily after 1816 was such that the emergence of private property and a free labor market could not bring private rates of return on economic activities into parity with social returns. In the end, they thwarted Sicilian economic development altogether. Second, the foregoing analysis challenges the widely held view that the basic explanatory variables for the governmental failures of the Bourbon and Italian states in Sicily, as in the South, are the numerical and ideological weaknesses of the bourgeois ruling class. It suggests, instead, that the relative failure and inconstancy of centralized authority was due more to its administrative structures than to the alleged incapacity of the social forces working through and upon those structures. The machinery of government was not a *neutral* device but a fundamental determinant of behavior itself. In brief, the iron circle can best be accounted for by the forced creation of unity through administrative measures and not by personality and class characteristics.

5

Life under National Jurisdiction

The changes in the organization and conduct of agricultural and communal activities resulting from the shift from baronial to national jurisdiction had profound consequences for the social life of Sicilian villagers. Before, the high degree of interdependence resulting from the organization of agricultural activities required villagers pursuing their individual interests to take into account a wider community of interests and a longer time horizon. Now, with the changes in property rights, each villager could disregard the interests of others. At the same time, the rules governing communal activities gave rise to a situation where the conduct of local affairs became the exclusive domain of a privileged few. Whereas before the development and maintenance of diverse social conditions depended principally on differentiation in land-based occupational skills and opportunities, after 1816 the continuance of different social conditions was reinforced by the lack of political rights for the great majority of villagers. To be sure, such conditions of life had existed under baronial jurisdiction. But the critical difference was that after 1816, baronial abuses became lawful private practices, governmental failures became proper governmental procedures, and no effective remedies were available to deal with such abuses and failures.

Control of public facilities was added to the control of agricultural resources as distinguishing characteristics of the dominant social aristocracy. In the absence of "voice" in the organization and conduct of public affairs and of an alternative to land-based production and occupational opportunities, a majority of people in the Sicilian countryside remained fixed in their subject status. Distinction between gentlemen (*signori*) and peasants continued to be made in terms of "hats" (*cappeddi*) and "caps" (*birritti*), but between and within these classes social differences became permanent and difficult to surmount. As a result, attempts to minimize exposure to adversities in the conditions of life resulting from national jurisdiction varied according to the social standing of individuals and over time.

Central jurisdiction from Naples served to make Sicilians aware of themselves as they had never been before, but also served to keep them apart. As islanders became united against what they regarded as their common enemy, their interests and motives for the overthrow of the Bourbon government had become so divergent that they proved difficult to reconcile once a revolt succeeded. In addition, the difficulties of translating a successful revolt into a viable expression of self-government were compounded by outside armed interventions. Thus we find a majority of Sicilians participating for different reasons in the revolts of 1820, 1848, and 1860. The 1820 and 1848 revolts failed; the 1860 revolt, consolidated by the intervention of Garibaldi's "Thousand Men," succeeded. But the ideals of Italian liberation and unification gave way to the exigencies of state making and state building, and, as a consequence, the 1860 revolt served to establish a more lasting "iron circle" around those individuals who had initiated it.

The Sicilian peasants found themselves excluded from the benefits deriving from the new national jurisdiction. The peasant strategy was to attempt to minimize their exposure to the play of a game in which they were constant losers. The more extreme the deprivations, the more willing the deprived became to use extreme measures in the absence of alternative methods of seeking more agreeable solutions. But these reactions brought counterreactions from state officials. Special government laws were, however, met by other "special laws." And it was in this sense that Sicily became "the Ireland of Italy" (Ferrara, 1860). Some Sicilians began to orient their search for a better life beyond their island. By 1900, thousands of descendants of earlier Sicilian colonists had become the new colonists of North Africa and the Americas.

Diverse Social Conditions of Camporano Villagers

The 230 families that peopled the Mogata fief between 1765 and 1790 and some additional families that went to Camporano by 1800 were relatively homogeneous in their social conditions. The division of labor inherent in the farming of the estate provided the basis for the development of different social classes among them and their descendants. The fixed amount of natural resources, the expanding peasant population, and the changes in the structure of basic social institutions after 1812 together solidified and fixed social differences in the nineteenth century.

The "Caps"

The overwhelming majority of villagers were peasants, divided between burgisi and *viddani* or *villani*. As the root words of these terms suggest, both terms must have been originally used interchangeably to refer to all local residents (see Sorge, 1910–1916: II, 72–74). By the nineteenth century, in Camporano they were used to refer specifically to two peasant strata. At the same time, to call a peasant a burgise became a privileged appellative, while *viddanu* became a pejorative one. Such differences have remained to present times. Within each substratum there were further social differences.

The burgise class was differentiated in terms of "higher" and "lower" subgroups. The higher burgisi were either small proprietors, the *enfiteuti*, or rentiers who acted as middlemen between the baron and the tenants. By the 1840s, there were at least six families of rentiers—at least three of these rentiers came from the outside to act as overseers of neighboring estates. By the 1860s, there were some ten families of rentiers in the village. The most prominent rentiers belonged to the Corona, the Fontena, the Igelo, and the Vallera families.

The lower burgisi were those individuals who tilled the land as sharecroppers and were known as *inquilini*, *metatieri*, or *terrazzani*. They were the largest group of burgisi. By the middle of the nineteenth century there were some three hundred families of lower burgisi. Each possessed at least a plow and two mules. Some of them possessed a yoke of oxen and held tracts of land under the emphyteusis lease.

The majority of peasants were viddani or agricultural laborers divided into at least three subgroups. The daily laborers, the jurnatari, who de-

67

pended entirely on their daily earnings, were the largest subgroup. They adapted themselves to any work that afforded them an opportunity to augment their slender incomes. The monthly and yearly laborers, the *misalori* and the *annalori*, respectively, did the same type of work except that they were assured of a monthly or yearly income. Possession of a mule or a donkey allowed a viddanu to be hired as a teamster. Such a villager would eventually be known as a *vurduranu* or *sciccharu* but remained a viddanu. Private guards came generally from this class of peasant.

The "Hats"

The baron as the local seigneur stood above members of the professional and the well-off (*possidenti*) classes. The original professional class, composed of an accountant, a notary public, a schoolteacher, and a doctor expanded over time to include communal and postal clerks and the agronomist-overseer of the Mogata estate, Vincenzo Vallera. By 1857, Camporano had its own lawyer, doctor, public notary, and pharmacist; also by that time there were sixteen well-off persons (*possidenti*) who came from rentier or burgise families. The rise of *possidenti* may account for an increase in the number of professional people. In 1887 Camporano had four lawyers, four doctors, five public notaries, and two pharmacists.

The Priestly and Artisanal Population

Churchmen, artisans, and merchants occupied a mixed social position. By the 1840s Camporanesi had their own priests and monks. Almost all the Camporano priests came from the burgise and the viddanu class yet, because of their office, they were regarded as "the first nobles of the village." As we shall see later, they came to occupy a strategic position beyond the administration of church sacraments.

During the nineteenth century, no Camporano house was without a shuttle or a spinning wheel. According to a government survey, at least until 1840 there were some 400 Camporano women earning wages from these activities (see Fiume, 1977, 1978). It is not unlikely that the third baron of Mogata, who introduced silkworms in the later 1820s, was one of their employers. Communal records for 1857 show sixteen spinners

68

paying consumption taxes on wine. After 1860 the term *artisan* in Camporano applied exclusively to male workers.

Artisans included barbers, blacksmiths, carpenters, harness makers, masons, quarrymen, shoemakers, and tailors. There was very little difference between these artisans and shopkeepers like butchers, bakers, and "clothiers." Artisans like harness makers and blacksmiths sold not only their labor but also their products, especially at country fairs in and around Camporano; shopkeepers like the two clothiers were also tailors. With the exception of the butchers who came from a single burgise family, all other merchants and artisans came from the viddanu population. Bakers continued to work as agricultural laborers or as Mogata tenants. But being a blacksmith, a harness maker, or a mason was more remunerative than being a barber or a shoemaker. As a result, social standing in the village varied accordingly. Each artisan or shopkeeper would "leave" his occupation to at least one of his sons. In 1978, at least four of the six butchers were still the direct descendants, and bearers of the same first and last names, of butchers in the 1850s.

After 1816, and especially after the unsuccessful attempt to compensate villagers for their lost common property rights in the early 1840s, the nature of social interdependence among villagers underwent drastic change. Distinction between gentlemen and peasants continued to be made in terms of "hats" and "caps," but between and within each stratum there developed such a diversity of interests that common action on behalf of shared interests became a difficult undertaking. The problem of translating successful uprisings into expressions of self-government places in sharp relief this growing diversity of interests and the attendant difficulties at common action.

Armed Reactions against National Jurisdiction from Naples

The imposition of a system of government alien to the Sicilian political tradition in 1816 caused confusion and ill feelings among all Sicilians. The majority of Sicilian barons resented the abolition of the Sicilian parliament and the presence of intendants. Publicists chafed under the abolition of the freedom of the press. Before, the rule of different royal houses had hardly affected the secondary laws and habits of islanders;

now, there was a wholesale remodeling of institutions. Lawyers were required to learn a new system of jurisprudence administered by French-trained officials. In the countryside, villagers, who had for the most part wrestled local liberties from the barons or self-perpetuating oligarchies, now found themselves deprived of any say in the conduct of local government. By taking over and then underproviding public security throughout the island, the central government produced additional resentment. In the face of strong opposition, conscription was withdrawn after the revolt of 1820. Defense of the island was left to mercenary soldiers, commanded by Northern Irish and Austrian generals.

Those who stood to gain from the extension of centralized government and administration from Naples became by 1848 dissatisfied. Jacobins shifted their support of centralized jurisdiction from the absolutist government of Naples to a government elected by democratic vote for the whole of Italy. Public officials and inhabitants of provincial towns discovered that their towns' "civic equality" with Palermo meant no other benefit. Merchants came to regard government regulations from Naples as interference in their work. As the professional class of each town expanded, some members found themselves continuously excluded from the private gains resulting from the control of local government.

By attempting to direct and supervise all the activities in the public and private sectors, the Neapolitan government found itself blamed for everything that went wrong in Sicily. Natural catastrophes as well as epidemics were blamed on the government. As a result, any protest or disturbance—however mild—went beyond determinate government policies to invest and to challenge the very foundations of the Kingdom of the Two Sicilies.

At the same time, attempts to ameliorate the social, economic, and political conditions of Sicilians compounded the difficulties of the Bourbon government. Measures to compensate villagers for their lost civic usufruct rights created more discontent about the government among potential beneficiaries as well as landowners. Villagers found that the measures were not effective enough to compensate them for their loss; landowners opposed the very idea of limitations on their rights of proprietorship. An office of statistics was established in 1832, but its journal, the *Giornale di Statistica*, provided the forum for political economists to conduct analyses of Sicilian issues that raised or implied serious questions about absolutist rule itself. When freedom of the press was reinstated, Sicilian publicists, with their concern for the conditions that give rise to and sustain "the spirit of association," provided the intellectual grounds for both the revolt of 1848 and the growth of the Italian school of public finance (see Buchanan, 1960: 73; Lanza di Scordia, 1842). After 1848, the Neapolitan government initiated several policies which led to a general economic improvement of all classes in Sicily (Giuffrida, 1968; Intendenti delle Provincie, 1851). But as their economic conditions improved, Sicilians tended to question and detest even more "the yoke of Naples." Thus by the middle of the nineteenth century, islanders of various classes came to regard the overthrow of that yoke as the solution to all their particular problems. At the same time, by imposing relatively mild penalties on unsuccessful revolutionaries in 1821 and 1849, Bourbon officials encouraged further attempts.

As they became united by a common dislike of Naples, Sicilians had, however, become separated by conflicting interests and motives. With each succeeding revolt, these interests and motives proved increasingly difficult to reconcile without falling back into a new form of tyranny and subjugation. The difficulties of translating a successful revolt into a viable expression of self-government were, in addition, compounded by external interventions. In 1820 and 1848, Sicilians discovered that they could not separate themselves from Naples without external support. The landing of Garibaldi's Thousand Men at Marsala in May 1860 hastened the collapse of Bourbon rule in Sicily but also served to alter the meaning of the Sicilian uprising from an attempt to produce specific and tangible results to a generic appeal for a united Italy. Consequently, the change from the Bourbon to the Savoy monarchy made Sicilians "Italians," but the iron law of oligarchy continued to prevail (Mack Smith, 1954; cf. Galasso, 1980: 16–18; Ragionieri, 1964: 72–73). As Tomasi di Lampedusa (1958) observed, things changed in order to remain the same, but in 1860 a united Italy à la Cattaneo could not be established either (Ganci, 1968; Sabetti, 1982). Archival papers and a local history published in 1900 are the primary sources for the reconstruction of how the revolts of 1820, 1848, and 1860 were reflected in Camporano.

The Revolt of 1820

With the end of the Napoleonic Wars, there was a general decline in the demand for Sicilian wheat and local prices fell appreciably. Expenditure by the British troops on the island, amounting to some £10 million a year, stopped with their withdrawal in 1815 (Mack Smith, 1968b: 355).

In addition, the introduction of a new system of government, including food impost and conscription, aggravated the situation. Throughout 1818, intendants reported numerous localized agitations, particularly against food impost and conscription.

It is against this backdrop that news of a revolt by Neapolitan liberals against the Bourbon government reached Palermo in July 1820. A revolt in Madrid aimed at curtailing absolutist prerogatives had given impetus to the Neapolitan liberals to seek a similar constitution from King Ferdinand (see Sartori, 1962). Neapolitan officials in Palermo announced that Sicily would also share in the benefits of the new Neapolitan constitution. They soon discovered, however, that what most Sicilians seemed to want was a constitution of their own—hence, "the first Sicilian separatist revolution" (Cortese, 1956).

On July 16, 1820, demonstrations against Naples and attacks on central government offices began. After several days of open warfare, the consuls of the workers' guilds, aided by the cardinal archbishop of Palermo, restored peace and order. Members of the nobility took part in the junta or council governing Palermo and the surrounding area. The news of the successful uprising spread to the countryside (see also Renda, 1968).

In the Mozarra province, local authorities suspended food impost on the eighteenth. On the nineteenth, in the town of Castelfrano, near Camporano, villagers took over the food impost offices, burning all the papers. While Camporano officials hesitated, a band of villagers guided by two peasants, a priest, the sacristan, and a schoolteacher were preparing to take over communal offices. On the twentieth, the commune was taken over; public officials were removed from office and communal papers burned. A "revolutionary committee," made up of representatives of the various classes, named Baron Udo to represent Camporano interests in Palermo.

By September 1820, some 140 communes representing over 50 percent of the Sicilian population sent delegates to Palermo. The Palermo junta soon, however, found itself unable to establish a united front against Naples as well as to collect sufficient funds and recruits to sustain the revolt. At the same time, the revolutionary government in Naples had problems of its own. In March 1821, Austrian troops invaded Campania and restored King Ferdinand and his government. In June 1821, Lord Bentinck presented a motion in the House of Commons calling upon the British government to intervene in the defense of Sicilian liberties, but the motion was defeated (Rosselli, 1956: 154–155; see also Romeo, 1955: 90, and note 106). Austrian troops were already garrisoning Sicily.

Food imposts were increased to meet the cost of the five-year military occupation. The hope of Messinese to have their city recognized as the leading city on the island was not realized; nor were the promised tax exemptions for Trapani in Western Sicily. In Camporano the old public officials resumed their posts. The participants and leaders of the local uprisings were left undisturbed. Only Baron Udo and his brothers were forced to go into exile for their part in the revolt.

Camporanesi had not taken part in the revolt until they perceived possible benefits to be gained as a result of the revolutionary activities. Different villagers reacted in the same way in 1848. But the basic difference is that in 1820 villagers had acted as a community in their reactions against food impost and loss of local self-government. By 1848 villagers had become so split up in their means of livelihood and social conditions that, as soon as the revolt succeeded, they experienced serious difficulties in reconciling the conflicting interests and motives that had led them to take part in the revolt.

The Revolt of 1848

Rumors of a revolt began spreading on the occasion of the celebration of the king's birthday on January 12, 1848. A riot developed in a poor district of Palermo, spreading throughout the city. As the revolt became successful, other citizens declared their support for it. Palermo intellectuals, liberals, and resident nobles joined. Committees were organized to keep order, to provide arms, to collect money, to arrange food supplies, and to spread the news throughout the island. When news of the Palermo revolt spread throughout the island, a majority of Western and Eastern Sicilians took up arms and scythes.

The reconstituted parliament made up of a House of Commons and a House of Lords opened its proceedings in March 1848. Proponents of a unitary republic and monarchy joined forces with proponents of a federal republic and monarchy to establish a coalition government. Independence from Naples was proclaimed but, in order to gain British support for the revolt, Sicily was declared a parliamentary monarchy. This proclamation was, in turn, accompanied by another proclamation affirming Sicily's readiness to join a federal union of Italian states—a reference to

73

other revolts taking place on the Italian mainland. The possibility of creating a United States of Italy offered to Sicilians prospects for regaining independence from Naples, for defending themselves against the recurrent problem of war, and for being part of a larger political community that respected the need for local and regional self-governing capabilities. In short, Sicilians in 1848 became Italian nationalists because of federalism (see Cattaneo, 1848; Ferrara, 1848; Romeo, 1950: 305–345; cf. Peri, 1970: 47–49, 57–75). But the revolutionary situation also provided limitations to the making of a United States of Italy that could not be overcome in a short time span. Conflicting interests and motives had allowed Sicilian revolutionaries to act with autonomy and self-reliance in liberating themselves but, after the revolt, these conflicting interests became increasingly difficult to reconcile. A view of the 1848 revolt from Camporano and Palermo reveals the salient features of this problematic situation.

Throughout the first part of the 1840s, there had been growing unrest especially among Camporano agricultural workers for the lack of compensation for the lost common property rights. The food impost was also resented and contraband was used to evade the excise men. The spark that eventually led villagers to side with the Palermo revolt occurred with the news reaching Camporano that a general amnesty had been declared for these crimes and that those jailed in Palermo had been set free on January 28.

At the time, a local agricultural worker was in the Camporano jail, seemingly for having stolen roots of licorice. His young brother wanted him to be set free. The local magistrate refused the request. On the evening of January 30, the brother of the jailed man together with relatives attempted to set him free. An armed conflict developed between this group and the jailer aided by his two sons. The next day the situation was becoming critical as other villagers joined this group of agricultural laborers. Local officials finally convinced the magistrate to set the jailed man free. Once free, he joined the group for more demands. Armed with rifles, scythes, and sticks with nails, the landless peasants took over the house that served as the office and residence of the local judge and his family. The royal papers were burned, while the lives of the judge and his family were saved through intercession of a priest and some high burgisi. Now Mogata tenants joined those who had taken over the magistrate's office. Some 150 low burgisi attempted to force the notary public to hand over the metateria deeds for Mogata. Leading members of the

74

professional class and five rentiers supported by several armed *campieri* succeeded momentarily in dissuading those Mogata tenants from carrying out their threats.

Soon afterward, the landed gentry, rentiers, and higher burgisi formed a committee of public safety to defend private property in land and to take charge of local affairs. On February 18, that committee headed by Mogata overseer Vallera strengthened its hold on local affairs by organizing a 140-man contingent of the national guard recruited among artisans and higher and lower burgisi. In June 1848, the offices of chief magistrate and jurors were resurrected to replace the committee of public safety but the "hats" continued to dominate those offices. The rentier Salvatore Fontena became the chief magistrate. At the same time, a priest was unanimously chosen by the male population to represent Camporano in the new House of Commons; the fourth baron of Mogata, by virtue of his hereditary privilege, became member of the new House of Lords.

These events did little to placate unrest among Mogata tenants and agricultural workers. On July 2, 1848, the Feast of the Holy Eucharist, some lower burgisi and viddani interrupted the religious procession to protest for different reasons against the landed classes. The local contingent of the national guard arrested the leaders of the protest amid shouts of "Down with the hats!" But there seems to have been no attempt on the part of lower burgisi and agricultural laborers to free those imprisoned or to continue joint action against "the hats." On October 25, a dispute between a viddanu and the son of Mayor Fontena in the main square took on the appearance of an armed conflict. Bloodshed was avoided through the intercession of some priests. As a means of calming unrest, local jurors decided to collect revenues in support of the revolt only among the well-to-do families. But the ill feeling among the various social classes remained.

Villagers had become so clearly split up in their means of livelihood and social conditions that it was as if within Camporano there existed several distinct communities, each calling for a government of its own. Local issues and problems appeared insoluble. The survival of the 1848 revolt in the form of a United States of Italy might have provided the basis for an eventual devaluation of rural proprietorship as determinant of authority and influence among villagers, for an extension of the civil and political rights to land workers and, ultimately, for villagers to act as a community. But the revolt was short-lived.

Parliamentary leaders in Palermo experienced serious difficulties in coping with a multitude of contrasting claims made by different social classes in the name of the revolt and in organizing an army against outside intervention. Seven different ministries succeeded each other without resolving the problem of collection of revenues, land rights, and defense. The hated food impost was abolished, but there was little argument about alternative sources of finance. Representatives of the landowning class tried to prevent the introduction of new taxes aimed at their interests. They also disliked discussions of limitations of their property rights—limitations that had served as the critical incentive for peasants to rise in the countryside. A national guard was created to balance the presence of the peasant squads. When in September 1848 a large Bourbon army attacked Messina, the problem of conscription was still being hotly debated in parliament. In February 1849, Eastern Sicilians were forced to surrender. By that time, leaders of the national guard and of the peasant squads in Western Sicily had different reasons to be dissatisfied with the outcome of the revolt. They independently began to parley with the Neapolitan emissaries. In March 1849, the imminent collapse of revolts on the Italian peninsula and the lack of international recognition of and support for Sicilian independence shattered the remaining hopes of Sicilian revolutionary leaders. When Bourbon troops finally reached Palermo, they met no resistance (see Chiaramonte, 1901; Mack Smith, 1968b: 415–425).

The net result of Bourbon restoration was tighter control from Naples. In Camporano, the mayor of prerevolutionary times took office again. Villagers who had participated in the Camporano revolt benefited from a general amnesty; only Baron Udo was forced to go into exile, where he died a year later.

The Revolt of 1860

The course of events that led to the overthrow of the Kingdom of the Two Sicilies and the establishment of the Kingdom of Italy began as an armed clash between the police and some Palermitans on April 4, 1860. News of the Palermitan disturbance spread throughout the island and, on April 8, the intendants reported riots occurring in the coastal towns and in the interior. These riots were again aimed at both governmental offices and landowners' property. As the police and army found it difficult to

76

squelch them, landowners began to lose confidence in the ability of the Bourbon government to protect their property. The May landing of Garibaldi's Thousand Men was initially viewed favorably by both those who desired protection for their property and by those who were rebelling for the possession of land. But, as Denis Mack Smith has observed, the very success of the revolt led Garibaldi "to recognize that [the support of property owners] was much more important to him in the long run than that of peasants" (1950: 236). *Garibaldini* began to suppress further agrarian outbreaks. Peasants stopped aiding them. Many years later, Garibaldi still did not understand why not a single peasant joined his volunteers in 1860 (Garibaldi, 1889: II, 147).

It would seem that the 1848 revolt had taught Camporano land workers not to participate in revolutionary activities. There is no record of any agitation in Camporano until May 28, 1860, the day before Garibaldi reached Palermo. The success of the revolt had already been secured when, according to an account, "all Camporanesi, including children, took to the streets to join in the fight for the redemption of Sicily." On May 29, the landed gentry once again established a committee of public safety headed by Vincenzo Vallera. On August 18, a new communal government issued a proclamation of thanks to Victor Emmanuel and Garibaldi. During a tour of the Sicilian interior in August 1862, Garibaldi visited Camporano as guest of the baron and the local "hats."

"Complete fusion" with Piedmont was accompanied by a wholesale remodeling of all the secondary laws and institutions, which aimed at changing the habits and customs of islanders. The events of 1816 were thus repeated between 1860 and 1865. More than the constitutional change itself, it was these changes in the structure of social relationships that produced great upheavals. While Piedmontese saw themselves as coming to deliver Sicily from bondage, Sicilians came to view the new institutions as a change from one "yoke" to another (see Brancato, 1956; F. Perez, 1862). Moreover, the confiscation of church property in 1867 alienated the Sicilian clergy and the peasants—the former for their continued support of the various revolts, the latter for the failure to receive land confiscated in their name (see also Composto, 1964; Li Vecchi, 1977). For most Camporano villagers and Sicilians, then, successive armed revolts had done little to reduce their exposure to a game of life in which they were constant losers.

Individualistic Reactions

The shift from the Bourbon to the Savoy monarchy did not fundamentally alter the institutional arrangements that governed agricultural and communal affairs. It served, instead, to strengthen the gross inequalities of conditions of the various classes and to increase the markedly asymmetrical interdependence already existing among villagers. The organization of the political economy permitted villagers to pursue their individual advantages and to disregard the consequences for others. As most Camporano peasants found themselves to be consistent losers whenever they had anything to do with landlords and public authorities, they came to rely upon the individual qualities of courage, self-respect, and self-reliance as strategies in taking care of their individual and family welfare, in maintaining a favorable balance of good will with those who were friends and in minimizing their exposure in dealing with others—in essence, by displaying the attributes typified by the original meaning of the Sicilian word *mafia*. At the same time, voluntary collective efforts to reduce the consequences associated with unrestricted individualistic choice ran against the constraints interposed by the instrumentalities of government.

Communal Politics

In the previous chapter I have indicated how the organization of local government after 1816 impeded local public officials from taking action on local problems and, at the same time, allowed them to use public offices for private gain. The only notable change resulting from the new national jurisdiction in 1860 was the creation of a communal council elected on a franchise limited to about 1 percent of the Camporano male population in the 1860s and extended to about 10 percent by the turn of the century. The right to vote placed, however, a burden on those having that right. As most of the new voters were Mogata tenants or lower burgisi, they now faced additional pressures from other villagers who provided them with the means for their livelihood. Until 1890, the prefect and not the communal council chose the mayor among those elected. But the electoral competition for the office of mayor before and after 1890 turned on obtaining most votes so as to force either the prefect or the communal councilors to appoint the person with the highest number of "preference votes." The selection of the mayor thus gave rise to further animosity among the professional and landowning classes and further discouragement about politics among all Camporanesi.

In 1876, during the first local election after the 1875 disturbance about the metateria contracts, of the two hundred electors only six voted for the baron. He was able, however, to induce members of the communal council to withdraw their support for the new mayor and by 1880 a prefectoral official was administering communal affairs. By this time members of the Udo and Vallera families had organized what became known as "the majority party"; professional and landowning villagers excluded from the majority coalition had organized a group of their own, which became known as "the minority party." But in the 1881 communal election, so unsure was the majority party of winning that its principal candidate, the first son of Baron Udo, had the Mogata private guards escort Mogata tenants when they went to vote. In the 1880s, both population growth and changing electoral qualifications served to raise the number of voters to about five hundred from about two hundred in 1870. As the number of electors increased, it became more difficult and costly to maintain control of each elector. As a result, leaders of the two electoral coalitions began to challenge voter enumeration itself. There took place innumerable and protracted court battles between the two groups about the proper voting qualifications of almost all the Camporano voters.

Being selected or elected mayor, however, was no assurance for the completion of the mayoral term. The design of communal government permitted a mayor to see himself with sufficient competence and authority to take unilateral actions and to expect routine approval for those actions by members of his communal coalition. But this was not always so in practice, as communal councilors clung to even the hollowest form of consultation in order to maintain a semblance of self-government. In fact, no sooner had a new mayor taken office than he experienced the same difficulties as the previous mayor—how to reconcile the pomp of office with the requirements for maintaining council support. At the same time, an incumbent mayor also faced pressures of resignation from the unsuccessful mayoral candidate as well as arbitrary dismissal from the prefect. Between 1868 and 1895 at least six mayors did not finish their terms of office; communal government had to be dissolved and placed in the hands of prefectoral functionaries at least four times; at least one duly elected mayor was dismissed by the prefect for hostility toward the government (also see Spreafico, 1965: 104–105).

There was an additional reason why the election of local officials bore no reference to local issues and problems. Throughout the second half of the nineteenth century, succeeding national governments—whether of the left or the right—found in the office of the prefect a useful instrument to establish their electoral majority in parliament. Thus the selection of the Camporano mayor, who could in turn provide votes for the deputy favorable to the national governing party, became of paramount importance to the prefect whose post and promotion depended on government leaders. Between 1868 and 1897 at least two prefects went in person to Camporano in order to organize communal elections on behalf of the national government (see also Pareto, 1893, 1894).

An item in a questionnaire of the Jacini parliamentary commission sent to all the district judges and prefects in 1883 ran as follows: "What conception of public authority do Sicilian peasants have?" The reply by the Camporano district judge noted: "Camporano peasants do not believe possible the exercise of public authority that does not have as its motive the self-interest of he who exercises that authority." As we have seen, this conception of public authority had an empirical base in the exercise of public authority in Camporano. Camporano peasants had, thus, correctly learned to calculate the consequences that flowed from the structure of local government. At the same time, communal politics, rather than generating a supply of good will, served instead to produce malevolence among villagers. By the 1880s Camporanesi had come to use the well-wishing phrase "May you become a mayor!" as a curse.

Agricultural Activities

The past chapter showed how the meaning of the Mogata fief changed from a bundle of rights enjoyed by the baron and villagers alike to a private property enjoyed by the baron alone and how various governmental attempts to limit the right of proprietorship failed. As a result, the baron found himself in the strategic position of having almost exclusive access to sources of wealth and subsistence. Through the overseer, he could now control the terms and conditions for working the estate. The great majority of villagers continued to depend for their livelihood upon work on Mogata and neighboring estates, but their relationships with the land had changed. The system of interdependence was markedly asymmetrical. The baron was dependent upon the peasants both to work his holdings and to pay him rent. But the landowner had a labor surplus from which to select replacements in case of a particular individual's refusal to abide by the terms of the agricultural contract. The peasant, however, depended on the baron for his very survival. In addition, crop yield was also subject to inclement weather and natural catastrophes. Recognizing this lopsided dependence, each tried to maximize his short-term gains.

I noted in chapter 4 the circumstances that led the fourth and fifth baron of Mogata to abandon the agricultural innovations of Epifanio Udo and to lease large tracts of Mogata land to local rentiers. Both the baron and the individual gabelloto derived a profit from the land with minimum investment in improvements and equipment. Profit derived from the land served either to purchase additional land from the 1867 expropriated church property in neighboring villages or to send children to private schools in Palermo. The protective tariffs on wheat started in the late 1870s gave additional incentives to Baron Udo and rentiers alike to treat land workers according to the classic definition of *latifundium*.

The amount of land that a sharecropper or *paraspolare* received under the metateria contract depended on the quality of terrain, the distance between the field and the village, and the extent of the competition for share tenancy. At least until 1870 every sharecropper received a salm of land for a two-year period; by 1883 Damiani reported that the contract had been reduced to half a salm for a one-year period. Given the insecure tenure and faced with the onerous agrarian contract, each sharecropper tended to underinvest in the factors of production and to derive as much yield as possible during his tenure. Manuring and deep plowing became rare; concealing and stealing the crop became annual occurrences. At the same time, by the 1880s the average yield per salm decreased from sixteen to ten quintals of wheat. A sharecropper would often be left without wheat to sow again. It became "customary" for the baron (and for the rentiers) to anticipate the seed in terms of two salms of wheat for every salm of cultivated land. But this also left most cultivators worse off.

The seed and a premium of four tumoli were returned at harvest time. However, the tumolo as a measure varied. When the peasant picked up the seed from the manor, the seed was measured with a small tumolo, the so-called clean tumolo (roughly eighteen kilograms). To prevent the peasant from taking part of the seed to the mill for his family use, copper sulfate (*'ncilistrata*) was mixed with it (see also Ziino, 1911). This reduced even more a tumolo of seed. The seed with the premium was re-

81

turned at the threshing area. There it was measured with a bigger tumolo, the so-called exigency tumolo (roughly twenty-eight kilograms). When the sharecropper borrowed the seed, he could use his own animal. When he returned it, however, the landowner's mules were used, for which the peasant paid one lira for every salm.

The jurnatari or agricultural laborers, who represented the majority of peasants, depended for their livelihood on both burgisi and "hats." A jurnataru did not have enough capital or work. Harvest time was the time when he worked the most. A village physician, writing on Camporano public health in 1886, described the jurnataru's work pattern as follows. He would travel with a sickle over his shoulder to neighboring towns in search of work and not return to his hut for weeks. His wife would on occasion find a burgise who allowed her to glean in the stubble. But if it was a bad harvest year, she was obliged to take home not more than one-third of the stalks gathered. Their children would also herd sheep for the burgisi in return for payment in kind. Each jurnataru family would attempt to have a goat whose milk, if there was enough to sell to neighbors, helped to augment the family income (see also Carini, 1894; Salomone-Marino, 1897).

Some of the agricultural laborers continued to enjoy civic usufruct rights with or without the complacency of the private guards or burgisi. In the discussion of the 1848 revolt, I have noted how this question contributed to the local uprising. A history of Camporano published in 1900 reported other such events. In July 1870, a jurnataru was caught gathering dead wood and was killed by a private guard. A few days later, as the guard was being arrested by the carabinieri, a son of the deceased shot the guard. In March 1875, two cousins were caught taking roots of licorice by another *campiere*, who denounced them to the carabinieri. The next day the guard himself was found dead on a nearby estate while the two cousins became fugitive. Apprehended some time later, they were condemned to seven and five years of prison, respectively. In September 1876 another private guard was mortally wounded in a vineyard.

As each individual laborer attempted to check the sources of his vulnerability vis-à-vis other villagers, he produced consequences that worsened his long-term net welfare. At the same time, if a jurnataru did not take advantage of the short-term gains, he also stood to lose (see also Arnone, 1910a: 548). Like most other villagers, the agricultural workers seemed to be locked in a many-person analogue to the prisoner's dilemma of modern game theory (Rapoport, 1960).

82

Peace and Security in the Camporano Countryside

In the previous chapter I noted the difficulties experienced by law-enforcement agencies of successive central governments to maintain peace and security in the Camporano countryside. I also suggested that public security provided by the brigade of mounted police and, later, by the carabinieri as well as various governmental policies ranging from food impost to conscription contributed to the rise of social banditry. At any one time between 1863 and 1900 there were at least four bands of brigands or social bandits roaming the Camporano territory (see also D'Alessandro, 1959). In such circumstances, the attainment of peace and security came to depend on the need and ability of each villager to defend his family and property.

The *campieri*, the Camporano private guards, sold security to the baron and rentiers, but police reports of the time suggest that they could not always insure adequate protection for their rentiers. In 1864 a Camporano rentier was kidnapped. He was released after his family had paid a ransom of some two thousand lire. In June 1870 another rentier was kidnapped on his way to a watermill in the neighboring territory of Torsa. He was later killed, apparently because his family could not, or refused to, meet a very high ransom demand. This killing induced several Camporano rentier and professional families to agree to purchase protection from one of the brigand bands of the area. But securing protection from brigands exposed members of these families to criminal charges from state officials. In September 1870, in a show of strength, an army and police contingent from Mozarra encircled Camporano and proceeded to arrest twenty-four wealthy and prominent villagers, including a former mayor, for abetting a criminal association. Most of them spent at least a few years in the Mozarra prison.

In the absence of law and order, wealth-producing activities were not the only liability, however. The strong measures used by police officials against captured brigands must have hardened the resolution of those still at large for, by the early 1870s, there began to appear newspaper reports of burgisi and viddani being victimized by brigands. Going to the field with a mule and even making the annual visit to the Shrine of Saint Calogero, a popular saint in Camporano, posed a danger. Until the turn of the century, villagers taking their wheat to the Torsa mill, which required almost a day's journey by mule through different neighboring territories, did so at their own risk. At the same time, there are also several

83

reported cases of agricultural workers and shepherds being arrested for refusing to report or signal brigand movements to law-enforcement officers (cf. Caico, 1910).

Once again Camporanesi—wealthy and poor villagers alike—faced a situation with few opportunities and remedies. Private provision of security was inadequate even for those who could afford it. Public provision by the state police posed as much danger as the brigands.

Voluntary Collective Reactions

Attempts were made to mitigate circumstances of communal life through a variety of voluntary collective efforts. But the relative success of these undertakings depended in turn on the extent to which they were permitted by political regimes that allowed only public officials to be concerned with public action. Thus there developed a situation whereby, as officials of the central government asserted their jurisdictional claims, they came to regard voluntary collective efforts undertaken by villagers on behalf of their common interests as direct challenges to their authority. For Camporanesi the difference between the Bourbon and Savoy monarchy came to mean the degree to which the organization of each political regime hindered the efforts of local residents to provide for themselves. Thus the success of voluntary efforts came to depend on the degree to which villagers could withstand the impediments inherent in the structure of government. The vehicles that permitted initial success in lawful concerted action were the local parishes. By 1890 exit from the village became the principal form of successful collective reaction to the iron circle.

The *Monte frumentario* as a Wheat Bank

The preamble to the charter of the *Monte frumentario* (literally, "mountain of wheat") created in 1814 alludes to a precursor established by local peasants around 1790. Although cited in other documents, there seem to be no extant records of that earlier undertaking. There are sufficient records of the 1814 wheat bank to illustrate its relative success and the conditions that led to its collapse by 1890.

The wheat bank was intended to create a supply of durum wheat for the peasants to borrow in times of need and at a cheaper rate than that

84

provided by the baron or rentiers. The maximum that a cultivator could receive at first was two salms per year, to be returned in August of the following year with a premium of one tumolo per salm borrowed. By 1870 the economic conditions of the wheat bank permitted its officials to increase the amount of wheat a cultivator could borrow to four salms at the same premium as before.

Four peasants helped to establish the Monte by pooling together a quantity of wheat from their harvest in August 1814. It is known, however, that local jurors took additonal steps to strengthen that initiative by levying a 5 percent tax on the 1814 harvest, amounting to ninety-four ducats. The tax collected and the wheat donated served to establish an initial wheat pool, to rent a storage space, and to hire a part-time accountant. A committee of local cultivators directed the wheat bank; every year two peasants took turns on the five-member committee.

In 1819 the Monte frumentario came under the supervision of the Central Office of Public Beneficence. Members of its executive committee now were the mayor, two peasants selected by the *decurionato*, and a priest appointed by the bishop. These changes do not seem to have affected the operation of the Monte. During an inspection in 1852, the intendant singled out the wheat banks of Camporano and Castelfrano, a nearby town, as the most prosperous in the province. In September 1855, a royal edict made the wheat bank a communal one without, however, affecting the composition of its administration or the nature of the service provided. In that year, the Monte storage place contained some 430 salms of wheat. In 1858, another intendancy inspector found the economic situation of the Camporano wheat bank "remarkable" and suggested to the Ministry of Sicilian Affairs that such local initiatives should be encouraged elsewhere.

Throughout this period, from 200 to 400 salms of wheat were borrowed every year by close to 300 burgisi. The records for 1849 indicated that some did not return the wheat borrowed with the accrued premium. While there were similar cases in other years, it would appear that they did not greatly hinder the operations of the Monte. In fact, it had become such a successful concern that at various junctures in the 1850s, its officials loaned funds to communal officials to carry out repairs on the water mains, to enlarge the cemetery, and to establish an initial fund of some 280 onze for the setting up of a communal loan bank, the *Monte di Pietà* (see also Di Matteo and Pillitteri, 1973). In 1871, the acting mayor warned the Mozarra prefect that the Monte needed auditing as too many cultivators did not return the wheat borrowed on time. But in 1878, a prefectoral inspection confirmed the florid economic conditions of the Camporano wheat bank. At that time some 550 salms were being loaned to some 440 cultivators; the Monte had some 700 salms of wheat as assets.

By 1895 another prefectoral official was reporting on the Camporano wheat bank. This time he was in charge of the almost bankrupt Monte. What conditions led to the decline of the once flourishing local enterprise?

A royal decree dated October 28, 1878, transferred the direction of the Monte from the mayor, local cultivators, and a priest to a communal relief agency directed by the mayor. The mayor was, in effect, given discretion to appoint members of his own choice to direct the bank—regardless of whether or not they were cultivators. From 1879, succeeding mayors were doing precisely that. By the early 1880s, the direction and operation of the wheat bank became increasingly divorced from its original purposes. Officials of the communal relief agency used the wider latitude of discretion allowed to them to disregard some peasants' demands while favoring others. At the same time, the control of the Monte became an issue of dispute among those villagers desirous of being elected mayor. They saw it as an additional source of authority and prestige of the incumbent mayor (see Sonnino, 1877: 260–261). It was these disputes that, in part, led to the placement of the communal relief agency under prefectoral trusteeship. Although they had hoped that the discretion allowed to officials of the Camporano relief agency could have been better used, provincial authorities found little illegality in the way that discretion had been used. The prefectoral functionary sent to the village in 1895 drew up a new charter for the wheat bank, but its funds and good name had been all but depleted. The 1814 Monte ceased to exist except on paper.

Agrarian Association

The metateria arrangement provided the conditions for the pursuit of individualistic action among landlords and sharecroppers. At the same time, the use among Camporano cultivators of such word phrases as *ad opra e rendita* denote informal, ad hoc concerted action such as helping each other in the field, pooling draft animals, or using each other's mule or donkey (see also Carini, 1894). In the fall of 1875 there was, how-

ever, an attempt on the part of some two hundred Mogata tenants to realize mutual interests by coming together in a fasces or league.

The aims of the organizers of the agrarian association were (1) to alter
the metateria contract so that the landlord and tenant would share the
costs of each of the factors of production in the same proportion in which
they would share the product, and (2) to establish the basis for long-term
benefits to local burgisi. The realization of the second objective was dependent upon the success of the first. However, by the time the league
was organized in 1875, the principal aim was changed to a demand for
an equal share of the product.

It is not clear how many Mogata tenants took part in organizing this
league. By September four or five tenants emerged as leaders of the association. Both they and association members belonged to church confraternities that served as mutual-aid societies. It is possible that participation in these confraternities helped Mogata tenants to develop the skills
and knowledge necessary to overcome individualistic action. At the
same time, Mancur Olson's analysis of *The Logic of Collective Action*
(1965) suggests that the face-to-face Camporano group was easier to organize than a larger group because (1) the benefits that were to be derived for a single member were of a sufficient magnitude to offset the cost
of that joint effort, and (2) each individual tenant was apt to see a direct
relationship between his individual contribution and its effect upon that
joint effort. It is also possible that a knowledge of the organization of
sharecropper leagues in neighboring towns gave Camporano tenants additional information about the potential benefits to be derived from this
kind of collective action.

Camporano peasant leaders were faced with the problems of how to
bring about changes in the metateria arrangement. Strikes were illegal
and it is now known that provincial police officials were ready to intervene in the case of a declared strike. Each association member was required to refuse to sign the existing share tenancy contract with the estate overseer. Two squads of league members made sure that this was
adhered to by Mogata tenants. As the loss of a whole year's crop was becoming a real possibility, the baron renewed his call to central government authorities in Mozarra to maintain the prerogatives of rural property
in Camporano. As secret depositions before the parliamentary commission in 1875 indicate, the high police officials in Mozarra were sympathetic to the claims of the Camporano workers but the very discharge of
their responsibilities implied a disregard for the aims of peasants. The

87

kidnap and eventual murder of the three-year-old son of a prominent villager in late September, although unrelated to the metateria dispute, gave central government authority in Mozarra additional incentives to intervene. Some time in October, an army contingent encircled Camporano and forcibly disbanded the agrarian association.

The old sharecropping arrangement was reinstated. Testifying before a parliamentary commission in December 1875, the mayor of Camporano, Ciro Vallera, and other members of the landed gentry, supported the proprietary rights of Baron Udo in relation to the labor force. By the late 1870s, metateria had been changed from two years to one year, with each cultivator still receiving one-third of the product. Relations between the landlord and tenants had worsened (Damiani, 1885: vol. XIII, book II).

The spread of new agricultural and artisanal workers' solidarity leagues throughout the Sicilian countryside by 1894 attests again to the self-organizing capabilities of Sicilian workers. Now it was the Sicilian prime minister, Francesco Crispi, who ordered their suppression. At least until 1894, the successful transformation of collective voluntary efforts into lawful viable concerns could not take place as long as these efforts aimed to introduce changes in the laws and arrangements that maintained and supported the iron circle.

Confraternities as Mutual-Aid Societies

Today, activities of the confraternities of the Holy Eucharist, of the Immaculate Conception, and of Our Lady of Sorrows are restricted to religious functions. Their members, totalling no more than seventy and wearing the different colors of the various confraternities, can still be observed accompanying a procession on the feast of the Camporano patron saint or a funeral train of a deceased member. Created in the course of the nineteenth century for the "greater glory of God," these congregations provided members with temporal as well as spiritual benefits. Today what remains of the temporal benefits is the right of burial in one of the three confraternity chapels (cf. Sleiter, 1974). Church and state papers suggest what Camporano confraternities did as mutual-aid societies.

One of the first Camporano-born churchmen helped to create the congregation of the Holy Eucharist. Its charter was formally approved by the Bourbon monarch in August 1841; its members came from the viddani class, the villagers who were particularly affected by the suppression of civic usufruct rights on Mogata. In part in recognition for his work among the poorest villagers, that priest was nominated by communal officials for the position of vicar in 1844. The second oldest confraternity is that of the Immaculate Conception, established in 1855. It was again started through the efforts of another churchman at a time when the conditions of Mogata tenants were deteriorating. While priests advanced in the church hierarchy, confraternity members gained temporal as well as spiritual benefits. These two societies set a pattern to follow for the organization and practice of other religious societies that were established in the 1880s.

The ability to provide benefits depended upon the financial resources of each congregation, which derived from an initial membership fee and an annual contribution from each member. The financial capabilities could easily be strained if all members of each association allowed some members to disregard the interests of others. That the congregations of the Holy Eucharist and of the Immaculate Conception continued to provide services to their members over a fifty-year period would indicate that this problem was successfully managed. The temporal benefits provided by these two confraternities included burial in the congregation chapels, financial help to the old, sick, and unable-to-work members, and some dowry (*maritaggio*) for the daughters of deceased members.

The meager financial resources of the Holy Eucharist and the Immaculate Conception were seldom sufficient to provide sickness, unemployment, or pension benefits to the chronically ill and elderly members, or "life insurance" benefits to all the unmarried daughters of deceased members. As a result, during the harvest season members of each confraternity took turns in visiting threshing areas in and around Camporano to gather donations in kind. Temporal benefits as well as dues were suspended at times of epidemics such as that of the cholera in 1867 and at times of bad harvests such as that of 1874. In that particular year, officers of the two congregations joined those of the wheat bank in a campaign to raise funds to distribute among the most indigent villagers. Some five thousand lire were collected and distributed. These efforts were, in turn, aided by the widespread religious practice of inviting the old and the poor for supper on the feast of Saint Joseph—a practice that is still observed.

Thus, the church-sponsored associations allowed villagers to realize mutual benefits and to participate in self-governing efforts to a degree not possible in communal affairs (see Grew, 1974: 255; and Renda, 1955: 619–620, and note 1). As the 1875 burgisi league suggests, membership in these associations also served to provide the primary political leadership for other types of concerted action. The work of Camporano priests on behalf of rural workers tends to support Sidney Sonnino's comments about the Sicilian clergy. His research on the Sicilian political economy led him to observe that

> civil society appears to the Sicilian peasant only in the form of rapacious landlords, tax collectors, conscription officers and police officials [carabinieri]. The priest is, instead, the only person who treats him with affection and charity; who, even when he cannot help, shares his suffering with him; who treats him as a human being; and who speaks to him of a future everlasting justice to compensate for the present earthly injustices. . . . In the church [culto religioso] the Sicilian peasant finds the ideal part of his life; outside of it, he finds nothing but toil, sweat and misery. (Sonnino, 1877: 145)

Christian precepts as well as advancement opportunities in the church hierarchy are, no doubt, the basic explanatory factors for the work of Camporano religious leaders on behalf of rural workers. But there were at least two other contributing factors.

First, practically all the Camporano priests, "the first nobles of the village," came from the same class of people they took such an active interest in—the Mogata tenants and the agricultural laborers. Unlike government offices, access to church offices continued to be relatively open to all villagers. While there were, as a rule, not more than six priests assigned to the village, at any particular time after 1860 there must have been at least twenty Camporano churchmen outside the village. After 1860, the church remained the only avenue of intragenerational mobility for young peasant villagers—even for those who never finished their seminary training (cf. Alvaro, 1930). Between 1840 and 1885 at least sixteen villagers went to the seminary eventually to return as elementary schoolteachers, clerks, and even lawyers. The chain migration to the United States in the late 1800s was due in part to a Camporano Jesuit who taught moral theology at the famous Jesuit college in Woodstock, Maryland, and in part to a former Camporano seminarian who was the Italian consular agent in several American cities, including Trenton, New Jersey.

Second, the work of Camporano priests on behalf of villagers was also

90

influenced by government regulations. The charters of the 1841 and 1855 congregations had to be approved by government authorities in Naples; articles of the charters could not be changed without the authority of state officials; priests acting as spiritual directors were required not to take part in the election of officials or any other nonreligious activity of those societies; congregants were also asked to promise "not to keep secrets from public officials." But having interposed these limits, Bourbon officials left the religious societies of Camporano alone. The expropriation of church property in Sicily in 1867 and the fall of papal Rome in 1870 produced a situation whereby the interests of Sicilian churchmen and the pope coincided in their mutual hostility or opposition toward the new Italian kingdom. In 1867, confraternities like those of Camporano came under the scrutiny of the prefect. At least until the 1890s there was an increasing concern in the annual report submitted by the commandant of the Camporano carabinieri about "the anti-state and pro-church activities" of the two congregations among "the wretched classes." In a report to the parliamentary commission in 1883, the district judge for the Camporano area noted disapprovingly that local peasants were still under the influence of priests who "continue(d) to spread the most absurd beliefs and superstitions" (Damiani, 1885: vol. XIII, book II). But, as long as there was no governmental attempt to suppress or alter religious associations, it was unlikely that the standing and influence of Camporano churchmen could be checked. Indeed, the 1880s was the period when several new church-sponsored associations were established.

A young priest, Giuseppe Riera, helped to found the new confraternities. The organization of these new societies followed the familiar principles of the two oldest congregations, with some modifications. There was more emphasis on temporal benefits. While the earlier sickness, unemployment, and "life insurance" benefits were increased, new ones were also added. For example, confraternity members tilling the land in the malaria-infested estate of a neighboring town were given a small dose of quinine (cf. Verga, 1881). A few years after it was established, the congregation of Our Lady of Sorrows alone had some 250 members among higher and lower burgisi, daily laborers, and artisans. Once again, it was church-sponsored associations that provided the context for Camporanesi of diverse social conditions to come together on matters of common concern—in essence, to act as a community. In part for this work, Riera was made vicar in 1885.

91

In 1890, central government authorities attempted to restrict church activities in Italian public life. Private associations such as confraternities, then numbering close to twelve thousand throughout Italy, were required to provide public assistance under the direction and supervision of communal relief agencies. In effect, these regulations transformed confraternities into public welfare agencies without, however, any change in the way confraternities gathered their funds. In such circumstances, it was difficult to expect confraternity members to fund the provision of temporal benefits to nonmembers as well. A decline of the Camporano confraternities as mutual aid societies followed. Efforts to circumvent government restrictions and to check the erosion of church confraternities led to the establishment of the congregation of the Holy Family as a "circle" in 1896, with more than five hundred members. By this time the changing political conditions in and beyond Sicily served to give radically new dimensions to Camporano parishes as agencies for championing "the real village" against "the legal village."

Chain Migration

The 1885 parliamentary report on Sicilian conditions noted no migratory movement among Camporanesi. But already by that time some villagers must have been orienting their search for a better life beyond the Camporano horizon, for by the end of the 1880s several villagers left Camporano. As was mentioned earlier, a priest and a former seminarian residing in the United States helped to give direction to this search. What began as an individualistic reaction to the iron circle soon became a mass exodus of almost Biblical proportions (see also Macdonald and Macdonald, 1964; Macdonald, 1956). In 1891 the Camporano correspondent for a Mozarra newspaper reported that in that year alone some 400 land workers had sailed for North African and North American shores. By 1898, as the chain migration from Camporano continued, a local newspaper correspondent reported that communal officials were expressing genuine fears about the very survival of Camporano (see Battaglia, 1895: 195; Sereni, 1947: 351). By 1900, Giuseppe Riera, now the village archpriest, could already appeal to Camporanesi living in the diaspora to help build a new church. In 1901, according to a report in a provincial Catholic newspaper, Camporano villagers living in Chicago, New York City, and Trenton organized as church-building committees, collected, and sent to Father Riera, relatively large sums of money. One single donation came from Buenos Aires.

In sum, chain migration was the principal form of voluntary concerted action that, unlike the wheat bank, the peasant association, and the confraternities, could proceed unhindered. The other successful local joint effort entirely free of governmental and political restrictions was the Camporano musical band. Composed of about twenty-five artisans and land workers at any one time, the band provided musical services for any occasion—from funerals to religious and national feasts, from celebrations of communal electoral victories to visits of the Mozarra bishop and prefect. Thus, at least until the early 1890s the long-term survival and success of voluntary collective efforts under the iron circle depended upon the extent to which these local ventures were entirely free from, or could withstand, governmental and political restrictions.

Conclusion

The reconstitution of the village political economy after 1816 provided little or no opportunities for villagers to act as a community. By 1848 Camporanesi had become so clearly split up into separate, antagonistic classes that it was as if within Camporano there existed several distinct communities. Reactions to the iron circle, or to the reconstitution of agricultural and communal activities as a function of centralized government authority, thus varied according to the relative position of individuals. At the same time, the successive armed revolts and voluntary collective undertakings revealed that, no matter how much villagers engaged in such efforts, it was events at the national level that ultimately determined the breakup of the iron circle in Camporano. Basic changes in the structure of the local political economy could come only from members of the ruling class. As Camporano peasants found themselves to be consistent losers whenever they had anything to do with landlords and public authorities, they came to rely upon individual qualities typified by the Sicilian word *mafia* in order to enhance their life prospects. Individualistic choice thus became the most "successful" long-term reaction to the iron circle. But, as noted, the more the incentives for the individual villager to take advantage of any opportunity available to sustain his family's livelihood increased, the worse off all

93

villagers became. It is in this sense that Gramsci's characterization of Southern Italy as "a general social disintegration" (1926: 42) applies to Camporano.

What are some other generalizations or hypotheses embedded in the analysis? First, the weight of evidence about voluntary collective efforts presented in this chapter suggests that people in the South did possess the knowledge and skills appropriate for concerted action and entrepreneurship. Prevented from cooperating, they became individualistic. Second, "general social disintegration" was not an inability to act but the presence of institutional arrangements for private property and public choice that created impediments to social aggregation. Third, the transformation of political authority between 1860 and 1865 did little to ameliorate conditions of life in the Sicilian countryside and in the South as a whole. This has often been viewed as part of the human price that had to be paid for the quickest and shortest road for Italy to the structure and characteristics of a modern country. Perhaps it had to be so. But the history of post-Risorgimento Italy suggests that when the victimization of a subset of the population is used as the means, or human price, to attain a desirable end, that future good may itself be permanently flawed. As Elinor Ostrom (1975: 468) has suggested in another context, an ethics appropriate to political analysis must include an *ethics of consequences* as well as an ethics of motives.

In any event, by the 1880s, the failure of the armed, individualistic, and collective efforts to alter radically village life must have brought Camporano peasants to resemble closely the description of the average Sicilian peasant that emerged in the Damiani parliamentary report. Damiani concluded that the Sicilian peasant was "somber like a hermit, patient like Job, wretched like Lazarus, and without a future like a Helot or a Fallah' (Damiani, 1884: vol. XIII, book I, 121). Yet the structure of government that had failed to enhance, if not served to diminish, the welfare potential of Camporano peasants had also fostered among them a spirit of independence and self-reliance that kept alive their sense of personality and self-respect. In the course of the nineteenth century, this spirit of mafia took on several manifestations, including exit from the village. In the twentieth century, it was to take on yet another form.

6

The Regime of Self-Reliance

Villagers attempted to obtain satisfactory remedies to local contingencies through a pattern of social organization outside of the formal institutions. This pattern of social organization is the outlaw regime of mafia or what a sociologist policeman characterized as "primitive self-government" (Alongi, 1887: 45)

The constitution of the Camporano outlaw regime took place precisely when the lawful regime was changing for the better. The rise of Christian Democracy in the 1890s served to renew and strengthen the concern of the Camporano clergy for the hardships of villagers. New and unprecedented church-sponsored associations were established with the purpose of interesting the greatest possible number of Camporanesi in matters of the commonweal. In 1896, the central government itself became infected with this spirit of change (Ganci, 1958). While the machinery of government remained as it was, many unjust, harsh, and arbitrary laws were leniently applied or left unenforced. Giolitti's advent to power in 1901 solidified, with almost a decade of rule, this New Liberalism. The labor shortages caused by chain migration and the remittances from abroad further enhanced the life prospects of Camporanesi who remained behind. The steadily increasing improvements that followed, however, far from tranquillizing villagers, drew attention to the as yet unremedied features of Camporano life and these now appeared even more intolerable. Villagers were thus emboldened to reject altogether official efforts to govern them—in essence, to extend the spirit of mafia or self-reliance from individualistic to collective efforts. Alongside the formal structure of government, there emerged by 1908 another structure of government, at once inlaw and outlaw, which excited the loyalty and interest of villagers.

The beginnings of the Camporano regime of mafia are associated with the rise of an economic entrepreneur, Mariano Ardena, in the late 1890s. The opportunities as well as limitations generated by the changing conditions provided the context for Ardena to become also a political entrepreneur or, in the words of a Camporano peasant turned merchant, "a profitable altruist," a villager who by helping others also helps himself. The radical thrust of Christian Democracy in Camporano lay in championing "the real village" against "the legal village" and in channeling the accumulated hostility toward the existing institutional arrangements into profitable altruism. If forces outside Camporano initiated the breakup of the iron circle, forces inside Camporano completed the breakup and gave it its local color.

Christian Democracy

During the course of the nineteenth century most Camporanesi had access only to their church as an instrument of collective action. By the early 1890s, however, another chain of events beyond the Camporano mountains provided novel opportunities for the local clergy to act on behalf of villagers.

Pope Leo XIII's encyclical *Rerum Novarum* in 1891 signaled the end of papal attempts to regain temporal power in Italy and ranged the church on the side of social reform. The encyclical, supported by the ban for Italian Catholics (*non expedit*) to vote or participate in national elections, stimulated the rise of Christian Democracy as a grass-roots movement capable of "reclaiming" the Italian working classes from both Liberalism and Socialism. Throughout the peninsula and particularly in Lombardy, Piedmont, and Veneto, the church-sponsored societies of the Congress Movement ceased to be the pope's organizational weapon for the restoration of his temporal government and became the organizational weapon of the nascent Christian Democracy (Jemolo, 1955: 46–79; cf. Diamant, 1960: 23–28; Salvadori, 1963: 373–378). In Sicily, the rich tradition of church involvement in community affairs and the afflic-

96

tion caused by the failure to intervene decisively against the suppression of the workers' solidarity leagues in 1894 led Catholic religious and lay leaders to accelerate their efforts on behalf of Christian Democracy.

In 1895, the First Sicilian Catholic Congress was held at Palermo. Anticipating some of the tenets of modern "liberation theology," the Congress asserted that Christian life was impossible without human dignity. Since human dignity was not possible for most Sicilians without basic structural changes, the fight for social, economic and political reforms was more urgent than traditional pastoral work. "Priests out of the sacristy!" was the directive that emerged from the gathering—a directive that had already been echoed by the Mozarra bishop in a pastoral letter to the clergy of his diocese in 1893. The main speaker at the First Sicilian Catholic Congress, Father Luigi Cerutti from Veneto, served as an example of what activist priests could do and of what support they could receive from the Church. Cerutti had organized several cooperative credit societies or rural banks (*casse rurali*) in Veneto with the backing of the Bank of Rome, established in 1880 by the Holy See in order to provide capital at low rates of interest for organizations of the Congress Movement. In 1899, a detailed Demochristian program was drawn up at Turin, calling for, among others, constitutional reforms to permit local self-government, bold social legislation to improve the conditions of the working classes and freedom of association for trade unions and cooperatives. In 1901, Prime Minister Giolitti formally recognized what by 1895 the central government could no longer effectively hold back— freedom of association. By 1903, thanks in part to the activities of a young Sicilian priest and nobleman, Luigi Sturzo (1871–1959), Christian Democracy in Sicily consisted of a vast regional network of peasant leagues, friendly societies, and cooperative credit institutions, supported by diocesan newspapers calling for local and regional self-government (see De Rosa, 1977: 53–117; di Giovanni and Palazzo, 1982; Guccione, 1974: 53–154; Naro, 1977; Renda, 1972; Sturzo, 1901).

For the Camporano priests, and particularly for Giuseppe Riera, who had helped to organize new confraternities in the early 1880s, this chain of events must have been an exhilarating experience (see also Bernanos, quoted in Fogarty, 1957: 342). The rise of Christian Democracy vindicated their earlier pastoral work. Assisted by his own brother priest, Efisio, Giuseppe Riera contributed to the work of Luigi Sturzo in several ways. With the aid of newspaper reports of the time and archival material

97

on church-sponsored mutual-aid societies, one can reconstruct some of Giuseppe Riera's activities.

In 1895, Riera established a wheat bank for the poor. The initial capital of thirty-five salms of wheat came from the one-year cultivation of five salms of land put at his disposal by a Mogata rentier in exchange for perpetual prayers for his soul. In the same year, he was instrumental in setting up a parish electoral committee among peasant and artisan voters in order to bring Christian Democracy into communal and provincial politics. In 1896, Father Riera helped to found another confraternity as the Circle of the Holy Family with temporal benefits that surpassed those already provided earlier by the extant confraternities, now almost exclusively concerned with spiritual benefits. In 1897, he convinced young peasants and artisans to form a social club, and in the same year that Catholic circle, named after Pope Leo XIII, had about two hundred supporters. In 1898, Riera took the lead in establishing, among Camporano burgisi and sharecroppers, what was to become the single most important Demochristian association—a cooperative credit society or rural bank (*Cassa rurale*) appropriately named after Saint Joseph, the patron saint of both Camporano and workers. In 1901, he secured the ground floor of a house to serve as a recreation circle or club for Camporano workers to gather in the winter months and chat about current events, to play cards, and to hear lecture series on the "evil of divorce," an issue then being debated throughout Italy.

To be sure, both Giuseppe and Efisio Riera exercised dominant influence in the operation of these Catholic societies (see also Cameroni and Cameroni, 1976). For his lead in organizing them, Father Giuseppe also advanced in the church hierarchy. He was named Camporano archpriest in 1897 and a bishop in 1910. Yet, the church-sponsored associations were so organized as to attract villagers to matters of mutual concern and to give each member a taste for authority and popularity in the conduct of local affairs. They became, in fact, an unfailing source of profit and interest to a vast number of villagers. Year by year, the activities of the Demochristian societies spread at an increasing tempo that by the early 1900s the whole village seemed to be in the throes of a rebirth.

For example, the *Cassa rurale* or Saint Joseph cooperative credit union, starting with no owned capital, in a few years of making loans and receiving deposits built up a large indivisible owned capital and reduced dramatically the dependence of Camporano sharecroppers on local usurers (see Costanzo, 1923). At the same time, according to some former

98

members of the *Cassa*, including Father Giacomo Nicosia, members used to view their cooperative credit society less as an economic institution and more as a social institution in the sense that mutual assistance also fostered individual self-esteem and community solidarity (see also Geertz, 1962: 243–246). In February 1901, members of the rural bank agreed to finance the establishment of a consumers' cooperative and by July of the same year it became operational. In September 1901, Mogata tenants and officials of the *Cassa* organized and led a strike of all the Mogata tenants using the rallying cry "Fair contracts or all to America!"

Going to America had already served to ease pressures on the land and to increase wages by one-third for the daily laborers who had stayed behind. By abstaining en masse from sowing their lots, Mogata tenants now compelled their landlords to consider agricultural production jointly with them. The interaction between the two groups led to a reciprocal modificaticn of expectations and action. By November 1901, the new Mogata proprietor, Princess Laura Gardena, and the local rentiers agreed to eliminate many of the unfair deductions that were made from the sharecropper's portion of the product. Mogata lots would now be divided into three kinds according to the quality of terrain, and only those of top quality carried with them a *terraggiolo* or land dowry deduction of about a salm of wheat for each salm of land. These modifications in the conduct of agricultural activities took on the semblance of a collective labor contract—prompting the Camporano correspondent for the Socialist journal *La Battaglia*, who also happened to be the only Camporano Socialist, to observe that local Demochristians were "implicit Socialists." What in 1875 another generation of Mogata tenants had tried and failed to achieve because of government intervention now could be achieved without fear of government intervention, thanks to New Liberalism and Implicit Socialism.

The success of the Saint Joseph cooperative credit union in stimulating and supporting mutual adjustment of expectations and behavior among Mogata tenants and landlords had other positive consequences. Princess Gardena began to take genuine interest in the life and problems of her Mogata tenants, even though, or perhaps because, the former fief was a very small part of her patrimony. In the summer of 1902, she reduced motu proprio the land dowry to four tumoli of wheat for each salm of land, appointed a new Mogata overseer, and leased several Mogata lots to the Camporano cooperative credit society acting as a collective landholding society (*gabella*). In the same year, Gardena donated religious vestments to the Camporano church and began to support financially the local institution for helping needy schoolchildren named after her (*patronato scolastico*). For their part, rentiers who were also professional people began to give lecture series to the peasant recreation circle on topics ranging from the value of education to the virtue of personal and public hygiene. The victory of the Demochristian slate of candidates in the July 1903 communal election signaled both the end of the majority and minority coalitions that had dominated local government after 1870 and the beginning of an interclass grand coalition that permitted peasants, artisans, and members of the former ruling class to act together in communal politics.

The pattern of mutual adjustment or reciprocal modification that accompanied the rise of Christian Democracy was becoming so much a part of village life that some members of the Igelo, Fontena, and Vallera families, who proclaimed themselves either Masons or freethinkers, tried to retain their traditional hold on Camporano peasants by establishing mutual-aid societies to compete with the church-sponsored associations. It is not clear, however, to what extent these members of the former ruling class had become seriously committed to the idea of village life "as a process of cooperating experience" (Follett, 1924: 30). For, according to reports in the Catholic newspaper *Il Sole del Mezzogiorno* of 1903, when their undertakings failed to attract the support of a relatively large number of Camporano peasants in order to become operational, they attempted unsuccessfully to have the Liberal central government dissolve the Camporano Catholic societies for their alleged antimonarchical and subversive activities. Yet, it would seem that the rise of Christian Democracy had by 1903 produced in Camporano what at least since the 1848 revolt had been difficult to realize and what later Gramsci in his well-known essay "The Southern Question" (1926) was to dismiss as an all-time impossibility in Southern Italy—a commonality or a progressive adjustment of interests between cultivators and landlords (see also Lupo, 1977).

At the same time, the very successful beginnings of Christian Democracy in and beyond Camporano laid bare insurmountable contradictions within the Italian Catholic world. As the manifold activities of the younger clergy and the laity on behalf of the working classes overflowed into the political realm, they took on markedly "secularistic" features and created a sphere of action outside of ecclesiastical control. As a result, the Demochristian movement threatened to make the *non expedit*

100

ban nugatory, to succumb to the modernist tendencies that were then infiltrating and subverting matters of the faith, and to deprive the church hierarchy of ultimate authority over the Catholic movement. Moreover, there were still Italian Catholics as intransigently opposed to the transformation of the Congress Movement into the organizational weapon of Christian Democracy as they were to the values and world of the Italian state and Liberalism. In such circumstances, the church in Italy could neither be a direct agent or organizer of social and political action nor tolerate a Catholic movement or party independent of itself. But, whereas Leo XIII sought to mitigate the fervor with which the younger clergy and many of the laity had flung themselves into realizing Christian Democracy, his successor, Pius X, stilled that fervor altogether. In 1904, Pius X dissolved the Congress Movement and almost all its constituent sections, placing economic and social organizations under the direct control of the church hierarchy. The threat of Christian Democracy becoming an Italian Catholic party before World War I was thus averted. As Sturzo was to recall these events during his exile from Fascist Italy, "(t)he term Christian Democracy then became empty of sense and was buried in silence" (Sturzo, 1938: 466; see also De Rosa, 1977: 123–126; Webster, 1960: 3–23).

These events had little or no adverse effect on the organization and conduct of the Camporano church-sponsored associations as such (cf. Guccione, 1974: 155–171). A provincial newspaper reported that as late as 1907 Camporano Catholics, like other Catholics in the Mozarra province, still celebrated the annual feast of Christian Democracy. In part for his leadership in organizing these societies and for his submission to papal authority, archpriest Riera was rewarded with a bishopric on the Italian mainland in 1910. But the stunted growth, or what Sturzo called "the emptying of sense and burial in silence," of Christian Democracy before World War I opened the way for more autochthonous values to take full possession of the process of cooperating experience in Camporano.

Profitable Altruism

Almost thirty years after his death, the overwhelming majority of villagers continues to maintain a high regard for Mariano Ardena's actions. Indeed, when villagers are confronted with problems they cannot solve, they are wont to say, "What we need is another Don Mariano." They

101

readily admit that, starting from modest conditions, by the time of his death Ardena had become a wealthy man. As a 1974 survey in a Catania newspaper suggests, most villagers would agree with the peasant turned merchant's assessment of Ardena's actions on behalf of Camporanesi as based on profitable altruism. However, there are today fewer opportunities and rewards as well as substantial constraints and costs for such a new entrepreneur to rise.

Ardena's Social Background

Mariano Ardena's biography is not difficult to sketch, as much of his life is a matter of public knowledge among old villagers of all social conditions. He was the first son of Salvatore Ardena and Rosalia Riera. Salvatore was a lower burgise who at times augmented his earnings by working as a laborer. He had married Rosalia Riera, who came from a similar background. Rosalia was the sister of Giuseppe and Efisio Riera. One of Mariano's brothers, Gaetano, was ordained to the priesthood in 1903 and lived in the village until his death in the 1950s. Mariano's only sister married into the Novara family which, although it had been one of the first families to settle on the Mogata estate in the 1770s, was of similar social class. One of her two sons, Franco Novara, who was born in 1903, graduated from the university with a degree in civil law. Eventually he served as aide to Mariano Ardena.

Unlike his brothers, Mariano did not go to school beyond the third grade. He worked in the fields with his father. Until his death, while in the village, Mariano wore a "cap," the traditional accoutrement of the Sicilian peasantry. Ardena's social background tends to support Henner Hess's observation that many, probably the majority of, mafiosi came from the lower rather than the middle stratum of Sicilian society (Hess, 1970: 44).

The Beginnings of Profitable Altruism

The first available police report on Mariano Ardena dates to the spring of 1897. The emphasis on the word *available* here is important, because popular accounts suggest that Ardena had earlier been involved in assaults against some villagers. Though I spared no effort in and outside of state archives, I cannot confirm or deny the accuracy of such accounts. Much has also been written in the popular press about Ardena's criminal

102

record after 1897, but popular accounts are neither accurate nor valid and should be viewed skeptically. My principal sources of information about the criminal record of Ardena and other Camporano mafiosi are newspaper reports of trial proceedings from 1903 on, accessible records of trial proceedings, and police (*questura*) background material on local mafiosi prepared in connection with the antimafia war of the 1960s.

In the spring of 1897, Ardena was nineteen years old and president of the local Catholic youth association named after Pope Leo XIII. Most likely, he was appointed to that position by his uncle, Archpriest Riera. The circle gathered some two hundred Camporanesi between the ages of twelve and twenty-one. Because of the then tense church-state relations, the carabinieri kept a close watch on such groups. One of their reports in 1897 noted that the circle headed by Ardena "exercised influence among the poor class." At about the same time, Ardena was taking part with other villagers in the search for cattlerustlers who had raided a villager's farm. The interplay between the persistent absence of law and order in the Camporano countryside and the lessons in working together that had been learned in the church-sponsored associations provided the context for Mariano Ardena to become a local entrepreneur and, eventually, a leader of the local mafia regime.

By the 1890s, it had become demonstrably clear to most villagers that if they valued public security, it would have to come about through their own efforts (cf. Osgood, 1929: 114–125). This situation provided the incentives for Mariano Ardena to organize, among members of the Catholic circle he headed, a group of two armed individuals to escort, at a price, villagers taking wheat to the mill in the territory of Torsa, a neighboring village in another province. This venture soon became a successful going concern. By 1900 it was expanded into a barter system. Villagers no longer needed to go to the distant mill. For a modest fee, they could exchange wheat for flour without leaving the Camporano area.

Already by 1898 Ardena and members of his protection group must have succeeded in obtaining immunity from the two brigand bands in the Terrano-Torsa area, for in that year they were arrested for collaborating with brigands. They were arrested for the same crime in 1903. By that time Ardena was no longer taking a direct part in the barter system. But in each case, Ardena and the other young villagers were released for insufficiency of proof. No villager furnished evidence against them.

During this time, some notable changes in the relative standing of Ardena and his group among villagers took place. The provision of security and the way the barter system was conducted gained them respect and esteem. The incarceration they suffered in 1898 and 1903 served to enhance the legitimacy and reasonableness of their actions. Now villagers began to go to Ardena with other problems. It was easy to see why people turned to Ardena's group and not to the government for protection. Although their activities were illegal, Ardena and his friends had gained the support of most Camporanesi. Peace and security were coming to rest to a very large degree on their actions. A sidewalk overlooking the village square soon became the meeting place where Ardena and members of his protection group held council and met other villagers in the early hours of the morning. These modest beginnings were transformed into a successful long-term enterprise.

The Authority Pattern of the Outlaw Regime

The configuration of voluntary efforts resulting from the interconnected rise of Christian Democracy and profitable altruism significantly amplified the patterns of joint efforts and reciprocity with one another that had existed in Camporano only in the microcosm of kinship and neighborhood groupings. This process of cooperating experience, together with the stunted growth of Christian Democracy, provided the context in which villagers gained information about the potential benefits to be derived from an extension of profitable altruism. Common reference to a distinct language pattern, coupled with the knowledge of the existence of outlaw regimes in the neighboring towns of Castelfrano and Terrano, must have facilitated that learning process (cf. E. Ostrom, 1968). Before long, leaders of the various voluntary associations clustered together to form a community superstructure of institutional arrangements that had all the characteristics of a formal system of government. Since this aggregate structure of decision-making arrangements was informal, it cannot be easily identified as involving named entities equivalent to offices in formal institutions of government. By 1908, its principal features appeared in all their magnitude to reveal an authority pattern that bore striking similarities to that observed by Llewellyn and Hoebel in their study of the law ways of the Cheyenne people—a council of chiefs and a military society (Llewellyn and Hoebel, 1941; see also Hess, 1970; and Lestingi, 1884). The presence of enforcers made this aggregate authority pattern an outlaw, extralegal regime of self-reliance (see also Nieburg,

104

1969; Pospisil, 1967). The sidewalk overlooking the village square became the seat of this informal government.

For his part in knitting together the network of voluntary undertakings into a common structure, Mariano Ardena became the principal leader of the Camporano mafia regime or the primus inter pares among council chiefs. The presence of priests in this council gave an aura of supernatural approbation to the authority pattern of the outlaw regime. But this primitive self-government was also grounded upon the accumulated political wisdom of villagers.

The Accumulated Political Wisdom of Villagers

One of the central features of the Sicilian political tradition was the emphasis on common understanding and common agreement as necessary conditions for entering into and sustaining political covenants between the monarch and the Sicilian barons and between each baron and settlers. The critical shortcoming in this political tradition was the absence of governmental structures either as means for attempting to reestablish the commonality of understanding and agreement or as means for sustaining the operability of covenantal arrangements under the conditions of partial misunderstanding and disagreement. The institutional changes that followed the establishment of centralized government and administration in 1816 accentuated the shortcomings of the earlier period by doing away completely with common understanding and common agreement as necessary conditions for political choice. By the 1890s, the wisdom or knowledge shared by most Camporano villagers included a lack of consensus about the authority structure of the state as well as normative rules of conduct reminiscent of the "calculus of consent" (Buchanan and Tullock, 1962) that was part of the pre-1812 political tradition.

In chapter 4, a basic disjunction between the language of officialdom and the everyday language of villagers was noted. This was further compounded by the presence of similar-sounding words that had, however, different meanings in Sicilian and Italian. Thus, for instance, for most villagers the word *government* meant first of all individual self-government. In chapter 1, the different meanings attached to the Sicilian and Italian terms *mafia* or *maffia* were noted. This lack of common understanding was reinforced by a lack of common agreement about the authority of the state. As discussed in chapters 4 and 5, the instrumentalities of government, including arrangements for the enforcement of rural

105

property rights, biased social relationships in favor of a subset of the population to dominate economic relationships. After 1860, the phrase "to make a united Italy" was used to refer to the incentives provided to public officials to use their offices for private ends. By the late 1880s, the well-wishing phrase "May you become a mayor!" was used as a curse.

If their distinct language pattern placed most Camporanesi at a relative disadvantage in dealing with the instrumentalities of government, it also served as a shield against public officials and as a basis for sharing a common understanding and agreement of terms, definitions, and expectations of words translated into action. But common agreement was not a necessary condition for a political association to exist. Coercive capabilities could be exercised to yield conformity to authority, regardless of whether or not this authority provided the basis for mutually productive relationships. The outlaw regime emerged as an expression of local self-government precisely because its authority pattern derived from, and was built upon, a calculus of consent that was absent in the lawful regime.

The need to check individualistic drives, to encapsulate interpersonal and property conflicts, and to find reasonable and just solutions to common problems in light of the awareness of the costliness of state solutions was expressed in a number of local sayings, gathered among old Camporano peasants. From these local sayings, taken as manifestations of the peasants' image of the world around them, there also emerges a conception of the individual and of interpersonal relationships in reference to events in the world (see also Guastella, 1884; Pitrè, 1913; Salomone-Marino, 1897).

Each villager was seen as capable of selecting alternatives that would enhance his expected net potential well-being: each individual has his own preferences (*nun tutti hannu lu stissu palati*); everyone is presumed to be the best judge of his own interest (*ognunu havi li so' gusti*); and everyone can be expected to advance his own interest (*ognunu tira pri lu so' caminu*). In fact, each person was, first of all, his own sovereign in the government of his own affairs (*ognunu cuverna a se' stissu e Diu cuverna a tutti*). These village norms were accompanied by the recognition that "anyone who governs himself, often errs" (*cui si cuverna iddu stissu, spissu sgarra*). Selfish interest as a rule for interpersonal relationships always betrayed a lack of consideration or ignorance (*cu l'amuri propriu e' sempri la 'gnuranza*). The basic normative rules of conduct were respect of every individual and the right of everyone to make a living (*campari*). But the markedly asymmetrical interdependence existing among villagers precluded most villagers from claiming or asserting the right of respect and the right of *campari*. In the absence of public facilities to determine and enforce these village, but also universalistic, values, Camporanesi had evolved individualistic constraints based on *omertà* and infamy (*'nfamità*).

Omertà derives from the Sicilian word for man, *omu*. A Camporano villager was not necessarily *omu*. *Omertà* meant the qualities that allowed, for example, a peasant to be a "man"—a self-reliant person or mafioso. Its connotations referred to one's individual efforts (1) to make himself respected; (2) to defend his property; (3) if necessary, to restore his honor and that of his family; and (4) to solve conflicts and problems without seeking the help of other individuals or having recourse to the instrumentalities of the state. In short, omertà was the antithesis of servility (see also Pitrè, 1889).

The ability to carry out successfully one's efforts to be a man rested on the tacit collaboration of others not directly involved. Thus an additional connotation of *omertà* was infamy (cf. Calisse, 1928: 423–425). It referred to the act of interfering with one's attempt to seek either reparation or self-redress. The translation of the state of being infamous (*'nfame*) into action varied according to particular circumstances. It ranged from personal contempt to property mutilation (*sfregio*) and to death.

As the analysis of village life under the iron circle suggests, however, *omertà* and infamy had proven to be inadequate arrangements for sustaining mutually productive relationships. Manifestations of agreement in order to become operable rules of conduct needed to be related to a common set of decision-making mechanisms. The superstructure of institutional arrangements that emerged from Christian Democracy and profitable altruism came to provide that common facility. The normative rules of conduct thus became the constitutional rules of the mafia regime (cf. Bailey, 1969: 5–7; Pigliaru, 1959).

The Council of Chiefs

The council of chiefs was the formal facade of the authority pattern of the Camporano outlaw regime. Vested with political and legal powers, this self-perpetuating body crystallized before the soldiers of the mafia began

107

to function as an important agent of social action. It was originally made up of officials of the various church-sponsored associations, including members of the clergy (see also Blok, 1969: 106 and note 26; Pecorini, 1967). The tradition of good behavior and careful politics required of chiefs was such that apparently not all the officials of the various church-sponsored associations, and especially members of the parish electoral committee, originally served on the council. Mafia chiefs were to do all their business by talking, yet they were expected to talk as little as possible. Mariano Ardena emerged as the principal leader of the mafia regime also because he exemplified in words and deeds the qualities of leadership required of council chiefs.

By the 1910s, the council consisted of former leaders of Demochristian associations as well as villagers not connected with those associations. Whereas the membership of former Demochristian officials and church leaders gave continuity to the functioning of this governing body, the membership of other villagers brought renewed vigor to it. By 1920, the council consisted of some thirty chiefs of diverse social conditions—almost one chief for every one hundred villagers.

The Military Society

The soldier society served as the police arm of the council of chiefs. Both council chiefs and soldiers were known as "men with a belly" (*omi di panza*)—individuals who knew how to keep things to themselves. But whereas council chiefs were "men of patience and self-command," soldiers were "men with a good liver"—men of direct action.

The original soldiers were Ardena's associates in the barter trade. One of them, Illuminato Carena, a young peasant who was both a low burgise and an agricultural laborer, became the chief soldier. Membership was voluntary and at the discretion of the individuals already members. Until the early 1920s, it had about six members. Bound by consanguineal and ritual kinship ties, mafia soldiers were socially equal to the overwhelming majority of villagers.

The introduction of constraint through the soldier society served to channel the more extreme manifestations of individualistic choice without submerging expressions of individual self-government. *Omertà* was maintained, though some of its connotations changed. Except for personal, usually sexual, honor, self-redress was no longer tolerated. Silence was continued while recourse to the instrumentalities of the formal government was allowed in cases where it did not produce infamy. Justification for extreme sanctions such as in cases involving infamy, now referring especially to state informers, was shifted to the soldier society. It was in this sense that the following sayings represented a measure of agreement about extreme sanctions imposed by the mafia soldiers: "Where there is wrong, there is the dead body" (*Un e' lu turtu, e' lu murtu*). "The dead is dead, now let us help the living [he who has done it]" (*Lu murtu e' murtu e s'havi a dari ajuti a lu vivu*).

The reach of the mafia soldier society became wide. Acting as law agents, its members imposed sanctions with a rigor that at times was harsh. It is in this sense that Anton Blok's characterization of mafiosi as "violent peasant entrepreneurs" also applies to Camporano mafiosi (Blok, 1974). But the imposition of sanctions on villagers who performed specific acts which had potential harm to others was based on the recognition that—at least in theory—similar sanctions would be imposed on anyone else who performed the same acts (cf. Schelling, 1960). Death was considered only as a last resort—when all other reasonable avenues had been completely exhausted. It was a measure not taken lightly by the mafia soldiers and not without a sensing of opinion by the council chiefs.

The sensing of opinion for the justification of sanctions revealed most clearly the careful politics involved in sustaining consensus regarding the reasonableness of actions taken on behalf of villagers. It represented a delicate equilibrium, for villagers neither acknowledged nor recognized radical differences between rulers and ruled—between what John R. Commons called "authoritative transactions" and "authorized transactions" (1924: 65–142). The Sicilian word *amicu* ("friend") was, in fact, used to refer to both mafia officials and villagers who, while not officials, "understood." It was in this sense that the phrase "friends of friends" came to refer to the political community of the Camporano mafia (cf. Blok, 1974: 151, note 9). Moreover, the word *cummanari* ("to order")—a favorite word among public officials—was a hated word among Camporanesi. To present days, the expression *cci aviti a cummanari* ("who do you think you can boss around?") is used in terms of "What do you have to say?" when one attempts to interfere gratuitously in other people's affairs.

The description of the authority pattern of the outlaw regime suggests some modifications in Charles Tilly's observation that "(u)nlike most governments . . . the (mafia) system has no accountability, no visibility, no means of representation for those under its control" (1974: xix). The same description does not, however, challenge the truth value of Tilly's observation in the sense that thus far I have been describing the formation of the mafia regime. Whether the Camporano mafia system turned out as well in practice as in project remains to be seen.

Conclusion

The breakup of the iron circle began at the very time when it appeared so indestructible. Chain migration itself produced the first symptoms of its disintegration as the labor shortages that ensued altered the lopsided dependence of cultivators on landowners and rentiers. The factors that significantly contributed to the collapse of the iron circle were the same factors that significantly contributed to the constitution of the mafia regime. In the interconnected rise of Christian Democracy and profitable altruism, one can observe the characteristic village individualism succumb to the equally characteristic village need for joint efforts and reciprocity with one another, the evolution of village wisdom into law and the appearance of a pattern of social organization, at once inlaw and outlaw, which excited the loyalty and interest of villagers—the regime of mafia or self-reliance (cf. Hirschman, 1970).

In rejecting the official effort of the state to govern them, Camporanesi established their "own self-government." That, however, posed the problem of how the condition of political constraint could be maintained concurrently and over time with a substantial measure of consensus about the legitimacy of actions taken on behalf of villagers. There was a potential source of conflict in the administration of sanctions as well as services for relatives of profitable altruists. There was a need to establish cooperative arrangements with leaders of neighboring outlaw regimes on matters of common concern. In turn, there was also the need to minimize the exposures inherent in, and the constraints imposed by, the instrumentalities of the formal government. At the same time, these efforts raised the additional problem of a potential collusion between state officials and large landowners, on one hand, and mafiosi, on the other, to the disadvantage of villagers. The likelihood of a transformation of local self-government into a shakedown racket or criminal association was substantial. The mafia system of Camporano could indeed be "more curious and more cruel than government itself" (Tilly, 1974: xix).

7

Life under the Dual Regime

The mafia emerged with its own network of community organizations. The presence of these decision structures and those of the formal government meant that villagers had recourse to different strategies as they moved from one decision-making context to another. Transactions conducted in reference to the mafia system took into account the formal system while, at the same time, transactions conducted by reference to the state came to take into account those of the outlaw regime. There thus developed a situation where particular actions represented simultaneous moves in these diverse decision-making arenas.

As the process of cooperating experience continued, without pause, to overlap and interconnect these arenas, the working arrangements of the Liberal state became congruent with those of the Camporano primitive self-government—obscuring the partition between lawful and unlawful conduct of both mafiosi and government officials. Thus attempts to deal with the Camporano outlaw regime as a police problem proved to be ineffective. At the same time, actions pursued under such conditions served to strengthen the autonomy and legitimacy of the outlaw regime and to reduce the accumulated hostility of villagers toward the lawful regime. Perhaps for the first time in the history of Camporano, villagers possessed instrumentalities of government that allowed them to be part of the larger political community without depriving them of opportunities to act as an autonomous local community.

The outbreak of World War I served to shatter the coexistence of this "division and cohesion" (Eckstein, 1966). By 1919, the uninterrupted onrush of new exigencies and circumstances brought into question the very appropriateness of the existing institutions of government for resolving issues and problems in both Camporano and Italy as a whole. In Camporano the surplus of good will or residual agreement about the structure of the community organizations permitted its officials to take considerable deterioration in stride as they searched for ways to overcome their crisis of regime. In Italy as a whole the very absence of such a surplus or residual about the Liberal state brought its crisis of regime beyond the recuperative capabilities of central government officials. The parliamentary monarchy collapsed precisely when the Camporano extralegal regime had been able to marshal from within and from without forces that ensured its functioning in the face of partial disagreement. The advent of Fascist rule revealed fully, and not without irony, how fragile and unsatisfactory an expression of self-government and even self-reliance the Camporano mafia group was without the instrumentalities of the Liberal state as its supporting structure. Life under the dual regime gave way to life *Under the Axe of Fascism* (Salvemini, 1936).

The Outlaw Regime in the Process of Cooperating

Villagers who were close to Mariano Ardena, and whose recollections flow back into the primeval years of the Camporano mafia as a going concern, like to recall many trouble cases in support of the claim that the outlaw regime oversaw, encouraged, and gave purpose to the work begun by Christian Democracy. Though many such episodes are probably magnified or exaggerated in the recollections of former council chiefs, credence is lent to their claim by the recollections of other villagers, checked against and supplemented by accessible newspaper accounts and public papers of the time.

The outlaw regime assumed a twofold function in village life before World War I: that of insuring law and order and of facilitating the pursuit of individual and joint or collective opportunities through its community organizations.

112

Life under the Dual Regime

Relationships with Other Outlaw Regimes

One of the problems of social organization faced by leaders of the Camporano mafia regime was the need to establish cooperative arrangements with neighboring mafia leaders on matters of common concern. The basis for mutually productive relationships came to rest on a common reference to the basic rules outlined in chapter 6.

Officials of diverse mafia groups were known among themselves and among their respective constituents also as *persone 'ntisi*, that is, persons who understand and are listened to. It was as *persone 'ntisi* that Ardena and other council chiefs succeeded in extending the reach of the Camporano soldier society beyond the Camporano territory. The meeting place was often the country fairs held in the summer months. It was in this sense that a police official correctly identified these meetings as "veritable interprovincial conferences" (Alongi, 1887: 136). These interprovincial conferences also served to regulate conflicts between and among diverse mafia groups.

It was as "a person who understood and was listened to" that Mariano Ardena, together with Illuminato Carena and other mafia soldiers, traveled to a relatively distant town sometime between 1905 and 1908 to arbitrate a dispute between two mafia factions. That dispute had already erupted in violence when the two sides agreed to seek a peaceful resolution of their conflict. Some years later, when the leader of that distant outlaw regime died a natural death, he was not buried until after Ardena arrived. In paying his last respects to the deceased, Mariano Ardena was also being shown respect. By this time Camporanesi as well as outsiders began addressing Ardena as Don Mariano. It marked the first time that a Camporano peasant was honored with a title of distinction generally used for noblemen, professional persons, and gentlemen of means.

The Private Provision of Public Security

Sometime before 1910, a Camporano sharecropper with the help of his wife was plowing a field that he shared with a relative. A band of mounted brigands approached them and requested food. The peasant at first refused and finally consented to give them what he and his wife had. Sometime later, a group of mounted carabinieri came to the field and asked the peasant in which direction the bandits had gone. Apparently at first the peasant refused but, as the police officers were about to arrest

113

him for reticence, he revealed the direction taken by the brigands. In the same day, an armed conflict took place between the bandits and the carabinieri. A few days later, a member of the same band of brigands returned to the field and killed the peasant. He shot the wrong person. That day the other relative was working the field.

It is not clear what functions the Camporano carabinieri detachment assumed in this event. What seems clear, however, is that villagers turned to council chiefs for action. Council chiefs faced the problem of deciding what to do. It was a situation that involved members of the same family. Moreover, a mafia soldier was a blood relative of the wife of the deceased sharecropper. The brigand had made the mistake of killing the wrong person but the villager had also broken *omertà*. Cries of vengeance were heard among those who accompanied the funeral cortege of the deceased villager. If one believes the recollections of several old villagers, how outlaw regime officials dealt with this problem illustrates a flexibility and sensitivity in adjusting available means to inflict penalties on violators without resorting to arbitrary decisions. It also points to how new rules of conduct were made.

Acting on behalf of council chiefs and assisted by neighboring mafia leaders, Ardena made contacts with the bandit leader and requested that the bandit who had mistakenly killed the villager should also be killed. Presumably this request was carried out, although villagers were not clear about this. At the same time, Ardena is reported to have told him that henceforth, no matter what any Camporano villager did to or said of brigands, no brigand could take "the law into his own hands." This was a new rule. It also applied to Camporanesi farming in neighboring territories and to officials of neighboring mafia regimes. Matters related to villagers from now on became the jurisdiction of the Camporano mafia. The phrase "I am from Camporano" became a measure of immunity for villagers farming and traveling in the area. Camporanesi could easily be distinguished from other villagers by the way they spoke Sicilian.

Having dealt with the problem of the brigand, there was now the problem of what to do with the relative of the deceased peasant. He had broken *omertà* and was now *'nfame*. The penalty was death. But council chiefs appeared reluctant to reach that decision. At the same time, while one mafia soldier, who was related to the wife of the dead tenant, was eager to apply that extreme sanction, the others were reluctant to carry it out. Representation was sought from villagers and the village square took on the appearance of a town hall meeting. "Let the wife of the dead

114

man decide" emerged as the communal decision. When the wife of the dead man was asked, she is reported to have said, "I do not want my nephews and niece also to be without a father." That decision was binding, but the facade of formal authority invested in the council of chiefs was maintained by having a council chief announce it to mafia soldiers. The man whose life was now spared came out of his two-room house to resume his field work.

This raised another problem, however. What to do with a villager who had not observed a principal rule of conduct of the community, but, by his presence, still claimed to be a member of that community? The overwhelming majority of villagers apparently refused to have any dealings with him. Sometime after the incident, the villager is reported to have left the village in search of a better life elsewhere.

With the presence of the outlaw regime, wealth-producing agricultural activities ceased to be a liability. Upper burgisi, rentiers, as well as large landowners could now obtain security at a price. But many potential wealth producers among the lower burgisi could not afford the money price of protection. Thus while upper burgisi, rentiers, and landowners paid in money or in kind, lower burgisi paid in terms of support and loyalty—lending their eyes and ears to the maintenance of peace and security in the Camporano territory.

Between the early 1900s and World War I, payment of different prices served both to insure a rough degree of fiscal fairness and to maintain peace and security as a preferred state of community affairs. In support of this state of affairs, old villagers like to mention the absence of cattle rustling throughout the Camporano area and the unhindered trips village people made on foot and by mule to a shrine in honor of Saint Calogero in a distant town (see Caico, 1910). As some mafia soldiers came by the early 1910s to take on the functions traditionally reserved to *campieri*, it is likely that they may also have acted like *campieri* and victimized some land workers.

Agricultural Activities

While mafia soldiers worked to insure peace and security in the Camporano countryside, other community organizations worked to realize individual and joint opportunities in agricultural activities. In 1907, officials of the Saint Joseph cooperative credit society renegotiated the lease of Mogata lots (*gabella*) that it had contracted as a landholding

115

society in 1901. The extension of the *gabella* for another six years was accompanied by the renewal of the 1901 tenancy agreement and both appear to have been continued until the outbreak of World War I.

The success of these efforts led Camporano cultivators to press for similar arrangements for land they farmed in neighboring estates. Acting on their behalf, and through the Saint Joseph credit cooperative, Ardena began to negotiate a collective lease with individual management of lots (*affittanza collettiva*) with the proprietor of the 1,200-hectare Anzalo estate in the valley below Camporano. Such a tenancy agreement would have meant little or no financial loss to the proprietor, but it would have displaced several Anzalo rentiers who were from the same town as the proprietor. Perhaps because of this, the landowner did not accede to Ardena's request. By 1908, one of the rentiers let his *gabella* lapse and in that year officials of the Saint Joseph credit union, acting on behalf of Camporano tenants, took over the cultivation of that *gabella* through an *affittanza collettiva*. Renegotiated at least once, this collective lease with individual management of lots lasted almost until the end of World War I (see also Arnone, 1910b; Colajanni, 1887; Lorenzoni, 1923; Prestianni, 1956; 106–107).

For his part in securing this tenancy agreement, Ardena was given by both the Anzalo proprietor and the Camporano tenants first choice of lots to cultivate. And it was by advancing the interests of others that Ardena advanced his own. His action received a sort of government recognition in 1910, when a report issued by the Faina parliamentary commission investigating rural conditions in Southern Italy identified him as a leading organizer of cooperative landholding societies in the Mozarra province.

Also in 1910, and perhaps because of the parliamentary inquiry, the Saint Joseph cooperative credit society received a prize of one thousand lire from the Ministry of Agriculture, Industry, and Commerce for raising "the material and moral conditions" of the Camporano population. The *Cassa* annual financial reports submitted to the provincial tribunal, together with reports of its activities that appeared in Mozarra newspapers, give additional indications of the functions the credit union had assumed in the Camporano political economy.

The *Cassa* membership increased from two hundred in 1901 to about four hundred in 1908 and reached seven hundred in 1915, to include almost all the Camporano cultivators. Starting with the capital derived from fees or shares paid by members, and augmented by deposits made by old and new members, the credit society had by 1915 almost half a million lire in small savings to function also as an intermediate banking institution of the Banco di Sicilia. Over the course of this period, the Saint Joseph *Cassa rurale*, while continuing to act as a rural bank, provided complementary functions for the benefit of its members—from the collective renting of land to the joint purchase of fertilizer and other agricultural requisites. But the local economy was not the only facet of village life that could reveal how cooperative activity had brought together and interwoven the instrumentalities of the legal and extralegal regimes to enhance the welfare potential of villagers.

Communal Government and Center-Periphery Relations

With the rise of Christian Democracy, the conduct of communal government had ceased to be the exclusive domain of a privileged few. What the mafia did as a going concern until World War I was to maintain the grand coalition of community interests put together by Christian Democracy in the 1903 local election, to nullify or remove almost all the institutional impediments to communal collective action interposed by or resulting from centralized government and administration, and to make Camporano an autonomous local periphery vis-à-vis the political center in Rome. This unorthodox self-rule or *autogestion* took several forms.

Mafia chiefs holding council near the village square, and not the prefect and the provincial control commission in distant Mozarra, gave villagers confidence and opportunity to maintain a "watching brief" on the activities of the communal government. This extended even to those who were formally excluded from voting for the preparation of the electoral list of the grand coalition—before and after 1912, when the Giolitti government extended manhood suffrage to all males who were thirty or who had served in the armed forces. Old villagers recall that now they could obtain papers and certificates from communal clerks without undue delay or fear of being asked to do too many errands and small services in return. Thanks also in part to the very difficulties in monitoring communal performance by distant officials, many cumbersome and even obnoxious communal regulations could now be left unenforced or safely ignored.

At the same time, the prefect now must have found it difficult to control Camporano votes for national and provincial elections, unless he too came to terms with the mafia. Electoral support varied according to the

117

potential benefits that potentially successful candidates could bring to the village as a whole. Thus in the provincial election of 1910, it was the lawyer and rentier Salvatore Vallera and not Ardena's cousin who received local support. His anticlericalism aside, Vallera was deemed more capable of representing Camporano interests before the provincial administration. Public works projects to improve the provincial road connecting Camporano to neighboring towns and Mozarra were attributed to his efforts.

Under these conditions, the machinery of the formal government permitted villagers to gain access to services that the Camporano mafia could not directly produce, without impairing or threatening the unusual "division and cohesion" that had emerged. In 1911, a public housing project was started for the Camporano poor; in 1914, a subsidy from the central government allowed communal officials to make extensive improvements in the existing water services. Also by this time, quinine was being distributed freely by the central government to those villagers who worked in malaria-infested areas like the Anzalo estate. The instrumentalities of the dual regime complemented one another to make of communal government and center-periphery relations a cooperative activity in the service of the commonweal. The only available evidence about this gives added meaning to the process of cooperating experience.

In chapter 6, I noted that not all the members of the rentiers and professional class, the "hats," had accepted, or adjusted to, the rise of Christian Democracy. Some members of the Igelo, Fontena, and Vallera families had sought to regain their hold on community life by trying to attract Camporano cultivators to their cooperatives. Their efforts failed and Christian Democracy eventually collapsed for other reasons. Now, the same individuals transferred their opposition to the outlaw regime—with the same degree of success. In 1910, they established a producer and consumer cooperative among their own tenants. Comprising not more than twenty members, this venture remained a "letterhead organization" operating, according to some, from a drawer in Salvatore Vallera's desk. Mozarra tribunal records show that it was formally closed in 1914.

Some of the dissident "hats" like Vallera were pamphleteers who were to gain a reputation for their ferocity and recklessness of prose. Yet, before World War I, they do not seem to have relied upon these means to attract attention to, and garner support for, their cause outside the village. In their published works they did not even use the term *mafia*, which had already pejorative connotations, to talk about the Camporano

118

outlaw regime. It would seem that opposing interests seldom reached the point of being irreconcilable interests. After he was defeated in his attempt to become mayor of Camporano, Vallera ran as a candidate against Ardena's cousin in the provincial elections for the Camporano-Castelfrano district, with the endorsement and support of the Camporano mafia.

There are also reported cases of failure to consider communal government as cooperative activity within the communal council itself. Between 1909 and 1914, there were at least two mayors who did not complete their term of office. Communal records and newspaper reports do not furnish information beyond terse announcements of resignation. It seems that all these instances involved mayors whom villagers had found to take too seriously the pomp of communal office and to see themselves with sufficient competence and authority to take unilateral action. When they apparently failed to reform their ways and to revert to behavior required for cooperative activity, council chiefs intervened to press for their resignation.

Thus, available evidence about partial disagreement and "errant behavior" enhances rather than diminishes "the social appropriateness" (Sproule-Jones, 1978) of the outlaw regime. The very discrepancy between how communal affairs and center-periphery relations were supposed to take place and how they actually took place now had given communal government some of the functions inherent in the original sense of the term *communal*.

World War I and the Onrush of Change

The congruence between the legal and the extralegal regimes had helped not only to foster local self-rule but also to reduce the accumulated hostility of villagers toward the formal institutions of government. One clear manifestation of this rapprochement was conscription. By 1910, military service was no longer detested and had, in fact, become part of a young man's life cycle. Indeed, so dishonorable had desertion or draft evasion become that it was not unusual for young villagers who had emigrated to North America or Africa to return home just to do their military service. The uninterrupted onrush of new exigencies and circumstances that accompanied the outbreak of World War I shattered the congruence between the legal and extralegal regimes, restored Camporano to its subor-

119

dinate position in the large encapsulating political structures, and brought into question the appropriateness of the authority pattern of the mafia regime itself. With the advent of Fascist rule, the period between 1915 and 1922 appears, in retrospect, but a transitional stage to the decline of village life.

War and the Breakdown of Consensus about the State

Italy's entry into World War I during the so-called radiant days of May 1915 was preceded by a national debate between advocates of intervention and advocates of neutrality. While the former saw the war as Italy's last war of unification or first war as a great power, the latter saw the war as a threat to parliamentary institutions or, in the famous words in 1917 of the new pope, Benedict XV, "a useless slaughter" (quoted in Webster, 1960: 51; see also Seton-Watson, 1967: 419–421).

Rural people were expected to shoulder the heaviest burdens of Italy's entry into the war in two ways: conscription and requisition of wheat and cattle. As a result, in Camporano, as in other parts of Sicily (Barone, 1977: 84–96), the national debate took the form of an almost plebiscitary rejection of the war as a useless slaughter. Only members of the Camporano professional and rentier class like the communal secretary, advocate Amilcare Fontena, and university students like Diego Consalvo and Liborio Cortale were also so interventionist as to volunteer to fight. Most villagers liked neither the draft nor the requisitioning of mules and wheat. In February 1915, the seven hundred members of the Saint Joseph cooperative credit society unanimously approved a resolution in favor of neutrality. This resolution was widely reported in newspapers as evidence of the diffused aversion to the war in the Sicilian countryside. It received added standing when, two months later, Camporano became the meeting place for a diocesan congress, which the Catholic journal *L'Aurora* of 14 April 1915 also reports as having come out against Italy's entry into the war. Exigencies of war led to the breakdown of consensus about the Liberal state and met varying degrees of opposition among Camporanesi.

The number of conscripted Camporano peasants who as infantrymen fought over the course of the war in the S-shaped frontier between Italy and Austria, the most difficult of the Western Front, is not clear, but it was more than two hundred. For the whole of Sicily, the war took away at least some four hundred thousand peasants out of its male peasant popu-

120

lation of some seven hundred thousand, including children over ten years old—leaving uncultivated some two hundred thousand hectares out of some six hundred thousand hectares used for wheat production. The food and labor shortages in Sicily were compounded by growing disaffection among the peasant soldiers, who represented more than half of those fighting on the Austrian front. The setbacks suffered by the Italian forces in 1917 heightened the possibility of mass desertion. In an attempt to reduce that possibility, the central government sent representatives to the war zone to assure peasant soldiers that their efforts would be compensated with land distribution at the end of the hostilities (Micciché, 1976: 9–17; Serpieri, 1930: chapter 1). This was what in 1917 Maffei Pantaleoni called "the promissory note for the peasants' sacrifices" (quoted in Papa, 1969: 15).

In spite of both the rigorous enforcement of general mobilization and the war promise "Land for the peasant soldiers!" at least fifteen Camporano peasants joined by 1917 more than twenty thousand Sicilian deserters and draft dodgers to make of the Sicilian countryside "a haven for deserters and draft dodgers" (General Luigi Cadorna, 1917, quoted in Bertrand, 1976: 3)—in brief, a field of operations for social bandits. There is no evidence about what functions the outlaw regime assumed in the general mobilization. But as a result of banditry, mafia soldiers experienced serious difficulties in insuring peace and security throughout the Camporano territory. During and immediately after the war, provincial and regional newspapers reported many petty thefts and at least three Camporano cultivators found dead at harvest season.

If general mobilization produced problems of law and order, requisition of foodstuffs and animals generated substantial incentives for black-market operations in and beyond Camporano. Evidence exists for the selling of mules and horses to the army.

As part of the war effort, army provincial commissions were set up throughout the countryside to requisition horses and mules for the front. Members of the Mozarra commission experienced considerable difficulties in locating mules and horses at the price set by the government. It is against this background that, through the office of his cousin lawyer residing in Mozarra, Ardena is reported to have approached army officers of the provincial commission. The Camporano mafia agreed "to facilitate" the commission's work by requisitioning the animals for them in the Camporano area. Similar arrangements were apparently made with officials of neighboring outlaw regimes.

An account of these transactions first appeared in a provincial newspaper in May 1915. Several other such accounts appeared again in 1917. These reports claimed that leaders of outlaw regimes had facilitated the work of the army commission in three ways: (1) they made it easier for owners of sick and old animals to have them requisitioned for the appropriate price; (2) they provided protection to villagers who owned animals that they did not want to be requisitioned; and (3) they sold at least one hundred mules to the army that were stolen outside of the province. The minister of war set up an inquiry to investigate these accounts. The result of that inquiry in 1918 found Ardena, his cousin lawyer, some fellow villagers, other villagers from throughout the province, together with some army officers, before a military court in Palermo charged with grave offenses against the nation at war.

At the trial, Ardena and fellow villagers were defended by a team of lawyers that included Salvatore Vallera, then apparently serving as provincial councilor from the Camporano district. This team of lawyers stressed the problem of enforcing requisition orders among a hostile population and their effects on wheat production. But the proceedings also revealed that Ardena had invested some of the money earned from these transactions in lawful business enterprises elsewhere in the province of Mozarra and on the Italian continent, and that most other villagers had profited from the same black-market operations—villagers whom Ardena and the other accused refused to identify. In the end, the court was forced to dismiss the charges against Camporanesi for insufficient proof but ordered the accused army officers to be retired from the armed forces.

This trial, rather than casting a shadow over the mafia regime, further enhanced its position among villagers. While most villagers had profited from black-market operations, only Ardena and aides had carried the burden of paying for those activities. The trial showed how far the exigencies of war had pulled apart the instrumentalities of the Camporano dual regime and how easy it was for the outlaw regime in such circumstances to degenerate into a "rent-seeking society" (Krueger, 1974).

Peace and the Breakdown of Consensus about the Mafia System

The announcement of the victorious end of the war in November 1918 was greeted in Camporano with ringing church bells as well as high hopes for a resumption of life as villagers knew it before the outbreak of hostilities. But the Camporano tenant farmers, *enfiteuti*, and agricultural

122

workers who had spent the war years in the trenches on the Carso line had been inoculated with a radically new set of ideas. They were now going back to Camporano motivated by aspirations and designs that could not easily be reconciled with a simple return to prewar village life.

Camporano ex-servicemen were eager to redeem the promissory note "Land for the peasants!" There was, however, no land they could freely receive or possess. Moreover, most uncultivated or poorly cultivated land had become so because of manpower shortages caused by the war. In part for these reasons, as late as the summer of 1919 national legislators experienced serious difficulties in translating the war slogan into public policy. Under these circumstances, land could be acquired only through an agreement with those who owned it. Yet, for the returning peasant soldiers, the desire for land took precedence of the desire for mutual agreement.

The ex-servicemen were returning to Camporano with other far more revolutionary ideas. Life in the trenches had both increased their dislike of wars and infused them with unprecedented patriotic feelings toward Italy as their common fatherland (see also Seton-Watson, 1967: 515–519; Webster, 1960: 51). The same villagers who had earlier inveighed against city people and *signori* for wanting the war were now drawing to Camporano "hats" like Diego Consalvo, Liborio Cortale, and several members of the Fontena and Igelo families who shared their wartime spirit of comradeship and nationalism. That some of these "hats" had been their front-line superior officers helped ex-servicemen to draw closer to them. Thus the war had served not only to make Camporano peasants feel Italian but also to overcome their resentment toward the local professional and rentier class.

With their sense of self-reliance heightened by a new spirit of comradeship and nationalism, demobilized Camporano infantrymen wanted more than simple redemption of their promissory note; they wished to get the administration of village affairs into their own hands (cf. Gentile, 1924, cited in Holmes, 1979: 136). With its very raison d'être grounded in mutual agreement and sustained now also by force, the mafia regime, far from promoting the revolutionary changes the ex-servicemen had in mind, actually appeared to impede them. That villagers like Ardena and Carena had legitimately been, or caused themselves through self-mutilation to be, exempted from war duties did little to make the old loyalty toward the outlaw regime compatible with the new loyalty toward the fatherland.

123

Force could not alter this situation. Mafia leaders brought into play all their statecraft in order to stem this trend of popular feelings. Council leaders who had also fought in the war, like council chief Isidoro Riera, were pressed into action to persuade fellow ex-servicemen to desist from precipitous moves. The number of officials of the various community organizations was enlarged to include young villagers who had distinguished themselves in the war, like lieutenant and physician Paolino Safavia. At the same time, an outside development recalling as it did prewar Christian Democracy, confirmed, invigorated, and gave center-periphery ties to mafia efforts. In January 1919 the Popular Party (PPI) was established, with the permission of the Vatican but independent of church control, under the leadership of Don Luigi Sturzo.

Preceded by what a local chronicler described as "febrile work," Father Gaetano Ardena and several other villagers, including some council chiefs and the local pharmacist, opened the Camporano section of the Popular Party or *Popolari* in May 1919. The occasion was used to recall and appeal to Demochristian loyalties. Proposals for the resolution of "the land-for-the-peasants question" were adopted in line with the Popular Party programs (see Webster, 1960: 61–64). While upholding rural property rights, Camporano PPI leaders came out in favor of dividing large estates to create small peasant holdings. Newspaper reports of the time confirm that they called upon, among others, Princess Laura Gardena to cede sections of the Mogata fief around the village, now held by rentiers, to ex-servicemen as a contribution to the restoration of social peace.

The *Popolari*'s proposal for meeting the war promise coincided not only with the principles of mutual adjustment but also with the growing appreciation by mafia leaders like Ardena of the value of private property, now that the earnings from black-market operations allowed them to become small land proprietors and businessmen. There is, however, no evidence that the Gardena family acknowledged or responded to this call. Moreover, the local PPI leaders established two other "Demochristian" groups: a Veterans Union (*Unione Reduci*) and an assistance center for returning soldier peasants—both, if we are to believe a newspaper report, with the overwhelming participation of ex-infantrymen. In August 1919, some of these veterans were part of a Camporano delegation that, according to another newspaper report, traveled to Mozarra to hear a speech by and meet with Giovanni Gronchi, a national Popular

124

Party representative and Catholic union leader who was to become president of the Italian Republic in 1955.

Thus all the available means had been employed to show a solicitude for the aspirations of former peasant-soldiers and a concomitant willingness to respect the right of large landowners in order to create convergences out of differences and to maintain the social appropriateness of the outlaw regime. By the fall of 1919, however, another chain of events had added new knots to the tangle of Camporano life, raveling every effort of council chiefs to stem the trend of popular feelings.

First, sometime between August and September 1919, former army officers Diego Consalvo, Liborio Cortale, and Onofrio Fontena joined with others to organize a local branch of the National Association of Combatants (ANC) and appealed to members of the local Veterans Union to join their group by describing it, correctly (Sabbatucci, 1974: 87–88), as the truly national movement of all the ex-servicemen in Italy. A principal aim of ANC was the realization of the war promise "Land for the peasant soldiers!" at all cost, including land assaults and invasions. This was something that neither the renascent Demochristian party, for its respect of private property, nor the Socialist party, for its emphasis on collectivization, was prepared to advocate (see Accati, 1970; Marino, 1976: 66–178; Miccichè, 1976: 17–37). In part because of this aim, ANC had by September 1919 become the association of almost all the ex-servicemen in the nearby town of Terrano, an event that all Camporanesi knew of and Consalvo, Cortale, and Fontena exploited fully to attract adherents from the Camporano Veterans Union.

Second, the success of ANC-led invasions in Latium and Apulia in the summer of 1919 prompted the central government to authorize prefects to requisition "uncultivated land" and distribute it to deserving claimants, provided they organize themselves in cooperative (the Visocchi law of September 2, 1919). But, given the fact that there was little or no uncultivated land that prefects could distribute, the government measure served, in effect, to sanction, and extend a protective cover to, the aims and activities of ANC groups like that of Camporano. Hence, mafia and Popular Party efforts at interactive adjustment appeared, at best, a defense of the status quo (see also Marino, 1976: 248; Rocca, 1920; Serpieri, 1930: 345–347).

Third, the decision of the national ANC leaders to present slates of candidates in the November 1919 general elections had the effect of placing the Camporano ANC group in direct collision with the mafia regime. It mattered little that some council chiefs made proclamations of electoral neutrality or pointed to a relative of Ardena who was running as an ANC candidate for the Mozarra district. The ties between the Popular Party and the local mafia were such that all the statecraft of Ardena and other council chiefs could neither insulate the community organizations from the agitations of election nor effect a rapprochement between the two groups. Factional ardor was redoubled by the new electoral system of multimember districts with proportional representation among party lists (cf. Hermens, 1951: 47–62). Not a single ANC candidate was elected in the Mozarra area and the very attempt to turn ANC into a political force met with failure in Italy as a whole (Sabbatucci, 1974: 222). But in Camporano the passions that a desire for land, patriotism, clericalism, and imagination could create were so agitated to evoke opposition to the Popular Party and, by implication, to the local mafia from almost half of the Camporano voters.

As a result of this convergence of events, it became impossible to maintain consensus about the appropriateness of the authority pattern of the mafia regime for resolving local issues and problems. Villagers had become so acutely conscious of their different loyalties and conflicting interests that they now split into two opposing camps. While the Camporano ANC emerged as a community organization in spite of the failure of its sponsoring national association to become a political party, the Camporano mafia changed from *the* organization of community organizations to an organization of community organizations at the service of the Popular Party.

Concordia Discors as Basis for a
New Process of Cooperating Experience?

The antagonism between the two groups became articulate in several different squabbles in the two years before the advent of Fascist rule. The land question and the control of the commune were the chief objects of controversy. Though the debate was repeated and amplified by eager and fervent newspaper correspondents on both sides, opposed interests seldom became incompatible and irreconcilable interests—or conflict, *guerre à outrance*. From newspaper accounts of the time and recollections by villagers from both sides, one can piece together at least three distinct but interdependent reasons why antagonism does not seem to have escalated beyond verbal confrontations.

First, even though more than one-third of villagers now rejected the appropriateness of the authority structure of the mafia regime for resolving local problems and issues, there was still a residue or surplus of good will among them about the mafia. Despite what one would believe from post-1922 declarations, only a few combatants appear to have then been prepared to deny altogether some form of historic legitimacy to the Camporano mafia group.

Second, there was a reciprocal recognition and acceptance of the fact that each group represented divergent but justifiable interests. Even though mafia leaders continued to maintain a numerically and militarily dominant position in village affairs, they did not force the other group into submission. It ran against village norms that served as basis of the outlaw regime itself to impose decisions on unwilling villagers or, in the language of modern Italian politics, to have recourse to "the brute use of majority power" (Fried, 1973: 206), and these shared values may in part account for the absence of outright attempts to exploit the dominant position. The growing fusion of the outlaw regime with the renascent Christian Democracy may have interposed additional constraints. At any rate, there is no available evidence to suggest that leaders and members of the two political communities threatened each other with extinction.

Third, the requirements of conflict did not dominate all other social considerations. Members of both political communities were still related to one another not only through an intricate network of familial, ritual kinship (*comparatico*) and friendship ties but also through reciprocal concerns. In August 1920, villagers, including members of the Veterans Union, joined together to take part in a civil and religious ceremony organized by the ANC to commemorate the thirty-eight Camporano war dead—even though it was an open secret that leaders of both groups were competing against one another to attract candidates for the September communal elections and that members of the combatants group were planning "a land invasion" in the fall. Throughout this period, dissident villagers also seemed to have continued to be members and to enjoy the benefits of the Saint Joseph cooperative credit society.

In sum, there were powerful common interests to exact convergence out of differences and to maintain a concordia discors that would permit reaching outcomes in village affairs not destructive to both sides. The conflict situations that existed between the outlaw regime and the ANC had the characteristics of what Thomas C. Schelling calls *"bargaining situations"* (1963: 6, emphasis in the original). These were manifest in dealing both with the land question and with communal politics.

The *affittanza collettiva* or collective lease with individual management of lots that Ardena and leaders of the Saint Joseph cooperative credit society had negotiated for the cultivation of the Anzalo and Mogata estates before the war came to an end sometime by 1917. This and the breakdown of consensus about the mafia regime opened the way now for the two Camporano groups to compete for the possession and cultivation of the former fiefs.

In January 1920, about thirty ex-servicemen of the Veterans Union, including council chief Isidoro Riera, together with Gaetano Ardena, who was proving to be just as energetic a social animator-priest as Giuseppe Riera had been, organized the Veterans Landholding Society. In order to encourage the voluntary transfer or sale of estates to actual farmers and to prevent speculations by land jobbers, this cooperative sought to purchase land itself with a view to dividing it up and reselling to its individual members (see *International Review of Agricultural Economics*, 1921a; Ruini, 1922). This aim, which was in accordance with the Popular Party program, was strengthened by the news in April 1920 of a government decree (the Falcioni law of April 22, 1920, no. 515), which set aside about $2.5 million to furnish favorable land and agricultural credit to cooperative credit societies and assigned loans in Sicily to the agricultural credit section of the Banco di Sicilia (see *International Review of Agricultural Economics*, 1921b). Yet the idea of "free land" propagated by the combatants group must have still exercised such an attraction or pull on members of the Veterans Union that they do not seem to have immediately or automatically joined the Veterans Landholding Society. At the same time, since the majority of ex-servicemen had joined the local ANC branch, the veterans leaders opened their cooperative to non-ex-servicemen and women in order to make it numerically strong and economically viable. For it was only by the end of July 1920 that this Demochristian venture was legally recognized by the Mozarra judicial authorities. By this time, the cooperative had about two hundred members.

The establishment of the Veterans Landholding Society, together with the news of the Falcioni law, which also applied to cooperatives that "had in *any way* obtained possession of land" (Hobson, 1926: 69; emphasis added), accelerated the efforts of combatants to organize and effect land invasions through a lawfully constituted landholding society of their own. But now these villagers faced the antithetical problem the veterans experienced earlier. Many more villagers than there were combatants wanted to receive free land. As a result, at least 50 of the 260 members of the Combatants Landholding Society were not ex-servicemen. This collective undertaking headed by former army officers like Diego Consalvo and Onofrio Fontena received legal recognition by the Mozarra authorities in September 1920.

The two groups were not, however, the only ones to make plans for the control of Mogata and Anzalo. Estate owners for the Camporano area helped to organize a Mozarra section of a Sicily-wide "party of landowners and cultivators" whose aim was to pressure prefects and other central government officials to protect their rights of proprietorship against land invasions. While they were not very influential with the Mozarra prefect, they did succeed in gaining the support of Popular Party leaders in and outside of Camporano as well as villagers like Mariano Ardena who were already sympathetic to their cause (see also Marino, 1976: 94). In a September 1920 meeting of the Mozarra branch of this "party," Ardena was made member of its nine-member provincial directorate. Also by this time, Camporano rentiers were attempting to prevail upon Princess Gardena to sell them the land they held in *gabella*, about five hundred hectares of the thirteen thousand hectares of Mogata.

This array of positions had created a situation whereby all the parties involved could neither act in solitary endeavor nor move unilaterally to advance their particular goals or interests—without being engulfed in mutually destructive relationships. For example, members of both landholding societies farmed Mogata and Anzalo. If outlaw regime and PPI leaders moved to regain control or secure the sale of either estate, they could not evict combatant-tenants who had been farming there for years without evoking stiff opposition and even armed reaction from the combatants association. If combatants leaders moved to invade or take over the same estates, they faced similar problems in the case of tenants from the other side. Since they were all *dependent upon* one another in their pursuit of gain or in their avoidance of loss, each was forced to take into account the potential actions of the other—creating, in essence, "a gamelike situation" (Rapoport, 1960). What must have helped to create this gamelike situation was the fact that, as we have seen, villagers from the two political communities were still connected with one another through common and overlapping interests.

The interdependent strategies and choices that went to transform a conflict situation into "a game" are not simple to trace or explicate even for some of the participants. The moves from a bargaining situation to mutual adjustment of expectations and action are not altogether clear—when and how, for example, leaders of the two groups agreed to lay claims to different estates, even though we know that a majority of combatants were Mogata tenants, that a majority of veterans were Anzalo tenants, and that Ardena himself held a small *gabella* on Anzalo. Events surrounding the outcomes are less difficult to trace and it is this knowledge that illumines, if it does not explicate, how concordia discors operated as a new process of cooperating experience.

In October 1920, as mafia leaders were still negotiating the sale of the Anzalo estate, combatants invaded the Mogata estate. Since most of these invaders were already Mogata cultivators, their land invasion followed a pattern that had become widespread after the Visocchi law. Under this law, uncultivated or poorly cultivated land could be requisitioned by ex-servicemen organized as cooperatives. But since there was little or no uncultivated or poorly cultivated land, one way of making it so was for tenants to stop sowing for a few days and then proceed to requisition the land they themselves had made uncultivated or poorly cultivated. In the fall of 1920 some 330 cooperative landholding societies in Sicily used this strategy to seize land, or a similar number of estates, comprising some ninety thousand hectares (Orsenigo, 1921; Prestianni, 1926; Schifani, 1954; see also Beals, 1923).

The invasion of Mogata evoked a strong letter of protest to the prefect and minister of the interior from at least one Mogata rentier who saw his negotiation with Princess Gardena for the sale of the land he held in *gabella* doomed. At the same time, the excitement generated by the "land assault" must have been difficult to contain by combatant leaders, for some combatants rushed down the valley below and occupied about one hundred hectares of the Anzalo estate. Soon, however, these passing exigencies of conflict gave way to the more lasting exigencies of concordia discors.

In November 1920, the Mozarra prefect recognized as lawful, and Gardena agreed to, the claim of the Camporano Combatants Landholding Society to take over the conduct of the Mogata estate. The prefect recognized as legitimate, and the combatants agreed to, the claim of rentiers like Vallera to purchase land their families held in *gabella* from Gardena, with the result that the territory of Mogata shrunk from thirteen hundred hectares to about eight hundred a few years later. At the same time, Mogata tenants belonging to the Veterans Landholding Society continued to farm their lots but all indications suggest that they had to belong to the other landholding society. The Mozarra prefect also permitted the combatants to hold portions of Anzalo they had invaded, about one hundred hectares, as "requisitioned land" for a period of five years, in return for a very small rent to the proprietor.

This course of events had the effect of convincing the Anzalo proprietor to accept the market-value purchase offer of the Camporano Veterans Landholding Society, said to be about three million lire. In the spring of 1921, the transfer of property took place in Palermo. The proprietor received a down payment of about 15 percent, which the veterans group obtained from the Saint Joseph cooperative credit society. He was expected to receive the rest of the purchase price within a year, as the cooperative applied for an interest-free loan to the credit section of the Banco di Sicilia in accordance with the Falcioni law. Delay in receiving the loan, in part resulting from conditions related to the crisis of regime of the Liberal state, threatened to nullify the sale. Ardena and some council chiefs attempted to convince the Anzalo proprietor not to adhere too strictly to the original agreement. It is not clear if this attempt meant force. After all, the Anzalo proprietor too had an interest in selling his property rather than seeing it "requisitioned" by some invaders. At any rate, it was not until well after the advent of Fascist rule that this landowner was paid in full with a loan from the Banco di Sicilia and that the transfer of property titles began to take place from the landholding association to individual farmers to create some three hundred small peasant landowners.

The sale was for 1,008.39 hectares and not 1,185, which represented, according to the cadastral map, the total hectares of Anzalo. A government investigation carried out in conjunction with "the Fascist struggle against the mafia" around 1926 revealed that the difference, some one hundred hectares, had been assigned to Ardena, his sister and at least three other mafiosi for their trouble in securing the sale of Anzalo. It was in this way that profitable altruism became a burden on great landlords and cultivators alike. There was no government action to dispossess these villagers of their property, however. This investigation also indicated that Ardena had been active in other landholding societies beyond the Camporano area but there does not seem to be evidence about these activities.

By 1922, the land question opened by World War I was being resolved in two ways: through a tenancy agreement of Mogata and through the sale of Anzalo. Both fiefs were being farmed as they had been before the war, with some notable changes. Mogata, now drastically reduced in size, continued to be farmed through an *affittanza collettiva* but under different management—from mafia leaders to the Combatants Landholding Society officials. Anzalo, now slightly reduced in size, was being divided by the Veterans Landholding Society among some three hundred small landowners. These different solutions took on radically new meanings and produced new problems for Camporano cultivators as Fascist rule gained hold of village life.

The breakdown of consensus about the authority pattern of the local mafia was accompanied by the breakdown of consensus in the grand coalition that had governed communal affairs since the turn of the century. But the Camporano electoral committee could still present, and muster electoral support for, a minimum winning coalition. A noticeable difference now was that the activities of the Camporano electoral committee were also carried out in the name of the Popular Party while the opposition organized by the local combatants branch became known as "the nationalist party." In the first and last communal election after 1919, that of September 1920, the *Popolari* ticket, headed by former army officer and local physician Paolino Safavia, obtained almost two-thirds of the votes and a majority of seats on the communal council.

Several affidavits placed before the Camporano district court suggest electoral intimidation against members of one another's party and in 1921 the communal council tried unsuccessfully to fire communal secretary Fontena and other employees for their "fifth-column" activities on behalf of "the nationalist party." Conflict between the two groups seldom became *guerre à outrance*, however. The very recourse to judicial and prefectoral authorities suggests a willingness to encapsulate the conflict and transform it into a symbolic one.

By 1922, the Camporano mafia had been able to marshal from within and from without forces that ensured its functioning in the face of partial disagreement. It is possible that the growing fusion with the renascent Christian Democracy might have led to another challenge to the mafia regime and to its very displacement in village life. Sturzo's opposition to the mafia was well known. The rise of the mafia regime had filled, in effect, the vacuum left by the collapse of the prewar Demochristian movement. But in 1922, with the crisis of regime of the Liberal state itself coming to an end, the newly repaired structures of what was once the "Camporano organization of community organizations" were to succumb to and be replaced by other inauspicious forces.

The Fascist Measures in the Last Struggle with the Mafia

At the time of the coup d'état in October 1922, Sicily was the least Fascist region in Italy. In the 1921 national elections, the Fascist party won not one parliamentary seat there. As late as May 1922 there were not more than ninety-five hundred Fascists in all of Sicily (Snowden, 1972: 288, note 68; see also Vetri, 1976a). Following a visit to the island in 1924, Mussolini announced "a war of liberation and redemption from the mafia." From 1924 until his abrupt dismissal in 1929, the prefect of Palermo, Cesare Mori, was in charge of that campaign (Mori, 1933; see also Petacco, 1975). In treating the presence of mafia regimes (the antistate) as an exceptional police problem (see Lo Schiavo, 1933; but cf. Puglia, 1930), the Fascist government was repeating what had been done in 1875–1876. That earlier effort had in part failed because, as noted in chapter 1, it was impossible to arrest every Sicilian villager who had engaged in some form of behavior that ultimately threatened or diminished the authority of the state. But the Fascist measures succeeded because they altered the political, economic, and social positions of all villagers. In this way, the Fascist "last struggle with the mafia" became part of the suppression of the parliamentary monarchy itself. The collapse of the Camporano dual regime followed (cf. Chapman Gower, 1935).

The Takeover of Communal Government

There were no "Fascists of the first hour" in Camporano, despite what one would believe from post-1925 embellishments of local Fascist history. It was not until after the march on Rome that leaders and adherents of the Camporano nationalist party joined the Fascist party and established a local Fascist headquarters. As Fascist leaders, former combat-

133

ant leaders Consalvo, Cortale, and Fontena gained new standing and prestige among all villagers. In the atmosphere of exalted patriotism generated by the union of nationalism and fascism, the conduct of Camporano communal affairs by Demochristian and mafia leaders came under attack.

As a decorated army officer and local physician, mayor Paolino Safavia now appeared somewhat out of place in the Popular Party and, fearing reprisals, resigned as mayor in 1923 (see also Marino, 1976: 288; Palidda, 1977). It was left to the acting mayor, Father Gaetano Ardena, to maintain a spirit of communal opposition to Fascist authorities. This opposition took several forms, if we are to believe villagers' recollections checked against and augmented by newspaper accounts and communal papers of the time. When in June 1923, the parliamentary undersecretary of public instruction stopped at the Camporano railway station on his way to Mozarra, Mayor Ardena sent no communal delegation to greet him. When in October of the same year, the Camporano commune received funds from the central government to improve water services, Mayor Ardena sent no idolatrous telegram of thanks to Mussolini, as was becoming the practice of most communal governments. As the Camporano ecclesiastical and secular leaders neither acknowledged nor praised the new central authority, local Fascist exponents engaged in a vigorous newspaper "assault" on the communal government and organized a cleanup campaign of the cemetery using the rallying cry "Make way for the competent!" (cf. Sarti, 1969). So well known had Camporano Fascist leaders become that they attracted the attention of regional and national Fascist leaders. When Mussolini visited Mozarra in the spring of 1924, a Camporano Fascist, Liborio Fontena, introduced him in a public meeting. The attempts to force the resignation of the mayor and the majority councilors failed, however. In 1924, the Fascist councilors abandoned in protest the biannual communal meetings (cf. Miccichè, 1976: 216–217; Vetri, 1976b).

It was not until after the promulgation of a law in December 1925 that empowered the central government to remove from office any public official who "took up an attitude incompatible with the general tendencies of the Government" (quoted in Salvemini, 1931: 26, note 6) that the duly elected Camporano authority was finally disbanded. The destruction of any semblance of local self-government and the establishment of *podestà* or communal dictators throughout Italy were hailed even in learned quarters as Mussolini's attempt "to carry on his modern revivification and unification" of Italy (Born, 1927: 871; see also analysts cited by Salvemini, 1927; and Sturzo, 1926).

In April 1926, acting mayor Ardena was replaced by former army officer Diego Consalvo as the first *podestà*, accountable only to the prefect and to the provincial Fascist leader. Consalvo's first act as *podestà* was to have pictures of Mussolini bought and placed in every Camporano communal office and schoolroom. But old villagers still remember his humanitarian efforts to attenuate the effects of directives from Rome for all villagers. In November 1931, Consalvo was replaced by Onofrio Fontena who remained *podestà* until the last hours of Fascism in Sicily.

Blood and Iron Methods

In the summer of 1924, Mussolini's antimafia war became part of the general war against "antistate elements" in Sicily. In 1925, Ardena and several other mafia leaders and soldiers were before a Mozarra court charged with belonging to a criminal association. But the Mozarra tribunal dismissed the charge against them for lack of criminal evidence. Similar dismissals took place before other courts in Western Sicily.

In 1926, the new government overcame the problems posed by existing legal measures by decreeing a special or exceptional law against the mafia. This decree established that "in order to insure public security in the Sicilian countryside any person indicated by public opinion as a leader, participant, accomplice, or abettor of criminal associations [was] subject to exile." "Public opinion" in this case meant police officials who could tell a mafioso by "intuition and smell" (Mori, 1933: 42). In one of Mori's roundups in 1926, five Camporano mafia chiefs and soldiers were arrested. In part as a result of "blood-and-iron methods," one mafia soldier died in prison; the others were exiled.

In his account of "the last struggle with the mafia," Prefect Mori correctly noted that the abolition of the electoral system deprived local mafia regimes of an essential source of influence and prestige among public officials (Mori, 1933: 155). But Mariano Ardena must have still been able to use his influence with police and other officials, for he was exiled for several years to an area where he had a relative. During that time he was prosecuted at least once for belonging to "the Mozarra commercial mafia" and was asked to testify against Mansueto Alois and other mafiosi of Terrano. Neither Ardena nor others volunteered much information about their activities, however. At the same time, police officials

135

found it difficult to apply new antimafia laws against each participant, accomplice, and abettor of the Camporano mafia. To do so would have meant the arrest of most Camporanesi. As a result, there could not be a complete social epuration of mafia elements in Camporano.

By 1930, Ardena was bankrupt. A Mozarra tribunal eventually declared him insolvent. During the 1930s, he and other Camporano mafiosi resumed their agricultural activities. Though they lived under police surveillance, former outlaw regime leaders continued to enjoy the esteem and respect of most villagers and to be feared by local Fascist officials.

Agricultural Policies

Amid the general wreck of the Camporano dual regime, some of the most fundamental organizations of the Camporano mafia still remained. It was not until the early 1930s that, following the Fascistization of most credit institutions, the Saint Joseph *Cassa rurale* and its consumer cooperative were disbanded or collapsed and their functions taken over by newly established local branches of the Banco di Sicilia (see also Schifani, 1950: 71). The Veterans Landholding Society continued throughout the 1930s to function as the agency through which the new small landowners of Anzalo completed payment of the loan they received from the agricultural credit section of the Banco di Sicilia. Strong circumstantial evidence suggests that officials of this landholding society diverted members' money to Ardena as he faced bankruptcy in the late 1920s. Post-1945 critics of the Camporano mafia did justifiably make much of the fact that the three hundred Anzalo small landowners had to pay at least twice part of the collective payment of the estate during the 1920s and that mafiosi like Ardena appropriated for themselves about 10 percent of the Anzalo estate. What most post-1945 critics fail to recall is what happened to members of the Combatants Landholding Society. It is this knowledge that helped many, if not all, of the Anzalo landowners to temper their criticisms of mafia leaders.

In August 1923, the Combatants Landholding Society joined the Fascist union of agricultural cooperatives. One of its leaders, Onofrio Fontena, was appointed to the directorate of the provincial union of those cooperatives. As a result, the encapsulation or suppression of voluntary collective ventures that followed the Fascistization of Sicilian life did not affect the *affittanza collettiva* of Mogata by the Combatants Landholding

Society. But not before long, the very protective cover of Fascist rule gave incentives to the new Camporano authority to disregard the interests of members of the Combatants Landholding Society. By the middle of the 1920s, some Camporano Fascist leaders began to appropriate the collective rent for themselves. When in 1930 two Mogata tenants demanded an account of how cooperative leaders were using cooperative funds, they were expelled from the landholding society and arrested for anti-Fascist sentiments. Also by that time, Princess Gardena had become unhappy about the *affittanza collettiva* of Mogata. By 1932, combatant leaders had exhausted both the capacity of Mogata tenants to pay rent and the patience of the Mogata proprietor to wait for it. Soon afterward, Gardena initiated legal proceedings against the landholding association and regained exclusive control of Mogata. After 1935, as members of the mafia-sponsored landholding society were becoming full proprietors of their Anzalo lots, members of the nationalist-sponsored landholding society were farming Mogata under the supervision of a new Mogata overseer. The new share tenancy for Mogata meant, in effect, a return to the pre-1901 metateria "contract." Tenants were now forced to bear almost all the costs of production, without any say in the selection of the crop or the method of work. Their share of the product amounted to no more than one-third. A system of private guards was now organized under the direction of the provincial police detachment. Against this backdrop, it is easy to see why most Camporano cultivators were, and still are, not as critical of the actions of local mafiosi before and during Fascist rule as post-1945 opponents of the Camporano mafia have been. Even at its worst, the Camporano mafia appeared to be the lesser of two evils.

At the time when agricultural economists had convincingly demonstrated the need for "a battle *against* wheat production," the new government initiated a "battle of wheat" to make the country self-sufficient—precisely when the price of wheat on the world market was declining. By the late 1930s, the battle of wheat did indeed raise production but at the cost of seriously imbalancing agriculture and of imposing heavy burdens on both peasants and consumers in general (see Checco, 1977; Salvemini, 1931; Schmidt, 1938; cf. Costanzo, 1926).

The establishment of a state wheat pool (*consorzio*) in Camporano as part of the battle of wheat tended to favor the large wheat producers. It narrowed the outlets for the small amounts of wheat the peasants had for sale. Whereas before the small peasants were able to sell in the village and country fairs at going prices, now they had these possibilities foreclosed. They could sell only to the state wheat pool (see also Amadei, 1971: 57 and note 2). By the middle of the 1930s black-market operations were resumed.

By 1936, each worker had to be registered with the local state employment office. He could no longer seek employment on his own; at the same time, employers too could obtain workers only through the local employment office. This left the director of the employment office in a position to decide who among those of the list of workers was first in line and where he should work. Under these conditions each villager negotiated as best he could with both the potential employer and the director of the employment office for any kind of employment opportunity. In the process, the director of the employment office became one of the most hated persons in the village.

Old peasants recall that there was a great deal of hunger in the village in the 1930s. In 1936 village women took to the streets to protest the flour shortage, with little effect. It was under these conditions that some villagers justify their participation as volunteers in the Ethiopian and Spanish wars. They saw these wars as sources of relief for unemployed people like themselves. By 1940, in an attempt to earn the loyalty of Sicilian peasants in the face of the impending Italian participation in the war, the Fascist government prepared a highly publicized "assault on the Sicilian latifundia" in the form of a land reclamation scheme (see De Francisci Gerbino, 1940; Fortunati, 1941). This attempt failed both to earn the loyalty of Camporano peasants and to alter agricultural conditions. Too late, Fascist officials realized that the common people of Sicily could not be so easily hoodwinked. When in the emergencies generated by World War II, Mussolini invoked their aid, only a few answered his appeal.

Conclusion

Thus Camporanesi experienced what Alongi had earlier called "primitive self-government" (Alongi, 1887: 45). By successfully meeting the problem of political constraint and by retaining an essential autonomy from state officials and great landowners, leaders of the mafia regime were able to provide the conditions for satisfactory remedies to local contingencies. It was in this sense that village life under the dual regime

138

was an "improvement" over village life under the iron circle. It was, however, an improvement along functionalist lines or à la machine politics that could neither be translated into self-government properly understood nor stand the test of changing times.

In emphasizing the absence of local self-government properly understood, I am not suggesting or implying that local self-government can stand by itself. In addition to opportunities for local self-government, there must exist some structure of overlapping regimes that will afford opportunities to resolve conflicts and reach appropriate judicial and legislative remedies to facilitate mutual interests. This is precisely what was missing in centralized government and administration. In such circumstances, what primitive self-government or any other similar system can do is to provide short-term remedies to government failures, but its very mechanisms of *autogestion* may create additional difficulties for a unicentric political system to correct its errors. The history of the United States suggests that government failures in federal political systems can also generate primitive self-governments at the local level. But their very polycentricity sharply curtails the reach of localized groups, without depriving the large political system of considerable error-correcting capabilities.

The uninterrupted onrush of new exigencies and circumstances that accompanied the outbreak of World War I revealed fully how easy it was for the Camporano mafia to become a rent-seeking society and another burden on peasants and great landlords alike. If the Camporano mafia system did not work as well in practice as in project, it had yet to become more curious and more cruel than government itself. The conclusion reached in chapter 6 still holds. The mafia in Sicily was not always an exploitative countergovernment by estate managers and their armed bands under the protection of large landowners.

Under the axe of fascism the Camporano mafia regime collapsed. But the relative position of Camporano peasants vis-à-vis large landowners and the factors of production was now reduced to a status of serfdom not very dissimilar to that brought about by the reconstitution of village relationships in 1816. Confident in the future, Camporano villagers exhibited a remarkable endurance of present adversities and a defiant silence that outside officials mistook for submission. What had been hailed as "the last struggle with the mafia" turned out to be an interlude that served to strengthen the legitimacy of the Camporano mafia system and to give unprecedented power and prestige to local mafiosi.

8

Life under the
Dual Family Compact

The Allied landing on the plain of Gela in July 1943 signaled the end of twenty years of Fascist rule in Sicily and the reconstitution of the Camporano mafia system. This time the mafia emerged without a network of community organizations, but recognition by and access to Allied officials gave Ardena and other mafia leaders authority and influence as they never had before. As Sicily once again was separated from the Italian mainland and ruled by new governors, the mafia became the lawful regime of Camporano.

As exigencies of peace began to take precedence over exigencies of war, the conduct of local affairs was soon plagued with the problem of how political constraint could be maintained concurrently and over time with a substantial measure of consensus about the legitimacy of actions taken on behalf of villagers. The return of the island to the civil administration of a new Italian government in March 1944 revealed fully the magnitude of this problem and exposed the Camporano regime to additional limitations. Under these changing conditions, the authority pattern of the Camporano mafia itself became, like after World War I, a source of problems. But, unlike World War I, now no amount of cajolery and even economics could maintain its legitimacy or establish concordia discors anew. Breakdown of consensus gave way to fundamental disagreement and conflict, and by 1946 villagers faced two opposing groups, each attempting to maintain or secure a dominant position in village affairs. These were the Ardena Family and the Vallera Family.

By 1948, the pursuit of opportunities by the Ardena Family came to correspond fully with the interests and activities of the ruling party and the official church. By contrast, the Vallera Family acted as the local Left bloc or Popular Front of the Socialist (PSI) and Communist (PCI) parties. In such circumstances a challenge to the political dominance of the Ardena Family came to represent a challenge to the ruling party and official church; in turn, a challenge to the political dominance of the ruling party and the official church came to represent a challenge to the position of the Ardena Family. It was in this sense that village life in the postwar period took the form of village life under the dual family compact rather than the dual regime.

To American readers, the term *family* will bring immediately to mind, and reinforce what they already know about, organized crime in the United States. To Italian readers, the use of the same term to characterize the Camporano mafia and the local Left bloc will seem strange, since mafia groups in Sicily have generally not been known as "families," and will seem controversial and even offensive, since Left parties can in no way be compared to mafia groups. I urge both sets of readers to hold their reactions in abeyance until they come to see why and how Camporanesi used the term *family* to characterize the mafia and its opposition. In turn, to Canadian readers, the term *family* will bring to mind a part of their history when a combination of the leaders of government, business and the Church of England controlled and dominated Upper Canada (Ontario) life and became in fact known as the Family Compact. More generally, those familiar with recent developments in the study of covenant and politics (e.g., Elazar, 1969; Freeman, 1980) will readily acknowledge that compacts, like covenants, have a dark as well as a bright side. For all these reasons, then, it seems proper to speak of village life under the dual family compact.

Throughout the postwar period, local problems and issues could not be disaggregated to permit the simultaneous pursuit of different policies. Instead, different problems and different issues became subject to simultaneous pursuits of similar rent-seeking strategies and policies. Government took on the features of a trading company whose every operation was directed to the benefits that each group could derive therefrom. To prevent misunderstanding from creeping in, I must again anticipate what will become evident later. Though both family compacts sought to provide selective benefits to their members, I am not suggesting that they were exclusively personalist and clientelistic factions. The two compacts were also factions of principles, or political associations of a sort.

Villagers who belonged to the two defunct compacts today speak of this period in terms of "old scars" and prefer not to show them. In fact, recollections of this period are especially painful for former members of the Left compact. The outcome of the struggle between the two groups, the resolution of the land question, and the recent application of anti-mafia laws against some villagers have forced them to reevaluate their early stand against the mafia system. Thus, accounts of village life under the dual family compact are but bits and pieces of data. They serve, however, to illustrate how villagers dealt with issues and problems under conditions of fundamental disagreement and conflict.

The Reconstitution of the Outlaw Regime

Popular accounts of the Allied invasion tend to stress that American officials deliberately brought the mafia back to facilitate the conquest of the island. This chain of events is plausible (cf. Campbell, 1977; Faenza and Fini, 1976: 9–13; Ganci, 1968: 278–286; Kefauver, 1951: 19–34; Servadio, 1976: chapter 6), but does not seem to have occurred at least in Camporano. There are two aspects of the reconstitution of the Camporano mafia that are often ignored in popular accounts. The first is the conditions existing in Camporano at the time of the Allied advance. The second is that the outlaw regime did indeed become the lawful regime under Allied rule but its reconstitution had little to do with American officials. The Allied invasion simply provided opportune conditions; villagers did the rest.

Camporano in the Theater of War

The Allied invasion began on July 10, 1943. American troops landed along the Southwestern coast and British troops landed along the South-eastern coast. On landing, American forces were greeted, as Ernie Pyle

142

correctly observed (1943: 88; see also Servello, 1979), more as liberators than as conquerors. As news of the Allied advance reached Camporano, however, residents, including city people who had sought refuge there, became apprehensive about nearby Axis positions, part of the defense system of Western Sicily. Already Allied planes had heavily bombarded a nearby defenseless city. At the same time, the inhabitants of Terrano, the center of the defensive positions, were directly exposed to such a clash.

Camporanesi vividly recall the situation. They knew that the commanding officer, a much-decorated Italian colonel, was inclined to defend his position at all costs. If Terranesi undertook some kind of concerted action to avert bloodshed and destruction, neighboring villages also stood to gain from it. However, Camporanesi feared that Terranesi might do nothing for that very reason. The traditional rivalry between Terranesi and Castelfranesi might serve "to bring everybody down." As a result, while Camporano officials began to wear civilian clothes and to remove Fascist buttons from their jacket lapels, villagers began to turn to Ardena and other mafia leaders to do something about it. Unknown to Camporanesi, similar pressures were being brought to bear simultaneously on other disbanded mafia leaders by villagers in neighboring towns. It is known that these pressures were especially exerted on Mansueto Alois, leader of the mafia group in Terrano. These simultaneous moves gave rise to developments that favored the reemergence of profitable altruism.

The Outlaw Regime as a Solution to Collective Inaction

By 1943, some of the officials of the disbanded mafia, like Illuminato Carena, had died. Others, like Ardena and council chiefs Gesualdo Avola, Placido Perosa, Isidoro Riera, and Rosolino Uria, were older men in their late fifties and sixties. Whereas Ardena remained the only leader of the Camporano mafia to be known and addressed as Don Mariano, the other chiefs had also reached a dignified age that entitled them to be addressed as uncle. Though mafia soldiers Calogero and Girolamo Mezzena and Tano Cusna had reached a dignified age, they were still known as men of direct action, "men with a good liver." Ardena's nephew, lawyer Franco Novara, who had come of age during the Fascist era, occupied a unique position. He could be courageous and

143

generous but was often prone to anger and irritation. As an expert in legal matters, however, he was needed, though he fancied himself too much as *omu spirtu*, as a clever and experienced person.

Former mafia leaders during the 1930s had continued to enjoy the esteem and respect of most villagers and to be feared by local Fascist officials. When war broke out between Italy and the United States, Len Albano, an American then visiting relatives in the village, faced detention as an enemy alien. Ardena discussed Albano's case with local Fascist officials, who agreed to obscure his presence from provincial authorities. Thus it was natural for villagers to turn to leaders of the disbanded outlaw regime to do something about the Axis positions. What also emerged from the actions taken by Ardena and Novara is a careful politics aimed at a general acceptance of their authority among villagers and at procuring agreement with leaders of neighboring mafia systems.

Ardena and former council chiefs proceeded to sense the opinion of other villagers not directly associated with either the collapsing Fascist regime or their earlier activities. The result was the establishment of the Camporano Committee of Liberation. Members of this committee included Mariano Ardena, Franco Novara, former council chiefs, the local priests, and Carlo Vallera, a thirty-year-old member of the landed gentry. The two Mezzena brothers were not members of that committee. As former soldiers of the mafia, they were charged with the task of recruiting new soldiers. At the same time, Ardena contacted neighboring outlaw regime leaders to come together to decide what to do to avert bloodshed.

As a result, meetings of the various liberation committees occurred in Ardena's farmhouse. Alois assumed responsibility for seeing to it that nothing happened in Terrano; in turn, Ardena agreed to use his influence with leaders of other neighboring mafia regimes to convince them to take part in the war of liberation. The American Len Albano's participation in these meetings encouraged and gave additional purpose to the planning of villagers. Direct action was planned to coincide with the news of the advance of Allied troops in the area, and this is what happened when the American troops, already in possession of the provincial capital, advanced toward Terrano by July 20. As a result, when American troops reached the area, they found little or no organized resistance. Mafia soldiers and villagers had taken care of most of it. In Terrano and Camporano they were greeted by villagers headed by Mansueto Alois and Mariano Ardena. The coming of the Allied troops signaled the end of

144

the war for people living in the Camporano area and the beginnings once again of the outlaw regime as a going concern.

The Mafia Regime as the Lawful Regime

In late July 1943, Ardena was appointed mayor of Camporano by the American officer directing the Civil Affairs Branch of the Allied Military Government (AMGOT) in the area, and it was in this sense that the outlaw regime became the lawful regime. General enthusiasm wreathed and crowned the occasion. Shortly afterward, Len Albano went to Palermo to work for the Civil Affairs Branch of the Allied Military Government headquarters—giving Camporano mafiosi unprecedented access to and influence with the new governors of Sicily. Now Ardena's initiative on Albano's behalf in 1941 was seen as a calculated move or felicitous intuition in anticipation of this unfolding of events. But it is doubtful that Albano was "planted" in Camporano by American intelligence officials in 1939 or that he worked as an American agent before July 20, 1943.

Following the initial period of jubilation, local leaders began to manage public affairs. One of the first acts of the new mayor was to order the release of Fascist party officials arrested earlier. Villagers like to recall that this act of pacification occurred precisely when in Rome Mussolini had just been deposed, the national Fascist party disbanded, and its officials arrested. However, on the same day the chief Allied officer authorized the marshal of the Camporano carabinieri to issue arms permits to mafia soldiers in order to be able to discharge authoritatively the tasks assigned to them by Mayor Ardena.

Communal affairs as such were not problematic and Ardena delegated most of his communal functions to Carlo Vallera and Franco Novara. It was in this capacity, for example, that Vallera during the summer took over a number of state and Fascist offices. In December 1943, Novara became mayor of Camporano. At the same time, local questions like that of mosquito control could now be solved thanks to the technological innovation introduced by the American forces. An extensive program for limiting the number of malaria-carrying mosquitoes was, in fact, initiated, and by 1946 malaria was no longer a major problem in the Camporano area. Other questions were more intractable, however, and by the spring of 1944 the conduct of public affairs was plagued with how

145

to maintain a substantial measure of consensus about the legitimacy and authority of the local regime itself.

Peace and the Transformation of the Lawful Regime

Some villagers pinpoint the breakdown of consensus about the legitimacy of the authority structure of the local regime to a disagreement between Franco Novara and Carlo Vallera in the fall of 1943 and tend to attribute this to their personalities. Both Novara and Vallera admit having restless and exuberant temperaments that contrast sharply with the calm and sparse manners of most other villagers. These differences do not seem, however, to have placed great strains on their interpersonal relationships as late as the spring of 1944. Other villagers, instead, tend to attribute the breakdown of consensus to a disagreement between Ardena and Vallera about black-market operations in the summer of 1943. But if such a disagreement did take place, it does not seem to have altered the relationship then. The chain of events that led to the breakdown of consensus and to irreconcilable and incompatible differences is difficult to sort out. The recent war on the mafia has served to sharpen contradictory recollections of the main participants, and some of these recollections are the subject of criminal libel suits. What began in an unthinking spirit of general agreement or friendly differences gave way to fundamental disagreement and, soon afterward, to irreconcilable opposition.

The Question of Sicilian Self-Government

The Allied landing provided, for the first time since Italian unification, unusual opportunities for Sicilians to determine their own future. No sooner had the Allies reached Palermo than they were presented a memorandum by the Movement for Sicilian Independence (MIS). The document reasserted the existence of a separate Sicilian nation and the inherent right of Sicilians to govern themselves. It further called upon the Allied governments to permit a plebiscite on the abolition of the Savoy monarchy and the establishment of an independent republic of Sicily— in effect, to undo the 1816 fusion of Sicily with the Italian mainland. The recognized spokesman for Sicilian independence was a parliamentarian of pre-Fascist Italy, Andrea Finocchiaro-Aprile. But the movement itself

146

was a federation of individuals and groups ranging from descendants of the old parliamentary barons to the Sicilian Communist party. The strongest support for MIS came from the Eastern provinces of Catania and Messina (see Barbagallo, 1974; Canepa, 1942; Carcaci, 1977; Cimino, 1977; Di Matteo, 1967: 103–112; Finocchiaro-Aprile, 1966; Ganci, 1968: 286–310; Marino, 1979; Reece, 1973).

In October 1943, AMGOT authorities received another memorandum, but from a newly formed Sicilian United Front. This memorandum reiterated the inherent right of Sicilians to govern themselves but challenged the idea of an independent Sicilian homeland. It suggested that Sicilians could best realize their inherent right of self-government within a postwar Italian state. The memorandum attempted to reconcile, in broad terms, a unitary state with regional autonomy. The signatories of the Sicilian United Front document included leaders of the renascent Demochristian party and dissident Communists and Socialists who opposed the independentist position taken by their respective parties. Of all the Sicilian United Front groups, only the DC could count on a rapidly expanding number of supporters in the Western Sicilian countryside (see Di Matteo, 1967: 181–206). The early Demochristian movement had emphasized local autonomy and even federalism, but now, faced with a separatist threat, the renascent DC favored regional autonomy in a centralized state. Some DC leaders now went as far as to deny the existence of a Sicilian nation (see Barbagallo, 1974: 148).

Camporano officials and villagers looked sympathetically to *both* causes. Most of them believed in the existence of a Sicilian nation. They knew personally some of the MIS leaders like Baron Guido de Requena who had visited Camporano as soon as Ardena became mayor to enlist his support to and aid for independence. At the same time, Sicilian United Front appeals for regional autonomy within a postwar Italian state whose very nature and future were in doubt made little or no impact on most Camporano residents. Yet such appeals could not be entirely brushed aside. Christian Democracy was part of the "institutionalized" (Barnes, 1977: chapter 2; see also Kjellberg, 1975) political tradition of Camporano. In turn, most of the leaders of the renascent Mozarra DC group were known to Camporano villagers either as former Popular Party adherents, or as neighboring villagers, or both. One of them, Salvatore Cedro, had already traveled to Camporano to pay homage to Ardena upon his becoming mayor. The spokesman for the DC group in Mozarra, Nunzio Lozano, had the reputation among Camporanesi of being "a little

147

people's lawyer." He was also a personal friend of Novara since their college days when they were both activists in the Catholic University Students Association (FUCI).

Faced with these conflicting preferences and loyalties as well as changing circumstances, local mafia leaders made no commitment to support either cause. Such a posture soon became untenable, however. By January 1944, when Allied officials formally lifted restrictions on the organization of political groupings and on the freedom of the press in Sicily, Camporano leaders were becoming committed to different solutions to the question of Sicilian self-government. Gaetano Ardena and Novara had joined the DC and were setting up a local Demochristian headquarters; a council chief had come out in support of independence and organized the local MIS section; Vallera, who had already been pulled away from separatism to autonomy by a relative from Palermo who was a dissident Communist, began to attract other villagers to what was then vaguely perceived as socialism. Only Mariano Ardena, though sympathetic to the MIS cause, did not commit himself to a specific political grouping.

In February 1944, the Allied governments, among others, agreed to turn over the civil administration of Sicily to the Italian government, and at the end of March the prefect of Palermo became the high commissioner of Sicily directly responsible to the Italian prime minister, then Marshal Pietro Badoglio. By that time, however, the monarchical form of the Italian state and the continuation of the Badoglio government were in question. The National Committee of Liberation, composed of all the anti-Fascist parties, claimed to represent the Italian nation. Thus the problematic situation at the national level reflected in a macrocosm what was taking place in Sicily.

The return of Sicily to Italian civil rule vindicated the early efforts of Sicilian DC leaders to present an alternative to the separatist movement and placed them in the strategic position to influence and direct the formation of the national Demochristian party and the staging of Italian affairs. These developments in Camporano enhanced Novara's position both as mayor and as DC representative. The return of Sicily to Italian rule had no immediate adverse effect on independentist activities as such, protected as they were by AMGOT authorities. In Camporano the small separatist group continued its sporadic activities unperturbed. By contrast, the same development caused problems for Vallera and other villagers who adhered to the dissident, autonomist, Communist-Socialist

148

group. The emerging PCI-PSI bloc or Popular Front—based as it was on the call for a republic, a general land reform, and the nationalization of "private monopolies"—ignored or glossed over the question of Sicilian self-government. Indeed, its emphasis was on a unitary political system (see Di Matteo, 1967: 27; Gaja, 1962: 217–220). As a result, Vallera was now forced to sever collaboration with the pro-autonomist DC group and to take up positions on local and regional issues in line with central directives.

As representatives of competing national party groupings, both Novara and Vallera were now compelled to ignore their common experience and even their family ties and to take mutually exclusive positions on issues and problems. As tension between their political affiliations increased, these Camporanesi became more and more separated by the conflicting ideologies of Christian Democracy and socialism or Marxism. Emboldened by the growing dissension among Camporano leaders, and still smarting from the loss of authority, some former Fascist officials in the summer of 1944 helped to organize a local Communist (PCI) party, with lawyer Antonio Fontena as its first secretary. Though this group had fewer than thirty adherents among artisans, shopkeepers, and landless peasants, it served to give support to Vallera's position by recognizing his leadership of the Camporano Popular Front.

Faced with a local government in the process of disintegration, mafia leaders pressed into service every point of mutual contact and credibility to effect a rapprochement. But as their conflicting loyalties became fixed and insurmountable, Camporanesi found it extraordinarily difficult to maintain mutual agreement about the legitimacy of the mafia system to function as the political instrumentality of the community. All the statecraft of Ardena and other mafia leaders could neither restore consensus nor find concordia discors among villagers. The management and cultivation of Mogata served as a point of convergence for these contrasting positions to intensify and clash.

The Land Question

The liberation of Sicily also reopened the question of rural property and proprietorship. But at least until the winter of 1943, this was not yet a pressing issue. For Camporano peasants a more immediate concern was how to take advantage of the new opportunities available to them. With the liberation of Sicily, they had stopped paying rent to the proprietor of

149

Mogata, bartering their food products for commodities ranging from discarded oil drums used to store water, to leather, and to gold. Black-market operations were expanded to supply local foodstuffs to distant parts of the island and even points beyond.

By March 1944, the Mogata overseer had been unable to obtain payments from all the Mogata tenants. Finally, the administrator of the House of Gardena turned to Camporano mafia leaders for help, appealing, in effect, to their profitable altruism. With a duly notarized act, Gardena in May 1944 turned over the management of the Mogata estate to "Ardena and company." Mafia leaders assumed responsibility for the annual collection of rents from sharecroppers, keeping about 20 percent of the collected rent in kind for their services.

This arrangement did not alter the terms of share tenancy, which remained those of Fascist times. However, those earlier terms, assigning almost all the cost of production and one-third of the product to the tenants, were inoperative by May 1944. If they were reinstated and enforced, Ardena and company stood to gain a sizable share of the collected rent but also to alienate most Mogata tenants, their single most important constituency of supporters. There is considerable uncertainty about whether or not the old share-tenancy arrangements were reinstated and enforced for the 1944 harvest season. But it seems clear and less subject to dispute that they were still in question throughout the summer of 1944 and until that year's sowing season. By that time the old terms of share tenancy were revised by the Italian minister of agriculture to make tenant farmers responsible for only half of the cost of production, while receiving more than half of the product. In the end, mafiosi decided—it seems—to abide by the new sharecropping regulation and to raise the collection fee for the landowner. Some villagers, in fact, allege that Gardena never received any portion of the rent, as a result. Whatever the case may have been for the Mogata proprietor, this turn of events was not entirely detrimental for Mogata tenants who, after all, were supposed to pay rent for the use of land not their own.

Among villagers opposed to the outlaw regime, the same turn of events was subject to different interpretations. Vallera and other Left leaders viewed these developments as an effort on the part of the largest Camporano landowner to preempt a possible land reform and as a stratagem on the part of Ardena and company to maintain the strategic position of the mafia system among Camporano peasants. They thus pro-

150

ceeded to exhort Camporano peasants to break the chains that kept them in bondage—even though Mogata represented only about one-fourth of the hectares farmed by Camporano cultivators. When these exhortations failed to move most Mogata tenants to his side, Vallera reached outside the village to vent his indignation in Left periodicals by picturing the village under the heavy hands of "hats, priests, and local officials."

In this atmosphere, the secular and ecclesiastical leadership of Camporano was in no mood to tolerate an opposition that appeared, to them, imprecisely partisan in charge, disrespectful of traditions, and reckless in its words or deeds. The net result was Novara answering Vallera's statements in the DC press with ad hominem attacks; and local priests thundering damnations from the pulpit against "local atheists," some of whom also appeared, in their eyes, "to lead scandalous personal lives." In August 1944, Andrea Finocchiaro-Aprile brought his campaign for Sicilian independence to Camporano. Though he failed to win the Camporano mafia to his cause, his visit served to give added prestige to local mafiosi and to start a chain of events that transformed fundamental disagreement into irreconcilable opposition.

In an attempt to enhance and strengthen their standing among villagers, local Left leaders proceeded to invite a high-ranking Left official, recently freed from Fascist prison, to speak in Camporano. Ardena is reported to have given his consent to the use of the sidewalk overlooking the square—the "private" territory of the outlaw regime—as the platform for the Left gathering, but outsiders remained unaware of or failed to appreciate this conciliatory move. After discussing land reform as a manifestation of the ongoing war of liberation and inveighing against the forces of oppression in general terms, the outside Left orator said that Camporano peasants were slaves of Laura Gardena and Ardena. At this juncture, Ardena, who was known for his calm and taciturn manners, shouted, "It's not true!" These few words sparked a chain reaction in the crowd that escalated into what has become known as "a mafia aggression and massacre." More than ten years of due process of law were necessary to unravel, somewhat, this event and to determine beyond reasonable doubt who did what wrong. Also by that time, however, due process of inquiry had, for the most part, given way to slogans, and these have, in turn, acquired, in Henner Hess's words, "their own historical legitimacy" (Hess, 1970: 93). Mafiosi or adherents from the Demochristian and separatist camps had indeed fired on the Left gathering, but a care-

151

ful reading of available judicial proceedings reveals a more complex and less dramatic unfolding of the so-called mafia massacre than appeared in the popular and Left press.

When Ardena interrupted the outside Left speaker, a Communist from Mozarra turned to him and, brandishing his walking stick, told Ardena to let the speaker finish. A villager nearby, probably one of Ardena's bodyguards, fearing that the outsider was striking Ardena, hit him first. Confusion developed, and at that moment someone from the Left group raised his pistol and fired a shot in the air in the hope of restoring calm. The shot had the opposite effect. Some mafiosi fired their pistols; others threw hand grenades toward the speakers' platform. This episode lasted no more than a few minutes as people, including Vallera (who had shared the platform with the orator), fled into houses and side streets near the square. However, eighteen people, including the orator, suffered minor wounds.

A special joint edition of Sicilian Left periodicals was issued on this "mafia and separatist aggression and massacre." Special editions of independentist and Demochristian papers followed to refute the charge of aggression and massacre. Telegrams urging prompt action against "mafia and separatist aggressors" reached the Italian prime minister, Left representatives in government, and the high commissioner of Sicily. A prefectoral functionary was sent to replace Novara as mayor. Ardena, Novara, five mafia chiefs, and ten other mafiosi were charged with massacre. Warrants for their arrest were issued. The accused became fugitive. The local mafia regime thus ceased to be the lawful regime. Although more recent references to the 1944 mafia massacre in the Left press tend to give exclusive prominence to the national Popular Front leader and to ignore Vallera (e.g., Macaluso, 1971), both of them then were hailed as heroes of the new antimafia war.

Jubilation by the Left over this chain of events soon became muted, however, for the accused successfully challenged the legality of the warrants and pressed charges against Vallera and others for having taken part in a massacre against them. The fugitives returned to the village. Now they would be tried without being detained, together with Vallera and the others. In the course of the legal proceedings, charges against the Left adherents were dropped while charges of massacre against seventeen mafiosi were changed to some form of private violence.

Life under the Dual Family Compact

The Mafia Regime and Its Opposition as Family Compacts

By the end of 1944, the problem posed by the breakdown of consensus had become an issue of what to do with irreconcilable opposition. There were some one hundred villagers determined to remain in the village and to vanquish the mafia regime. This was unprecedented. The case of World War I combatants discussed in chapter 7 furnished no guidance on how to deal with the current crisis, as they had not sought to displace the mafia system. Moreover, were these dissident villagers still subject to *omertà*? Breaking *omertà* meant being *'nfame* which carried the penalty of death. Thus the situation facing leaders of the Camporano mafia was without precedent and fraught with new sources of violent conflict.

The sidewalk overlooking the village square now became the center of a buzz of activities. There, for everyone to see, Ardena, Novara, and the chiefs met to hold council, to sense the opinion of villagers, and to plan what to do. What emerged illustrates a flexibility and sensitivity in adjusting available means to meet new circumstances. A decision was made to extend the principles of how individual villagers dealt with those who broke village norms to the declaration of defiance posed by Left adherents. It appeared to have all the form of the following rule: "Some villagers say that they are no longer with us. So be it—no-longer-with-us-they are" (Llewellyn and Hoebel, 1941: 125). By implication, dissident villagers were also exempt from *omertà*. This exclusion rule was subsequently used to deal with other villagers, including Salvatore Albano, a nephew of a mafia chief, who refused to conform. Thus this new rule was used to avoid force in the resolution of conflict and to maintain the mafia system in the face of irreconcilable opposition and "miscreancy."

The political community of the mafia regime, now more restrictively defined, comprised about two-thirds of the village population. It included most peasants and artisans, communal employees and a few members of the professional class such as the local physician and the midwife. With the collapse of the independentist movement by 1947, its Camporano supporters also came to be identified with the Demochristian party and ideology. But the principal political values or ideas of most mafia supporters were still grounded upon, and sustained by, a strong spirit of local patriotism and self-reliance. As a general rule, a villager who valued self-reliance was more apt to join or lend his support to the mafia group than to the Left group. Unlike Christian Democracy, Marx-

153

ism or socialism appeared too much of a "foreign" and authoritarian phenomenon to most villagers. In fact, no organism was surer of earning villagers' suspicion than what appeared to be an externally directed and voiced Left movement. Here was everything that a typical or average Camporano villager disliked: property and its attributes contested; a foreign dialectic transported into the village and nourished by appeals to religious antagonism; and a rejection of accommodation or compromise that also implied a potential for violence. The congealing of differences among villagers had the effect of making mafia leaders and members of their political community act as if they were a single family—"that darned family" (*a famighiazza*), as dissident villagers began to say. Soon, however, members of the Ardena Family began to refer to dissident villagers as members of the Vallera Family.

The developments associated with the 1944 incident and the ability of the mafia regime to act as "a united family" served to strengthen Vallera's standing among dissident villagers and regional and national Left parties officials. His claim that he alone was in a position to direct and to gather support for the Popular Front in the dual struggle against the Camporano mafiosi and Demochristians appeared justified. He faced, however, the problem of how to put together the components of an organization that could translate his claim into reality, *without* that organization's becoming a mirror image of what he sought to destroy.

Vallera's first efforts were directed to the creation of a highly disciplined organization capable of directing the struggle against the Camporano mafia. Six individuals selected among the early Left adherents served as members of his command apparatus. They included a lawyer, a merchant, an elementary schoolteacher, and his brother. Membership in this bloc implied unquestionable recognition and acceptance of the authority of Vallera as well as basic agreement with and adherence to Socialist and Marxist ideas. Membership carried a promise of selective benefits that would result from the takeover of the commune and the Mogata fief from the Ardena camp. Slogans such as "To the commune!" and "Land to the landless peasants" were in fact used to attract members, especially among landless peasants. Such slogans were not, however, sufficient to obscure or conceal the irony inherent in the circumstance. The Camporano mafia, and not the Left group, was organized and supported largely by people associated with the "caps" or those who were of true peasant origin. The leaders of the antimafia opposition, and not mafia chiefs, came from the "hats" or the overseer and supervisory

154

class in the old estate (cf. Tarrow, 1967: 281; White, 1980). By 1946, and in spite of the return of prisoners of war and the coming of age of other villagers, the political constituency of the Left bloc consisted of not more than one-third of the Camporano adult male population.

Villagers between the Two Political Compacts

By 1946, Camporano became divided into two camps. For villagers it was difficult to remain neutral. A discussion of the alternatives confronting villagers serves to contrast the opportunities and limitations inherent in the organization of each group.

The rule dealing with those who proclaimed to be outside of the jurisdiction of the local mafia group did not preclude the possibility of admission and readmission. The road for admission or readmission of a dissident villager was wide and open. It took many forms—from a deferential salutation to a council chief, to a request for help and counsel to Ardena. It ran against village norms to refuse to acknowledge a sign of respect and to deny help or counsel to a villager in strained circumstances. After 1948, admission or readmission in the mafia camp took the form of an application for membership in the local DC; one would always find a fellow villager ready to sponsor that application. Irrespective of the form, the action taken by a "miscreant" villager and the response given by a member of the mafia tacitly served, especially after 1946, to bury past "errors" and to renew pledges of good will. Thus, bitter enemies became members of the same political community.

This membership policy stood in sharp contrast with that adopted and pursued by the Left compact. Vallera proclaimed that members of his bloc should have nothing to do with mafiosi—a term now beginning to encompass anyone who disagreed with him or questioned his judgment. He threatened to move "like a steamroller" against them. This precluded any possibility of allowing dissatisfied members of the Camporano mafia to join the Left camp. There were several supporters of the mafia group who by 1948 had developed a strong dislike of Novara and some of the mafia soldiers. Joining the Left bloc seemed to them a remedy worse than the ill they already knew. At the same time, such a proclamation went against the habits and norms of most Left supporters who were related to supporters of the other side through an intricate network of familial, *comparatico*, and friendship ties. But the threat, containing a dynamic mechanism of its own (cf. Boulding, 1963), gave rise to a situation

155

whereby villagers began to spy on each other's activities. The association between the Vallera-directed Left bloc and the national Popular Front served not only to maintain Vallera's hegemony vis-à-vis the local Communists but also to preempt the rise of other channels of opposition to the local mafia.

The rift between members of the two political communities widened even more significantly after 1946, when the requirements of organization and membership confronted struggles over communal affairs and land reforms. Thus in the postwar period communal party politics and agricultural affairs were principal arenas of conflict as well as critical tests for the viability of each "family compact." By that time, mafia leaders had overcome the problem of peace and security in the Camporano countryside as a challenge to their authority.

The Struggle for Peace and Security in the Countryside

The opportunities to engage in black-market operations provided by the collapse of Fascist rule and the reestablishment of the mafia system had been interpreted by some villagers as a general absence of "law and order." They had engaged in individualistic action for themselves and their families but this, however, caused hardship and injury to others and endangered the safety of the community as a whole. When by the fall of 1943 at least three villagers failed to reform their ways, mafia chiefs intervened to force them out of the Camporano area.

By the spring of 1944, these villagers attracted individuals in similar circumstances from other villages to form two brigand bands, the Tarsia and the Pezzana bands, operating in areas not too distant from Camporano. The Tarsia band took over a hamlet and forced the major landowner to accept its protection. The Pezzana band was in similar circumstances on the other side of Terrano and Camporano. Both bands operated in areas free from jurisdictional claims of neighboring mafia regimes.

By the fall of 1944, in part as a way of evading conscription in the army and in part as a way of taking advantage of the incentives existing for pursuing outlawed activities, individuals from neighboring villages and towns formed at least four other groups of "social bandits." These bands now roamed the same countryside as that of the Tarsia and

Pezzana bands. From time to time they also made incursions into the Camporano area. So immune had these bandits become that many of them could spend the cold winter months not on the run in the mountains but with their families in their natal towns or in the hamlet occupied by the Tarsia band, resuming their activities in the spring or harvest season.

By 1944 the provision of public security throughout the Camporano and neighboring territories was entrusted to a thirty-man interprovincial detachment of carabinieri and polizia with headquarters in Terrano. A May 1944 circular issued by the minister of the interior, then the Sicilian Salvatore Aldisio, ordered such interprovincial detachments to stamp out promptly "all manifestations of criminality"—from black-market operations, mafia, and separatism to petty crimes, and acts of banditry. But from the perspective of field officers, to stamp out *all* the illegal activities was clearly infeasible. Moreover, police officers themselves depended on black-market operations to sustain their individual and families' livelihood, since their monthly salaries had not kept up with the exigencies of the war (see also Di Matteo, 1967: 137, 260–262; Gaja, 1962: 160–162; Maxwell, 1956; Nicolosi, 1976; Sansone and Ingrascì, 1950). As a result, the Terrano interprovincial detachment of carabinieri and polizia concentrated on stamping out bandits as a way of establishing public security in the countryside. This task was not an easy one, however.

The success of this police work depended in large measure on gaining the cooperation of persons who either had been victimized or had knowledge of the territories in which bandits operated. Yet the need to gain information and cooperation ran against the professional nature of their work. These police officers were expected to remedy their ignorance of territories and language and to generate cooperation without somehow being exposed "to the air they were breathing" (see report cited in Di Matteo, 1967: 429–434). As a result, they had become increasingly isolated from the communities they were supposed to serve. They had remained largely inactive or when active had found it easier to concentrate on enforcing petty regulations against villagers they were supposed to protect. Their own presence had in large measure generated a hostile environment that was counterproductive for securing peace and security in the countryside—replicating almost exactly the situation that had existed in the nineteenth century.

By the end of 1944 the failure to establish public security revealed the magnitude of the problems police officers faced. As the number of bandits increased, their areas of operation became congested. Indiscriminate raids on isolated settlements, cattle rustling and highway robbery were now added to the list of other criminal activities. What had in the past been sporadic incursions in the Camporano area now became regular events. Cases of villagers being deprived of their wheat on the way from the neighboring estates of Kirie, Kamma, and Anzalo became the order of the day. Another indication of the high level of personal insecurity was evidenced in the fact that Camporano women cancelled plans to travel on foot to the Shrine of Saint Calogero that June as devotion to that saint required.

If this intensification of insecurity underscored the problems that plagued the work of the regular police forces, it also exposed fully other kinds of problems that plagued the police force of the mafia regime. As was shown in chapter 6, Ardena's profitable altruism began by offering protection to villagers. Though by 1944 the mafia regime had ceased to be the political instrumentality of the community, its social appropriateness and legitimacy were still in part dependent upon securing peace and security in the Camporano countryside. Yet the common soldiers and chiefs were apparently reluctant to engage in actions against bandits during most of 1944.

The killing of a close relative of Ardena in a highway robbery between Mozarra and Camporano in December 1944 served to dramatize the challenge to the authority of the Camporano mafia, to reveal most clearly that things were getting out of hand, and to mobilize Camporano "mafia soldiers" to action. Also by this time, the intensification of acts of banditry led the central government to renew its concern for a prompt restoration of law and order in Sicily. Not later than the first week of November 1945, a high police official, member of a newly created agency for "the war against all the manifestations of banditry," and Ardena also representing other mafia groups came together to prepare a joint plan of action.

The cooperative nature of the operations against bandits makes it difficult to sort out how this concerted action took place. Early in 1947, all the members of the Tarsia band were apprehended by a combined "operation" of Camporano and Terrano mafia soldiers and mounted police. With the arrest and imprisonment of the Tarsia band, the bandits' challenge to the authority of the Camporano mafia system came to an end.

Communal and Party Struggles

Following the 1944 incident, the conduct of communal affairs in Camporano was in the hands of prefectoral functionaries. The March 24,
1946, local election signaled the full resumption of communal and party
politics. It was the first time that women were allowed to vote. The conduct of communal affairs on the basis of electoral success served to
transform the rivalry between the mafia and its opposition into a struggle
for the "privatization" of the decision making.

The postwar control of communal government by the mafia assumed
all the characteristics of communal government of a century earlier, with
a modern twist—a majority rather than a minority of villagers now
earned rates of return or profits from the exercise of public authority.
Government took on the features of a huge trading company whose every
operation was directed to the benefits of its members and supporters.
While the growing correspondence between the Camporano mafia and
the ruling party sustained, encouraged, and gave meaning to this privatization of public goods and services, the full correspondence between the
Camporano Left compact and the national Left bloc generated additional
misery among dissident villagers.

The First Communal Election

The March 4, 1946, local elections took place before the national referendum on the monarchical or republican form of the Italian state and the
national election for the Constituent Assembly. Thus the local elections
provided an early indication of the relative strength of the political parties. In Camporano this first electoral contest was also an occasion for
the expression of popular judgment for or against the mafia. The DC list
was in fact headed by Novara and included mafia chiefs as well as two
priests. The Left bloc list was headed by Vallera and included his
closest aides.

The electoral competition was carried out under an electoral law that
for communes like Camporano gave a slate of candidates receiving a
simple plurality of votes four-fifths or sixteen seats on the twenty-
member council. At the same time, the ballot form which contained the
names of all the candidates was so arranged that each elector might either vote simply for the party symbol or vote for individuals distributed
among different party lists (panachage). Once it was established which

159

list had the majority, individual candidates would then be elected according to their separate totals of preference votes. Panachage, used only in 1946, was designed to provide both stable majority and liberty of choice, but in Camporano generated other results as well.

Of the 2,156 valid votes cast, the DC list received 1,861 (86 percent) while the Left bloc or Popular Front received 298 (14 percent). Novara was thus elected mayor with a fifteen-member majority. For an overwhelming majority of the Camporano population, the electoral result represented the reaffirmation of the legitimacy of the outlaw regime following the breakdown of consensus. This overwhelming support for the mafia was also used to affect the choice of the four opposition councilors drawn from the electoral list presented by Vallera.

Confident that the DC list already had minimum winning support, mafia leaders exhorted—it seems—some of their own supporters to choose the three or four last "dummy" candidates on the Left list as their individual preferences. The aim was to exclude Vallera and the first three real candidates on the Left list. This strategy succeeded. Soon at least three "dummy" councilors began to side with the majority of councilors and by the end of their terms had stopped attending the twice-a-year council meetings. Hence, the first electoral contest served to enhance further the position and authority of the Camporano mafia. The resolution of the question of Sicilian and Italian self-government in the same year shaped subsequent manifestations of communal and party struggles.

The Regionalist State and Demochristian Rule

According to a police report, by 1945 some five hundred thousand belonged to the Movement for Sicilian Independence. Separatist leaders experienced, however, serious difficulties in their efforts to translate this support into a Sicilian state enjoying a form of "sovereignty-association" with Italy and a future federal Europe. In an attempt to overcome Italian government opposition, independentist leaders appealed for support to the governments of the Allied troops still in Sicily, but these appeals produced the opposite results. Appeals to the United Nations then assembled in San Francisco to recognize the right of self-determination of Sicilians also went unheeded, as the Italian government pressed into service every means at its disposal to nullify the separatist move. As these peaceful attempts by Andrea Finocchiaro-Aprile failed, other MIS

160

leaders sought armed solutions. Uprisings, however, intensified dissension among the disparate elements of the MIS and evoked military and police repression from Italian officials. For all these reasons, by 1946 the struggle for Sicilian independence—or what Sicilian separatists called "the Idea"—had almost come to an end (Barbagallo, 1974; Carcaci, 1977; Finocchiaro-Aprile, 1966; Ganci, 1968: 310–337).

At the same time, the activities of the independentist movement had the effect of altering the stands taken by central government and national parties officials on the question of Sicilian self-government. By the end of 1945, central government and Left parties officials had, gradually and reluctantly, moved from a rigid centralist position to the autonomist position of the Demochristian party. As a result of this emerging consensus, the solution to the question of Sicilian self-government reached by 1947 was a special provision or charter for regional government—leaving the basic structures of the unitary, but no longer monarchical, state unchanged.

Under these circumstances, the establishment of regional government added new constraints to the conduct of communal affairs in Sicily. Communal services would now have to be carried out in relation to formal rules and regulations promulgated by both the central government and the regional government. Communal authorities had no essential control over the national and regional bureaucracy. Both central and regional governments now had a monopoly of authority over the supply of public goods and services at the communal level. Access to the exercise of this monopoly of authority was dependent upon winning national and regional elections. The national party organizations and the electoral system of proportional representation provided the nexus between the two levels of government in "the regionalist State" (Mack Smith, 1974: 144) and the procurement and delivery of public services at the local level in Sicily.

Between the 1946 and the 1952 communal elections, four other elections took place: the 1946 and 1948 national elections and the 1947 and 1951 regional elections. The interplay between national and regional party organizations became evident with the first regional elections in April 1947. By election time, the Left bloc parties were still in the Demochristian-led national coalition government, and this served to attract voters to the Left regional organizations in that first election. The possibility to form a DC-Left coalition government in Palermo was shattered when the DC-Left coalition government in Rome broke up in preparation for the 1948 national election and in response to American pressures on the Italian prime minister against the Left presence in government. As a result, Sicilian Demochristian leaders turned to the Right in order to form the government and to maintain majority legislative support.

The passing of the land reform law in 1950 deprived the Left parties of a major campaign issue, and by the 1951 regional election the DC regional government had acquired roughly the same majority support that the DC national government had. This correspondence remained until the late 1950s, making the relationship between the two levels of government one of mutual support. The connection between national and regional party organizations and national and regional elections had critical consequences for the two Camporano groups.

The Mafia in National and Regional Politics

The electoral work of Novara and the local clergy on behalf of the DC in the national and regional elections was constrained by the need to maintain the viability of their going concern in light of the diversity of party preferences among their supporters. Though the DC party lists in national and regional elections always received a majority of votes, non-Left support was dispersed among several party lists. Most if not all the Camporano separatists and monarchists were, for example, either supporters or officials of the mafia. The 1946 local election results were more an affirmation of the legitimacy of the Ardena group than support of the Demochristian party as such. This diversity of party preferences was, in turn, enhanced by the electoral laws. What contributed to make the Camporano mafia an electoral agency of DC candidates for the national and regional elections was the system of voter preference within each party list (cf. Zuckerman, 1979: 64–68, 204–205).

To simplify the analysis I shall refer only to the elections of DC national and regional "deputies," but the argument also applies to the elections of DC senators. For the national elections Camporano was part of the twenty-one-member and, by 1948, twenty-six-member electoral district of Palermo; for the regional elections, it was part of a five-member district in the Mozarra area. The preference system within party lists was introduced in part as a way of facilitating the choice for electors in such multi-member districts. It determined who among candidates from the same party list would be elected. For example, in the 1946 national

162

election, the nine seats assigned to the DC party went to those with the highest proportion of preference votes; similarly in the 1948 national election, thirteen Demochristian deputies were also so elected there. The same electoral law applied to the regional elections.

Preference voting required discriminating choices among voters who had little or no opportunities to know about each candidate of the same party. Faced with the costly prospect of securing such information, voters were apt to vote simply for the party list and, in the process, increase the likelihood of electoral success of those candidates who managed to secure even relatively few preference votes. As a result, for most parties two contests occurred in each national and regional election: an interparty contest and an intraparty contest. Candidates from the same party faced the problem of how to reach and attract party voters in view of similar attempts by other party candidates. At the same time, preference votes were easier to get in small communes than in large communes, but each candidate could not directly negotiate with each party sympathizer. In the case of the Palermo electoral district, both the diversity of the 169 communities and the distance between the four provinces posed serious constraints to intraparty contests. It was these calculations that led at least two not so well known Demochristian candidates, Salvatore Cedro and Melchiorre Perez, who had in 1946 succeeded in having their names placed on the party list, to enlist the aid of the Camporano mafia in their attempt to attract voters. In turn, there were ideological and personal reasons why these candidates expected aid from Camporano leaders.

Salvatore Cedro came from a neighboring town. As a physician fresh from medical school, he had briefly served as a health officer in Camporano immediately before the war. But during the war he had been involved with villagers like Gaetano Ardena in clandestine activities of the renascent Demochristian party; in 1943 he had visited Camporano when Ardena became mayor. Melchiorre Perez also came from a small town but in another province. Roughly the same age as Ardena, he had taught jurisprudence at several universities. Novara had been one of his students, and so now it was natural for Perez to ask Novara to help him win his own cause. In addition to Cedro and Perez, mafia leaders also supported another DC candidate, Emanuele Altura, who for his Popular Party past was well known throughout Western Sicily and as such did not need Camporano preference votes to be elected. But for the Camporano secular and ecclesiastical leaders, Altura's candidacy had special meaning. Most of them knew him from the pre-Fascist years of the Popular Party, and so their campaign on his behalf in 1946 represented a spontaneous manifestation of their long-standing support for his efforts and ideas.

It was for reasons of principle and friendship that Cedro, Perez, and Altura, and not other DC national candidates, received the endorsement and help of Camporano mafiosi. The Ardena group also functioned as an electoral agency of Demochristian candidates in the 1947 and 1951 regional elections. For these elections Camporano was part of a five-member district. Nunzio Lozano, whom Camporanesi already knew as "the little people's lawyer," was one of the two Demochristian candidates elected with the support of the Ardena group.

The electoral work of the Camporano leaders was aimed less at trying to change the choices of those already known to sympathize with the Left and more at convincing DC or undecided electors that a vote for the DC party list alone was a "wasted vote." At the same time, for members of the Ardena camp voting as instructed by a priest, a council chief or Ardena himself was another way of demonstrating support for their own political community, and most if not all the Camporano DC voters in the national and regional elections exercised their preference options accordingly. By 1948 most Camporano villagers viewed Altura, Cedro, and Perez as their national deputies and Lozano as their regional deputy. And so it was in this way that, in spite of an array of party lists and party candidates, national and regional elections became meaningful and made sense to most Camporano voters—hastening the advent of "party clientelism" (cf. White, 1980; Zuckerman, 1979).

The April 1948 national election, the first national election under the republican constitution, took place against a backdrop of local, regional, national and international events that served to intensify the rivalry between the two Camporano groups. First there was the 1947 regional election, with Lozano and Vallera as opposing candidates for the Camporano area district. As could be expected, that electoral campaign soon took the form of who between the two represented, or was least tainted with, the mafia. The campaign also escalated into fistfights between supporters of the two candidates; and it is exceedingly difficult to know who started such physical confrontations. One of these confrontations further escalated into an armed clash between Novara and a close aide of Vallera. The situation became so critical that when Lozano and Vallera closed their campaigns in Camporano, a contingent of riot police from

164

Mozarra occupied the village. The intervening factors in the intensification of rivalry between the two family compacts must have been the ongoing court proceedings about the 1944 incident and the on-going struggle for the control of Mogata. At the same time, the February 1948 coup d'état in Prague followed by the presentation throughout Italy of Popular Front or Left bloc lists aggravated the fears of a possible Communist takeover in Rome. As Norman Kogan has observed, that election campaign "was immediately turned into a struggle of apocalyptic proportions, and the vote was depicted as a telling climax in the battle between Christ and anti-Christ, between Rome and Moscow" (Kogan, 1966: 51). United States and Vatican officials mobilized their resources to stem the apparent Red tide (see Faenza and Fini, 1976: chapter 9).

As a result, during the 1948 electoral campaign, mafia leaders sided squarely on the Demochristian side, employing all their resources in the battle against "Anti-Christ and Moscow." For example, the ease with which communal clerks acceded to villagers' requests for public services such as communal papers and certificates now depended on villagers' party affiliation. Strict adherence to bureaucratic rules was used as a means to penalize Left-wing adherents. This adherence to "work rules" was also evidenced in the delivery of mail. However, the same stratagems were not used to victimize a grain merchant and some tenants of the Mogata estate known for their adherence to the Left compact; these villagers attribute this to village norms giving anyone the right to *campari* or the essential means of livelihood. In turn, support of the Demochristian party by the church hierarchy justified and invigorated the pro-DC stand taken by the Camporano clergy. Hence, withdrawals of church sacraments, from baptism to extreme unction, were used as additional means to sanction the electoral work of the mafia and to undermine that of the Left bloc. Similarly, both the midwife and the physician used all their influence to advance the cause of Christian Democracy. As communal officials, some mafiosi availed themselves of the prerogative to name presiding officers of the polling stations and thus monitor more directly the success of their pressures on undecided and poor voters.

When the Camporano election returns were in, the percentage of votes received by the DC had increased to about 70 percent from 49 percent in the 1947 provincial election. But the Red scare had served to draw votes more from the right-of-center parties than from the Left bloc parties, whose electoral support remained almost fixed at about 30 percent. Somewhat similar results were registered at the national level to permit the Demochristian party to be able to form a one-party government. The Demochristian leader De Gasperi preferred, instead, to continue the coalition government with the small center parties in order to retain a measure of relative autonomy and independence from United States and Vatican officials. By contrast, the same election identified and fused the interests of the Camporano mafia with the interests of the Demochristian party to make it difficult over the long run for Camporano leaders to retain a measure of relative autonomy and independence from national and regional DC officials. From 1948 on, membership in the political community of the mafia system became equivalent to membership in the dominant national and regional party.

The Left Compact in National and Regional Politics

The full correspondence between the Vallera-directed Left compact and the national Popular Front gave Camporano Left adherents strong center-periphery ties. Nevertheless, the PCI presence in the Camporano Left bloc created the belief among villagers that Vallera as the local leader would have to convince the small group of PCI sympathizers about the appropriateness of actions to be taken in relation to the local political economy. But, with his election to the regional assembly in 1947, Vallera was able to maintain his hegemonic position among Left adherents and, symbolically, to recoup from the battle lost in the 1946 communal election.

By 1949, however, there was growing dissension in the Left bloc as a result of Vallera's actions concerning the land struggle. By 1950, the emerging PCI leader, Salvatore Albano, succeeded in attracting new members to his party from both the DC and the PSI. A report in the Sicilian PCI organ, *Il Siciliano Nuovo*, for February 1950 showed that 110 Camporano members had renewed their party cards and that 140 more landless peasants had bought their first party cards; female party activists had increased "400 percent."

These developments did not seem to have affected Vallera's leadership of the Camporano Left, for he relied less on the consensus of Left adherents and more on the requirements of maintaining a united Left Front in Camporano. Though on occasions Communist national and regional leaders intervened in Camporano Left affairs on the side of the local PCI by forcing Vallera to sign statements of understanding (*giunta d'intesa*) aimed at preventing him from "riding roughshod" over local PCI

166

adherents, they did not seem to have monitored the extent to which those statements of understanding were in fact adhered to by leaders of the local Left compact. Vallera continued to enjoy the support of important Communist regional and national leaders and the superior authority that derived from such leverage. His hegemonic position remained unchanged even after 1951, when, fearing defeat, he did not run for reelection in the regional assembly. Thus during the post-1946 period, whereas the Camporano mafia was slowly absorbed by the Demochristian party, the Camporano Popular Front was constantly plagued with internal disagreement and conflict. The second communal election also illustrates this evolving situation.

The Second Communal Election

The May 1952 communal election did not radically depart from the previous national and regional elections, in both campaign tactics and results. The electoral law, now without panachage, transformed the 65 percent DC votes into a sixteen-member majority and the roughly 35 percent Left bloc votes into a four-member opposition on the communal council. By this time, the old Camporano outlaw regime could no longer muster the plebiscitary support it did in the first postwar communal election.

At the same time, there were two other aspects that made the 1952 communal election different from the 1946 election. First, the DC provincial secretary began "to intrude" in local Demochristian affairs by claiming the right of final authority over the composition of the communal DC list. Second, Albano succeeded, on behalf of the local Communists, in having his and several other names placed on the Left list prepared by Vallera and became one of the opposition councilors. Neither development augured well for the long-term survival of the two family compacts.

Communal Government as a Trading Company of the Mafia

I have already noted how in the course of the 1948 national election access to communal services became dependent upon membership in the Demochristian party. Also by 1948, the communal building itself came to be viewed as the local headquarters of the Demochristian party. The structure of governmental arrangements placed local officials in a posi-

167

tion of relative immunity vis-à-vis dissident villagers. The only lawful recourse for those deprived of public services was to seek remedy from officials of the central and regional governments. Between 1947 and 1951 Vallera raised these problems in the regional assembly; national Left legislators brought them to the attention of members of the Chamber of Deputies. But the requirements of winning elections permitted leaders of the ruling party to exercise their monopoly of central and regional authority to allow the transformation of the communal government into a sort of trading company of the Camporano mafia. It was in this way that public services became private services, leaving at least one-third of villagers without any lawful remedy—confirming, in effect, Tocqueville's observation that "(t)he extension of judicial power in the political world ought . . . to be in the exact ratio of the extension of elective power; if these institutions do not go hand in hand, the state must fall into anarchy or into servitude" (Tocqueville, 1835: I, 77). Access to public services by those deprived took place more as expressions of political humanitarianism or philanthropy than as rights to equal municipal or public services.

Between 1948 and 1954, Camporano local officials working with DC national and regional deputies were able to attract roughly 200 million lire from the European Recovery Program (see also Jenness, 1950; Palazzolo, 1958: 80–82; Tarrow, 1977b: 205, note 7). The public works that followed included the construction of a slaughterhouse and two public housing projects, the paving of the main square and three streets whose original stone pavements dated back to some fifty years before, the erection of new walls around the expanded cemetery, and the addition of a stone road on a sheep walk. Most of these works were done through public tenders from outside. But the construction and use of each public work reproduced in varying degrees the conditions that existed in the provision of communal services.

For example, the Ardena supporter in charge of the Camporano employment office used the discretion inherent in his authoritative position to rig the hiring process for the projected public works in favor of those who belonged to his political constituency (see also Greco, 1970: 21). Deprivations imposed on Left adherents resulting from the exercise of official discretion were strengthened by legal provisions dating back to the Fascist period that placed severe legal restrictions for Camporano workers to find employment beyond the boundaries of their own village (see Clark, 1954; Einaudi, 1955). Once again, relaxations of these laws

168

took place more as expressions of political humanitarianism or philanthropy than as rights to equal employment opportunities. At the same time, the nature of public works such as the village square and the streets made it infeasible to exclude any villager from enjoying their use. Similarly, the construction of the stone road on that sheep walk was made to allow vehicles to reach the Ardena farmhouse but, once built, the road also allowed vehicles such as threshing machines to reach other farms. By contrast, in the case of the two housing projects it was easier to indulge some and to deprive others.

Entrenched in their powers, Camporano leaders treated public affairs only insofar as they could be turned into private profit for themselves and their followers. Under these conditions, voting served to emphasize the disjunction existing between participation in the electoral process and articulation of preferences for public services. Agricultural activities provide additional evidence of how far conflict had pushed villagers against one another.

Land Struggles

As I have noted, the management of the Mogata fief became a principal source of conflict. Each family compact mobilized its capability to impose a constraint upon the other: one to maintain the control of Mogata it had, the other to wrest and replace that control with its own. The struggle for the control of Mogata took on the form of simultaneous "stamped papers offensives"—legal efforts on the part of all concerned either to promote or to prevent the enactment and application of land reform legislation. The reopening of the land question resulting from the full resumption of party politics in 1946 allowed local Left leaders to couch the struggle for the management of Mogata within the general context of the struggle for agrarian reform. Control of Mogata became a social imperative. At the same time, however, the reopening of the land question also permitted Left adherents such as Salvatore Albano to challenge the Vallera leadership and to pursue a course of action in opposition to both the mafia and the Left compact. Under these conditions, slogans became substitutes for reason, while the vicious circle of escalating threats and counterthreats extended beyond the resolution of the Mogata question to envelop all other agricultural activities.

169

The Stamped Papers Offensive and Counteroffensive

In March 1945, Vallera appealed to the dormant Board for the Colonization of the Sicilian Latifundia to expropriate the estate of Princess Gardena. She had failed to build some sixty farmhouses for Mogata sharecroppers as required by a February 13, 1933, law later incorporated in the January 2, 1940, law on "The Colonization of the Sicilian Latifundia." Failure to comply with any article of the 1940 law exposed landowners such as Gardena to expropriation of their estates. But, as indicated in chapter 7, the Fascist "assault on the latifundia" in 1940 had been simply a last-minute effort to win the loyalty of the Sicilian peasants in the face of World War II. By 1945, regional and national Left leaders were already calling for a general land reform that went beyond the land reclamation policy of the Fascist regime. Against this backdrop, Vallera's request for the application of a "regressive" Fascist policy was not well received in Palermo. As a result, the high commissioner of Sicily turned down his request.

By 1946, the land question in Italy once again became part of the exigencies of peace. In an effort to meet this question, the DC minister of agriculture, Antonio Segni, prepared legislative measures legalizing land invasions. In a move reminiscent of the Visocchi law of 1919, the Segni law of September 6, 1946, permitted peasants organized as cooperatives to be appropriate agencies for the cultivation of "uncultivated or poorly cultivated lands" either as individual lots or as single production units. The problems that had accompanied the application of the Visocchi law were now compounded by the presence of parties whose claims on behalf of peasants, with or without land, far exceeded those of the post–World War I combatants association (ANC). In order to mobilize and attract peasants to their cause, Left leaders became the most strenuous advocates of private ownership of land (cf. Hajda and Leonardi, 1978: 7–9).

Starting on September 10, 1946—well before prefects in Sicily had had an opportunity to become fully cognizant of the September 6, 1946, law—small landowners, tenant farmers and agricultural workers mobilized by Left activists began to invade a number of estates. On September 28, the Left parties organized a general strike throughout Sicily to protest delay in the implementation of the Segni law and to reiterate the call for a total restructuring of rural property rights as a social imperative. In an attempt to deflate what appeared to be an explosive situation, the new commissioner of Sicily held a number of meetings with leaders of the landowners' and peasants' associations. On November 5, 1946, he secured "a pact of friendship and collaboration between landowners and rural workers." This pact or accord guaranteed peasants tenure of lands they already occupied, assured landlords a rent, and helped to accelerate the work of the provincial commissions. At the same time, this agreement also reaffirmed the abolition of the gabelloto as an intermediary institution between landowners and those who tilled the land. These national and regional developments served to renew the stamped papers offensive, to enhance the strategic position of the Camporano mafia, and to intensify the disagreement that had begun to afflict the Camporano Left.

Leaders of the Ardena group found it easy to organize a distribution cooperative in accordance with the requirements of the Segni law and the actions of the high commissioner of Sicily and on February 2, 1947, it was so established. Composed of Mogata tenants, the association took the name of the Cooperative of War Veterans, recalling the Veterans Landholding Society founded in 1920. On March 20, 1947, the management of the Mogata estate was duly transferred from mafia leaders to cooperative leaders—in effect, a move in stamped papers only since the transfer involved almost the same persons. Except for an individual fee that went to support the DC-sponsored Regional Association of Agricultural Cooperatives (ARCA) to which the local organization belonged, tenants continued to farm Mogata as they had before.

It was not until March 20, 1947, that Vallera was able to put together a cooperative, called the Emancipation Cooperative and composed, it seems, of at least one hundred members, that could compete with that of the mafia. Delay in establishing the cooperative was apparently due to disagreement that existed among Left adherents on how best to wage the struggle for Mogata. Whereas Salvatore Albano envisaged a land invasion, Carlo Vallera urged, instead, the continuation of the stamped papers offensive through his cooperative. With the superior support of national and regional Left leaders, Vallera's judgment prevailed. The cooperative became a member of the Left Regional Union of Agricultural Cooperatives (USCA). By March 29, however, its very raison d'être had already been preempted by the transfer of Mogata to the Cooperative of War Veterans. In April 1947, Vallera was elected regional deputy but, even from his new position, he could not obtain what he sought either through personal intercession, with Princess Gardena carrying a promise of a rent higher than she was alleged to receive from the other coopera-

171

tive, or through legal recourse to the Mozarra commission for uncultivated or poorly cultivated lands. By 1949 a turn of events involving USCA
itself further undermined his efforts.

By 1947, 153 of the 264 cooperatives in the Sicilian countryside belonged to USCA. Financed in part by contributions of member cooperatives and in part by loans from state agencies, USCA officials had by 1948
established a network of structures ranging from legal aid to banking facilities for Left cooperatives. But, as this regional union of cooperatives
became a viable and successful concern, Left leaders began to require
its financial administrator to allocate sub rosa parts of the USCA funds for
electoral and other petty expenses. These secret and unlawful manipula-
tions of USCA funds also gave substantial incentives to the USCA financial
administrator to direct some funds for his own stock-market operations.
When in early 1949 one of these operations failed, that official abandoned his post, taking with him all the available USCA cash, some fifty
million lire (then equaling close to one hundred thousand dollars in
United States currency). The USCA was bankrupt and by the end of 1949
was liquidated, causing the demise of many local cooperatives that had
entrusted it with the deposit and transfer of rent to landowners. As a distinguished lawyer who had lent his skills to Sicilian peasants involved in
land invasions was to recall later, "with the [USCA] collapse there began
the end of the (Left) cooperative movement" (Sorgi, 1959: 633; cf.
Schneider and Schneider, 1976b). Soon afterward, the Emancipation
Cooperative ceased to be even a letterhead organization.

Land Invasion

The failure of Vallera's stamped papers offensive now gave Albano and
other PCI adherents an opportunity to organize a land invasion, a course
of action "vetoed" by Vallera two years earlier. But by 1949, a land invasion in the Camporano territory had little prospect of success. The
lawful operation of Mogata by the Cooperative of War Veterans was now
backed up by the coercive capabilities of both the police force of the
state and the soldiers of the Camporano mafia regime. Moreover, similar
arrangements now applied to neighboring fiefs farmed, in part, by
Camporano tenants. The only exception to this general situation was the
Kirie estate located in the territory of a neighboring town. But in the case
of this estate, Albano and PCI adherents faced other constraints.

First, villagers used the term *estate* or *fief* to refer to Kirie, but Kirie

172

was an estate or fief in name only. Originally a fief covering some one thousand hectares, it had been subdivided in the course of the eighteenth and nineteenth centuries to single cultivators. By the 1940s what remained of that estate was some 180 hectares on the side of a mountain, owned by a lawyer from a family of Camporano rentiers, Ciro Corona, and cultivated by Camporano agricultural workers. Second, a justification for "land invasions" was grounded in part on the existence of "uncultivated or poorly cultivated" lands. Yet this was not the case of Kirie, as market demands for wheat were giving rise to its *overcultivation*. A third constraint faced by Communist leaders had to do with land invasion itself. A successful land occupation and parcelization of Kirie required the establishment and maintenance of some kind of organization in accordance with the Segni law of 1946. Yet by 1949 the collapse of both the regional union of the Left agricultural cooperatives and the Emancipation Cooperative had produced much disillusionment about formal voluntary associations among Left adherents. Most landless peasants were now in no mood to lend their name and efforts to establish a new cooperative venture.

These constraints were, however, overridden by the need of Camporano Communists to do something on their own. Led by the PCI secretary and a student studying to become a land surveyor, and accompanied by their wives, a number of landless peasants invaded and occupied almost half of Kirie in November 1949. The mafia soldier who acted as the *campiere* and the land workers then preparing the land for sowing abandoned their fields. After several days on Kirie, the invaders, if one believes the recollections of some of the participants, became concerned about a confrontation with mafia soldiers. The landowner pressed charges against some twenty villagers for having led the occupation or invasion of "other people's lands with the intention of appropriating them or drawing profit from them." At the same time, Vallera and his emissaries began to urge members of the PCI group to farm their Kirie lots through the disbanding Emancipation Cooperative in order for the land invasion to have legal standing. By the spring of 1951, a district court dismissed charges against the participants of the Kirie invasion. Land occupations with the aim of promoting their legal cession fell within the strictures of the law and more specifically within the provisions of the Segni law of September 6, 1946. In an effort to retain possession of Kirie, the land invaders agreed to farm their part of the "estate" through the disbanded Left Cooperative.

173

But less than a year later, Corona regained all of Kirie. Disagreement between Vallera as president of the cooperative and PCI adherents as members of that cooperative had apparently become such that the original invaders voluntarily relinquished the cultivation of Kirie. Whereas Vallera wanted to cultivate Kirie as a collective farm under the direction of the Emancipation Cooperative, the invaders wanted to cultivate Kirie as private, individual, lots. It is possible that the cultivators began to abandon Kirie also because of the possibilities they perceived coming from the 1950 regional land reform.

Private vs. Public Land Reform

In preparation for a national land reform, the National Institute of Agricultural Economics (INEA) conducted between 1946 and 1947 a detailed survey of the distribution of land property throughout the Italian mainland and islands (INEA, 1947). This survey revealed the extraordinary number of private land holdings, the very small size of most properties, and the relatively small extent of genuinely large holdings, prompting Luigi Einaudi to observe that "a problem of latifondo does not exist in Italy, not even in its classic regions, the *Mezzogiorno* and Sicily. There exists instead many diverse problems . . . not to be resolved with 'land reform' but with the particular measures adapted to places, types of culture and social organization" (Einaudi, 1948: 1; see also Medici, 1945; Vanzetti, 1948). Moreover, the rapid industrialization then taking place in Northern Italy stood to provide powerful incentives for people to leave the rural areas and thus to undermine the land reform premise that a large number of people should "remain on the farm." But, under pressures from the Left parties, land reform came to be accepted by most Italian politicians as a major remedy for the ills affecting Southern Italy—or, in the words of John Montgomery, land reform as an example of "a principle which has been tested and has survived, though its effects have rarely been reported or explained" (Montgomery, 1972: 62). I report and explain some of its effects in Sicily.

The year 1950 was the year of land reform legislation in Italy. In May of that year, the national parliament approved a land reform law entitling Calabrian landless peasants to ownership of land on the Sila plateau. In October, this law was extended to other parts of the South. On December 27, 1950, the legislation introduced by the DC regional government became the lawful means to effect agrarian reform in Sicily (text of the law

174

and subsequent amendments in Tramontana, n.d.). Though the regional government sought to initiate a land policy that went beyond the simple redistribution of rural property rights initiated by the central government, the proposed transfer of land ownership involving large estates in excess of two hundred hectares affected not more than some one hundred and fifty thousand hectares out of some two million hectares of farm land in Sicily (e.g., Diem, 1961, 1963).

The eight hundred hectares of Mogata and at least some four hundred other hectares farmed by Camporanesi in neighboring estates came under the jurisdiction of the Sicilian land reform act. This law stood to affect adversely the proprietary claims of large landowners, the strategic position of the mafia, and the agricultural activities of most Camporanesi.

The limitation to own not more than two hundred hectares of contiguous rural property was accompanied by a substantial loss in the compensation of expropriated land. Article 42 stipulated that landowners were to be compensated for expropriated land in accordance with the national taxation value based upon pre-1940 taxable income and were to be paid in 5 percent state bonds redeemable in twenty-five years. Because of the use of low taxation value and the low market quotation of the state bonds, the compensation stipulated in article 42 equaled, in effect, not more than 40 percent of the average market value of expropriated land. Of all the large landowners in the Camporano and neighboring areas, the proprietor of Mogata, now Princess Vittoria Gardena-Manresa, heiress of Laura Gardena deceased in 1949, stood to incur heavy losses. She had inherited several thousand hectares of land but now she stood to retain not more than three hundred hectares of noncontiguous properties. All of Mogata was expected to be expropriated. For mafia leaders, the parcelization of Mogata meant the disbandment of their cooperative venture as well as the loss of an essential source of both profit and influence.

Camporano cultivators also stood to lose if the land reform was implemented. Article 39 of the reform act specified that those eligible to receive land were *only* heads of peasant families with less than 100 lire of taxable income and without a criminal record of any kind residing in the commune where land was to be divided. Plots of land would then be assigned by means of an official lottery. Article 38 specified that the size of each plot to be turned over to each peasant was to be not less than three hectares (seven acres) and not more than six hectares (fifteen acres). Lots of less than three hectares were to be allowed in cases involving land

175

"extremely fertile" or situated in the immediate vicinity of towns and villages. As a result, Camporano peasants who were farming estates in neighboring territories appeared to be automatically excluded from the list of potential beneficiaries for those estates. The allocation of Mogata lots based upon the requirements of a taxable income less than one hundred lire meant the eviction of most if not all the tenants farming Mogata. At the same time, Camporano agricultural workers with less than one hundred lire of taxable income faced other kinds of restrictions. The number of eligible Camporano landless peasants was reduced to about 348. Now, if all the arable land of the nearly eight hundred-hectare Mogata estate was divided, as the law required, into holdings of at least three hectares each, there could be only about two hundred and fifty such holdings, leaving still some one hundred landless agricultural workers without any ownership of land. At the same time, there would be at least some four hundred Camporano tenants dispossessed of their holdings in and beyond the village territory because of the land reform. In sum, the law appeared to impose deprivations on all those the land reform was intended to benefit (cf. Blok, 1966; Franklin, 1969: 160–163; Rochefort, 1961; Shearer, 1968).

A knowledge of the consequences that were likely to flow from the parcelization of estates in the Camporano and neighboring territories brought together Vallera, who was then a member of the regional assembly, and Albano to blame the DC regional government for the bad reform law and at the same time to urge the prompt application of that reform law (see Cipolla, 1954; Formiggini, 1954; Scaturro, 1956). The same knowledge, however, gave the Mogata proprietor, administrator, and tenants substantial incentives to explore ways to reduce or to nullify the potential deprivations they stood to suffer.

The December 27, 1950, law (article 30) stipulated that any voluntary parcelization of land in excess of two hundred hectares undertaken by landowners after December 31, 1949, was null and void. However, the second sentence in the same paragraph introduced a number of exceptions that served to relax the declaration of nullity. The exceptions included the following: (a) land donations to public and private welfare agencies and to heirs who were contemplating matrimony; and (b) land sales for the establishment of "small peasant handholding farms." The first exceptions were based upon the civil code, the second were based upon the June 26, 1948, law and "successive extensions" aimed at establishing viable family farms or small peasant landholdings (*la piccola*

176

proprietà contadina). These national laws could not be countervened by any regional law. At the same time, the successive extensions of the 1948 law were open to different and contrasting interpretations (see Landi, 1953). As a result of these national laws, the regional government could not, in part, formulate a clearly understandable set of legal prescriptions for the land reform. Several consequences followed.

Two days after the enactment of the December 27, 1950, agrarian reform law, Princess Gardena-Manresa transferred the Mogata estate to Novara as president of the Cooperative of War Veterans. The purpose of the duly notarized sale was the creation of small peasant landholdings precisely in accordance with the 1948 national law of such landholdings and its successive extensions. The sale of Mogata to individual members of the mafia cooperative took place through the emphyteusis lease. If, however, the copyhold lease assured a speedy transfer of Mogata and opened the way for individual control and use of each lot, it also carried a higher annual rent than the share-tenancy rent to be paid to the proprietor through the cooperative, either in perpetuity or until the encumbrance was redeemed (*affrancamento*). In addition, the land tax would now have to be borne by each cultivator. It was in this way that the design of the land reform could be thwarted. This stratagem was for most Mogata cultivators a choice of the lesser evil.

This course of events evoked different reactions from Camporano Left leaders. They urged their adherents who were also Mogata tenants not to sign the emphyteusis lease with Novara. They claimed that the transfer of Mogata, taking place two days after the agrarian legislation had become law, was not valid; that the 1948 law on which the transfer had been based either had expired or was inapplicable to the Camporano situation. As a member of the regional assembly, Vallera appeared to these villagers to have more access to valid information than they or Novara and Ardena. Moreover, Vallera's arguments were now also supported by Albano. At least thirty-seven Mogata tenants are reported to have found these arguments convincing enough to refuse to accept land from the mafia and to press charges against the Cooperative of War Veterans. But, while their claims were being considered by judicial authorities in Mozarra, they could watch other Camporano villagers furrow their former lots in the winter of 1951.

A year later, a regional government report on the application of the agrarian reform act (Regione Siciliana, Assessorato Agricoltura e Foreste, 1952) confirmed what Camporanesi already knew. A private rather than public land reform had occurred in Camporano. The burden now was upon regional government officials to translate into reality their own version of the expropriation and subdivision of Mogata. By 1952, however, these officials were also under pressures from Left members of the regional assembly to revise the original agrarian reform act. And it was in such a climate of uncertainty that private land reform prevailed upon public land reform at least in Camporano.

Conflict and All Other Agricultural Activities

In the course of this period, conflict between the two groups also came to dominate all other agricultural activities. Exchange labor such as mowing, pruning, weeding, or tidying a vineyard continued to take place but only among members of the same political community. There were, however, other agricultural activities such as threshing and grazing that required a high level of interaction or interdependence, not necessarily divisible according to membership in the same political community. The difficulties of sustaining this high level of interdependence were now compounded by conflict. Disagreement about work schedule among peasants took on the form of symbolic confrontations between the political compacts.

Since the 1930s, threshing was done for the most part with machines from neighboring towns. During this period, several sites in the Camporano and neighboring area had come to be used as appropriate places for peasants to take their wheat sheaves. The work of feeding the machines from the stacks, carrying the sacks from it to the weighing machines, and making the stack of chaff were done jointly by all the peasants. However, several work characteristics of threshing could easily give rise to dispute and quarrels. It was, for example, difficult to adhere to strictly equivalent work since some cultivators were apt to have larger stacks of wheat than others. The order in which stacks were threshed was also likely to be a matter of dispute, since some people were inclined to do less work after their own wheat had been threshed than before. Each peasant assumed the direction of the work while his own wheat was threshed, and this too was apt to be resented by some. The availability of pitchforks and knives could transform a dispute or a misunderstanding into potentially dangerous incidents (see also Davis, 1973: 101–103).

In the past, considerations of mutual interests had attenuated these problems. Some peasants had assumed on an ad hoc basis general supervision by shifting rounds to see that everyone was doing all the necessary work. Now the exigencies of conflict between the two camps served to exclude considerations of mutual interests and to compound disputes and quarrels. Between 1945 and the early 1950s, pitchfork incidents involving adherents of the two groups became part of almost every threshing season. The only persons who would now interfere to stop such fights were women who would disarm their husbands and push them apart. One of these women recalls each threshing season as "her annual calvary."

Verbal and physical confrontations also took place in the case of grazing cattle straying on neighboring lands. The most vivid trouble case involves two villagers with adjacent and unfenced lands. Antonio Caldera, who belonged to the political community of the mafia, used his lot to cultivate alternately wheat and legumes; Calogero Ceras, who belonged to the political community of the Left bloc, used his lot instead to graze cattle. As a way of dealing with crop damages resulting from occasional straying of sheep and calves, Ceras had agreed to compensate Caldera with an unclear number of sheep cheeses and ricotta and perhaps even a lamb every year. This arrangement, negotiated every year, represented, in effect, a solution to "the problem of social cost" (Coase, 1960).

It seems that during the campaign for the April 1947 regional election these two villagers had an argument in the village square about Vallera's anti-DC speeches. As a result, Caldera rescinded the grazing arrangement with Ceras; he would no longer permit any straying of Ceras's cattle. Several days later, in the early hours of the morning, Caldera passed through his land on the way to the Anzalo estate and discovered Ceras's sheep "all over his field." Both villagers apparently agreed "to fight it out" at a specific location sometime that day. It is not clear what "to fight it out" meant, however. But only Ceras went to the meeting place armed. When Caldera reached the spot, Ceras opened fire with his pistol. One of the shots killed Caldera. Fearing reprisal from the mafia, Ceras surrendered to the marshal of the carabinieri. He was later sentenced to life imprisonment but was set free many years later.

Leaders of the two compacts spread the word to their respective constituency that any provocation from the other side should be first reported to them. But, as in the case of the threshing incidents, such provocations were as difficult to resist as they were easy to provoke.

Interpersonal Relationships

In the analysis thus far, I have indicated how the exigencies of conflict between the two groups served to regulate and shape the conduct of the local political economy. Exigencies of conflict also came to dominate all other social calculations. Villagers abandoned efforts or strategies to maintain cordial or at least neutral relationships with each other. The critical variable that guided social intercourse among kin and neighbors in the postwar period was membership in one of the two political communities.

Relationships among members of the two political communities came to be based upon avoidance relations or what villagers characterized as "walls of silence." Thus blood relatives ceased to speak with one another. For instance, Novara's sister who was married to Vallera's brother severed relationships with her own family; Albano and his mafia uncle became estranged. Villagers earlier attached great value to maintaining good relations with the other villagers living in the same neighborhood; now they ceased to speak to and to help one another. Women who used to cooperate in many ways—from sharing utensils to fetching water and from "taking the sun" together to keeping the neighborhood streets clean—no longer did so. Similarly, children could play and even share the school benches only with other children whose parents belonged to the same political community. The village square now became divided between the territory of the mafia and the territory of the Left. There was no neutral space in the piazza, but one of the three cafes came to serve that purpose.

There were exceptions to these walls of silence, however. The local clergy, and particularly the priest Gaetano Ardena, were known to listen to, and to act upon, complaints from villagers of the other side against any member of the mafia society. Moreover, as indicated earlier, all villagers knew that it ran against the village norms of the old Camporano mafia for individuals like Ardena and Novara to deny help to any villager in strained circumstances. In fact, Ardena could always be so approached in the early hours of the morning on the sidewalk overlooking the village square. But such a course of action from Left adherents countervened one of the essential rules of the Left compact. There were, however, several such exceptional cases. One case involved an adjutant of Vallera who went as far as to rely on Ardena's automobile and driver when his wife needed to undergo an emergency operation in a Palermo hospital. It is cases such as this that veterans of the postwar struggles between the two compacts like to recall as "flashes of light" in an otherwise dark period of village life.

Conclusion

The vicissitudes of World War II provided the conditions for the reconstitution of the Camporano mafia as a lawful regime. But the conditions that provided unprecedented opportunities at self-rule soon gave rise to unprecedented limitations. The reemergence of local and Sicilian problems, suppressed or ignored during the Fascist era, together with the dominant position being acquired by new political groupings in the staging of postwar Sicilian and Italian affairs, made it extraordinarily difficult for villagers to maintain consensus about the old mafia system as the political instrumentality of the community. All the statecraft of the mafia leaders could neither insulate the local regime from the conflicting ideologies of Christian Democracy and socialism nor find a new concordia discors. Following "the 1944 mafia massacre," Camporanesi confronted two groups of villagers, each united as a family compact. Postwar life took place as these two political compacts threatened each other with extinction. In these circumstances, the village norms of humanitarianism and compassion probably spared Camporano mafiosi from becoming truly "violent peasant entrepreneurs" but could not prevent many villagers from being victimized. Other distinct but interrelated generalizations suggest themselves.

First, the Camporano mafia was organized and supported largely by people associated with the "caps" or those who were of true peasant origin. By contrast, the agents of the opposition who chose to use the political alliance of the Left came from the "hats" or the overseer and supervisory class in the old estate. The people of peasant origin placed greater emphasis upon self-reliance and tended to build their alliance with the church and Christian Democracy, "outside forces" with a record for respecting and promoting self-help; members of the overseer and supervisory class were more oriented toward securing the leverage to be derived from superior authority, and to do that required building a coalition with opposition elements in national politics. Moreover, it is possible for personalist or clientele compacts to be factions of principles or political ideas as well. The historical perspective of DC-mafia relationships, rather than mere "party clientelism," may go a long way in explaining contemporary Sicilian politics.

Second, for a majority of villagers the condition of political constraint of the mafia was maintained concurrently with a substantial measure of consensus about the legitimacy of actions taken on their behalf. Entrenched in their powers, mafia leaders treated local affairs only insofar as they could be turned into private profit for themselves and members of their political community. In this petty prosperity, they easily forgot and betrayed the very origins of the outlaw regime. As the old Camporano mafia came more and more to be an instrument of political privilege rather than an expression of primitive self-government, its dominant position in village affairs did indeed become more curious and more cruel than government itself. The postwar Camporano mafia thus fits and supports the conventional view of Sicilian mafia groups, but it was a criminal association that victimized the largest landowner as well as a minority of villagers.

Third, the willing support of the mafia system by a majority of villagers and the antimafia war waged by the Left joined together to fuse the interests of the mafia with the interests of the ruling party, to escalate the vicious circle of threats and counterthreats between members of the two political communities into a recurrent exchange of bads, and to reveal fully the internal disagreement and conflict that plagued the Left bloc itself. As this *guerre à outrance* came to dominate all other social calculations, the social cost inherent in maintaining the viability of the two compacts reached dramatic proportions to obscure and confound the exploited from the exploiters, the oppressors from the oppressed. This conclusion supports what has almost become a truism in social science. It is exceedingly difficult for groups locked in combat with one another not to tend to acquire similar characteristics.

Fourth, events surrounding the land struggles provide additional support for what Robert C. Fried in another context has described as "a general dilemma of the Italian Left: that its programs, involving massive intervention by public authorities, must depend for their execution on existing bureaucratic agencies in which the Left has little confidence and over which it has had little control" (Fried, 1973: 67). The same Sicilian events suggest an even more fundamental problem for the Left in the postwar period: that its cure for remedying the ills of Southern Italy appeared to many potential beneficiaries not better than the disease. Existing bureaucratic agencies can compound, but cannot always be blamed for, the difficulties Left programs and activists have had in succeeding as carriers or agents of positive change.

Finally, village life under the dual family compact was hardly an improvement over village life under the dual regime. Villagers—mafiosi and nonmafiosi alike—were trapped in a web of relationships that produced outcomes which they did not themselves value so highly as possible alternatives. For several reasons, then, postwar Camporano politics does not quite match the patrons and partisans model that emerges from the study of other Southern Italian *comuni.*

9

The New Order of
Village Relationships

In the immediate postwar period, leaders of the outlaw regime had successfully overcome several critical tests. They had met the defiance of
bandits and helped to restore peace and security to the Camporano
countryside; they had solved the problem of what to do with irreconcilable opposition and surmounted the challenge posed by the local Left
bloc in agricultural and communal activities. The complete correspondence or fusion with the Demochristian party reaffirmed and sustained
these efforts. The judicial proceedings for the 1944 armed incident
were still on, but the relationship with the ruling party posed little
threat from state officials. Though the old Camporano mafia had come
more and more to approximate and fit the conventional image of a Sicilian mafia group, its dominant position in Camporano life seemed
indestructible.

Yet the collapse of the Camporano mafia began at the very time when
it appeared so indestructible and, by the middle of the 1950s, the regime
that had weathered so many storms in the past collapsed suddenly and
catastrophically. This event was soon followed by the exhaustion of the
local Left bloc. The requirements of national and regional interparty and
intraparty politics served both to bring about the collapse of the two
groups and to clear the way for an *"effective presence"* (LaPalombara,

1971: 207) of the regionalist state in Camporano, some ten years after it was established in Sicily.

At the same time, the consequences of the conflict between the two family compacts led villagers to reorient their search beyond the world around Camporano for ways to cope with the contingencies of life for themselves and their families. Legally trapped in the village by some Fascist laws that still remained in force, Camporanesi ignored those laws and began to exit illegally. Thus the collapse of the two groups was accompanied and reinforced by what became known as "the hemorrhage of emigration" or simply "the exodus." In the solitude of strange cities on and beyond the Italian continent, Camporanesi from both compacts buried their enmity and learned to appreciate anew the village, but also universal, norms of mutual help and mutual respect.

The changes of the period profoundly altered the conditions of life of those who remained behind. By the middle of the 1970s, almost all the Camporano residents possessed, or had within affordable reach, amenities of modern life. Such an equality in material well-being or in access to desired consumer goods is unexampled in the two-hundred-year history of Camporano and even unimaginable to villagers who, thirty years ago, left Camporano never to return. Yet these very signs of progress have served to place in sharp relief other features of modernity. The regional government acquired an effective presence in Camporano precisely when the requirements of national and regional interparty and intraparty politics, while keeping its original form, were draining it of its substance—in essence, making the regionalist state work as an "imperial state." As ruling parties and ruling bureaucracies gained full hold of the Camporano structure of basic social institutions, villagers were pulled into a new order of relations that bore innumerable resemblances to village relationships of a century earlier. Once again villagers came to rely upon individualistic choice as a strategy in taking care of their individual and family welfare, in maintaining a favorable balance of good will with those who were friends, and in minimizing their exposure in dealing with others.

From the Family Compacts to the Imperial State

It is relatively difficult to pinpoint the dates of the collapse of the mafia and, correlatively, that of the Vallera group. It is clear, however, that whereas the mafia ceased to be a going concern by 1955, the Vallera group ceased to be a going concern by 1956. Available evidence permits one to piece together the salient features of the different and similar conditions that brought the authority structure of the two compacts beyond, in Albert O. Hirschman's words, "repairable lapses" (Hirschman, 1970: 1).

The Demochristian Party Displaces the Mafia

The complete correspondence or fusion of the mafia with the Demochristian party in 1948 served to give Ardena, Novara, and other mafia chiefs authority and influence as they never had before in peacetime but also served to undermine that autonomy and legitimacy of their concern. Entrenched in their powers, Camporano leaders do not seem to have discerned or realized their impending ruin—until it was too late.

By 1951, control over the organization and conduct of the regional Demochristian party had become a source of intraparty differences between such national Sicilian leaders as Salvatore Aldisio, Bernardo Mattarella, and Mario Scelba, and regional leaders such as Giuseppe Alessi and Franco Restivo. At issue was whether national leaders should have greater control over the regional party organization and whether the set of leaders that gained greater control over the regional party organization should also have greater say over the policies of the regional government, then headed by Restivo. These regional intraparty differences were, in turn, reinforced by national intraparty differences about De Gasperi's leadership as party secretary and prime minister. At issue was the nature of both the national party organization and the national government policies.

De Gasperi represented the dominant or centrist view that the DC should continue to rely upon the mass organizational support of the church hierarchy, large and small business associations, and spontaneous local civic groups. Governmental policies should continue to be aimed first of all at insuring an interparty anti-communist movement for the preservation of parliamentary democracy. A circle of mainly second-generation Demochristian leaders ranging from Amintore Fanfani to Aldo Moro contended, instead, that the party should cease to be a sort of aggregative federation of diverse groups and become an autonomous, independent, and capillary organization in order to compete with the Communist party. Drawing upon the theories of Keynes and Beveridge as

186

well as papal encyclicals, these second-generation Demochristians proposed a policy of reform and modernization both to meet social and economic problems and to preserve parliamentary democracy from Communist avalanches (see Galli, 1978: 97–151; Galli and Prandi, 1970: 79–80; Zariski, 1965: 7–9).

The superimposition of regional and national intraparty differences produced a matrix of intraparty factions in Sicily that both reinforced and cut across regional and national divisions (Di Fresco, 1976: 32–47). If questions of principles go a long way in accounting for the rise of intraparty divisions, exigencies of intraparty rivalry, or the logic of the system, soon colored and infused those divisions with "interest" or "convenience" factionalism (Sartori, 1971). The case of "the Camporano deputies" reveals how and why this transformation took place.

By 1952 the national and regional deputies supported by the Ardena group had become members of the complex matrix of DC intraparty factions. Melchiorre Perez adhered to the dominant centrist faction headed in Sicily by Scelba, minister in the national government, and by Restivo, president of the regional government. Salvatore Cedro belonged to the minority Left faction headed in Sicily by national deputy Mattarella and regional deputy Giuseppe La Loggia. The position of the other two Camporano deputies, Emanuele Altura and Nunzio Lozano, cut across the centrist and Left factions. Altura shared Perez's position on governmental policies and Cedro's position on the party organization but placed more value on the autonomy of action of regional Demochristian leaders. Lozano agreed with Cedro's position on both the organization and policies of the Demochristian party but, like Altura, placed more value on the autonomy of action of regional party leaders. Because of these overlapping interests, Altura and Lozano came together to support a third faction being established within the Demochristian party in Sicily, that of national deputy and minister Salvatore Aldisio and of regional deputy and minister Giuseppe Alessi.

Camporano national and regional representatives thus developed powerful incentives to secure and strengthen their individual basis of support among Camporano villagers. Two other factors contributed to the spread of "the politics of factions" (Zuckerman, 1979). Deputies like Cedro and Perez had become relatively well known among Camporano residents to be able to dispense with "letters of introduction" from local mafiosi in order to reach or be reached by villagers. At the same time, by relying less on, and by not being seen with, people like Ardena, the

187

same deputies also aimed to reduce their exposure to Left charges of conniving with the mafia (cf. Alessi, 1949; Barrese, 1973: 16–22; Li Causi, 1966: 210–211). Moreover, the cases of Cedro and Lozano suggest how, by advancing the interest of their factions, they helped to undermine the spirit of local patriotism and self-reliance that characterized and sustained the old Camporano mafia.

For example, Cedro, as a member of the DC parliamentary group that claimed to represent the interests of peasants, directed his efforts toward establishing a Camporano direct cultivators association linked with the DC national Confederation of Direct Cultivators led by Paolo Bonomi (see also LaPalombara, 1964: 236–246; Sacco, 1955). The establishment of the peasant association sometime before 1952 received the support of mafia leaders, and a peasant relative of Ardena became its first president. But it was clear that the potential benefits Camporano cultivators stood to gain from the association derived more from their electoral support of Cedro and Cedro's parliamentary activities on their behalf and less from their association with and support of Ardena, Novara, and other mafia chiefs. Such was the case, for example, when sometime before the end of 1952 members of this peasant association received a newsletter from Cedro describing, correctly, how Communist and Socialist efforts in the parliamentary committee on labor and social security had blocked his and Bonomi's bills seeking to extend the provisions of the national compulsory insurance against sickness and disease to direct cultivators.

Nunzio Lozano engaged in somewhat similar calculations. In 1952, he called Liborio Imera, a relative of Novara, to the regional ministry he was heading in Palermo. Already in the 1951 regional elections Imera, then a university student, had demonstrated his organizational skills by helping to manage Lozano's campaign throughout the Mozarra district. As regional minister and faction leader, Lozano needed capable assistants like Imera both to help supervise the work of former colonial administrators assigned to the regional bureaucracy by the central government and to maintain close links with communal officials and voters in the Camporano area.

The spread of factionalism coincided with and was accompanied by efforts on the part of the DC provincial secretary to assert his authority over the composition of the Camporano DC list in the 1952 communal election. At the same time the provincial secretary's concern for less visible candidates corresponded with the need by mafia leaders to put together a slate of candidates with a high probability of success. However, the claim and exercise of final authority over Camporano DC affairs by the Mozarra Demochristian official underscored the fact that Camporano leaders no longer possessed autonomous authority in party and communal activities.

In sum, the requirements of Demochristian party life had by 1952 led to the development of more inclusive loyalties among leaders and supporters of the local mafia. This development stood to displace altogether local patriotism and self-reliance that—however transformed into perverse manifestation now—were still the very foundation and strength of the Camporano mafia. Yet, the consequences of Demochristian intraparty rivalry were not yet felt, as the momentum of success in agricultural and communal affairs carried the local regime forward.

The DC slogans and speeches in the 1953 national election echoed those of the two previous national elections. Behind the facade of familiar campaign appeals urging the strengthening of De Gasperi's centrist government and designed for interparty rivalry, Demochristian supporters and sympathizers faced for the first time another set of appeals resulting from intraparty rivalry. Following the 1952 national DC congress, the Left minority faction organized "a party within a party" by the name of Democratic Initiative. Now members of the various DC factions intensified their preemptive activities in order to secure dominant positions in the future national government. The intensification of intraparty rivalry in Sicily was reflected in the Mozarra area in the competitive rivalry among Altura, Cedro, and Perez.

By Easter Sunday, two months before the 1953 national election, the Camporano deputies were pressing leaders of the mafia to take sides. But, already by that time, intraparty differences had so penetrated the political community of the Ardena compact that the choice of any leader to act as an electoral agent for a particular set of candidates had little or no prospect for emerging and being enforced as a group decision. Ardena was being pulled by "ancient PPI loyalties" to support Altura. Novara was having difficulties in reconciling his preference for the centrist position represented by Perez and the Sicilian position represented by Altura. Though Ardena and Novara no longer supported Cedro, other mafia chiefs still preferred him over the others. The local midwife and health officer had already declared their unconditional loyalty to Cedro, openly disagreeing with Ardena and Novara. Moreover, the political community had become divided equally between those who favored the

189

faction represented by Altura and Lozano and those who favored the Democratic Initiative faction represented by Cedro. Support for Cedro was particularly strong and intense among members of the DC peasant association he had helped to establish.

It was only at this juncture that apparently Ardena, Novara, and other mafia chiefs discerned the way events were shaping and the ruin that threatened their going concern. They attempted to reduce the opposition of interests and to enhance the mutuality of interests among themselves and their political community, with little success. Not even the conciliatory skills of the local clergy, Gaetano Ardena included, could check the claims of more inclusive loyalties from taking full and complete precedence over those toward the local regime. The local patriotism and self-reliance that the old Camporano mafia promoted had passed away even among mafia leaders. The encapsulation of the outlaw regime by the Demochristian party was such that before the electoral campaign was over, the Ardena group slithered into the same vortex of internecine conflict that had plagued the Left bloc since 1946. But, whereas common agreement was not a necessary condition for the Left group, the very authority pattern of the Camporano mafia derived from and was built upon a calculus of consent. As a result, while the absence of consensus had failed to dissolve the local Left bloc, the breakdown of consensus among mafia chiefs and their constituency of supporters melted the very innards of the mafia system.

The electoral results did not radically affect the fortunes of the various Demochristian candidates acquired in the 1946 and 1948 elections. But the electoral campaign revealed and finalized the inner and unavoidable decadence of the old Camporano mafia. The architects and builders of what had once been a network of community organizations were thus left with the shreds and tatters of a broken "family." Giving a sense of timeliness to this chain of events, Mariano Ardena died of old age. Thus the Camporano mafia appeared to have lasted as long as Ardena, even though it was in ruins before his death.

Novara pressed into service all his personal contacts in the Demochristian party to succeed in becoming a member of the central committee of the Mozarra DC federation. Novara sought to rely upon that strategic position as a point d'appui for maintaining the mafia system. In effect, this was how Vallera was sustaining his authority among Left adherents. But Novara's elevation to the provincial DC federation occurred at the very time when the control of the provincial and regional party organization was changing from the centrist or De Gasperi group to the Democratic Initiative or Fanfani group. As the new party secretary, Fanfani turned to the task of translating into reality the Democratic Initiative conception of the DC as an autonomous, independent, and capillary organization capable of competing on its own terms with Left parties. In such "organizational renewal" (Galli and Prandi, 1970: 82) there was, however, no place for individuals like Novara. Not before long, Novara ceased to be a member of the central committee of the DC provincial organization. The replacement of the centrist control over the DC by the Fanfani group sealed the end of the Camporano mafia.

Divested of political power, Novara and other mafia leaders no longer felt bound by their obligations toward their political community. Hence they began to use their strategic positions in communal and agricultural activities to advance their individual welfare without taking into account the welfare of others—in effect, by abandoning even the pretension or self-deception of being profitable altruists. Novara succeeded in having himself appointed "technical adviser" to the Camporano commune, amid the protest of four DC councilors who by the summer of 1955 resigned. In this new position, Novara acquired a reputation that helped to destroy almost completely his prestige among villagers, without in any way halting the collapse of mafia fortunes. In 1956, he was charged with fraud. As president of the Cooperative of War Veterans, he was alleged to have exacted extra sums of money from Mogata cultivators as part of the emphyteusis leases they were paying. In part for this reason the Mozarra prefect ordered the disbandment of the cooperative in 1958. The complete end of profitable altruism swept away the final or last residues of the Camporano mafia system.

The chain of events came to a close in 1958 when a high court found Ardena, Novara, council chief Uria, and several mafia soldiers responsible for the 1944 incident and sentenced each to six years in prison. While Ardena had already been set free by death, those still living were set free as a result of a general amnesty from the president of the Republic. Also by this time, Mariano Ardena's priest brother died. His death signaled the collapse of the church as a political influence in Camporano life. Having become an appendage of the mafia and, ultimately, a ward of the ruling party, the Camporano ecclesiastical authority ceased to be the great force it was in the nineteenth century. Though individual priests like Archpriest Pietro Valle continued to have some influence in Demochristian party politics until the middle of the 1960s, the Cam-

191

porano church no longer possessed an independent and even credible moral authority in modern Camporano public life.

The Loss of Raison d'Être by the Camporano Left Compact

The collapse of the mafia deprived the Left group of an essential raison d'être. But the villagers who had earlier denounced, and sought to vanquish, the Camporano mafia now were the same persons who had considerable stake in keeping it alive. As a former principal adjutant of Vallera now freely admits, "By 1954 we needed the mafia more than the DC did." But another chain of events helped to bring the exhaustion of the Left compact beyond repairable lapses.

By the early 1950s, the outside conditions that maintained the viability of the Vallera group in the face of internal disagreement and conflict were subject to increased stresses and strains. With the defeat of the Popular Front in the 1948 national elections, some Socialist leaders began to fear that the continuation of the Popular Front would lead to the encapsulation and absorption of the PSI by the PCI—a trend already discernible in the trade-union movement. By the early 1950s, these Socialists organized themselves into an autonomist current and succeeded in convincing the party national secretary, Pietro Nenni, to run independent party lists wherever elections were held under proportional representation. The 1953 electoral results revealed that, since 1946, the PSI had lost almost a million and a half votes while the PCI had gained almost two million votes. The very survival of the Socialist party necessarily implied the breakup of "the unity of the working-class parties." It was not until after the publication of Khrushchev's secret report on *The Crimes of the Stalin Era* to the Twentieth Congress of the Soviet Communist party and the suppression of the Hungarian uprising in 1956 that a PSI congress formally abolished the unity-of-action pact with the PCI. But, by 1955 the national Popular Front was already moribund. In the spring of 1955, the PSI congress endorsed Nenni's offer of collaboration to Demochristian leaders for a DC Opening to the Left. A first sign of this collaboration was evident in the very same year when Nenni mobilized his party's support behind, and negotiated with, DC leaders for the election of Giovanni Gronchi, the DC president of the Chamber of Deputies, as president of the Republic (see Kogan, 1966: 95–102).

As evidence of the disintegrating Left unity in Camporano, local Communists like to recall that already by 1955 they had ceased to share the

192

same headquarters with the local PSI. But the breakup of the working-class unity at the local level, unlike that at the national level, gave local Communist leaders an opportunity to assert their autonomy and independence from the Socialist party. From now on, Vallera could neither assert his hegemonic authority over local Communist officials nor present his group as the vanguard of the Left in Camporano.

Some thirty Mogata tenants dispossessed of their lots had, at the urging of Vallera, sought legal remedies against both the Mogata proprietor and the president of the Cooperative of War Veterans. In 1954, while the legal claims of these villagers as well as the counterclaims of Princess Gardena-Manresa and Novara were still under consideration by Mozarra judicial officials, the regional minister of agriculture declared void the private land reform of Mogata and approved plans to divide the former fief according to criteria of land parcelization, then being discussed in the regional assembly. The minister's decisions acquired legal standing when they were published in the regional *Gazzetta Ufficiale* that summer, but Gardena-Manresa and Novara successfully appealed them as the question was still sub judice.

Sometime in 1956, the courts ruled in favor of maintaining the present division and cultivation of the Mogata estate until the regional assembly and the national parliament clarified and harmonized the terms and conditions of their respective laws concerning rural property, land tenure, and agrarian reform. It was not until the early 1960s that the uncertainties concerning the regional land reform were removed somewhat. But, following the 1956 judicial decision, Left peasants, who had refused land from mafiosi, were now definitely without land to farm. Moreover, those who had also challenged the private land reform were now further burdened with judicial expenses. A threnody of regret and of helplessness followed as the shattered Left adherents recalled their adamantine reliance upon Vallera's judgment. They concluded that they had been cozened by Vallera to refuse land from, and to seek legal recourse against, Novara and others just to serve as his "projectiles" against the mafia. These villagers' conclusion was unfair to Vallera, but the circumstances were such that it was easier to blame an individual than a bad law. However, it was difficult for regional legislators to come up with a land reform law that under the circumstances could not but be, in Hobbes's words, a "trap for money" (1651: 254).

Vallera and his principal aides attempted to overcome the disintegration of their concern in at least two ways. First, Vallera prevailed upon

193

PSI regional leaders to allow him to run in the 1955 regional election for the Camporano area district. Second, he encouraged a social activist from another town to do community-action work in the Camporano area. The success of either effort was expected to give a new raison d'être to the Left compact. But Vallera was not elected. In turn, most Camporano Left adherents refused to give their support to a community development group that appeared to shore up Vallera's authority.

Thus no effort could avoid the dissolution of the Left compact. This did not mean the collapse of socialism as such, for many villagers still remained loyal to their ideals. At the same time, the collapse of the Vallera united front took place precisely when there was increasing dissatisfaction among villagers about Demochristian control of communal affairs and when the Communist alternative represented by Albano was suffering a setback from events taking place in Eastern Europe. As a result, in the May 1956 communal election the slate of Socialist candidates presented by Vallera obtained 44 percent of the votes, an increase of 10 percent in Left support since the 1952 election. Though this electoral showing failed to dislodge the DC group from the commune, it helped to reveal fully the end of the Left compact. The increase in PSI votes had come, in part, from villagers whose past association with or support of the Camporano mafia had secured them sufficient rates of return or benefits to remain in the village while many of the early adherents to the Left compact had by 1956 been compelled by the very success of the Camporano mafia to "vote with their feet" (Tiebout, 1956).

Chain Migration as Exit from the Two Compacts

In the immediate postwar period some villagers are reported to have emigrated to North America in part to avoid the exigencies of conflict between the two opposing camps. By the early 1950s, the departure of villagers became a veritable "hemorrhage of emigration." The end of the warring compacts was accompanied and reinforced by the exit of villagers from Camporano.

"The American roots" in the village established by the previous chain migration were reactivated to ease what Cronin titled *The Sting of Change* (Cronin, 1970; see also Zimmerman, 1955). Between 1952 and 1956, at least two hundred Camporanesi are reported to have emigrated to places like Montreal, Quebec; Trenton, New Jersey; and Rochester, New York. Those who did not have relatives who could sponsor their

194

move to North America oriented their search for "bread and work" toward West European cities such as Munich and Zurich. Italian cities closer to the French and Swiss border were expected to be places for villagers to prepare for the last trek—where they could acquire new occupational skills, useful foreign words and, if necessary, forged papers for crossing the borders. Yet, because of existing laws against internal migration, villagers could not reside in cities like Como, Milan, San Remo, or Turin. They were legally trapped in Camporano. As a result, local residents ignored these laws and began to exit illegally (see also Fried, 1967: 510; Galtung, 1962).

Between 1952 and 1956, there were at least one thousand villagers who left the village illegally. It is not clear how many reached their European destinations, however. Some, in fact, never crossed the Alps. Once settled in North Italian cities, villagers began to call others. This chain migration became of great concern to communal and trade-union officials in North Italy who feared that the presence of "foreigners" like Camporanesi would alter the social fabrics of their communities, magnify the already inadequate provision of public services, and threaten occupational opportunities of local workers (see also Anfossi, 1962; Cavalli, 1964). Hence, Northern officials urged a strict application of existing legislation against internal migration and labor mobility. In 1955, the mayor of a Northern city near the French border took the unprecedented step of writing directly to the mayor of Camporano urging him to tell the local population to "stop once and for all flocking" to his city. In 1956 the police chief for the Mozarra province urged the Camporano mayor to initiate "an intense propaganda and persuasion campaign" to emphasize the risks and difficulties that villagers faced in exiting from Camporano. Though the police surveillance units experienced problems in enforcing antimigration laws, at least eight Camporanesi living illegally in North Italian cities are reported to have been apprehended during police dragnets and forcibly repatriated to Camporano by 1956.

Public exhortations, legal impediments, and even forced repatriation did not, however, stop the exit of villagers from Camporano. By 1958, leading protagonists of postwar village life like Albano, Novara, and Vallera sought a better future elsewhere. The laws against internal migration and labor mobility were finally repealed in 1961 (Ribolzi, 1962). But by that time, a new census revealed that the residents of Camporano were not more than thirty-five hundred—a decrease of some fifteen hundred residents since 1951.

195

The Affirmation of the Imperial State

Electoral politics in Sicily and the formation and conduct of successive regional governments became subject to electoral and legislative requirements of national government coalitions. Moreover, the establishment of regional ministries to coincide with the central government ministries was accompanied by a transfer of state administrative personnel to the regional bureaucracy. Faced with the requirements of national party politics and the problems of bureaucratic dysfunctions, Demochristian regional officials proceeded by 1953 to transform the regional bureaucracy into a workplace for party functionaries. As was observed in the discussion of the displacement of the mafia group by the Demochristian party, among these party functionaries was a Camporano villager, Liborio Imera, who was eventually assigned to "the regional ministry of the interior." The informal and personal networks that developed among officials of ruling coalitions cut across ideological and intergovernmental barriers to become fairly responsive to the articulation of demands for services by citizens and communal officials (cf. Di Palma, 1977a: 268–271; Serio, 1966a). Thus patterns of intergovernmental relations among central, regional, and communal authorities took on the appearance of a "pluralist" or polycentric rather than a consolidated, monocentric ordering. But this polycentricity accrued from informal efforts to overcome dysfunctions in consolidated and hierarchic levels of government and *not* from a design of self-governing, independent levels of government with overlapping jurisdictions—in effect, making a vice of what under federalism is often a virtue (cf. Barnes, 1976; Elazar, 1977; V. Ostrom, 1972; Tarrow, 1974).

With the "organizational renewal" (Galli and Prandi, 1970: 82) brought about by the capture of the DC organization by the Democratic Initiative faction in 1954, the new party secretary, Amintore Fanfani, sought to control, through a chain of subordinate officials, local, provincial, and regional Demochristian as well as governmental activities in Sicily. By 1958, Fanfani appeared to have achieved this aim. He was not only party secretary but also prime minister as well as minister for foreign affairs. He seemed to be, in the words of one observer, "the real boss of Italy" (Ottone, 1966: 110). In that year, however, some regional Demochristian deputies refused to recognize the party central executive's claim to designate the head of the Demochristian regional government and were expelled from the party. These events led to a constitu-

196

ency revolt which, in turn, gave rise to an independent Sicilian Catholic Social party led by Silvio Milazzo (Chilanti, 1959). By the end of 1958, the program of this new group, known pejoratively as *Milazzismo*, was attracting sizable grass-roots support throughout the Mozarra area. In Camporano at least seventy-five persons resigned from the DC to become members of the nascent autonomist party.

At the regional level, leaders of this new Sicilian party proceeded to form a coalition government with Communists, Socialists, Monarchists, and Neofascists. Whereas on the Italian mainland this alliance was deemed "unnatural" and seen as proof of Sicilian political immaturity, in Sicily it was seen as a rejection of the national ruling coalition and as an expression of a common interest for Sicilian home rule (see *Economist*, 1958; Renton, 1959; Macaluso, 1970: 75–124; cf. Kogan, 1959; Mack Smith, 1974: 144; Serio, 1966b: 81–84). This fundamental identity of interests reaching across a very diverse array of regional legislators gave rise to the possibility of a political stalemate between the central government and the regional government that would have provided the conditions for a reformulation of Sicilian autonomy.

By the spring of 1959, this Sicilian revolt provided an opportunity to third-generation members of the Democratic Initiative faction to challenge the position that second-generation Democratic Initiative members had acquired within the DC party with Fanfani as party secretary, prime minister, and foreign minister. Fanfani was forced to resign from all three posts. By the end of the same year, the continued dependence of some regional party organizations composing the regional government coalition on central party headquarters joined with negotiations for a national Opening to the Left by the new Demochristian leaders to undermine the possibility of a political stalemate between the central government and the regional government.

By 1960, the unnatural alliance collapsed. In 1961, the legislative support of the Socialist (PSI) regional party organization served both to reestablish Demochristian hegemony over the formation and conduct of Sicilian regional government and to open the way for the Opening to the Left. This Opening to the Left in Sicily and on the continent was expected to initiate a policy of institutional reform. Instead, it served to extend the dominant position of the Demochristian party and factions over the machinery of the regionalist state in Sicily to the Socialist party and factions (Serio, 1967; see also Rizzi, 1974).

A constituency revolt within one party organization was insufficient to

197

establish regional autonomy in the formation of regional governing coalitions. As long as the hegemony of central party headquarters and factions prevailed over a majority of regional party organizations and as long as the central bureaucracy prevailed over the regional bureaucracy, it was difficult to alter the structure of regional government (cf. Maranini, 1969; Pignatone, 1973). Thus the collapse of the dual family compact in Camporano resulted from and was accompanied by the affirmation of the imperial state in Sicily. And it is against this backdrop that modern village life has taken place.

The Reconstitution of Communal and Party Politics

The reconstitution of Camporano communal and party politics that followed the transition from the dual family compact to the ruling parties and ruling bureaucracies was characterized by several factors. First, there was the village normative or belief system that assigned a high value for the respect of every individual as a human being and for social and political equality among villagers. Common agreement and mutual adjustment were regarded as necessary conditions for approximating optimality in social relationships. The high regard that present-day villagers still have for the defunct Camporano mafia is in large measure a reflection of the extent to which it was constituted and worked according to these community, but also universalistic, norms.

Second, the operation of communal government provided villagers with their only opportunity to shape events within their grasp. Yet the structure of communal government in the regionalist state was still organized in such a way as to suppress the practice of common agreement and mutual adjustment in favor of a centrality of communal decisions. In spite of some changes in the structure of Sicilian communal government in the early 1950s, the mayor and the communal government as a whole still remained, in the words of an Italian constitutional scholar, "in a state of legal incapacity" (Miele, 1956) in relation to the production and delivery of most public services. Communal authorities continued to have no essential control over the national and regional bureaucracies as they operated at the local level.

Third, the displacement of the mafia by the Demochristian party and the breakup of the Left bloc were accompanied by sharpened and exten-

198

sive readjustment in party politics. Former members of the defunct mafia compact were now fully and without any local counterpoise integrated in the Demochristian party factions. Former members of the defunct Left compact ranged across a party spectrum that included the Social Democratic, Neofascist and, by the late 1960s, the Proletarian Socialist (PSIUP) parties—providing the conditions for Vallera and Albano to reassert their influence over the loyalist PSI and PCI adherents, respectively. The Opening to the Left in the early 1960s gave powerful incentives to Imera and Vallera to monitor and intervene in Camporano politics as members of both the ruling parties and ruling bureaucracies. A discussion of communal elections and communal government illustrates how the complex interweave of village norms for social relationships, the design of local government institutions, and the interaction between local, regional, and national party activities shaped modern Camporano political authority.

Communal Elections

Between the middle of the 1950s and the early 1970s, there were four communal elections—in 1960, 1964, 1968, and 1973. In each case, the Demochristian party lists received a plurality of votes and retained control of the communal government. The erosion of DC electoral support registered in the 1956 communal election continued, however. By 1964, the DC list gained a majority of communal seats with a plurality of thirteen votes; in 1968, this plurality was reduced to only three votes, to increase to thirty-two votes in 1973. Faced with this growing erosion, more and more outside Demochristian officials descended on the village to campaign on behalf of the local DC list. The regional ministry for communal affairs became, like the prefecture used to be in pre-Fascist times, the chief electoral agency of the ruling national and regional coalition.

The declining support for the DC communal lists from one election to another was due to the very conduct of succeeding DC groups as they became the communal government. Yet the continued control of communal government by successive DC lists was due principally to the extent to which the fiercely rivalrous DC officials charged with the preparation of slates of candidates were able to reconcile the requirements to organize combinations of voters sufficient to win elections with the need to meet the conditions of common agreement and mutual adjustment among DC factions and sympathizers. Though villager Liborio Imera from the re-

199

gional ministry of the interior exercised dominant influence in local DC affairs as the chief vote getter or "mushroom picker" for the Fanfani faction throughout the 1960s and the 1970s, he seldom imposed his authority to exclude candidates who supported other DC factions. In fact, most mayoral candidates tended to support third-generation Demochristians, the so-called *dorotei* center-right group represented by Cedro.

By contrast, leaders of the opposition parties did not or could not reconcile the requirements for a minimum winning coalition with national interparty differences. For example, in 1960 the sensing of opinion among villagers indicated strong dissatisfaction with the Demochristian communal government. Vallera, who had returned from the city to prepare the PSI slate of candidates, and the local PCI secretary, representing Albano, could not agree among themselves about the composition of a joint or civic list. In turn, each Left leader was precluded from entering into an electoral alliance with the very small group of MSI supporters who had remained loyal to the Fascist ideals of their youth.

As a result, there were three opposition lists in the 1960 election—the PSI, MSI, and a PCI-organized civic group. Though the PSI and the PCI lists together obtained 58 percent of the popular vote, the electoral law transformed the simple plurality of DC votes, 38 percent, into an 80 percent Demochristian representation on the communal council. Vallera, his brother, and two other Socialist candidates were elected opposition councilors. In the first communal meeting, it became somewhat clear why the Socialist group had earlier refused to be part of a joint Left list. Nicola Vallera proposed a Demochristian and Socialist coalition government as a means of anticipating the regional and national Demochristian Opening to the Left. The Demochristian majority flatly rejected his offer of collaboration but a less probable offer could have been scarcely imagined since the DC majority included three former mafia chiefs, Gesualdo Avola, Girolamo Mezzena, and Placido Perosa. As a result, Vallera's Opening to the DC, though in line with national PSI policy, was used by the local Communists as evidence that local Socialist leaders were prepared to betray their past in order to become part of the governing class.

It was not until the 1968 communal elections that, for the first time since 1956, villagers were confronted with only one slate of opposition candidates—a PCI-PSI civic list headed by Salvatore Albano who, perhaps for the first time since the early 1950s, had returned from Palermo to take charge of the local PCI campaign. In 1967, a revolt against the mayor among Demochristian councilors forced the disbandment of the council.

200

A joint Communist-Socialist list in 1968 was thus expected to benefit from internal Demochristian disagreement and to wrest the commune from "DC clutches." However, in preparing the Left ticket, Albano and local Socialist leaders failed to consult Vallera who, by that time, had left the PSI to run, successfully, for the regional assembly on the Communist party list. Thus while Camporano Socialists were not obliged to consult him, Camporano Communists were. But since Vallera's election to the regional assembly had been imposed on Mozarra area Communists by central party headquarters, Camporano PCI leaders used the local election to show their displeasure of PCI national leaders by excluding Vallera from having any say in the preparation of the joint Left list. This chain of events led Vallera, in turn, to characterize the Camporano Left ticket as "full of mafiosi" and to urge his loyalist supporters to vote for the DC list. The PCI-PSI electoral alliance fell short of winning the election by only three votes, making Vallera's withdrawal of support appear clearly responsible for the Left defeat. The Camporano commune continued to be in "the clutches" of the Demochristian party.

Communal Government as Mayoral Philanthropy

Communal elections, without the two warring compacts, provided each villager with a definite opportunity to air his views, to influence the preparation of different slates of candidates, and to choose the communal council. Yet the election of the communal council was but an empty show of freedom; communal councils have no real authority. For though village norms require common agreement as a basis for joint action, the design of communal government permitted a newly elected mayor to see himself with sufficient competence and authority to take unilateral actions and to expect routine approval for his actions from the majority councilors. For though the mayor could give voice to his and the council's wishes for essential public services, he had neither the authority for putting them into effect nor the control over the regional and national public service delivery systems. Thus the pomp of communal office was accompanied by a benevolent despotism without legal powers. Under these conditions, each mayor attempted to conceal or reduce his legal incapacity by pressing his authority over communal affairs in order to satisfy the preferences of individual villagers and by relying upon his relationship with leaders of the governing party in order to raid the public treasury of superior levels of government—in effect, by transforming

201

communal and intergovernmental activities into mayoral philanthropy.

One manifestation of mayoral philanthropy involved issuing communal documents or papers to villagers. Communal papers—from birth to death certificates to statements of celibacy and profession—are essential prerequisites for dealing with national and regional bureaucracies and private companies. Villagers, including those residing in other parts of Italy, must rely on such papers for an array of activities ranging from employment applications to educational opportunities; expatriate villagers, in fact, like to think of communal papers as the chain that links them to Camporano for life even though they may never return there (cf. Sciascia, 1969: 70). Until the early 1970s, communal certificates were also required especially for mules and horses. Caught in an almost constant need of communal papers, villagers tended to turn to the mayor to insure prompt and accurate service from communal employees. In turn, this is a domain of jurisdiction that permits any mayor to demonstrate unhesitatingly both his command of the communal bureaucracy and his responsiveness to villagers' requests. In the early 1970s, it was not uncommon for people going to the commune to observe the then mayor, Calogero Sala, preparing these papers himself. During his mayoralty his office became a sort of referral agency for all sorts of issues and problems villagers faced in dealing with higher levels of government.

Intergovernmental relations revealed other examples of mayoral entrepreneurship. The communal taxing power, involving local property, consumption, and family taxes, has generally been insufficient to generate revenues to cover the operating expenses of the Camporano commune. Faced with this problem, each mayor found it easier to convince national and regional officials that he needed more public funds than to convince villagers that the benefits from additional local taxes would exceed costs. Whereas in the early 1960s state subventions covered almost half of the annual communal expenditures (some forty million lire), by the early 1970s state subventions covered the entire annual communal expenditures (some eighty million lire). At the same time, the availability of state and regional "functional" and "bloc" grants designed to get communal governments to undertake actions they could not otherwise undertake contributed to enhance mayoral philanthropy as well as to distort local needs and priorities.

During the 1960s, Camporano acquired, among other things, a public rest room, a modern slaughterhouse, and a sewage treatment plant. But, by the end of the 1970s, these public works projects were still in disuse for lack of water or operating funds (cf. LaPalombara, 1966: 45, 119). In the early 1970s, mayor Sala found it easier to obtain public funds for the "beautification" of village streets with palm trees and flowers and for the construction of an aqueduct to tap Camporano water springs all villagers knew were not of potable quality than for other more pressing local priorities. As a result, the commune continued to be short of rooms; some of the streets behind the village square, originally paved fifty years earlier, remained badly in need of repairs; the road leading to the cemetery was still the old *trazzera* or sheep walk, and the old aqueduct, which already in 1965 had been found inadequate by a public health inspector, could not be repaired for lack of appropriate funds. By 1978, the new aqueduct was still inoperative because of the poor water quality, while the small dose of water received from the Sicilian Water Agency had become a trickle because of lack of repairs on existing water mains and pipes.

In the early 1970s, there began another kind of mayoral philanthropy—the expansion of the public employment rolls as part of the new regional policy aimed at modernizing communal bureaucracies. Whereas until 1972 there was just one communal guard charged with the enforcement of local ordinances, upon his retirement in 1973, three young villagers were hired to replace him. Two were from the *doroteo* faction and one was from the friends of Fanfani faction, appropriately reflecting *The Politics of Faction* (Zuckerman, 1979) that took place in the Camporano Demochristian group. Whereas in 1952 there were two municipal guards for a population of about five thousand, in 1974 there were three municipal guards for a population half that number—without, however, any noticeable benefits for the population as a whole.

The state functional and bloc grants did, however, provide short-term employment opportunities to villagers, and it is in this sense that the transformation of intergovernmental relations into mayoral philanthropy was most beneficial. As a result, during the course of the 1960s and 1970s, succeeding mayors tended to interpret the preferred state of communal affairs in terms of their own philanthropy—while pressing local issues remained unsolved.

The confusion of communal and intergovernmental activities with mayoral philanthropy evoked, however, contradictory responses from communal councilors and supporters of the majority party to generate both frustration and ill-will among all villagers. Whereas communal councilors tended to plot and intrigue against an incumbent mayor for both his "dictatorial powers" and his inaction on local issues and problems, villagers tended to support the same mayor for both his efforts to meet the requests of individual villagers and his ability to derive some success from the game of grantsmanship with regional and national government agencies. Whereas communal councilors tended to inveigh against "ignorant" villagers for their support of an incumbent mayor, villagers tended to inveigh against "rebellious" councilors for their efforts to unseat an incumbent mayor.

Since the collapse of the mafia, the conduct of communal affairs by successive DC mayors has been inherently unstable. Between 1956 and 1973, at least four mayors were forced to resign and the commune was taken over by regional functionaries. But, no sooner did a new mayor take office than he confronted the same issues and problems that had led the previous mayor to resign from office or withdraw from politics. While successive mayors, successive communal councilors and village residents continued to share a general concern for local needs and problems, the opportunities and constraints inherent in the design of governmental arrangements and in the logic of party politics have joined together to keep this general concern from being properly channeled into public or collective efforts—to remain, in Harold A. Innis's words (1936), an "unused capacity." In the early 1970s one could still hear old villagers recall the well-wishing phrase "May you become a mayor!" as a curse, just as their forefathers had done in the nineteenth century.

The Reconstitution of Agricultural Activities and the Modern Village Economy

As discussed in the preceding chapters, the history of the Camporano economy is essentially the history of land-based production and occupational activities. The collapse of the two compacts and the reconstitution of village relationships that followed pulled agricultural activities away from a zero-sum game but also undermined the very basis of the Camporano economy.

The uncertainty surrounding the private land reform of Mogata was put to rest in the early 1960s. In an effort to harmonize the differences between the 1950 Sicilian land reform act and the 1948 national legislation for the creation of viable family farms, the regional assembly finally passed a law in 1960 (law of July 27, 1960, no. 25) recognizing the superiority or supremacy of the 1948 national legislation over the 1950 land reform legislation—in effect, acknowledging the validity of the land reform carried out by Camporano mafiosi. At the same time, copyhold leases between cultivators and Princess Gardena-Manresa were rescinded, while the "rent" paid by cultivators was calculated as payment for the regional land agency encumbrance on the subdivided estate. Since many of the original Mogata assignees had either emigrated or ceased to be direct cultivators, the new law proceeded to make tenants or sharecroppers (*coloni, mezzadri,* or *affittuari*) farming Mogata lots for at least five years proprietors of the land they tilled. At least 191 of the 400 Mogata lots immediately changed ownership. Though the contradictory claims of the "old" and "new" proprietors of remaining lots still awaited final legal settlement as late as 1978, the Mogata fief, like other estates in neighboring territories, ceased to be a source of intense conflict for the first time since the 1830s.

The July 27, 1960, regional law that helped to regularize the former Mogata fief was part of a reordering of national land policy goals. By the end of the 1950s there was a general recognition that the postwar land reform laws had failed to realize their objectives in part because they had been based upon the incorrect assumptions that a large population should be maintained on the land (hence the continuance of Fascist laws against internal migration and rural mobility) and that there was sufficient land to be equitably shared by all who wanted to till it. Rapid industrialization was also attracting rural people to the urban areas (Franklin, 1969: 160). As a result, in 1959, the Demochristian-led national government formulated a Five-Year Plan for the Development of Agriculture, aimed at increasing productive efficiency. Enacted in 1961 and renewed in 1965 this plan, known as the Green Plan, amplified the 1948 law for the promotion of viable family farms by providing grants and cheap loans to farm operators and cooperatives for practically every kind of agricultural investment aimed at improving production—from the creation, consolidation or enlargement of farm units to new farm equipment (see McEntire and Agostini, 1969; Perez, 1971). Green Plans were, in turn, accompanied by other plans. Social security measures, including disability pensions, already effective in the industrial and governmental sectors, were fully extended to the agricultural sector as part of the conditions for the Socialist party entry into the national government (see Clark, 1977). A new share-tenancy law (law of September 15, 1964, no. 736) substantially enlarged the rights of tenants under existing contracts (see Scalini, 1976). Tenants were, in fact, given possession of the land for as long as they desired—a complete revolution from the share tenancy of a century earlier that had served to reduce tenants to a condition of serfdom. Rural land had changed, in Karl A. Wittfogel's words, from "strong property" to "weak property" (1957: 228).

All these changes aimed at keeping people on the land came too late, at least for Camporanesi. Remittances resulting from the hemorrhage of emigration and public aid resulting from mayoral philanthropy stimulated more service-oriented rather than land-based activities among Camporano residents during the 1960s. Following the relatively massive public capital input in the establishment of development poles in Sicily during the 1960s, many young Camporanesi succeeded in becoming or "were available to become" industrial workers or public enterprise employees. Never before had the interests and fortunes of Camporano individuals become so bound up with those of the state and, in effect, with those who controlled the instrumentalities of the state. With the Opening to the Left in the early 1960s, the Socialist party card became what the DC party card already was—a bread card (see also Evans, 1976: 90–91, 100–101; Hilowitz, 1976; Gross, 1973: 259–261).

The reduction in the village population and the rural work force was thus accompanied by a relative increase in both the inactive population and the so-called industrial work force. Whereas in 1951 the rural work force consisted of some 1,260 villagers (80 percent) of the entire active population of some 1,600 villagers, in 1961 it consisted of 650 villagers (55 percent) of a reduced work force of some 1,100 villagers. By 1971 those engaged in agricultural activities numbered not more than 349 (43 percent) out of a further reduced active population of about 800. The decrease in the rural work force takes on added meaning when the age group of those who continued to till the land is examined. By the early 1970s over 45 percent of the Camporano residents were over forty-five years old, as opposed to 20 percent in 1951. The agricultural work force consisted essentially of villagers, male and female, from this age group.

The extension of elementary schooling from grades five to eight, the knowledge of better employment opportunities in the industrial and public sector, gained in part through school, television, and expatriate and commuting villagers, had by 1971 led young villagers to turn away from the pursuit of agricultural activities. The Camporano farmer mentioned in chapter 2 as the only local producer of cheese predicted in 1972 that local cheese-making would end with him. In spite of the very steady and

206

high profit that such activity generated, not one young villager had shown an interest in cheese making. One of that farmer's sons developed such an "allergy" to milk animals that he even refused to sleep on mattresses or pillows made with home-spun sheep wool—long used by villagers as a measure of family means or refined manners—and slept on mattresses made with corn husks and pillows made with chicken feathers, long used by villagers as a measure of poverty or primeval manners. In May 1972, about one hundred schoolchildren almost unanimously described the rural work schedule as "a life of mud and beast." The overriding orientation toward agricultural work among young villagers in the early 1970s is best captured by Joseph Lo Preato's words, *Peasants no More!* (1967; see also Cornelisen, 1976: 126; *Corriere della Sera*, 1973).

As a result, 1978 communal data reveal a further decrease in the agricultural work force of Camporano. Yet, though agriculture has been declining as a viable means of supporting the local population, the 1978 communal data may not accurately reflect the rise of a new Camporano work force, that of the part-time farmer or peasant worker (see also Barberis, 1970). As Camporano became a client of the imperial state, the governmental failures or mismanagement of public finance that formerly had caused hardship only in certain spheres of villagers' life or affected only the state administration, now caused hardship in every facet of villagers' life and stood to ruin many homes. By 1975 the relative failure of the development poles to absorb new industrial or state workers and the acute wheat shortages that began to follow every harvest season (see Hytten and Marchioni, 1970; *L'Ora*, 1973) revealed fully how far most modern villagers had been pulled into a state of dependency that, though new, had all the characteristics of the lopsided dependence their forefathers experienced under the iron circle.

As a result, modern villagers have all rediscovered the value of subsistence agriculture in permitting them not only to survive even under the harshest of conditions but also to maintain some autonomy vis-à-vis agents of ruling coalitions (cf. Schneider, 1980: 174–175). Even those with steady jobs in the public service system have now found it useful not to lose their hold on agriculture. The cheese maker's son has managed to overcome his "allergy" and helps his father make cheese. Land around Camporano continues to be farmed, and in the late 1970s young and old peasant-workers established two sales cooperatives for tomatoes. Even the local pharmacist now tends personally to his vineyard—some-

207

thing that twenty years ago he would have found below his social standing. For these reasons, the earlier orientation of young villagers toward agricultural activities has changed as the prediction about the end of Camporano agriculture voiced by many villagers in 1971–1972 is no longer made. In this way, modern villagers derive benefits from the imperial state without being totally subservient to it.

Modern Efforts to Remedy the Sicilian Problem

As I have indicated, communal and party politics before and after the collapse of the two family compacts generated consequences not too unlike those of communal politics of a century earlier. At the same time, the shift in the basis of the village economy, including the almost complete displacement of family structures in the provision of intergenerational transfer of income, reduced "the precarious employment" (Sylos-Labini, 1964) so characteristic of agricultural activities but also strengthened the hold of ruling parties and ruling bureaucracies over village life. Thus, improvements in living conditions, including access to modern means of communication, have not been accompanied by a reduction in some of the principal characteristics of the Sicilian problem—governmental failure and citizen alienation. During this period, there were, however, at least two efforts to remedy these problems. The first, by central government officials, took the form of a new "last struggle with the mafia"; the second, and more recent one, by Camporano villagers, took the form of a revolt against Demochristian hegemony of communal affairs.

The Struggle against the Mafia

By the early 1960s, the problem of peace and security in Sicily was essentially restricted to the urban areas, now undergoing rapid economic growth, urbanization, and building explosion. The crisis of law and order experienced by law-enforcement agencies was part of a larger crisis that invested most other governmental mechanisms as they tried (1) to maintain some semblance of earlier delivery of public services; (2) to meet the demands and needs of new waves of urban or metropolitan residents; and (3) to realize forced industrial growth. These goals were in turn compounded by the fiercely competitive rivalry among the ruling parties and

208

factions for the colonization of communal, regional, and central government departments and agencies and among all the major party and faction leaders for the staffing and management of administrative offices through their respective public employee unions. The informal and personal networks that had earlier cut across ideological and intergovernmental barriers, thus assuring some governmental responsiveness to the articulation of demands for services by urban-area residents, had by the time of the Demochristian Opening to the Left in the early 1960s become so overloaded or exhausted as to be beyond the reach of those who led the governing coalition. The instrumentalities of government in Sicily were taking on the appearance of an archipelago of private empires or trading companies. As the largest city and provincial and regional capital, Palermo manifested most clearly the realities of life under an archipelago of private governments (see Capurso, 1964; Mariotti, 1967).

This state of affairs was not, however, confined exclusively to Palermo or the Sicilian urban scene. Serious problems of institutional weakness and failure and different levels of government acting as trading companies of ruling parties and ruling bureaucracies could be observed in urban areas of the Italian peninsula as far north as Rome and Milan (see Evans, 1967: 134; Fiorentino Sullo, quoted in Fried, 1973: 185; Galli and Prandi, 1970: 162; Montanelli et al., 1965; Passigli, 1963: 728–730; Ronchey, 1980). To be sure, in the absence of an additional layer of government like regional government for most of the Italian peninsula, the markedly private economy of most Northern cities, and the antagonistic position between PCI-controlled urban governments and DC-led national governments contributed to attenuate or minimize the "public pathologies" that in Sicily were reaching staggering proportions (see Sbragia, 1979). What differentiated the Sicilian urban scene from the rest of the Italian urban scene was the identification of a single factor or variable that, it was alleged, accounted for most if not all the public service failings and urban problems in Sicily—mafia clientelism. If only this clientelism could be eliminated, then governmental failure in Sicily would also be eliminated—and the statute of regional autonomy would finally and truly become operative. Such an assessment had by 1960 become a fixed plank in the PCI and PSI national and regional policy statements (see Barrese, 1973: 37–49; Berti, 1960; Pantaleone, 1962: 235–236).

During the 1950s, several calls were made for a parliamentary inquiry into the phenomenon of the mafia in Sicily, but these received little or no support from the DC-led regional and national governments. By 1962, the displacement of local mafia groups like that of Camporano by the Demochristian party, the difficulties experienced by DC national and regional leaders in controlling the instrumentalities of the regionalist state in Sicily, the Opening to the Left, and the very identification of governmental failure with such an elastic term as *the mafia*—all joined together to sway national DC leaders to heed the Left and launch the *first* parliamentary inquiry to deal exclusively with the phenomenon of the mafia. A potential impediment was removed when in March 1962 the DC-led regional assembly approved a motion urging the national government to initiate such an inquest.

The establishment and operation of the antimafia parliamentary commission proceeded with speed and dispatch. Created with a law in December 1962, this joint commission of the Chamber of Deputies and the Senate became operational in February 1963. Supported by almost unlimited financial and personnel resources, the commission was under the formal direction of a Northern DC senator and former jurist and under the "moral leadership" of a Sicilian Communist senator distinguished for his antimafia past. The commission set out to use its wide powers to investigate "pathologies" in Sicilian life—from banks to the administration of justice, from city retail and wholesale markets to the instrumentalities of communal, provincial, regional, and national governments.

Clearly, such an investigation, even if restricted to the Western provinces, could not be completed in the course of a few years. Moreover, it was difficult to expect Demochristian and Socialist national parliamentarians to investigate government activities that, for the most part, served as basis of their own power and influence in Sicily and in Italy as a whole. Soon it became eminently clear that, while "the mafia" had been a politically expedient slogan and rhetoric, it was of no great use in making sense of, let alone proposing remedies to, what was or went wrong in Sicilian public life. As Anton Blok has observed, "If mafia is as pervasive as suggested by Senator Pafundi [the president of the commission], comprising all instances of corruption and illegality, one cannot reasonably expect that the Anti-mafia Commission will be able to complete its task, that is, 'to report to Parliament on the most suitable remedy' " (Blok, 1974: 228).

A gang war in the Palermo metropolitan area in the summer of 1963 helped to sharpen the focus and direction of the antimafia commission

210

work. The commission issued a report to parliament suggesting, among other things, (1) the strict enforcement of existing laws against Sicilians deemed by law-enforcement officials to be "predisposed to commit crimes"; (2) the application of existing criminal association measures against those found not guilty either during pretrial investigations or in courts of law; and (3) the enactment of exceptional laws to deal with those deemed predisposed to commit crimes or judged to be members of criminal associations (cited in Pantaleone, 1969: 163–164; see also Poma and Perrone, 1964: 64–125). The translation of these recommendations into public policy meant in effect that until the commission completed its inquiry, governmental failures and citizen alienation in Sicily would be treated as a police problem. The burden of overcoming these problems thus came to rest upon the same law-enforcement agencies that were already experiencing serious organizational difficulties. As a result, the very difficulties in waging this new "last struggle" on all fronts and the need to achieve quick results prompted police officials to concentrate their police work in areas with a high visibility profile (see *Il Mondo*, 1973). Under these circumstances, places like Camporano became easy targets for waging a modern last struggle with the mafia.

By the beginning of the 1960s, most of the former leaders of the old Camporano mafia had died of old age. Of those still living, some like Novara had moved away from Camporano; of others remaining in the village, very few were involved in community activities, now increasingly confined to communal and party politics. Also by this time, villagers had had opportunities to reevaluate the "wounds" inflicted upon one another as members of the two warring compacts. Though communal and party politics were creating new wounds, most village residents were making conscious efforts to insure that these wounds would not leave permanent scars. Villagers like to refer to Sunday strolls in the village square and marriages across former compact lines as telling evidence of the new community life. For example, Nicola Vallera, the brother of Carlo Vallera, could now be seen together with erstwhile arch-enemies, with whom he was related through his wife, Novara's sister. Nicola Vallera's son married a daughter of former mafia chief Mezzena, who could now be seen with his nephew Salvatore Albano, the PCI leader, who, in turn, had renewed social relations with his first cousin, the Demochristian Liborio Imera, a high administrative official in the regional government.

For most villagers, the new antimafia war had the effect of reopening old wounds as well as creating new ones. For villagers like Carlo

Vallera, the same phenomenon represented a vindication of their past antimafia activities and a justification to renew those activities, this time with the support of the national government and law-enforcement agencies.

Sometime in 1963 Vallera, who was then a communal councilor, charged that the Camporano commune was in the hands of the mafia. As evidence of this state of affairs, he drew particular attention to a member of the communal executive council (the *giunta*), Gesualdo Avola, former associate of Ardena. As indicated earlier, in 1961, councilor Nicola Vallera had offered "this mafia" his group's collaboration for a local Opening to the Left. Moreover, the drawing of public attention to Gesualdo Avola appeared, to most villagers, puzzling, since he was not the only ex-mafia chief to be on the communal council. There was at least another former associate of Ardena on the council, but this man happened to be the father-in-law of one of Carlo Vallera's nephews. As a result, whereas most villagers tended to dismiss Vallera's claim that the commune was in the hands of mafiosi as "selective indignation" or personal antipathy toward Avola, outsiders interpreted the claim as part of the campaign against criminality in Sicily. The Left press and Left national and regional deputies raised questions about how DC-led national and regional governments could reconcile their avowed support of the antimafia commission with mafia-controlled communal governments like that of Camporano. They succeeded in pressing the national and regional ministers of the interior into action. Local and regional Communists, Albano included, who knew exactly what the situation was in Camporano, do not seem to have intervened to give better direction to the antimafia war. But if they had intervened, they would have risked being mistaken for "friends of the mafia."

First, the commandant of the Camporano detachment of carabinieri was replaced. No sooner had the new carabinieri commandant, a brigadier, arrived in the village than he recommended the application of existing criminal association laws against several villagers. In February 1964, Gesualdo Avola, Mansueto Avola, Saro Cusna, Placido Perosa, Rosolino Uria, and another villager residing in Mozarra, Diego Folenga, were *diffidati* or placed under a mild form of house arrest by the provincial police chief (*questore*). They had, it seems, committed no recent criminal act, but because of their mafia past, they were presumed to be "predisposed or inclined to commit crimes."

The response of the regional minister of the interior was also prompt.

He selected and authorized, with the consent of Left regional deputies and leaders, two regional "above-suspect-and-suspicion" functionaries to investigate Camporano communal affairs. These inspectors reached Camporano in June 1964. After an exhaustive investigation of communal affairs, including auditing financial transactions, the two inspectors submitted a not-so-secret report of over a hundred single-spaced legal-size typewritten pages to the regional minister of the interior. The report provides a fascinating glimpse of intracommunal and intergovernmental relations, mayoral philanthropy that tended to verge on political corruption, and petty bureaucratic infractions like not keeping all the archival papers in proper order. But there was no evidence whatsoever about the commune of the 1960s as a trading company of the Camporano mafia. No criminal charges followed, in fact. But in the antimafia climate that existed in Sicily, the inspectors' report became less important than the fact that the Camporano commune had been subject to antimafia investigation. The investigation itself, coming after the police measures, was sufficient to confirm and fuel outside suspicion of modern Camporano as a mafia stronghold.

A second wave of police measures began after the August 1963 recommendations of the antimafia parliamentary commission were translated into a new exceptional law in 1965 (law of May 31, 1965, no. 575). In the fall of 1968, the Mozarra provincial police chief proposed to the president of the Mozarra provincial court that the Avola brothers, Cusna, Folengo, Perosa, who was by now in poor health and living in retirement with his sons in Mozarra, and Uria be banished from Sicily for at least three years. The earlier *diffida* or police surveillance was used to justify the harsher measures. The Avola brothers and Perosa were further accused, in the words of the *questore*, "by Camporano public opinion" of being involved in international drug smuggling and of living beyond their means of direct cultivators or retired persons. Novara, then living elsewhere in Sicily, was also proposed for exile.

All the accused appealed these charges, with some success. By 1970, banishment for Cusna, Folengo, and Novara was reduced to a form of house arrest for at least two years. In the case of the Avola brothers, Perosa and Uria, their defense lawyer introduced reports from Internal Revenue officials (*guardie di finanza*) showing that the accused were not living beyond their means and affidavits from eighteen above-reproach-and-suspicion Camporanesi suggesting that Camporano public opinion found without foundations the *questore*'s charge. A relative of the Avola brothers living in Montreal, Quebec, had indeed returned to the village for brief visits twice in the late 1960s; a very old female relative of Perosa had indeed revisited her one-time place of residence in New Jersey—but no right-thinking villager could regard them as drug couriers. This challenge to the police claim failed to convince the Mozarra court, itself under investigation by the antimafia commission for being soft on alleged criminals. The villagers were banished from Sicily for three years.

It is difficult to account for the different sentencing. Most villagers are inclined to explain the different application of antimafia measures to the standing of the defense lawyer or to the influence possessed by the accused. Whereas Folengo and Novara could afford the service of a prominent Italian criminal lawyer and politician, the Avola brothers, Cusna, Perosa, and Uria, could not. Although Cusna had an influential relative, the Avola brothers, Perosa and Uria had no influential relative or friend. Though these explanations of selective indignation remain conjectures or speculations, the unequal punishment for a similar past served to increase the sense of injustice already generated by the earlier antimafia measures.

Moreover, former associates of Ardena were not the only villagers to be subject to antimafia measures. Between 1965 and 1968, at least nine other villagers, including a retired agricultural worker and brother of the local PCI secretary as well as an unemployed agricultural worker and local activist for the small Proletarian Socialist Party (PSIUP), were placed under police surveillance for a period of at least a year. These villagers could in no way be linked with either Mariano Ardena or still-living associates of Ardena. Some of them had belonged to the Vallera-led Left compact. In the past, they had, however, committed either some illegal act like stealing chickens or canvassing too close to the electoral polling stations, or some other act which, though not illegal, had incurred the displeasure of carabinieri officials and villagers influential for their antimafia work. The unemployed rural worker and PSIUP activist had done both, it seems. As a young man he had stolen some chickens, and as a PSIUP activist in the late 1960s he had raised some questions about the antimafia work in a public speech.

This chain of events led most villagers to fear that anyone, and particularly those with some kind of criminal record or with relatives in North America, was exposed to antimafia measures. The case involving a villager emigrating to the United States illustrates both the extent of this fear and the range of strategies available to Camporanesi as they sought to reduce their exposure to the caprice of public authority and to minimize the incentives for malevolence provided by the antimafia war.

In June 1972, Pio Gambara, peasant turned construction worker, was preparing to emigrate to an American city with his family. Before leaving Sicily, however, he wanted to say good-bye to Antonio Tarsia, the villager turned bandit (described in chapter 8), recently released from prison. Gambara had never been associated with him or with mafiosi. In fact, he was and remained a staunch Socialist. However, some ten years earlier, Tarsia's son, Gaetano, had been a source of companionship and help to him when they were both working in France. Gambara had been involved in a serious construction accident and Gaetano Tarsia's visits to him in a French hospital had attenuated his despair and loneliness. Now as he was leaving Camporano, perhaps forever, he wanted to signal to Gaetano Tarsia that he had not forgotten his help, by saying good-bye to his father living in a nearby town. However, Gambara knew that the former bandit was still living under a form of house arrest and feared that his visit might create some last-minute impediment to his and his family's imminent departure for North America. Faced with this dilemma, he sought a way of minimizing as much as possible whatever risk the meeting with a former bandit might entail. He knew that an outsider from the United States, then temporarily residing in Camporano, had expressed an interest in meeting Antonio Tarsia. If that outsider agreed to go with him, then his visit with Tarsia might be "beyond reproach and suspicion." And so it was on this basis that Gambara was able to say good-bye to Tarsia and that outsider was able to meet a former bandit.

With the publication of the documentary and "preliminary final" report, the work of the parliamentary commission came to an end by 1972. The commission concluded, in effect, that "mafia by its very nature defies any remedy" (Blok, 1974: 228; Ciuni, 1972; cf. *Panorama*, 1976). Though this report failed to meet the original intent of the inquiry ("to report to Parliament on the most suitable remedy"), it revealed two other aspects of the modern antimafia war in Camporano. The first aspect involves one of its research papers, which reads in part that "to represent the traditional mafia of the Mozarra area in the high echelons of the regional government is . . . Liborio Imera, nephew of Franco Novara." Of course, "the traditional mafia" had collapsed long ago in Camporano.

Moreover, as discussed earlier, Imera was appointed to his post by the DC regional deputy Nunzio Lozano in 1952. Presumably, then, that Demochristian deputy should also have been implicated for appointing Imera. Yet, the report made no reference to Lozano who, by that time, was an important national parliamentarian. This situation is not as revealing or incongruous as it first appears. The report was in part drafted by a non-DC deputy who had relied on an influential villager for information about the "traditional Camporano mafia." Moreover, by this time, Imera himself had shifted his support from Lozano's faction to the Fanfani faction. Thus, although the citation caused Imera public embarrassment, and eventually a demotion of a sort in the regional bureaucracy, it did not start police action against him, since it was known that the antimafia inquiry had become part of interparty and DC intraparty politics in and beyond Camporano.

Another facet of the work of the parliamentary commission involved Vallera himself. He too was part of the antimafia investigation. Segments of the dossier on him collected by the parliamentary commission became public in the middle of the 1970s. For the most part, they contain the same kind of allegations about his life and activities that had been conjured up about some of his fellow villagers. The antimafia campaign had thus come almost full circle in Camporano.

In sum, the modern struggle against the Camporano mafia took place almost twenty years after it was really needed. Occurring at the time it did, this struggle provided incentives not only to resurrect the old Camporano mafia but also to create a new Camporano mafia. Yet this does not seem to have been a unique or ad hoc incident. A study of the application of the same antimafia measures in villages and towns of a West Sicilian province suggests somewhat similar results for almost that *entire* province (Limuti, 1971; see also the case cited by the then PCI senator Nicola Cipolla, in Commissione Parlamentare d'Inchiesta sul Fenomeno della Mafia in Sicilia, 1972: 297).

Whereas the success of this new antimafia war confirmed the outsiders' view of Camporano as a mafia stronghold, the same success strengthened villagers' contention that it is state officials and politicians, more generally, who are the members of a "Grand Criminal Association"—a conclusion that, as indicated in chapter 1, had been reached by Napoleone Colajanni at the turn of the century. Instead of remedying governmental failure and citizen alienation, the antimafia war had become, at least in Camporano, a source of new governmental failure and citizen alienation in Sicily.

The Breakdown of Demochristian Hegemony

The continued Demochristian hegemony over Camporano communal affairs rested in part on the extent to which local DC leaders were able to put together successive slates of communal candidates with a high probability of success. The same happened in the 1973 communal election—with a difference. Though the party list was headed by the incumbent mayor of the *doroteo* or center-right faction, Calogero Sala, the slate of candidates also included a young villager adhering to the *base* or Left-wing faction, Lino Ventura. Soon after the election, serious policy differences emerged between Mayor Sala and Councilor Ventura. Whereas Sala charged Ventura of *arrivisme*, Ventura charged Sala of immobilism or, in Giuseppe Di Palma's words, *Surviving without Governing* (Di Palma, 1977b, see also 1980). As Sala continued the practice of mayoral philanthropy, Ventura succeeded in convincing half of the DC majority councilors to his views. In 1975, the dissident DC councilors provoked the resignation of Mayor Sala and the executive council.

The situation appeared somewhat like previous occasions when dissident councilors had forced incumbent mayors to resign. Only that this time the general context and the participants of the revolt gave it a new color. By 1975, with the collapse of the Opening to the Left, the "creeping compromise" (Di Palma, 1977a: 153) between Demochristian and Communist leaders had ceased to be a conjecture. This national event together with the "progressive" position taken by Ventura and his group led the PSI-PCI communal councilors to support Ventura in his bid to put an end to surviving without governing. In spite of the opposition from the provincial DC secretary, Ventura proceeded to form "a programmatic majority" with the PCI-PSI councilors and became mayor in March 1975.

During his tenure, as brief as it was exciting, Ventura made a determined attack on some long-standing Camporano problems—the lack of adequate school facilities, the necessity to repair the existing water mains and pipes and to resolve the issue of the still-inoperative aqueduct, the need to build new stone pavements on the streets behind the main church. He initiated talks with mayors of neighboring communes

217

on matters of common interest. He began to hold popular assembly-type meetings outside the commune to allow more citizen participation in communal matters. So involved did he become in affairs of the commonweal that he fell behind in his university studies and had to interrupt them. Yet Ventura's efforts soon revealed how difficult it was for a Camporano communal government to translate common interests shared by villagers into public policies without an essential control over the national and regional bureaucracy—without, in effect, evoking some form of governmental philanthropy from members of ruling coalitions in order to overcome bureaucratic inaction.

Thus, precisely when Mayor Ventura had come to appreciate the strategies and predicament of his predecessor, he and the other dissident DC councilors had become further isolated from the rest of the Demochristian majority. At the same time, Ventura found that reliance upon Communist and Socialist councilors insured his programmatic majority in the council but also gave Left councilors, for the first time since 1946, credibility to form a communal government of their own. As a result, when the time came for the preparation of slates of candidates for the 1978 communal election, Ventura and other dissident DC councilors were excluded from the DC list for "lack of orthodoxy," while the PCI-PSI group, now led by Albano, who had returned from Palermo to take charge of Communist affairs, established a "programmatic majority" list of their own. The orthodox slate of DC candidates was defeated by the Communist-led coalition by forty-one votes, roughly the same proportion of votes that had maintained Demochristian control of the commune since the late 1960s.

In the summer of 1978, Mayor Albano, still reveling in the defeat of the DC ticket, spoke eloquently about the end of Demochristian hegemony over the commune as also the end of government failure and citizen alienation in Camporano. The 1978 electoral results represent, however, not the end but a breakdown of Demochristian rule, for in the June 1979 national election the DC list still received a larger number of Camporano votes than all the other parties put together. It remains to be seen whether the breakdown of Demochristian rule—the splitting of support for the DC at the national and regional level and for the PCI-led coalition at the local level—can persist over time to allow the new programmatic majority to survive. It also remains to be seen whether the national and regional structures of the Communist party, including the control of some communes around Camporano, can serve as the organizational weapon of

218

the new Camporano authority to overcome its lack of control over the national and regional bureaucracy and to remedy governmental failure and citizen alienation. The new Camporano authority in 1978 was confident that it could release the "unused capacity" of villagers at self-government and make the Demochristian practice of surviving without governing a thing of the past. By 1979 there was, however, at least one feature of the old order that appeared to continue under the new—a renewed expansion of the communal bureaucracy.

Conclusion

Between the early 1950s and the end of the 1970s, Camporano village life continued to undergo radical transformations. These transformations appear, in retrospect, as the inevitable outcomes or sequences of the process of change in village relationships that began with the emergence of national party organizations as the artificers and matter of the postwar reconstruction of Italian and Sicilian political economy. The Demochristian political tradition of Camporano itself facilitated and, at the same time, obscured the integration and marginality of villagers in the modern political economy of mass parties. The passion and ardor that accompanied the transformation of the mafia regime and its opposition into two family compacts strengthened as well as made less discernible the way events were shaping. The struggle between the two groups still provided possibilities for a majority of villagers to be part of the larger political community without foreclosing opportunities to act as an autonomous local community. But such "division and cohesion" could not coexist for long. The hegemony of the national and regional ruling coalitions over village life could not be deflected. By the middle of the 1950s, the local patriotism and self-reliance that the old Camporano mafia had typified, fostered, and promoted were completely displaced by more inclusive loyalties. The mafia, which had become another burden on villagers, passed away. At the same time, the collapse of the Left bloc resulted from inner decadence or defects inherent in its very organization. In this sense, then, the mafia and its opposition, instead of vanquishing one another, vanquished themselves.

The factors that significantly contributed to the collapse of the two family compacts were also those that significantly contributed to pull villagers into a new order of relationships which bore striking resemblances to that of a century earlier, with two crucial differences. First, the localized majority and minority "parties" of one hundred years before had given way to the national and regional factionalism of modern mass parties. But this factionalism did not derive exclusively from personalism, clientelism, or rent seeking. It was grounded in and promoted by issues of principle as well. Second, more than the land reform itself, changes in the legal basis of land use, such as tenancy laws, assured the transformation of the prerogatives of landowners from "strong" to "weak" property rights (Wittfogel, 1957: 228). But the destruction of property in land as a critical determinant of authority and control over the work force and village life also brought with it a structure of incentives inimical to agricultural productivity itself. As the instrumentalities of the imperial state became the chief employer of labor or provider of income in Camporano, agricultural activities, which had been a source of dependency and subjection a century earlier, now became the primary source that allowed villagers to maintain some autonomy vis-à-vis "foreigners" who came as members of the ruling parties and ruling bureaucracies.

Efforts to remedy government failure and citizen alienation under the imperial state have produced mixed results. The antimafia war demonstrated, once again, how righteous *and* wrong remedial policies can be when they lack empirical validity. The breakdown of Demochristian hegemony over communal affairs has helped to foster the belief among villagers that they can realize their unused capacity at self-government. But it remains to be seen whether this unused capacity can be translated into collective efforts on behalf of common interests shared by villagers, in the present institutional framework and circumstances. At any rate, the breakdown of Demochristian hegemony, however transitory, coming when it did, served as a fitting close to the Camporano political economy experience in which it played not an insignificant part.

10

Epilogue:
The Past as the Future?

To the traveler in Sicily who today chances to pass through Camporano, the depopulated and calm look of the town will give no hint of its rich and agitated two-hundred-year history. In this book I have charted and examined that history in order to unravel and explain the Sicilian problem. Like frontier communities in North America or older Sicilian towns, Camporano was never an isolated whole. The first Mogata settlers and successive generations of Camporano villagers were always part of the modernity and developmental sequence of their time. To give contextual mapping to the Camporano experience, I have thus followed outside events, circumstances, and traditions that, since the first settlers reached Mogata in the late 1760s, critically affected and shaped the initiative and response of villagers to contingencies of life.

As noted in chapter 1, this kind of longitudinal analysis has its hazards. The relatively little material before the abolition of feudalism in 1812 and the introduction of national jurisdiction in 1816 does not permit a "before-after" evaluative study of the impact those changes had on village life. Though every effort has been made to reduce uncertainties in written and oral trouble cases, the nature of this kind of research precludes any full assurance that no errors of detail, perhaps even of important details, remain. In order to trace the dynamics of these events, it was necessary, in Philip Selznick's words (1966: 250; see also Kjellberg, 1975: 126–127) "to attempt a reconstruction, which is to say, a theory of the conditions and forces which appear to have shaped the behavior of key participants." Selznick notes that such a reconstruction, even if it involves only a particular historical event, is always hazardous.

Yet the very strategy of research has, in part, compensated for these difficulties. By tracing how villagers "suffered" as well as "made" history over the course of almost two hundred years, there are many case studies of the Sicilian problem at adjoining points in time and under varying conditions. By relying on a multiplicity of archival sources and people for the reconstruction of most Camporano trouble cases, I have made every effort to insure the reliability of the events portrayed. The constellation of historical episodes depicting villagers as they confronted different task environments gives some measure of confidence about the warrantability of the analysis sustained in preceding chapters. In short, I believe that I have provided a substantially correct picture of about two hundred years of experience concerned with efforts to sustain village life. The same constellation of historical episodes suffices to cast doubt on widely accepted hypotheses and maxims and to direct attention to new and more plausible generalizations about governmental failures, general social disintegration and outlaw societies in Sicily. The way I have unraveled the Sicilian problem within the context of a single community suggests how subsequent research can be carried out to confirm or disconfirm my generalizations.

Camporano, the Sicilian Problem and Social Organization

The Camporano political economy experience confirms and strengthens the principal thesis of the study: that the Sicilian problem is ultimately grounded in the structure of authority relationships that impinges upon the pursuit of both individual and joint or collective opportunities. But the way organization is established, maintained, and altered over time and under varying conditions reflects in part the continuing interplay between economic and political factors. In reviewing the principal conclusions of the study, other parts of the world, Italian and otherwise, are suggested that share Sicily's situation and call up helpful analogies, comparisons, and further research on the problem of social organization.

Epilogue: The Past as the Future?

State Making and Political Development

The analysis I have made of the Sicilian political economy tradition until the early nineteenth century challenges the view of the Sicilian people lost in a servitude to successive conquerors or being "their own worst enemies." It also suggests some modifications in the often-expressed view that "in few countries of the Western world is the past so much a part of the present as in Italy. . . . In the arts the Italian past is a goad, a glorious and live tradition, a yardstick; in politics it is largely a burden, something to be overcome, a fountain of disunity and bad habits" (Barnes, 1966: 306, and 1976: 99). The influence of the model history of European sovereign states aside, it is not always clear why one should accept, in Denys Hay's words (1961: 27), "the need to explain the diversity of Italy as though unity were the norm." As for bad habits, Sicily's past reveals some of the worst but also some of the best features of the Italian and Western political tradition. For example, the parliament, baronial jurisdiction, and local laws and privileges, commonly described as feudal, kept alive a spirit of independence and self-reliance as well as a sense of the Sicilian nation. They also deserve some credit for checking imperial conquest and financial extraction. In part because of these institutions, Sicily bypassed altogether the so-called age of absolutism, generally viewed as a necessary condition of European or Continental modernization and political development. Baronial jurisdiction as an economic and political enterprise provided the rudiments of self-government to Camporano villagers.

As a corrective to any tendency to idealize the pre-1816 Sicilian political tradition in retrospect, it would do well to reiterate that the tradition had critical shortcomings. Efforts to remedy those shortcomings in 1812 failed. But that failure was the outcome of a complex matrix of choices involving internal and external events and circumstances. Though it is difficult to predict, it is possible that if the 1812 constitutional experiment had run its course, it might have led to "incremental modernization" appropriate to the realization of the self-governing and self-organizing capabilities of diverse communities in Sicily. The history of "incremental democratization" (Powell, 1973) in Britain suggests this much. Sicilian leaders in the eighteenth and early nineteenth centuries did not simply want to imitate the British when they looked to British history for support and confirmation of their own reform efforts. Sicily's constitutional development appeared closer to the British than to the French.

Furthermore, Sicily's pre-1816 constitutional development is useful for another, more general, reason. It calls up Tocqueville's observation that the transition from feudalism to modernity did not always have to follow the pattern of development suggested by the model history of unitary states: "Transported overseas from feudal Europe and free to develop in total independence, the rural parish of the Middle Ages became the township of New England. Emancipated from the seigneur, but controlled at every turn by an all-powerful government, it took in France . . . the form of 'paternal government' " (Tocqueville, 1856: 48, 51). The differences that the township of New England and the "paternal government" of France made in the realization of the self-governing capabilities of communities of people are well known, but some of them, emphasized by Tocqueville, are worth repeating here:

> The township of New England possessed two advantages . . . namely independence and authority. . . . The New Englander is attached to his township not so much because he was born in it, but because it is a free and strong community, of which he is a member, and which deserves the care spent in managing it. In Europe the absence of local public spirit is a frequent subject of regret to those who are in power; everyone agrees that there is no surer guarantee of order and tranquility, and yet nothing is more difficult to create. If the municipal bodies were made powerful and independent, it is feared that they would become too strong and expose the state to anarchy. Yet without power and independence a town may contain good subjects, but it can have no active citizens. (Tocqueville, 1835: I, 69)

Against this backdrop, the creation of a legal-rational order à la Weber in 1816 represents a breakdown and *not* the beginning of modernization in Sicily. Rather than facilitate individual and collective efforts on behalf of common interests shared by islanders, it created an antithesis of interests between rulers and ruled, and between landowners and landless. The antithesis evolved into successive revolts, culminating in the very collapse of the Kingdom of the Two Sicilies and the creation of the Kingdom of Italy in 1860–1861. But the iron law of oligarchy inherent in the forced creation of unity through centralized government and administration remained, just as the proprietary claims of great landowners continued to be determinants of the human condition in the countryside.

The unification of Italy in the early 1860s could not be achieved in

collapse of Sicilies

any other way. As a result, there followed another antithesis of interests between rulers and ruled, between landlords and peasants, which baffled people in both classes about the proper remedy to their predicament. As a leading Italian statesman, Sidney Sonnino himself became locked into the same structure of authority relationships he had earlier analyzed in Sicily. Indeed, even a cursory examination of the parliamentary debates between 1870 and 1914 will reveal that members of the governing class were themselves critically aware of the shortcomings in the structure of basic social institutions for advancing human governance and welfare. But changes in the instrumentalities of government and in the institutional arrangements in society would have given support to localized groups intent on asserting an inherent right of self-government and demolished the work of the fathers of Risorgimento or unification. Post–World War II national leaders faced a similar predicament. Thus, amid name changes from the Bourbon to the Savoy monarchy, from Fascist Italy to Republican Italy, the structure of basic social institutions has remained essentially invariant. The structure of basic social institutions, rather than being an instrument for advancing human welfare, has been an essential source of frustration, conflict, repression, and apathy—of human adversity among Sicilians. This conclusion requires some elaboration here. The relationship between property rights in rural land and economic development will be discussed in the next section.

First, as Italian political scientists have turned their attention to the making of united Italy, some have coined the phrase *il vizio d'origine* to suggest critical flaws in that statemaking (Zincone, 1980). The notion of *il vizio d'origine*, which resembles somewhat Lipset's theory of formative events, has elicited stiff criticism (Zincone, 1980). Nevertheless, if the *vizio d'origine* has any shred of validity as a concept, in the case of Sicily it is more applicable to the making of the Kingdom of the Two Sicilies, in the sense that the key ceasure occurred between 1812 and 1816. The circumstances and events created and shaped by the Bourbon state weighted the constitutional outcome of the Risorgimento in the direction of centralization. At the same time, by shifting the focus of historical investigation from the making of Italy as a preordained unitary state to the making of Italy as an experiment in constitutional choice, it becomes easier to understand and appreciate critical problems in developmental efforts.

It is entirely possible for fallible human beings to formulate explanations and to use those explanations for undertaking political and social

225

experiments that do not work in anticipated ways. Witness the attempts of French and Latin American revolutionaries. The reiteration of unitary and hierarchical principles of organization led Tocqueville to the conclusion that "in France there is only one thing that we cannot make: a free government; and only one thing that we cannot destroy: centralization" (Tocqueville, 1848: xviii). The failure of successive struggles to reform, overcome, or otherwise destroy the Latin American variant of the French bureaucratic phenomenon has led Claudio Vértiz to speak of "the centralist tradition of Latin America" (Vértiz, 1980). These points have been well understood by modern revolutionaries like Milovan Djilas (1969) and Amilcar Cabral (Morgado, 1974)—as they witnessed or anticipated attempts to create new societies and new social orders in Eastern Europe and Africa. Federal political systems have not been free of *vizi d'origine* either. The history of the Canadian Confederation, at least until 1981, is not only the history of what Mr. Justice Berger calls "fragile freedoms" (1981) but also the history of a political system that did not work as its creators had intended, of constitutional reform efforts that ended in stalemate, and of analysts "fallen into speaking the language of doubt when describing their society" (Bell and Tepperman, 1979: 6). The failure to extend the logic of the constitutional formula reached at the Philadelphia Convention to *all* people in the United States had the consequences of sustaining a "race problem" as a persistent issue in American history (V. Ostrom, 1971). Moreover, highly federalized political systems like the United States are susceptible to the so-called vicious circle of decentralization (Crozier, 1964: 236; see also McConnell, 1966). Thus every collective endeavor to realize developmental opportunities is subject to limitations.

The Sicilian problem elucidates, in fact, a crucial problem that confronts people engaged in the constitution or reconstruction of political order: namely, to know how different sets of principles articulated in correlative forms can be expected to yield different results. Federalist and autonomist principles of organization led Carlo Cattaneo and Francesco Ferrara to argue that the nature of the country, the political consciousness of its people and local and regional loyalties could be made to work for the commonweal under appropriate institutional arrangements. Instead, unitary principles of organization led Cavour and others to ignore or try to suppress them. In the end, unitary principles of organization prevailed. Many modern analysts have attributed remarkable intuition to Cattaneo and Ferrara for their capacity to anticipate patterns of Italian

226

development, which occurred long after their works were published. My analysis (see also Buchanan, 1960) suggests an alternative explanation: Cattaneo and Ferrara used a mode of reasoning or a theory of institutional design and analysis which enabled them to anticipate the direction that centralized government and administration would take in Italy. Their mode of reasoning was in part built upon the recognition that "the essential problem in the theory of organization is (1) to anticipate the consequences that follow when (2) self-interested individuals choose maximizing strategies within (3) particular organizational arrangements when applied to (4) particular structures of events" (V. Ostrom, 1974: 55).

Second, in saying that the structure of basic social institutions has been a critical source of human adversity among Sicilians, I am not suggesting or implying that somehow Bourbon and Fascist rule was the same as that of Liberal and Republican Italy. Nor am I discommending the improvements in public and private life that resulted from regime change in 1860 and in 1946. What I am suggesting as an hypothesis for further research is this: the programmatic, ideological, and personnel variations that accompanied the change from the Bourbon to the parliamentary monarchy and from Fascist to Republican Italy were insufficient to overcome the institutional weakness and failure of centralized government and administration.

A counterargument might take the following form. Granted the limitations in bureaucratic administration, the fact remains that the French state has been very effective. In many developing countries some form of development administration has provided more equal access to basic public services and nutritional needs of human beings than ever before. Therefore, governmental failures in Sicily do not dispose of the case *for* centralized government and administration elsewhere. Indeed, it can be argued that what Italy as a whole needs is a more consolidated system of government. Therefore we should be seeking answers to the following question: "Why has the Italian state been so inefficient, and the French state so efficient?"

To raise this question and to supply routinely the standard answer to it is to slide unwittingly into an unperceptive and unimaginative way of thinking. Just as the efficiency of bureaucratic structures is a necessary but insufficient condition for a productive *and* responsive public service economy, so the criterion of efficiency is necessary but insufficient for a proper evaluation of the performance of bureaucratic administration in a

227

democratic society. As has been noted, "producer efficiency in the absence of consumer utility is without economic meaning" (V. Ostrom, 1974: 62). Responsiveness, error-correcting capabilities, and justice as fairness are among the evaluative criteria that in a democratic society need to be employed simultaneously alongside administrative efficiency. Failure to consider and apply the same set of multiple evaluative criteria has led some to celebrate the French state and to lament that the Italian state has often been incapable of mounting effective repression. In short, there is a need to balance the record of comparative analysis of centralized government and administration in France and Italy. As for the other parts of the world, development by administration has produced quite impressive results in mobilizing resources and human beings for industrialization and modernization, but the cost has been, more often than not, "nation-destroying" rather than "nation-building" (Connor, 1972).

Third, the structure of government that failed to enhance, if not diminished, the welfare potential of most Camporano villagers made Italy, in some important respects, highly unstable. Yet the "flaws" that made Italy highly unstable also served to foster among its people a spirit of independence and resilience which kept alive their sense of personality and self-respect. Most Italians retained their essential humanity even under fascism and during the last year and a half of World War II—hindering the mounting of effective repression. As Robert C. Fried notes in *Planning the Eternal City* (1973: 107), "the compassion that today spares from demolition the thousands of illegally built homes that cover the Roman suburban landscape is the same that once saved the lives of antifascists and Jews in Rome in the days of the Nazi terror." A critical issue in Italian state making has been how to reflect and incorporate fully in the structure of authority relationships the almost automatic general humanity of an old and civilized people—in essence, how to link power and justice, politics and ethics and self-rule with shared rule (Elazar, 1979). The history of Camporano suggests that state making and development *can* take place independent of the values, living conditions, and dreams of human beings, but at the risk of becoming a new form of antidevelopment.

Rural Property Rights and Economic Development

Marxist and non-Marxist scholars alike have tended to regard, albeit for different reasons, the fall of feudalism as a necessary step in the eco-

228

nomic growth of the Western world. Private property rights in rural land together with a free labor market, it is argued, placed capitalization on a stronger basis to spur, assure, and sustain industrialization. The abolition of feudalism in Sicily in 1812 signaled the full and complete emergence of private property in rural land and a free labor market. But rather than progressing, Sicily's economy sank more deeply into backwardness, to become after 1860 part of the so-called Southern Question. In short, Sicily, like the rest of the South, does not fit the Western pattern of economic development. Several, at times contradictory, explanations have been used to account for this state of affairs.

In Sicilian historiography the abolition of feudalism itself has often been viewed as a critical explanatory factor of underdevelopment: "The 1812 parliament claimed to have freed a population from serfdom when, in fact, it was already free. . . . The truth is that the Sicilian barons took away that freedom and, in return, gave nothing to the population" (Salvioli, 1902: 339). There is some truth in this argument, but it is not the whole truth. The abolition of feudalism did indeed (1) countervene the long-standing canon in Sicilian jurisprudence that no prince or assembly could take away civic usufruct or common property rights from villagers without their consent, (2) transform fiefs into alodial or private properties, and (3) give barons extensive proprietary authority over natural resources. But the abolition of feudal laws and privileges also gave barons very limited scope and domain of authority over the local population. A free labor market together with communal government and parliament recast on the principles of self-government could seriously "devalue" rural proprietorship as a determinant of the human condition and bias agricultural development toward a wider community of interests and a longer time horizon. But, as we have seen, the creation of the Bourbon state prevented all this from happening. While the post-1816 central government dominated the structure of legal relationships without, however, any effective legal remedies for governmental failures, the landowners, secure in their prerogatives as private proprietors, extended their control over the labor force and rural life more generally. Hence, more than the 1812 abolition of feudalism as such, it was the creation of the Kingdom of the Two Sicilies that deprived agricultural activities of supporting institutional arrangements for bringing private rates of return on economic activities into parity with social returns (cf. Davis, 1979).

With the unification of Italy, explanations have tended to focus on whether agrarian reform is a prerequisite to successful economic development. Two principal explanations or polemics exist in the literature (Cammett, 1963; Gerschenkron, 1961). One, generally associated with Gramsci, argues that the failure of the Risorgimento to alter the legal prerogatives of landowners and to improve the conditions of life of the work force in the South goes a long way in explaining economic retardation. The other, generally associated with Rosario Romeo, argues that this was not a failure. The postponement of basic changes in property rights in rural land and the repressive or regressive labor and tax policies of post-1860 Italian governments on the rural population were an effective way of mobilizing capital for industrialization in the North. Basic changes in the legal basis of agricultural activities would have, perhaps, advanced rural development but at the risk of seriously retarding the transformation of Italy into a modern industrial country. In challenging Marxist analysis of the prerequisite for industrial development, Romeo advanced a general proposition that has received considerable attention in Latin America: namely, that the road to successful economic development does not have to pass through an agrarian reform.

Romeo's explanation may be more convincing than Gramsci's, but the transformation of Italy into a modern industrial country through what in Israel has been called Sapirism served to increase North-South differentials and to tighten the iron circle around communities like Camporano. However plausible Romeo's explanation may be in economic terms, the lesson from Sicily, as well as from modern Israel, is that old and new "Sapirism" cannot be strongly defended on political and ethical grounds. Gramsci's concern for rural development is a more defensible one. Gramsci correctly identified property rights in rural land and governmental arrangements for determining, enforcing, and altering the legal basis of those institutions as critical explanatory factors for both economic retardation and general social disintegration. The problem in Gramsci's analysis lies in its prescription: that in order to solve the Southern Question, Southern peasants should entrust all their aspirations and needs to a national party organization acting as an enlightened and benevolent modern Prince (see also Pinna, 1971). In fact, difficulties in mobilizing Southern peasants or in translating Gramsci's conception of party into reality have wrongly assumed the status for many analysts of adequate and reliable indicators of the associational incapacity and civic vices of Southern villagers (cf. Hirschman, 1971: 337). At the same time, Romeo's proposition acquires valence when it is checked against agrarian reforms and rural labor laws like those discussed in

chapters 8 and 9. Those post-1946 changes weakened, if not emascu-
lated, property rights in rural land, without in any way realizing their
policy objectives—to improve performance in the agricultural sector *and*
to improve the welfare of the rural workers.

The post-1812 Camporano agricultural experience viewed as a whole
suggests the following proposition: a landholding problem, or retardation
of economic development in rural lands, can result from weak as well as
strong property rights. This means that property in the means of agricultural production, like property in the means of industrial production,
does not necessarily entail a uniform and invariant bundle of legal and
customary claims. Just as the proprietary claims in rural land can determine the human condition in the countryside, so governmental regulations, taxation, and labor legislation can determine the nature, distribution, and exercise of the proprietary claims themselves—as the struggle
in the Chilean countryside between 1919 and 1973 further attests
(Loveman, 1976b). The continuing interplay of economic and political
factors at the local, regional, and national level has far more profound
implications for rural development or inertia than landholding as such
(see also Bates, 1978; Colburn, 1982; Hirschman, 1971; Thomson,
1973, 1976).

Voluntary Collective Action, Inlaw and Outlaw

Sicilian peasants and artisans have been prisoners of the institutional
arrangements that govern their communal and agricultural activities and
not of their culture or ethos. It is in this sense that Ferrara's prediction in
1860—that Sicily would become the "Ireland of Italy"—is valid. Over
more than a hundred years, successive generations of Camporano villagers have shown themselves to possess the skills and knowledge necessary to organize collective enterprises and yet, for the most part, they
have been *lawfully* prevented from putting those self-organizing capabilities to use.

The forced creation of Italian unity through administrative measures
and the near exclusion of Sicilian peasants, and the people of the South
more generally, from the benefits deriving from that unity have often
been justified, in part, on the assumption that in Sicily, as in the South,
there were no traditions of self-government on which Italian unification
could have relied, short of the mafia and the old notables. The presumptive knowledge one uses in thinking about political affairs is a critical

231

tool for deciding what one should believe and how one should act in relating to the larger community. Is there a danger that presumptive knowledge about the people and the history of Southern Italy may not be empirically warrantable? (see also Briggs, 1978; Salvemini and La Piana, 1943: 53–62). In that case, one might be led to accept incorrect assertions and to reject correct assertions. Furthermore, one might make incorrect diagnoses and prescribe the wrong remedies. Analysts rarely kill their patients; but they can make life miserable.

The analysis of voluntary collective efforts in Camporano suggests that human beings find solutions to problems of organization where and when they are able to engage in joint efforts and maintain reciprocity with one another. Such patterns may exist only in the microcosm of kinship and neighborhood groupings but such patterns can be used to build the configuration of other enterprises and associations beyond the local level to reach the region or the nation as a whole. This is what the spread of the Sicilian *fasci* or workers' solidarity leagues in the early 1890s reveals before it was forcibly checked by state authorities, and this is what the example of Zapata and the Mexican revolution (Womack, 1968) teaches about collective action in the countryside.

The analysis further suggests that when human beings are prevented from cooperating, they necessarily become individualistic. Individualistic action and even so-called amoral familism can thus become a way of life generated by the pursuit of strategic opportunities available to people as prisoners of the legal order governing public and private activities. These circumstances bear some resemblance to what scholarly studies of the development of African and Israeli political societies call the two publics—one public sector, founded in indigenous tradition and culture, is identified with primordial groupings and activities; the other, the civil public sector, is associated with the state administrative structures from which one seeks to gain, if possible, in order to benefit the primordial public (Segre, 1980: chapter 3). The same circumstances can, in turn, generate a crisis of identity as well as foster a logic of corruption and even shadow governments.

To a reader of contemporary Italian newspapers, mafias as shadow or outlaw governments seem to dominate public and private activities throughout the peninsula and islands. The use of the term *mafia* in Italian public discourse is exaggerated, but does not depart too much from usages elsewhere. Today one speaks not only of the Italian-American Mafia but also of many other mafias—from the Japanese Mafia in inter-

232

national organized crime (*Guardian* [Manchester], 1979) and the Donegal Mafia in Irish politics (Sacks, 1976) to the ethnic and regional Mafias that run the literary world and the publishing and communications industries in the United States (Podhoretz, 1979). In short, "mafia" has acquired such criminal or pejorative connotations in and outside of Italy that it can hardly be made neutral by definitional fiat. And yet, what emerges from the time-series analysis of the Camporano mafia regime—from the 1890s to 1907; from 1908 to 1914; from 1915 to 1918; from 1919 to 1926; from 1943 to 1944; from 1944 to 1955—suggests that a general condemnation of the mafia as outlaw concerted action is as inappropriate as general approbation. The development of the mafia in Sicily arose from a self-help tradition which, in the course of time, became corrupted, and, ultimately, an additional burden on villagers.

The rise of the Camporano mafia as an expression of self-rule and self-reliance can be largely explained in terms of both the failure of the official government and the stunted growth of Christian Democracy before World War I. It is possible that the rise of mafia groups as regimes of self-reliance in towns with a strong Socialist tradition may have been in part due to the suppression of workers' solidarity leagues throughout the second half of the nineteenth century. This, of course, does not rule out the possibility of mafia groups as criminal and parasitic institutions ab origine, but due process of inquiry requires that such possibilities be investigated and not assumed ab initio. By disaggregating the Camporano mafia system between how and why it was constituted and the actions taken postconstitutionally and by turning the focus of research to a consideration of that system in action within the larger context, I have demonstrated that due process of inquiry can apply to outlaw societies. The research places in sharp relief the paradoxical situation that self-help efforts face when they are constrained or forced to take on outlaw forms. As I speculated in chapter 1 and observed in chapters 6, 7, 8, and 9, such efforts are apt to experience considerable difficulties in remaining true to their origins. They can easily succumb to inner decadence or defects inherent in their very organization. The paradox of the sword or Faustian bargain inherent in the constitution of political order is perhaps nowhere more evident than in unorthodox or perverse forms of self-government. By becoming a burden and parasite on villagers, the Camporano mafia vanquished itself, but this may not always be so for other, larger, parasitic institutions in society.

To judge unilaterally a particular type of action as criminal just because it is labeled mafia is contrary to basic precepts of justice. The antimafia war in Camporano during the 1960s suggests how righteous *and* wrong public policy can be when it is based upon righteous indignation. The Camporano mafia had already ceased to be part of the Sicilian problem when the antimafia war resurrected it and created a new Camporano mafia—with somewhat tragic consequences. Appeals to the mafia to explain or account for governmental failures and even criminal activities in Sicily should be generally treated as mere confessions of ignorance because they avoid the investigation needed to show their empirical warrantability. Such appeals may unwittingly serve both to misdirect public concern about the course that the fight against crime should take (cf. *Attenzione*, 1980) and to provide a handy cover for ignoring "the practice of empire" or "bureaucratic free enterprise" among those who occupy public positions. It should be perfectly possible to remove the shadows and false lights that obscure the general view of mafia groups without diluting these mafia groups either into "mafia mystique" (Smith, 1975) or, by way of a functionalist argument, into veritable *onorate società*.

General social disintegration in Sicily is not an inability to act but the presence of institutional arrangements that create impediments to voluntary collective actions rather than facilitating those actions. The Sicilian case further suggests that human beings can abandon individualistic action in favor of other strategies, such as voluntary concerted action, when they have reasons to believe that such strategies would enhance their mutual, individual or family welfare. But this is not simply another case in support of Popkin's *Rational Peasant* (1979). It is also one in support of the thesis advanced by James C. Scott in *The Moral Economy of the Peasant* (1976). Sicilian villagers tend to act in a rational and moral way—signifying, in effect, that rationality and morality as truths and as rules of conduct need not be at variance with one another (see Colburn, 1982: 449). In any event, the history of Camporano reveals that the common people of Sicily do not fit in either Karl Marx's "sack of potatoes" (1852: 124) or Benedetto Croce's "inert and heavy and reluctant mass" (1925: 195).

Party Politics and Self-Government

Political parties like the Communist party have been generally hailed as the new agencies of political expression and representation for the true integration of Southern villagers in modern politics. Chapters 8 and 9 highlight some of the strength and weakness of this thesis. The requirements of national and regional party politics in Camporano did lead to the destruction of local patriotism, the collapse of the mafia, and the true integration of Camporano villagers in modern politics. But as a result of the dominance of party entrepreneurs and party leaders over the conduct of local affairs, the adaptive potential of an autonomous and self-reliant people has been lost in servitude to a new ruling class.

Modern Camporano has become marginal precisely because it is fully integrated into the political economy of mass parties. This does not deny the importance of economic factors in reducing communities, like those in Southern Italy, to "historical marginality" (Pizzorno, 1966). It simply alerts us to the possibility that historical marginality can be grounded in political factors as well. The preceding chapters point to at least two other sets of generalizations about party politics and self-government.

Southern Italy has often been singled out as a classic case of clientelist and personalist politics. The patrons of earlier times have now been replaced and displaced by mass parties like the DC, but politics there still goes on along particularistic rather than universalistic lines. The analysis suggests that there is something to this argument but it is not quite right. The existence of political clienteles, dispensing selective benefits and acting as rent-seeking societies, does not necessarily imply—as the literature would have one believe—that Southern Italians (1) lack universalistic values, (2) have a proclivity for particularistic politics, and (3) do not fight intraparty and interparty struggles on questions of principles. Events discussed in chapters 8 and 9 indicate that the universalistic values of liberal democracy are very much part of Southern villagers' belief and value systems, and that political ideas are not minor components of intraparty rivalry there. Furthermore, Zuckerman observes that "although particular arrangements and ties may change, there is much evidence that clientelism as a form of political association neither requires social disorganization nor is necessarily replaced with the spread of industrialization" (1979: 27–28). The point, then, is not why Southern Italian politics is characterized by clientelist and personalist factions but, rather, why the politics of factions takes the particular form it does there. This has already been dealt with by Zuckerman (1979), but I can amplify his discussion somewhat.

There is a tendency in much of the literature on modern Italian politics to assume too sharp a distinction between the politics of particular-

235

ism (selective economic or material benefits) and the politics of universalism (the collective good or the public interest). As a result, research on Italian party politics has taken on some of the characteristics of Pigovian welfare economics criticized by James M. Buchanan:

> The orthodox implication of Pigovian welfare economics follows only on the assumption that individuals respond to *different* motives when they participate in market and in political activity. The only behavioral model appropriate to the Pigovian analysis is that which has been called "the bifurcated man." Man must be assumed to shift his psychological and moral gears when he moves from the realm of organized market activity to that of organized political activity and *vice versa*. Only if there can be demonstrated to be something in the nature of market organization, as such, that brings out the selfish motives in man, and something in the political organization, as such, which in turn, suppresses these motives and brings out the more "noble" ones, can there be assumed any "bridge" between the orthodox externality analysis and practical policy even apart from problems of specific policy prescription. (1962: 23–24)

The notion of "the bifurcated man" is as inappropriate to the study of politics as it is to the study of economics. If social scientists were to analyze the strategies Southern Italians utilize when confronted with different types of joint decision-making mechanisms *separately* from the structure of individual internal value systems, the actions of individual Italians in different arenas might appear more logical and less traditional, and hence more universalistic and less particularistic (see also Benjamin, 1980: 3–4; E. Ostrom, 1966; Popkin, 1979: 244–245).

At this juncture one may summon the chicken-and-egg puzzle to question my assessment. The different types of joint decision-making mechanisms that exist in Italy are themselves not only causal phenomena but the product of decisions by political leaders. Therefore one may ask, Which came first? Decision rules or political clienteles? And, following this line of reason again, one may answer, The political clienteles came first. I disagree, and suggest, instead, that the chicken-and-egg puzzle may be no puzzle at all if one is willing to make the analytical distinction that public choice scholars make between constitutional choice and actions taken postconstitutionally. The value of this distinction is that it enables one to indicate whether or not the process of constitutional choice for the making of either the Kingdom or the Republic of Italy ar-

236

ticulated an awareness of the consequences that were to be associated with the way the exercise of and access to political authority was organized. Substantial data now exist about the performance of the constitutional proposal acted upon in 1860–1865 and in 1946. By bringing together the constitutional and the operational levels of analysis one can reach conclusions about whether or not, or the extent to which, joint decision-making mechanisms have yielded consequences consistent with expectations. This is the closest that human beings can come in establishing and examining governments as experiments in reflection and choice (see also V. Ostrom, 1971, 1974 and 1980).

The genius of the eighteenth-century philosophers was to reject the model of the bifurcated man and to recognize, instead, that the self-interest of individuals can be made to serve and advance the commonweal under the appropriate institutional arrangements. The genius of the authors of *The Federalist* and the participants of the Philadelphia Convention was to apply that lesson to the reformulation of the American constitutional system. By contrast, the contribution of eighteenth-century political thought to questions of institutional design and analysis has not been well received in Italy. Cattaneo, Colajanni, Einaudi, Ferrara and Salvemini are among the few "men of thought and action" to contribute to that tradition, but neither their thought nor their action became truly *filosofia militante* (Bobbio, 1971). The modeling and remodeling of the machinery of Italian government have generally proceeded on the assumption that the self-interest of individuals cannot or should not be made to serve and advance the commonweal—in the famous words of Vittorio Emanuele Orlando, "all political, sociological, economical considerations should be expunged from the pure science of law" (quoted in Ferraresi, 1982: 8). It is not without irony that the system of government which succeeded in theory to expunge "all political, sociological, economical considerations" from its administration should have become the opposite in practice. But let there be no misunderstanding. I am not trying to assign all the faults to political institutions. What I suggest for further research is this: that the structure of incentives inherent in the design of, say, American and Italian governments may go a long way in accounting for the different manifestations of clientelism that can be observed in the two countries; and that, as hinted in chapter 8, Southern Italian villagers and officials may be forced to behave in an institutional framework that produces outcomes (clientelism and the like) which they may not themselves value so highly as possible alternatives.

237

A second set of speculations derived from the preceding chapters relates more specifically to the relationship between local, regional, and national self-government. The failure of various voluntary and public efforts at community development in Camporano over the course of the nineteenth and twentieth centuries suggests that in addition to opportunities for local self-government, there must exist some structure of overlapping regimes which will afford opportunities to resolve conflict and reach appropriate judicial and legislative remedies to facilitate mutual interests. This is precisely the point regarding the failure of center-periphery relations in centralized regimes. Resolution of the Sicilian problem requires not only capability for local self-government but the capability to participate in larger, regional, national, and international communities that also respect the need for local self-governing capabilities—what Aaron Wildavsky characterizes as "a bias toward federalism" (1976; see also Bognetti, 1980; Rougemont, 1977).

This bias was anticipated in 1848 by demands of Sicilians for a United States of Italy and continuously reiterated by Sicilian autonomist publicists before and after Italian unification. It was shown, albeit in an unorthodox way, by the functioning of the Camporano mafia regime before World War I. The independentist movement after World War II, the Sicilian revolt in the Demochristian party in 1958, and the ongoing collective and self-help efforts in the earthquake-stricken Belice Valley, so tellingly described by Lorenzo Barbera (1980), represent different expressions of the same concern. In an analysis of alternative prospects for the future development of the Italian South, a one-time associate of Danilo Dolci in Western Sicily, Eyvind Hytten, reached similar conclusions when he observed that " 'the raw material' for a social reawakening [in the Italian South] is not missing. What is missing are the instruments and the institutions that could enhance it in a proper way, without exploitation from any quarter [*senza strumentalizzazione e senza tendenze eversive*]" (Hytten, 1969: 64; see also *L'Espresso*, 1979; Salvemini, 1973). The critical problem is how to move in this direction as long as the choices about basic policies and the availability of different organizational arrangements for pursuing developmental opportunities continue to reside with members of ruling parties and ruling bureaucracies, where local public employees are not accountable to local constituencies but to central and regional officials accountable to national mass parties.

The Past as the Future?

In the course of the second half of the nineteenth century and until Fascist rule, Sicilian publicists such as Napoleone Colajanni and Edoardo Pantano likened proposals to decentralize central and communal government authority to attempts to shorten the handle of a hammer when the hammer of central bureaucracy itself was the problem (see Ganci, 1958, 1973; Lupo, 1977). These analysts were skeptical about the capabilities of such efforts to correct the malfunctioning of the national system of public administration. At the same time, they were aware that the transformation of a centralized state into a state based upon a radically different design could occur only over a long period of time. Hence, they came to view proposals to shorten the handle of the bureaucratic hammer as opportunities that might provide the conditions leading to a transformation of the Italian state into a different system of government. This different system of government, they anticipated, would be based upon an extension of individual self-government to towns, villages, cities, regions, and to the nation. These Sicilian publicists used the writings on democracy in America by Madison and Hamilton and Tocqueville to support their contention that such a design of government was conceptually and operationally feasible (Colajanni, 1883; Ganci, 1973: 51–69, 261–285, and 1980).

If the scourge of war can now be avoided for several generations, then the extension of the regionalist state to the rest of Italy, the establishment of neighborhood councils in large communes, and the presence of a superstructure of institutional arrangements at the European community level may provide the conditions for a gradual transformation of the Italian public service system to emphasize service rather than control or philanthropy. If urban neighborhood councils succeed in restructuring their position from advisory councils to self-organizing, autonomous neighborhood governments with overlapping jurisdictions, if a revolt of constituencies succeeds in restructuring the major political parties, and if efforts are made to provide the European Economic Community with the necessary means to carry its agency to the persons of citizens of its member states, opportunities may then exist to transform the imperial state into one that allows Sicilian people to be part of larger political communities without depriving them of opportunities to act as autonomous local communities.

239

I have no interest in straitjacketing, albeit if only with the power of words, the future of Italy. I am not unmindful of Milovan Djilas's observation that "history does not exactly abound with instances of thinkers' predictions having come true, least of all those relating to social patterns and peoples' attitudes and ways of life" (1969: 150). The adaptive potential of a resilient people should always encourage "a bias for hope" (Hirschman, 1971). And yet, as long as the hegemony of the national ruling coalition prevails over local and regional party organizations, it is difficult to anticipate changes in the central government dominance over the service structures in communal and regional governments. Competitive rivalry among members of the ruling coalition and a transition from Demochristian hegemony to Communist hegemony need not radically alter these conditions (cf. Bartoli, 1981; Bognetti, 1978; Di Palma, 1978: 48–58; Lange and Tarrow, 1980; Penniman, 1981; Tarrow, 1977a: 255–258). The leaders of each major party have incentives to preserve the prerogatives of the central government over the instrumentalities of the imperial state as soon as they become the government and can exercise those prerogatives. Moreover, as long as the Europeanization of the Sicilian problem or the Southern Question excludes institutional considerations bearing upon a restructuring of decision-making capabilities available to individual citizens, it is difficult to anticipate changes in the present structure of the imperialist state and its satraps who dominate regional and local development. Hence, short of conditions that threaten the survival of the parliamentary regime itself, leaders of each major Italian party have little or no incentives to alter the structure of government to facilitate self-government in the different towns, villages, cities, and regions of Italy.

Political authority in Camporano is but an instance of a larger problem. The past is the future when history repeats itself. The Sicilian problem can be solved when the Sicilian people have the power to transform their own conditions and make their own history both as they come to terms with their own problems and have their share in shaping the history of Italy and that of Europe.

Bibliography

List of Works Cited

Accati, Luisa
1970   "Lotta rivoluzionaria dei contadini siciliani e pugliesi nel 1919–1920." *Il Ponte* 31 (October): 1263–1293.

Albini, Joseph L.
1971   *The American Mafia: Genesis of a Legend.* New York: Appleton-Century-Crofts.

Alessi, Giuseppe
1949   *Mafia banditismo e riforma agraria.* Palermo: Pezzino.

Aliberti, Giovanni
1967   "Il dazio sui consumi dopo l'Unità." *Nord e Sud* 14 (August–September): 218–250.

Alongi, Giuseppe
1887   *La mafia (fattori—manifestazioni—rimedi)* Palermo: Remo Sandron, 1904.

Alvaro, Corrado
1930   *Revolt in Aspromonte.* Trans. by Frances Frenaye. New York: Golden Eagle Press, 1962.

Amadei, Giorgio
1971   *Cooperazione per una agricoltura in trasformazione.* Bologna: Il Mulino.

Anfossi, Anna
1962   "Differenze socio-culturali tra gruppi piemontesi e meridionali a Torino." In AA.VV., *Immigrazione e industria.* Milan: Edizioni di Comunità.

Arnolfini, G. A.
1768   *Giornale di viaggio e quesiti sull'economia siciliana.* Caltanissetta: Salvatore Sciascia, 1962.

Arnone, Salvatore
1910a   "Il latifondo e le cooperative in Sicilia." *Rivista Internazionale di Scienze Sociali e Discipline Ausiliarie* 18 (August): 544–556.

1910b   "Il latifondo e le cooperative in Sicilia." *Rivista Internazionale di Scienze Sociali e Discipline Ausiliarie* 18 (September): 20–49.

241

Asor Rosa, Alberto
1975   *Storia d'Italia dall'Unità a oggi. La Cultura.* Vol. IV. Turin: Einaudi.
Attenzione
1980   "Mafia Myths and Mafia Facts: A Symposium." (February): 51–59.
Bagehot, Walter
1867   *The English Constitution.* London: Oxford University Press, 1968.
Bailey, F. G.
1969   *Stratagems and Spoils: A Social Anthropology of Politics.* New York: Schocken Books.
Balsamo, Abbé Paolo
1809   *A View of the Present State of Sicily: Its Rural Economy, Population, and Produce, Particularly in the County of Modica.* London: Gale & Curtis, 1811.
1848   *Memorie segrete sulla istoria moderna del Regno di Sicilia.* Palermo: Edizioni della Regione Siciliana, 1969.
Barbagallo, Salvo
1974   *Una rivoluzione mancata.* Catania: Bonanno.
Barbera, Lorenzo
1964   "L'enfiteusi in Sicilia dalle origini ad oggi." In *L'Enfiteusi in Sicilia.* Atti del I Convegno Regionale, Alleanza Coltivatori Siciliani e Centro Studi e Iniziative per la Piena Occupazione (October). Palermo: Tipografia Luxograph, 1965.
1980   *I ministri dal cielo. I contadini del Belice raccontano.* Milan: Feltrinelli.
Barberis, Corrado
1970   *Gli operai contadini.* Bologna: Il Mulino.
Barnes, Samuel H.
1966   "Italy: Oppositions on Left, Right and Center." In Robert H. Dahl, ed., *Political Oppositions in Western Democracies.* New Haven: Yale University Press.
1976   "The Dark Side of Pluralism: Italian Democracy and the Limits of Political Engineering." In John H. Halowell, ed., *Prospects for Constitutional Democracy: Essays in Honor of R. Taylor Cole.* Durham: Duke University Press.
1977   *Representation in Italy: Institutionalized Tradition and Electoral Choice.* Chicago: University of Chicago Press.
Barone, Giuseppe
1977   "Ristrutturazione e crisi del blocco agrario: dai fasci siciliani al primo dopoguerra." In G. Barone et al., *Potere e società nella crisi dello stato liberale.* Catania: Pellicanolibri.

Bibliography

Barrese, Orazio
1973   *I complici: Gli anni dell'antimafia*. Milan: Feltrinelli.

Bartoli, Domenico
1981   *Gli anni della tempesta: Alle radici del malessere italiano*. Milan: Editoriale Nuova.

Bates, Robert H.
1978   "People in Villages: Micro-level Studies in Political Economy." *World Politics* 31 (October): 129–149.

Battaglia, Aristide
1895   *L'evoluzione sociale in rapporto alla proprietà fondiaria in Sicilia*. Palermo: Libreria Carlo Clauden di Alberto Reber.

Baviera Albanese, Adelaide
1974   *In Sicilia nel sec. XVI: Verso una rivoluzione industriale?* Caltanissetta: Salvatore Sciascia.

Beals, Carleton
1923   "Absenteeism, Kissed and Crowned." *The Freeman* 7 (March 14): 10–12.

Bell, David, and Lorne Tepperman
1979   *The Roots of Disunity: A Look at Canadian Political Culture*. Toronto: McClelland & Stewart.

Benjamin, Roger
1980   *The Limits of Politics: Collective Goods and Political Change in Postindustrial Societies*. Chicago: University of Chicago Press.

Berger, Thomas R.
1981   *Fragile Freedoms: Human Rights and Dissent in Canada*. Toronto: Clarke, Irwin & Co.

Berti, Giuseppe
1960   "Per una inchiesta parlamentare sulla mafia di Agrigento." *Cronache Meridionali* (September): 539–552.

Bertrand, Charles L.
1976   "War and Subversion in Italy: 1917–1918." Paper. Montreal: Concordia University, Department of History.

Binder, Leonard, Lucien W. Pye, James S. Coleman, Sidney Verba, Joseph LaPalombara, and Myron Weiner.
1971   *Crises and Sequences in Political Development*. Princeton: Princeton University Press.

Blok, Anton
1966   "Land Reform in a West Sicilian Latifondo Village: The Persistence of a Feudal Structure." *Anthropological Quarterly* 39: 1–16.
1969   "Mafia and Peasant Rebellion as Contrasting Factors in Sicilian Latifundism." *Archives Européennes de Sociologie* 10: 95–116.

1972   "The Peasant and the Brigand: Social Banditry Reconsidered." *Comparative Studies in Society and History* 14 (September): 494–505.

1974   *The Mafia of a Sicilian Village, 1860–1960: A Study of Violent Peasant Entrepreneurs.* New York: Harper & Row.

Blum, Jerome

1978   *The End of the Old Order in Rural Europe.* Princeton: Princeton University Press.

Bobbio, Norberto

1971   *Una filosofia militante: Studi su Carlo Cattaneo.* Turin: Einaudi.

Bognetti, Giovanni

1978   "Stato ed economia in Italia." *Il Politico* 43: 85–105.

1980   "L'esperienza federale americana e l'attuale vocazione italiana al federalismo. Una riflessione comparatistica." *Jus* 27 (fasc. III): 214–251.

Bonfadini, Romualdo

1876   *Relazione della Giunta per l'inchiesta sulle condizioni della Sicilia.* Reprinted in Salvatore Carbone e Renato Grispo, eds., *L'inchiesta sulle condizioni sociali ed economiche della Sicilia (1875–1876).* 2 vols. Bologna: Cappelli, 1968.

Born, Lester K.

1927   "What Is the Podestà?" *American Political Science Review* 21 (November): 863–871.

Boulding, Kenneth E.

1963   "Toward a Pure Theory of Threat Systems." *American Economic Review* 53: 424–434.

Brancato, Francesco

1946–   "Il commercio dei grani nel settecento in Sicilia." *Archivio Storico*
1947   *Siciliano* (serie 3): 247–274.

1956   *La Sicilia nel primo ventennio del Regno d'Italia.* Bologna: Cesare Zuffi.

Briggs, John W.

1978   *An Italian Passage: Immigrants to Three American Cities, 1890–1930.* New Haven: Yale University Press.

Brogger, Jan

1971   *Montevarese: A Study of Peasant Society and Culture in Southern Italy.* Oslo: Universitetsforlaget.

Bruccoleri, Giuseppe

1913   *La Sicilia di oggi: appunti economici.* Rome: Athenaeum.

Buchanan, James M.

1960   "La Scienza delle finanze: The Italian Tradition in Fiscal Theory." In his *Fiscal Theory and Political Economy.* Chapel Hill: The University of North Carolina Press.

1962   "Politics, Policy and the Pigovian Margins." *Economica* 29 (February): 17–28.

Buchanan, James M., and Gordon Tullock

1962   *The Calculus of Consent: Logical Foundations of Constitutional Democracy.* Ann Arbor: University of Michigan Press.

Caico, Louise

1910   *Sicilian Ways and Days.* London: John Long.

Caldo, Costantino, ed.

1977   *I comuni in Sicilia: problemi sul riassetto territoriale comunale e intercomunale.* Palermo: Stampatore Tipolitografi Associati.

Calisse, Carlo

1887   *Storia del parlamento in Sicilia dalla fondazione alla caduta della monarchia.* Bologna: Forni, 1973.

1928   *A History of Italian Law.* Trans. by L. B. Register. Boston: Little, Brown & Company.

Cameroni, Silvana A., and Giovanni Cameroni

1976   *Movimento cattolico e contadino: indagine su Carlo De Cardona.* Milan: Cooperativa Edizioni Jaca Book.

Cammett, John M.

1963   "Two Recent Polemics on the Character of the Italian Risorgimento." *Science and Society* 27 (Fall): 433–457.

Campbell, Rodney

1977   *The Secret Wartime Collaboration of the Mafia and the U.S. Navy.* New York: McGraw-Hill.

Cancila, Orazio

1974   *Gabelloti e contadini in un comune rurale (secc. XVIII–XIX).* Caltanissetta: Salvatore Sciascia.

Candida, Renato

1956   *Questa mafia.* Caltanissetta: Salvatore Sciascia.

Canepa, Antonino

1942   *La Sicilia ai siciliani.* Reprinted in F. Gaja, *L'esercito della lupara: baroni e banditi siciliani nella guerriglia contro l'Italia.* Milan: Area Editore, 1962.

Capurso, G. L.

1964   "Cronache amministrative: Palermo." *Nord e Sud* (July): 52–56.

Carcaci, Duca di

1977   *Il movimento per l'indipendenza della Sicilia.* Palermo: Flaccovio.

Carini, Isidoro

1894   "La questione sociale in Sicilia." *Rivista Internazionale di Scienze Sociali e Discipline Ausiliarie* 2 (March): 395–423.

Cattaneo, Carlo
1848   *Stati Uniti d'Italia.* Turin: Chiantore, 1945.
Cavalieri, Enea
1925   "Prefazione alla seconda edizione." In Leopoldo Franchetti and Sidney Sonnino, *La Sicilia.* 2 vols. Florence: Vallecchi.
Cavalli, Luciano
1964   *Gli immigranti meridionali e la società ligure.* Bergamo: Franco Angeli.
Chapman Gower, Charlotte
1935   *Milocca: A Sicilian Village.* Cambridge: Schenkman, 1971.
Checco, Antonino
1977   "Le campagne siciliane e gli indirizzi di politica agraria del fascismo, (1922–1943): ipotesi e linee di ricerca." *Incontri Meridionali* (January–March): 108–117.
Chiaramonte, Socrate
1901   "Il programma del '48 e i partiti politici in Sicilia." *Archivio Storico Siciliano* 26: 110–221.
Chilanti, Felice
1959   *Ma chi è questo Milazzo?* Florence: Parenti.
Cimino, Marcello
1977   *Fine di una nazione.* Palermo: Flaccovio.
Cipolla, Nicola
1954   "La lotta per la terra dei contadini siciliani." *Riforma Agraria* 2 (October): 10–12.
Ciuni, Roberto
1972   "I mafiosi ringraziano." *Giornale di Sicilia* (June 4): pp. 1, 18.
Clark, M. Gardner
1954   "Governmental Restrictions on Labor Mobility in Italy." *Industrial and Labor Relations Review* 8 (October): 3–18.
1977   *Agricultural Social Security and Rural Exodus in Italy.* Western Societies Program Occasional Papers, no. 7. Ithaca: Center for International Studies, Cornell University.
Coase, R. H.
1960   "The Problem of Social Cost." *Journal of Law & Economics* 3 (October): 1–44.
Colajanni, Napoleone
1883   *Le istituzioni municipali: cenni ed osservazioni.* Piazza Armerina: Tipografia di Adolfo Pansini.
1885   *La delinquenza della Sicilia e le sue cause.* Palermo: Tipografia del Giornale di Sicilia.
1887   "Di alcuni studi recenti sulla proprietà collettiva." *Giornale degli Economisti* 2: 519–532.

1895   *Gli avvenimenti di Sicilia e le loro cause.* Palermo: Remo Sandron.

1900   *Nel regno della mafia: La Sicilia dai Borboni ai Sabaudi.* Palermo: Editrice I. L. A. Palma, 1971.

1905   *Come si amministra la giustizia in Italia.* Rome: Presso la Rivista Popolare.

Colburn, Forrest D.

1982   "Current Studies of Peasants and Rural Development: Applications of the Political Economy Approach." *World Politics* 34 (April): 437–449.

Commissione Parlamentare d'Inchiesta sul Fenomeno della Mafia in Sicilia

1972   *Relazione sui lavori svolti e sullo stato del fenomeno mafioso al termine della V legislatura.* Doc. XXIII, no. 2–septies. Rome: Stabilimenti Tipografici Carlo Colombo.

Commons, John R.

1924   *Legal Foundations of Capitalism.* Madison: University of Wisconsin Press, 1957.

Composto, Renato

1964   "Fermenti sociali nel clero minore siciliano prima dell'unificazione." *Studi Storici* 5 (April–June): 264–279.

Connor, Walker

1972   "Nation-Building or Nation-Destroying?" *World Politics* 24 (April): 319–355.

Cornelisen, Ann

1976   *Women of the Shadows.* Boston: Little, Brown & Company.

Corriere della Sera

1973   "Frenare l'esodo dei giovani per salvare l'agricoltura." (January 9): 5.

Corriere di Girgenti

1913   "Il Problema della irrigazione nel Mezzogiorno d'Italia." "Il Problema dell'acqua potabile e l'interesse contrario dei latifondisti." Reprinted in Giovanni Raffiotta, *La Sicilia nel primo ventennio del secolo XX.* Palermo: Industria Grafica Nazionale, 1959.

Cortese, Nino

1956   *La prima rivoluzione separatista siciliana 1820–1821.* Naples: Libreria Scientifica Editrice.

Costanzo, Giulio

1923   "The Principal Types of Agricultural Cooperative Society in Italy." *International Review of Agricultural Economics* 1 (new series): 50–80.

1926   "The Wheat Campaign in Italy." *International Review of Agricultural Economics* 4 (new series): 70–86.

Crivella, Alfonso
1593   *Trattato di Sicilia.* Caltanissetta: Salvatore Sciascia, 1970.
Croce, Benedetto
1925   *History of the Kingdom of Naples.* Edited by H. Stuart Hughes. Chicago: University of Chicago Press, 1970.
Cronin, Constance
1970   *The Sting of Change: Sicilians in Sicily and Australia.* Chicago: University of Chicago Press.
Crozier, Michel
1964   *The Bureaucratic Phenomenon.* Chicago: University of Chicago Press.
D'Alessandro, Enzo
1959   *Brigantaggio e mafia in Sicilia.* Messina: Casa Editrice G. D'Anna.
Damiani, Abele
1884 & *Atti della Giunta per la Inchiesta Agraria sulle condizioni della*
1885   *Classe agricola, La Sicilia.* Vol. XIII. Rome. Forzani e C.
Davis, J.
1973   *Land and Family in Pisticci.* London School of Economics Monographs on Social Anthropology, no. 48. New York: Humanities Press.
1978   "The Value of Evidence." *Man* 13 (September): 471–473.
Davis, John A.
1979   *Società e imprenditori nel Regno Borbonico 1815–1860.* Bari: Laterza.
De Francisci Gerbino, G.
1940   "Una grande riforma agraria: la colonizzazione del latifondo siciliano." *Giornale degli Economisti* (January–February): 67–87.
De Mattei, Rodolfo
1927   *Il pensiero politico siciliano fra il Sette e l'Ottocento.* Catania: Tip. Crescenzio Galatola.
De Rosa, Gabriele
1977   *Luigi Sturzo.* Turin: U.T.E.T.
De Stefano, Francesco, and F. L. Oddo
1963   *Storia della Sicilia dal 1860 al 1910.* Bari: Laterza.
De Viti De Marco, Antonio
1898   "Le recenti sommosse in Italia: cause e riforme." *Giornale degli Economisti* 16 (June): 517–546.
Diamant, Alfred
1960   *Austrian Catholics and the First Republic: Democracy, Capitalism and the Social Order, 1918–1934.* Princeton: Princeton University Press.

248

Bibliography

di Castro, Scipio
    1601   *Avvertimenti di Don Scipio di Castro a Marco Antonio Colonna Quando Andò Vicerè di Sicilia.* Rome: Edizioni di Storia e Letteratura, 1950.

Diecidue, Gianni
    1966   "I Consigli Civici a Castelvetrano nei Secoli XVI–XVIII." *Archivio Storico Siciliano* 16 (3): 89–151.

Diem, Aubrey
    1961   "Land Reform and Reclamation in Sicily." Ph.D. dissertation. University of Michigan.
    1963   "Land Reform and Reclamation in Sicily." *Canadian Geographical Journal* 66: 88–91.

Di Fresco, Antonio Maria
    1976   *Sicilia. 30 anni di regione.* Palermo: Vittorietti.

di Giovanni, Alberto, and Antonio Palazzo, eds.
    1982   *Luigi Sturzo e la Rerum Novarum.* Milan: Massimo.

Di Giovanni, Vincenzo, ed.
    1876   *Capitoli gabelle e privilegi della città di Alcamo ora per la prima volta pubblicati preceduti da notizie storiche.* Palermo: Tipografia di Michele Amenta.

Di Matteo, Salvo
    1967   *Anni roventi: la Sicilia dal 1943 al 1947. Cronache di un quinquennio.* Palermo: Denaro.

Di Matteo, Salvo, and F. Pillitteri
    1973   *Storia dei Monti di Pietà in Sicilia.* Palermo: Flaccovio.

Di Palma, Giuseppe
    1977a   "Christian Democracy: The End of Hegemony?" In Howard R. Penniman, ed., *Italy at the Polls: The Parliamentary Elections of 1976.* Washington, D.C.: American Enterprise Institute for Public Policy Research.
    1977b   *Surviving without Governing: The Italian Parties in Parliament.* Berkeley: University of California Press.
    1978   *Political Syncretism in Italy: Historical Coalition Strategies and the Present Crisis.* Berkeley: Institute of International Studies, University of California.
    1980   "Da un regime all'altro." *Biblioteca della Libertà* 17 (April–September): 115–132.

Djilas, Milovan
    1969   *The Unperfect Society: Beyond the New Class.* New York: Harcourt, Brace & World.

Dolci, Danilo
1966 *The Man Who Plays Alone*. Trans. by Antonia Cowan. New York: Pantheon Books, 1968.
Eckstein, Harry
1966 *Division and Cohesion in Democracy: A Study of Norway*. Princeton: Princeton University Press.
Economist (London)
1958 "Sicilian Revolt." 189 (November): 618.
Einaudi, Luigi
1948 "Proprietari e latifondisti in Italia." *Corriere della Sera* (May 1): 1.
1955 "Servitù della gleba." *Lo Scrittoio del Presidente*. Turin: Giulio Einaudi, 1956.
Elazar, Daniel J.
1969 "Federalism and Covenant." In Daniel J. Elazar, ed., *The Politics of American Federalism*. Lexington: D. C. Heath.
1977 "The Compound Structure of Public Service Delivery Systems in Israel." In Vincent Ostrom and Frances Pennell Bish, eds. *Comparing Urban Service Delivery Systems: Structure and Performance*. Beverly Hills: Sage Publications.
1978 "Covenant as the Basis of the Jewish Political Tradition." *Jewish Journal of Sociology* 20 (June): 5–37.
Elazar, Daniel J., ed.
1979 *Self-Rule/Shared Rule: Federal Solutions to the Middle East Conflict*. Ramat Gan: Turtledove Publishing.
Ente di Sviluppo Agricolo (E.S.A.) Regione Siciliana
1969 *Piano di sviluppo agricolo della zona*. 2 vols. Palermo (October).
Evans, Robert H.
1967 *Coexistence: Communism and Its Practice in Bologna 1945–1965*. Notre Dame: University of Notre Dame Press.
1976 *Life and Politics in a Venetian Community*. Notre Dame: University of Notre Dame Press.
Faenza, Roberto, and Marco Fini
1976 *Gli americani in Italia*. Milan: Feltrinelli.
Fanfani, Pietro
1885 *Novissimo vocabolario della lingua italiana scritta e parlata*. 6th ed. Naples: Cav. Antonio Morano.
Fenoaltea, Stefano
1975 "The Rise and Fall of a Theoretical Model: The Manorial System." *Journal of Economic History* 35 (June): 386–409.
Ferrara, Francesco
1848 "Unione non unità." Reprinted in his *Opere complete*. Vol. 1, Part

Bibliography

1. Rome: Associazione Bancaria Italiana e della Banca d'Italia, 1965.

1860   "Brevi note sulla Sicilia." In *Camillo Cavour. Carteggi. La Liberazione del Mezzogiorno e la formazione del Regno d'Italia.* Vols. 1–2. Bologna: Zanichelli, 1949.

Ferraresi, Franco
1982   "Bureaucrats, Clients and Politicians: The Deflection of Change in Italian Bureaucracy." Paper prepared for the Conference on Organizational Responses to Change, Montreal (April).

Ferrigno, Giovanni Battista
1915–   "Un contratto di pace tra Donna Antonina Contessa d'Aragona e la
1916   Università di Terranova nel 1516." *Archivio Storico Siciliano* 40: 118–146.

Finocchiaro-Aprile, Andrea
1966   *Il movimento indipendentista siciliano.* Palermo: Edizioni Libri Siciliani.

Fiume, Giovanna
1977   "Il lavoro della donna nella Sicilia dell'Ottocento (la tessitura)." *Nuovi Quaderni del Meridione* 15 (October–December): 435–452.
1978   "Il proletariato femminile in Sicilia prima dell'Unità." *Nuovi Quaderni del Meridione* 16 (January–March): 69–95.

Fogarty, Michael P.
1957   *Christian Democracy in Western Europe 1820–1953.* Notre Dame: University of Notre Dame Press.

Follett, Mary Parker
1924   *Creative Experience.* New York: Longmans, Green & Co.

Formiggini, Giorgio
1954   "La lotta per la realizzazione della riforma agraria in Sicilia." *Cronache Meridionali* (July–August): 526–530.

Fortunati, Paolo
1941   *Aspetti sociali dell'assalto al latifondo.* Quaderni di Cultura Politica. Serie 11, no. 3. Sancasciano-Pesa, Florence: Stab. Tip. Fratelli Stianti.

Franchetti, Leopoldo
1877   *Condizioni politiche e amministrative della Sicilia.* Florence: Vallecchi, 1925.

Franklin, S. H.
1969   *The European Peasantry. The Final Phase.* London: Methuen.

Freeman, Gordon
1980   *The Dark Side of Covenant.* Workshop on Covenant and Politics Publications, no. A-36. Philadelphia: Center for the Study of Feder-

alism, Temple University.

Fried, Robert C.
1963   *The Italian Prefects: A Study in Administrative Politics.* New Haven: Yale University Press.
1967   "Urbanization and Italian Politics." *Journal of Politics* 29 (August): 505–534.
1973   *Planning the Eternal City: Roman Politics and Planning since World War II.* New Haven: Yale University Press.

Gage, Nicholas
1971   *The Mafia Is Not an Equal Opportunity Employer.* New York: McGraw-Hill.

Gaja, Filippo
1962   *L'esercito della lupara: baroni e banditi siciliani nella guerriglia contro l'Italia.* Milan: Area Editore.

Galasso, Giuseppe
1977   "Un Secolo di Presenza Siciliana nella Cultura." *Archivio Storico Siciliano* 3 (serie 4): 493–507.
1980   "Il potere e i rapporti tra le classi." In Nicola Tranfaglia, ed., *L'Italia Unita nella storiografia del secondo dopoguerra.* Milan: Feltrinelli.

Galli, Giorgio
1978   *Storia della D. C.* Bari: Laterza.

Galli, Giorgio, and Alfonso Prandi
1970   *Patterns of Political Participation in Italy.* New Haven: Yale University Press.

Gallo, Corrado
1969   "Dell'inutile referendum del 1698 circa il sito della riedificanda città di Noto alla definitiva decisione del Cardinale Giudice." *Archivio Storico Siciliano* 19 (serie 3): 117–225.

Galtung, Johan
1962   "Componenti psico-sociali nella decisione di emigrare." In AA.VV., *Immigrazione e industria.* Milan: Edizioni di Comunità.

Ganci, S. Massimo
1958   *Il Commissariato del 1896 in Sicilia.* Palermo: M. Sciascia.
1964   "La mafia nel giudizio di Napoleone Colajanni." *Nuovi Quaderni del Meridione* (January–March): 50–71.
1968   *L'Italia antimoderata. Radicali, repubblicani, socialisti, autonomisti dall'Unità a oggi.* Parma: Guanda.
1973   *Da Crispi a Rudinì: la polemica regionalista, 1894–1896.* Palermo: Flaccovio.
1980   "Aspetti storici del federalismo e dell'autonomia." In Nicola

252

Bibliography

Tranfaglia, ed., *L'Italia Unita nella storiografia del secondo dopoguerra.* Milan: Feltrinelli.

Garibaldi, Giuseppe
1889   *Autobiography.* Vol. II. Trans. by A. Werner. London: Walter Smith & Innes.

Garufi, Carlo Alberto
1908   "Un contratto agrario in Sicilia nel secolo XII per la fondazione del casale di Mesepè presso Paternò." *Archivio Storico per la Sicilia Orientale* 5: 11–22.
1922   *Roccapalumba dal feudo alla abolizione de la Feudalità.* Palermo: Stabilimento E. Priulla.
1946   "Patti agrari e comuni feudali di nuova fondazione in Sicilia: dallo scorcio del secolo XI agli arbori del settecento." *Archivio Storico Siciliano* 1 (serie 3): 31–111.
1947   "Patti agrari e comuni feudali di nuova fondazione in Sicilia: dallo scorcio del secolo XI agli arbori del settecento." *Archivio Storico Siciliano* 2 (serie 3): 7–131.

Gattuso, Ignazio
1976   *Economia e società in un comune rurale della Sicilia (secoli XVI–XIX).* Palermo: Tumminelli.

Geertz, Clifford
1962   "The Rotating Credit Association: A 'Middle Rung' in Development." *Economic Development and Cultural Change* 10: 241–263.

Genuardi, Luigi
1911   *Terre Comuni ed Usi Civici in Sicilia prima dell'abolizione della Feudalità.* Palermo: Scuola Tip. "Boccone del Povero."
1921   *Il Comune nel Medioevo in Sicilia.* Palermo: Società Orazio Fiorenza.
1924   *Parlamento siciliano.* Bologna: Zanichelli.

Gerschenkron, Alexander
1961   "The Industrial Development of Italy: A Debate with Rosario Romeo (with a Postscript)." In his *Continuity in History and Other Essays.* Cambridge: Harvard University Press, 1968.

Ghisalberti, Carlo
1963   *Contributi alla storia delle amministrazioni preunitarie.* Milan: Giuffré.

Giarrizzo, Giuseppe
1966   "Paolo Balsamo economista." *Rivista Storica Italiana* 78 (March): 5–60.

Giuffrida, Romualdo
1968   *I Rothschild e la finanza pubblica in Sicilia (1849–1855).*

Caltanissetta: Salvatore Sciascia.

Goodwin, John
1842   "Progress of the Two Sicilies under the Spanish Bourbons from the
        Year 1734–35 to 1840 (Part II)." *Journal of the Statistical Society* 5:
        177–207.

Gramsci, Antonio
1926   "The Southern Question." Reprinted in his *The Modern Prince &
        Other Writings*. New York: International Publishers, 1967.

Greco, Gioacchino
1970   "Potere e parentela nella Sicilia nuova." *Quaderni di Sociologia* 19
        (no. 1): 3–41.

Greenfield, Kent Robert
1934   *Economics and Liberalism in the Risorgimento. A Study of National-
        ism in Lombardy 1814–1848*. Baltimore: The Johns Hopkins Uni-
        versity Press.

Grew, Raymond
1974   "Catholicism in a Changing Italy." In Edward R. Tannenbaum and
        Emiliana P. Noether, eds., *Modern Italy: A Topical History since
        1861*. New York: New York University Press.

Gross, Feliks
1973   *Il Paese. Values and Social Change in an Italian Village*. New York:
        New York University Press.

Guardian (Manchester)
1979   "The Japanese Mafia: Crime Goes International" (May 20): 14.

Guarino, Crescenzo
1949   "Ho attraversato da solo la 'casbah' di Partinico." *Corriere della Sera*
        (September 1): 3.

Guarnieri, Andrea
1889   "Un diploma di grazie e privilegi municipali concessi nel 1393 dai
        magnifici Conti di Peralta alla città di Calatafimi." *Archivio Storico
        Siciliano* 14: 293–314.
1892   "Alcune notizie sovra la gestione d'una casa baronale e sull'am-
        ministrazione della giustizia in Sicilia verso la fine del secolo
        XVIII." *Archivio Storico Siciliano* 17: 117–150.

Guastella, Serafino Amabile
1884   *Le parità e le storie morali dei nostri villani*. Palermo: Edizioni della
        Regione Siciliana, 1969.

Guccione, Eugenio
1974   *Ideologia e politica dei cattolici siciliani da Vito d'Ondes Reggio a
        Luigi Sturzo*. Palermo: Renzo Mazzone.

Hajda, Joseph, and Robert Leonardi
1978   "A Eurocommunist Approach to Agricultural Development: The

Italian Experience." Paper delivered at the annual meeting of the American Political Science Association, New York (August–September).

Hay, Denys
1961　*The Italian Renaissance in Its Historical Background.* Cambridge: Cambridge University Press.

Hermens, Ferdinand A.
1951　*Europe between Democracy and Anarchy.* Notre Dame: University of Notre Dame Press.

Hess, Henner
1970　*Mafia and Mafiosi: The Structure of Power.* Trans. by Ewald Osers. Lexington: D. C. Heath.

Hilowitz, Jane
1976　*Economic Development and Social Change in Sicily.* Cambridge: Schenkman.

Hirschman, Albert O.
1970　*Exit, Voice and Loyalty: Responses to Decline in Firms, Organizations, and States.* Cambridge: Harvard University Press.
1971　*A Bias for Hope: Essays on Development and Latin America.* New Haven: Yale University Press.

Hobbes, Thomas
1651　*Leviathan, or the Matter, Forme and Power of a Commonwealth Ecclesiastical and Civil.* New York: Collier Books, 1962.

Hobsbawm, Eric J.
1959　*Primitive Rebels: Studies in Archaic Forms of Social Movement in the 19th and 20th Centuries.* Manchester: Manchester University Press.

Hobson, Asher
1926　"Collective Leasing and Farming in Italy." *Journal of Land and Public Utility Economics* 2 (January): 67–72.

Holmes, Stephen Taylor
1979　"Aristippus in and out of Athens: Reply to James H. Nichols, Jr." *American Political Science Review* 73 (March): 134–138.

Hytten, Eyvind
1969　*Esperienze di sviluppo sociale nel Mezzogiorno.* Rome: Giuffrè SVIMEZ.

Hytten, Eyvind, and Marco Marchioni
1970　*Industrializzazione senza sviluppo. Gela: una storia meridionale.* Milan: Franco Angeli.

Il Mondo
1973　"Ventimila sospetti in Sicilia." (December 3): 7.

INEA
1947　*La distribuzione della proprietà fondiaria in Italia e la Sicilia.* Rome:

Edizioni Italiane.

Innis, Harold A.
1936   "Unused Capacity as a Factor in Canadian Economic History."
         Canadian Journal of Economics and Political Science 2 (February):
         1–15.

Intendenti delle Provincie
1851   *Discorsi pronunciati dagl'Intendenti delle Provincie dei Reali
         Domini al di là del Faro nell'apertura de' consigli provinciali del
         1851*. Palermo: Stabilimento Tipografico dell'Armonia.

International Review of Agricultural Economics
1921a   "Cooperative Land-Holding Sociéties—Italy." 12 (October):
         488–503.
1921b   "The Agricultural Credit Provided by the Bank of Naples and the
         Bank of Sicily." 12 (November): 582–592.

Jemolo, Arturo Carlo
1955   *Chiesa e stato in Italia dalla unificazione ai giorni nostri*. Turin:
         Einaudi, 1977.

Jenness, Diamond
1950   "The Recovery Program in Sicily." *Geographical Review* (July):
         355–363.

Kefauver, Estes
1951   *Crime in America*. Garden City: Doubleday.

Kjellberg, Francesco
1975   *Political Institutionalization. A Political Study of Two Sardinian
         Communities*. New York: Wiley.

Koenigsberger, H. G.
1951   *The Government of Sicily under Philip II of Spain: A Study in the
         Practice of Empire*. London: Staples Press.
1971   *Estates and Revolutions: Essays in Early Modern European History*.
         Ithaca: Cornell University Press.
1978   "The Italian Parliaments from Their Origins to the End of the 18th
         Century." *Journal of Italian History* 1 (Spring): 18–49.

Kogan, Norman
1959   "The Sicilian Regional Election of 1959." *Italian Quarterly* (Fall):
         58–65.
1966   *A Political History of Postwar Italy*. New York: Praeger.

Krueger, Anne O.
1974   "A Political Economy of the Rent-Seeking Society." *American Eco-
         nomic Review* 64 (June): 291–303.

La Colla, F.
1883   "La storia delle municipalità siciliane e il 'Libro Rosso' della Città
         di Salemi." *Archivio Storico Siciliano* 8: 416–434.

Bibliography

La Loggia, Enrico
1894   "I moti di Sicilia." *Giornale degli Economisti* 8 (March): 211–234.
1955   "Sintesi in dati comparati di alcune condizioni ambientali della Sicilia e indirizzi di politica regionale." *Notiziario economico finanziario siciliano.* Palermo: Banco di Sicilia.

La Lumia, Isidoro
1881– *Storie siciliane.* 4 Vols. Palermo: Edizioni della Regione Siciliana,
1883   1969.

Landi, Guido
1953   "La riforma agraria in Sicilia." *Rivista di Diritto Agrario* 32 (October–December): 315–353.
1977   *Istituzioni di Diritto Pubblico del Regno delle Due Sicilie (1815–1861).* 2 Vols. Milan: Giuffrè.

Lange, Peter, and Sidney G. Tarrow, eds.
1980   *Italy in Transition: Conflict and Consensus.* London: Frank Cass.

Lanza di Scordia, Pietro
1842   *Dello spirito di associazione nella Inghilterra in particolare. Saggio politico ed economico.* Palermo: Tipografia di Bernardo Varzì.

LaPalombara, Joseph
1964   *Interest Groups in Italian Politics.* Princeton: Princeton University Press.
1966   *Italy: The Politics of Planning.* Syracuse: Syracuse University Press.
1971   "Penetration: A Crisis of Governmental Capacity." In Leonard Binder, Lucien W. Pye, James Coleman, Sidney Verba, Joseph LaPalombara, and Myron Weiner, *Crises and Sequences in Political Development.* Princeton: Princeton University Press.

L'Espresso
1979   "Discussioni / I Meridionali affossano l'Italia?" (June 10): 220–228.

Lestingi, F.
1884   "L'associazione della fratellanza nella provincia di Girgenti." *Archivio di Psichiatria Scienza Penale e Antropologia Criminale* 5: 452–463.

Lewis, Norman
1964   *The Honoured Society: A Searching Look at the Mafia.* New York: Putnam.

Li Causi, Girolamo
1966   *Girolamo Li Causi e la sua azione politica per la Sicilia.* Palermo: Edizioni Libri Siciliani.

Limuti, Emanuele
1971   *Criminalità e mafia in Sicilia. Un decennio di misure di prevenzione.* (Estratto da *Rassegna di Studi Penitenziari*, fasc. 3) (May–June). Rome: Tipografia Delle Mantellate.

Li Vecchi, Alfredo
1975 *Caltanissetta feudale*. Caltanissetta: Sciascia.
1977 "Introduzione" to Simone Corleo, *Storia della enfiteusi dei terreni ecclesiastici di Sicilia*. Caltanissetta: Sciascia.
Llewellyn, K. N., and E. Adamson Hoebel
1941 *The Cheyenne Way. Conflict and Case Law in Primitive Jurisprudence*. Norman: University of Oklahoma Press.
Lombroso, Cesare
1879 *Sull'incremento del delitto in Italia e sui mezzi per arrestarlo*. Turin: Bocca.
Longo, Giuseppe
1957 "La nostra cara mafia." *Osservatore Politico Letterario* (April): 49–62.
Lo Preato, Joseph
1967 *Peasants No More. Social Class and Social Change in an Underdeveloped Society*. San Francisco: Chandler.
L'Ora (Palermo)
1973 "Prezzi: il grano imboscato." (August 29): 13.
Lorenzoni, Giovanni
1910 *Inchiesta parlamentare sulle condizioni dei contadini nelle provincie meridionali e nella Sicilia. Sicilia*. Vol. 6. Rome: Tipografia Nazionale di Giovanni Bertero.
1923 "Latifundia in Sicily and Their Possible Transformation." *International Review of Agricultural Economics* 1 (new series): 316–349.
Lo Schiavo, Giuseppe G.
1933 *Il reato di Associazione per delinquere nelle provincie Siciliane*. Reprinted in *La Giustizia Penale* 52 (part 1, 1952): 14–32.
Loveman, Brian
1975 "Can Development Be Administered?" Paper delivered at the annual meeting of the American Political Science Association, San Francisco (September).
1976a "The Comparative Administration Group, Development Administration and Antidevelopment." *Public Administration Review* (November–December): 616–621.
1976b *Struggle in the Countryside: Politics and Rural Labor in Chile, 1919–1973*. Bloomington: Indiana University Press.
Lupo, Salvatore
1977 "La 'questione siciliana' a una svolta. Il sicilianismo tra fascismo e dopoguerra." In G. Barone et al., *Potere e società nella crisi dello stato liberale*. Catania: Pellicanolibri.
Lupori, Nello
1960 "Il Catasto italiano a cento anni dall'unificazione. La situazione

agricola della Sicilia e gli accertamenti catastali." *Rivista del Catasto e dei servizi tecnici erariali* 15: 50–69.

Macaluso, Emanuele
    1970   *I comunisti e la Sicilia.* Rome: Editori Riuniti.
    1971   *La mafia e lo Stato.* Rome: Editori Riuniti.

McConnell, Grant
    1966   *Private Power and American Democracy.* New York: Vintage Books, 1970.

MacDonald, John S.
    1956   "Italy's Rural Social Structure and Emigration." *Occidente* 12: 437–456.

MacDonald, John S., and Beatrice D. MacDonald
    1964   "Chain Migration, Ethnic Neighborhood Formation and Social Networks." *The Milbank Memorial Fund Quarterly* 42 (January): 82–97.

McEntire, D., and D. Agostini
    1969   "Land Policies in Italy." In D. McEntire, ed., *Toward Modern Land Policies.* Padua: Institute of Agricultural Economics and Policy, University of Padua.

Mack Smith, Denis
    1950   "The Peasants' Revolt of Sicily in 1860." In AA.VV., *Studi in onore di Gino Luzzatto.* Milan: Giuffrè.
    1954   *Cavour and Garibaldi 1860. A Study in Political Conflict.* Cambridge: At the University Press.
    1965   "Latifundia in Modern Sicilian History." *Proceedings of the British Academy* 51: 85–124.
    1968a   *A History of Sicily: Medieval Sicily 800–1713.* New York: Viking Press.
    1968b   *A History of Sicily: Modern Sicily After 1713.* New York: Viking Press.
    1974   "Regionalism." In Edward R. Tannenbaum and Emiliana P. Noether, eds., *Modern Italy: A Topical History Since 1861.* New York: New York University Press.

Maranini, Giuseppe
    1969   "Le regioni tradite." *Corriere della Sera* (May 10): 11.

Marino, Giuseppe Carlo
    1976   *Partiti e lotta di classe in Sicilia.* Bari: De Donato.
    1979   *Storia del Separatismo Siciliano.* Rome: Editori Riuniti.

Mariotti, Delio
    1967   "Ricordare Palermo." *Nord e Sud* 14 (January): 8–16.

Marx, Karl
    1852   *The Eighteenth Brumaire of Louis Bonaparte.* New York: Interna-

tional Publishers, 1969.

Maxwell, Gavin
1956   *God Protect Me from My Friends*. London: Longmans, Green & Co.

Medici, Giuseppe
1945   "Italy and Land Reform." *Journal of Land and Public Utility Economics* 21 (February): 2–11.

Micciché, Giuseppe
1976   *Dopoguerra e fascismo in Sicilia*. Rome: Editori Riuniti.

Miele, Giovanni
1956   "Il nuovo ordinamento degli enti locali in Sicilia." *Rivista Trimestrale di Diritto Pubblico* 6: 278–298.

Montanelli, Indro, Alberto Cavallari, Piero Ottone, Gianfranco Piazzesi, and Giovanni Russo
1965   *Italia sotto inchiesta: Corriere della Sera 1963/65*. Florence: Sansoni Editore.

Montgomery, John D.
1972   "Allocation of Authority in Land Reform Programs: A Comparative Study of Administrative Processes and Outputs." *Administrative Science Quarterly* 17 (March): 62–75.

Morgado, Michael S.
1974   "Amilcar Cabral's Theory of Cultural Revolution." *Black Images* 3 (Summer): 3–14.

Mori, Cesare
1933   *The Last Struggle with the Mafia*. Trans. by Orlo Williams. London: Putnam.

Mosca, Gaetano
1884   *Teorica dei governi e governo parlamentare*. Milano: Giuffrè, 1968.

Mueller, Denis
1979   *Public Choice*. Cambridge: Cambridge University Press.

Naro, Cataldo
1977   *Il movimento cattolico a Caltanissetta (1893–1919)*. Caltanissetta: Edizioni del Seminario.

Nicolosi, Salvatore
1976   *Di professione: brigante*. Milan: Longanesi.

Nieburg, H. L.
1969   "Violence, Law, and the Informal Polity." *Journal of Conflict Resolution* 13: 192–209.

North, Douglass C.
1981   *Structure and Change in Economic History*. New York: W. W. Norton & Co.

North, Douglass C., and Robert Thomas
1971   "The Rise and Fall of the Manorial System: A Theoretical Model."

Bibliography

Journal of Economic History 31 (December): 777–803.
1973   *The Rise of the Western World. A New Economic History*. Cambridge: Cambridge University Press.

Novacco, Domenico
1964   "Bibliografia della mafia." *Nuovi Quaderni del Meridione* (January–March): 188–239.

Olson, Mancur, Jr.
1965   *The Logic of Collective Action*. New York: Schocken Books, 1968.

Orsenigo, L.
1921   "Note sull'invasione delle terre in Sicilia." *L'Italia Agricola* 58 (February 15): 33–40.

Osgood, Ernest Staples
1929   *The Day of the Cattleman*. Chicago: University of Chicago Press, 1970.

Ostrom, Elinor
1966   "Strategy and the Structure of Interdependent Decision-Making Mechanisms." Bloomington: Department of Government, Indiana University.
1968   "Some Postulated Effects of Learning on Constitutional Behavior." *Public Choice* 5 (Fall): 87–104.
1975   "Righteousness, Evidence, and Reform: The Police Story." *Urban Affairs Quarterly* 10 (June): 464–486.

Ostrom, Vincent
1971   *The Political Theory of a Compound Republic*. Blacksburg: Center for Study of Public Choice, Virginia Polytechnic Institute and State University.
1972   "Polycentricity." Paper presented at the annual meeting of the American Political Science Association, Washington, D.C. (September).
1974   *The Intellectual Crisis in American Public Administration*. 2nd ed. University: The University of Alabama Press.
1977   "Structure and Performance." In Vincent Ostrom and Frances Pennell Bish, eds., *Comparing Urban Service Delivery Systems*. Vol. 12, Urban Affairs Annual Reviews. Beverly Hills: Sage Publications.
1980   "Artisanship and Artifact." *Public Administration Review* 40 (July–August): 309–317.

Ottone, Piero
1966   *Fanfani*. Milan: Longanesi.

Palazzolo, Salvatore
1958   *La mafia delle coppole storte*. Florence: Parenti.

261

Palidda, Rita
1977   "Potere locale e fascismo: i caratteri della lotta politica." In G.
        Barone et al., *Potere e società nella crisi dello stato liberale*. Catania:
        Pellicanolibri.
Palmeri, Nicolò
1826   *Cause e rimedi delle angustie dell'economia agraria in Sicilia*.
        Caltanissetta: Salvatore Sciascia, 1962.
Panorama (Milan)
1976   "Mafia: lo Stato si arrende." (January 27): 38–42.
Pantaleone, Michele
1962   *Mafia and Politics*. London: Chatto & Windus, 1966.
1969   *Antimafia: occasione mancata*. Turin: Einaudi.
Pantaleoni, Maffei
1891   "Delle regioni d'Italia in ordine alla loro ricchezza ed al loro carico
        tributario." *Giornale degli Economisti* 2 (January): 48–89.
Papa, Antonio
1969   "Guerra e terra 1915–1918." *Studi Storici* 10: 3–45.
Pareto, Vilfredo
1893   "The Parliamentary Regime in Italy." Reprinted in V. Pareto, *The
        Ruling Class in Italy before 1900*. New York: S. F. Vanni, 1950.
1894   "Cronaca: allora ed ora." *Giornale degli Economisti* 8 (January):
        92–98.
Passigli, Stefano
1963   "Italy." *Journal of Politics* 25 (April): 718–736.
Paternò Castello, Francesco
1848   *Saggio storico e politico sulla Sicilia del cominciamento del secolo
        XIX al 1830*. Palermo: Edizioni della Regione Siciliana, 1969.
Paton, W. A.
1898   *Picturesque Sicily*. New York: Harper & Brothers.
Pavone, Claudio
1964   *Amministrazione centrale e amministrazione periferica da Rattazzi a
        Ricasoli (1859–1866)*. Milan: Giuffrè.
Peattie, Lisa Redfield
1968   *The View from the Barrio*. Ann Arbor: University of Michigan Press.
Pecorini, Giorgio
1967   "Chiesa e mafia in Sicilia." *Comunità* 21 (January–April): 49–68.
Penniman, Howard R., ed.
1981   *Italy at the Polls, 1979: A Study of the Parliamentary Elections*.
        Washington: American Enterprise Institute for Public Policy Re-
        search.
Perez, Francesco
1862   *La centralizzazione e la libertà*. Palermo: Stabilimento Tipografico di

Bibliography

Francesco Lao.

Perez, Rita
1971   *Aspetti giuridici della pianificazione in agricoltura*. Milan: Giuffrè.

Peri, Illuminato
1965   *Il villanaggio in Sicilia*. Palermo: Manfredi.
1970   *Dal viceregno alla mafia*. Caltanissetta: Salvatore Sciascia.
1978   *Uomini città e campagne in Sicilia dall'XI al XIII Secolo*. Bari: Laterza.

Petacco, Arrigo
1975   *Il prefetto di ferro*. Verona: Mondadori.

Petino, Antonio
1946   *La questione del commercio dei grani in Sicilia nel Settecento*. Catania: Azienda Poligrafica Editorale.

Pigliaru, Antonio
1959   *La vendetta barbaricina come ordinamento giuridico*. Milan: Giuffrè.

Pignatone, Francesco
1973   "Autonomismo, povera fiaccola sotto il moggio. . . ." *Giornale di Sicilia* (August 26): 1.

Pinna, Luca
1971   *La famiglia esclusiva. Parentela & clientelismo in Sardegna*. Bari: Laterza.

Pitrè, Giuseppe
1870–   *Usi e costumi credenze e pregiudizi del popolo siciliano.* Vol. XV. Bo-
1913   logna: Forni, 1969.
1889   "L'omertà." *Archivio di Psichiatria, Scienza Penale & Antropologia Criminale per il servizio allo studio dell'uomo alienato e delinquato* 10: 1–7.
1913   *La famiglia, la casa la vita del popolo siciliano.* Vol. XXV. Bologna: Forni, 1969.

Pitt-Rivers, Julian
1954   *The People of the Sierra*. Chicago: University of Chicago Press, 1963.
1978   "The Value of Evidence." *Man* 13 (June): 319–322.

Pizzorno, Alessandro
1966   "Amoral Familism and Historical Marginality." Reprinted in M. Dogan and R. Rose, eds., *European Politics: A Reader*, Boston: Little, Brown & Co., 1971.

Podhoretz, Norman
1979   "How the North Was Won: Excerpt from Breaking Ranks: A Political Memoir." *New York Times Magazine* (September 30): 20.

Poma, R., and E. Perrone
1964   *Quelli della lupara*. Florence: Casini.

Pontieri, Ernesto
1943   *Il tramonto del baronaggio siciliano.* Florence: Sansoni.
1961   *Il riformismo borbonico nella Sicilia del sette e dell'ottocento: saggi storici.* Naples: Edizioni Scientifiche Italiane.
Popkin, Samuel L.
1979   *The Rational Peasant: The Political Economy of Rural Society in Vietnam.* Berkeley: University of California Press.
Pospisil, Leopold
1967   "Legal Levels and Multiplicity of Legal Systems in Human Societies." *Journal of Conflict Resolution* 11 (March): 2–26.
Powell, G. Bingham
1973   "Incremental Democratization: The British Reform Act of 1832." In Gabriel A. Almond, Scott C. Flanagan, and Robert J. Mundt, eds., *Crisis Choice and Change: Historical Studies of Political Development.* Boston: Little, Brown & Co.
Prestianni, Nunzio
1926   "Quotizzazioni del latifondo." *La Terra* (March 15): 145–148.
1956   "La cooperazione agricola in Sicilia." *Sicilia al Lavoro* (November–December): 104–112.
Puglia, Giuseppe Mario
1930   "Il 'mafioso' non è un associato per delinquere." *Scuola Positiva* 1: 452–457.
Pupillo-Barrese, Antonino
1903   *Gli usi civici in Sicilia. Ricerche di storia del diritto.* Catania: Giannotta.
Pyle, Ernie
1943   *Brave Men.* Westport, Conn.: Greenwood Press, 1974.
Ragionieri, Ernesto
1964   "Politica e amministrazione nello stato unitario." Reprinted in his *Politica e amministrazione nella storia dell'Italia Unita.* Bari: Laterza, 1967.
Rapoport, Anatol
1960   *Fights, Games and Debates.* Ann Arbor: University of Michigan Press, 1970.
Reece, J. E.
1973   "Fascism, the Mafia and the Emergence of Sicilian Separatism." *Journal of Modern History* 45: 261–276.
Regione Siciliana, Assessorato Agricoltura e Foreste
1952   *Relazione nell'applicazione della legge 27 dicembre 1950.* No. 104. *Riforma agraria in Sicilia.* Palermo (September).
Reid, Ed
1964   *Mafia.* New York: New American Library.

Bibliography

Renda, Francesco
1955   "Origini e caratteristiche del movimento contadino della Sicilia occidentale." *Movimento Operaio* 7 (May–August): 619–666.
1963   *L'emigrazione in Sicilia*. Palermo: Edizioni Sicilia al Lavoro.
1968   *Risorgimento e classi popolari in Sicilia 1820–1821*. Milan: Feltrinelli.
1972   *Socialisti e cattolici in Sicilia 1900–1904: le lotte agrarie*. Caltanissetta: Salvatore Sciascia.
1974   *Baroni e riformatori in Sicilia sotto il ministero Caracciolo (1786–1789)*. Messina: Editrice La Libra.

Renton, Bruce
1959   "Trouble in Sicily." *New Statesman* (June 6): 788.

Restifo, Giuseppe
1976   *Sottosviluppo e lotte popolari in Sicilia 1943–1974*. Cosenza: Pellegrini.

Ribolzi, Cesare
1962   "La legislazione italiana in tema di migrazioni interne." In AA.VV. *Immigrazione e industria*. Milan: Edizioni di Comunità.

Riccobono, S.
1918   "La colonizzazione interna della Sicilia e la viabilità rurale." *Atti, Congresso Agrario Siciliano*. Palermo (September).

Rizzi, Felice
1974   "From Socialist Unification to Socialist Scission 1966–69: Socialist Unification and the Italian Party System." *Government and Opposition*: 146–164.

Rocca, G.
1920   "L'occupazione delle terre incolte da parte delle associazioni di agricoltori." *Riforma Sociale* (May–June): 221–252.

Rochefort, Renée
1961   *Le travail en Sicile: Etude de géographie sociale*. Paris: Presses Universitaires de France.

Romano, Salvatore Francesco
1958   *La Sicilia nell'ultimo ventennio del secolo XIX*. Palermo: Industria Grafica Nazionale.

Romeo, Rosario
1950   *Il Risorgimento in Sicilia*. Bari: Laterza, 1973.
1955   "Momenti e problemi della restaurazione nel Regno delle Due Sicilie (1815–1820)." Reprinted in his *Mezzogiorno e Sicilia nel Risorgimento*. Naples: Edizioni Scientifiche Italiane, 1963.
1980   "Potere, classi sociali, sviluppo economico." In Nicola Tranfaglia, ed., *L'Italia Unita nella storiografia del secondo dopoguerra*. Milan: Feltrinelli.

Ronchey, Alberto
1980   "La 'Lottizzazione.' " *Corriere della Sera* (October 12): 3.
Rosselli, John
1956   *Lord William Bentinck & the British Occupation of Sicily.*
Cambridge: Cambridge University Press.
Rougemont, Denis de
1977   *L'avenir est notre affaire.* Paris: Stock.
Ruini, Meuccio
1922   "The Italian Cooperative Movement." *International Labour Review*
(January): 14–33.
Saba, Andrea, and Sebastiano Solano
1966   "Lineamenti dell'evoluzione demografica ed economica della Sicilia
dall'Unificazione ad oggi." In Paolo Sylos-Labini, ed., *Problemi
dell'economia siciliana.* Milan: Feltrinelli.
Sabbatucci, Giovanni
1974   *I combattenti nel primo dopoguerra.* Bari: Laterza.
Sabetti, Filippo
1977   "The Structure and Performance of Urban Service Systems in Italy."
In Vincent Ostrom and Frances Pennell Bish, eds., *Comparing
Urban Service Delivery Systems.* Vol. 12, Urban Affairs Annual
Reviews. Beverly Hills: Sage Publications.
1982   "The Making of Italy as an Experiment in Constitutional Choice."
Publius: The Journal of Federalism 12 (Summer): 65–84.
Sacco, Leonardo
1955   "Una fabbrica di voti." Reprinted in his *Sindaci e ministri.* Milan:
Edizioni di Comunità, 1965.
Sacks, Paul Martin
1976   *The Donegal Mafia. An Irish Political Machine.* New Haven: Yale
University Press.
Salomone-Marino, Salvatore
1897   *Costumi ed usanze dei contadini di Sicilia.* Palermo: Remo Sandron.
Salvadori, Massimo
1963   *Il Mito del buongoverno: la questione meridionale da Cavour a
Gramsci.* Turin: Einaudi.
Salvemini, Gaetano
1927   *The Fascist Dictatorship in Italy.* New York: Henry Holt & Co.
1931   "Mussolini's Battle of Wheat." *Political Science Quarterly* 46
(March): 25–40.
1936   *Under the Axe f Fascism.* London: Victor Gollancz.
1973   *Movimento socialista e questione meridionale.* Milan: Feltrinelli.
Salvemini, Gaetano, and Giorgio La Piana
1943   *What to Do with Italy.* London: Victor Gollancz.

Bibliography

Salvioli, Giuseppe
1902   "Il villanaggio in Sicilia e la sua abolizione." *Rivista Italiana di Sociologia* 6: 371–401.
1909   "L'origine degli usi civici in Sicilia." *Rivista Italiana di Sociologia* 13: 154–179.

Sansone, V., and G. Ingrascì
1950   *Sei anni di banditismo in Sicilia.* Milan: Le Edizioni Sociali.

Santacroce, D.
1907   "La genesi delle istituzioni municipali e provinciali in Sicilia." *Archivio Storico per la Sicilia Orientale* 4: 30–74.

Santamaria, Nicola
1881   *I feudi, il diritto feudale e la loro storia nell'Italia meridionale.* Naples: Ricc. Marghieri di Gius. Editore.

Sarti, Roland
1969   "Fascist Modernization in Italy: Traditional or Revolutionary?" *American Historical Review* 74 (April): 1029–1045.

Sartori, Giovanni
1962   "Constitutionalism: A Preliminary Discussion." *American Political Science Review* 56 (December): 853–864.
1971   "Proporzionalismo, frazionalismo, e crisi dei partiti." In Giovanni Sartori, ed., *Correnti, frazioni e fazioni nei partiti politici italiani.* Bologna: Il Mulino, 1973.

Sbragia, Alberta
1979   "Not All Roads Lead to Rome: Local Housing Policy in the Unitary Italian State." *British Journal of Political Science* 9: 315–339.

Scalini, Paolo
1976   *Impresa e contratti agrari. Proroga—equo canone—contratti dei salariati fissi in agricoltura.* Milan: Giuffrè.

Scarlata, Francesco
1904   *Le associazioni per delinquere. Studio sociale e giuridico.* Girgenti: Stab. Tip. Carini e Doma.

Scaturro, Girolamo
1956   "L'esperienza siciliana nella lotta per la terra." *Riforma Agraria* 4 (November): 436–440.

Schelling, Thomas C.
1960   *The Strategy of Conflict.* New York: Oxford University Press, 1966.

Schifani, Carmelo
1950   "Sulla cooperazione agricola in Sicilia nel periodo fra le due guerre e dopo la seconda guerra." *Rivista di Economia Agraria* (no. 1): 67–92.
1954   "Sullla cooperazione agraria in Sicilia." In AA.VV. *Scritti in onore di Enrico La Loggia.* Palermo: IRES.

Schmidt, Carl T.
1938   *The Plough and the Sword: Labor, Land and Property in Fascist Italy.* New York: Columbia University Press.
Schneider, Jane, and Peter Schneider
1976a   *Culture and Political Economy in Western Sicily.* New York: Academic Press.
1976b   "Economic Dependency and the Failure of Cooperatives in Western Sicily." In J. Nash, J. Dandler, and N. A. Hopkins, eds., *Popular Participation in Social Change.* Amsterdam: Mouton.
Schneider, Peter
1980   "Burgisi, civili e artigiani nell'Ottocento: ipotesi di ricerca." In *La cultura materiale in Sicilia.* Quaderni del Circolo Semiologico Siciliano 12–13. Palermo: STASS.
Sciascia, Leonardo
1969   *Salt in the Wound.* Trans. by Judith Green. New York: The Orion Press.
Scott, James C.
1976   *The Moral Economy of the Peasant: Rebellion and Subsistence in Southeast Asia.* New Haven: Yale University Press.
Segre, Dan V.
1980   *A Crisis of Identity: Israel and Zionism.* New York: Oxford University Press.
Selznick, Philip
1966   *TVA and the Grass Roots: A Study in the Sociology of Formal Organization.* New York: Harper & Row.
Sereni, Emilio
1947   *Il capitalismo nelle campagne (1860–1900).* Turin: Einaudi.
Sergio, Vincenzo E.
1777   *Lettera sulla pulizia delle publiche strade di Sicilia.* Reprinted in C. Trasselli, ed., *Un secolo di politica stradale in Sicilia.* Caltanissetta: Sciascia, 1962.
Serio, Ettore
1966a   "Burocrazia in Sicilia." *Nord e Sud* 13 (June): 51–57.
1966b   "Il PCI in Sicilia." *Nord e Sud* 13 (November): 78–87.
1967   "Partiti in Sicilia." *Nord e Sud* 14 (April): 27–35.
Serpieri, Arrigo
1930   *La guerra e le classi rurali italiane.* Bari: Laterza.
Servadio, Gaja
1976   *Mafioso: A History of the Mafia from Its Origins to the Present.* New York: Dell.
Servello, Giuseppe
1979   "Quella notte in cui sbarcarono in Sicilia." *Giornale di Sicilia*

Bibliography

Settimanale (July 22–28): 9.

Seton-Watson, Christopher
1967   *Italy from Liberalism to Fascism: 1870–1925*. London: Methuen.

Shearer, Eric B.
1968   "Italian Land Reform Reappraised." *Land Economics* 44 (February): 100–106.

Sleiter, Rossella
1974   "Confraternita: fratelli di soldi." *Il Mondo* (November 14): 12.

Smith, Dwight C., Jr.
1975   *The Mafia Mystique*. New York: Basic Books.

Snowden, Frank M.
1972   "On the Social Origins of Agrarian Fascism in Italy." *European Journal of Sociology* 13: 268–295.

Sonnino, Sidney
1877   *La Sicilia nel 1876. I contadini* (libro secondo). Florence: Vallecchi, 1925.

Sorge, Antonino
1910–   *Mussomeli. Dall'origine all'abolizione della feudalità*. 2 Vols.
1916   Catania: Giannotta.

Sorgi, Antonino
1959   "Quindici anni di lotte contadine." *Il Ponte* 15: 620–635.

Spreafico, Alberto
1965   *L'amministrazione e il cittadino*. Milan: Edizioni di Comunità.

Sproule-Jones, Mark H.
1972   "Strategic Tensions in Political Science: An Essay for Philomphalasceptics." *British Journal of Political Science* 2 (April): 173–191.

1978   "The Social Appropriateness of Water Quality Management for the Lower Fraser River." *Canadian Public Administration* 21 (Summer): 176–194.

1983   "Institutions, Constitutions and Public Policies: A Public Choice Overview." In Michael M. Atkinson and M. A. Chandler, eds., *Canadian Public Policy: A Comparative Approach*. Toronto: University of Toronto Press.

Starrabba, Raffaele
1879   "Capitoli della Terra di S. Michele (1534)." *Archivio Storico Siciliano* 4: 347–364.

Sturzo, Luigi
1901   "Nord e Sud: Decentramento e federalismo." *Il Sole del Mezzogiorno* (March 31–April 1): 1.

1926   *Italy and Fascismo*. New York: Harcourt, Brace & Co.

1938   *Church and State*. Notre Dame: University of Notre Dame Press,

1962.

Sylos-Labini, Paolo
1964   "Precarious Employment in Sicily." *International Labour Review* 89: 268–285.

Tarrow, Sidney G.
1967   *Peasant Communism in Southern Italy.* New Haven: Yale University Press.
1974   "Local Constraints on Regional Reform: A Comparison of Italy and France." *Comparative Politics* 7 (October): 1–35.
1977a   *Between Center and Periphery: Grassroots Politicians in Italy and France.* New Haven: Yale University Press.
1977b   "The Italian Party System: Between Crisis and Transition." *American Journal of Political Science* 21 (May): 193–223.

Testa, Giuseppe
1973   *Il Principato di Campofranco nel feudo 'Fontana di li Rosi.'* Agrigento: Tipografia Primavera.

Thomson, James T.
1973   *Trouble Case Investigation of a Problem in Nigerian Rural Modernization: Forest Conservation.* Studies in Political Theory and Policy Analysis, Department of Political Science. Bloomington: Indiana University.
1976   "Law, Legal Process and Development at the Local Level in Hausa-Speaking Niger: A Trouble Case Analysis of Rural Institutional Inertia." Ph.D. dissertation. Bloomington: Indiana University.

Tiebout, Charles M.
1956   "A Pure Theory of Local Expenditures." *Journal of Political Economy* 66 (October): 416–424.

Tilly, Charles
1964   *The Vendée.* Cambridge: Harvard University Press, 1968.
1974   "Forward" to Anton Blok, *The Mafia of a Sicilian Village 1860–1960.* New York: Harper & Row.

Titone, Virgilio
1955   *La Sicilia dalla dominazione spagnola all'Unità d'Italia.* Bologna: Zanichelli.
1961   *Origini della questione meridionale. Riveli e platee del Regno di Sicilia.* Milan: Feltrinelli.
1964   *Storia Mafia e Costume in Sicilia.* Milan: Edizioni del Milione.

Tocqueville, Alexis de
1827   "Voyage en Sicile (1826–1827)." In J. P. Mayer, ed., *Voyages en Sicile et aux Etats-Unis.* Paris: Gallimard, 1957.
1835 & *Democracy in America.* 2 Vols. Ed. by Phillips Bradley. New York:
1840   A. A. Knopf, 1955.

1848   *Recollections.* Ed. by J. P. Mayer and A. P. Kerr. New York: Doubleday.
1856   *The Old Regime and the French Revolution.* New York: Doubleday Anchor Books.

Tomasi di Lampedusa, Giuseppe
1958   *Il Gattopardo.* Milan: Feltrinelli.

Tramontana, V.
n.d.   *I contratti e la riforma agraria. Legislazione completa della regione siciliana coordinata con le leggi statali in vigore al 15 luglio 1951.* Caltanissetta: Salvatore Sciascia.

Tricoli, Giuseppe
1966   *La deputazione degli Stati e la crisi del baronaggio siciliano.* Palermo: Flaccovio.

Tullock, Gordon
1967   "The Welfare Costs of Tariffs, Monopolies and Theft." *Western Economic Journal* 5 (June): 224–232.

Ulisse
1969   "The mafia." 22 (April).

Vanzetti, Carlo
1948   "La riforma fondiaria nel pensiero degli economisti agrari italiani." *Rivista di Diritto Agrario* 27 (July–December): 154–162.

Verdirame, Gaetano
1904a   "Le istituzioni sociali e politiche di alcuni municipi della Sicilia orientale nei secoli XVI, XVII, XVIII: Introduzione." *Archivo Storico per la Sicilia Orientale* 1: 105–118.
1904b   "Le istituzioni sociali e politiche di alcuni municipi della Sicilia orientale nei secoli XVI, XVII, XVIII: l'ambiente sociale ed economico." *Archivio Storico per la Sicilia Orientale* 2: 313–333.
1905   "Le istituzioni sociali e politiche di alcuni municipi della Sicilia orientale nei secoli XVI, XVII, XVIII: Imposte e tasse." *Archivo Storico per la Sicilia Orientale* 2: 19–60.
1905b   "Le istituzioni sociali e politiche di alcuni municipi della Sicilia orientale nei secoli XVI, XVII, XVIII: Continuazione v. fasc. prec." *Archivio Storico per la Sicilia Orientale* 2: 121–134.
1906   "Le istituzioni sociali e politiche di alcuni municipi della Sicilia orientale nei secoli XVI, XVII, XVIII: Appendice." *Archivio Storico per la Sicilia Orientale* 3: 70–80.

Verga, Giuseppe
1881   "Malaria." Reprinted in his *The She-Wolf and Other Stories.* Berkeley: University of California Press, 1973.

Vértiz, Claudio
1980   *The Centralist Tradition of Latin America.* Princeton: Princeton Uni-

versity Press.

Vetri, Giuseppe
1976a "Le origini del fascismo in Sicilia (I)." *Nuovi Quaderni del Meridione* 14 (January–March): 33–81.
1976b "Le origini del fascismo in Sicilia (II)." *Nuovi Quaderni del Meridione* 14 (July–September): 295–315.

Vile, Maurice J. C.
1967 *Constitutionalism and the Separation of Powers.* Oxford: Clarendon Press.

Villari, Pasquale
1878 "La Mafia." In Bruno Caizzi, ed., *Nuova antologia della Questione Meridionale.* Milan: Edizioni di Comunità, 1970.

Waern, Cecilia
1910 *Mediaeval Sicily: Aspects of Life and Art in the Middle Ages.* London: Duckworth.

Webster, Richard A.
1960 *The Cross and the Fasces. Christian Democracy and Fascism in Italy.* Stanford: Stanford University Press.

Whitaker, Gordon P.
1978 "Citizen Participation in the Delivery of Human Services." Paper presented at the Conference on Participation and Politics, Tutzing Akademie für Politische Bildung, Tutzing, Bavaria (June).

White, Caroline
1980 *Patrons and Partisans. A Study of Politics in Two Southern Italian Comuni.* Cambridge: Cambridge University Press.

Wildavsky, Aaron
1976 "A Bias Toward Federalism." *Publius: The Journal of Federalism* 6 (Spring): 95–120.

Wittfogel, Karl A.
1957 *Oriental Despotism: A Comparative Study of Total Power.* New Haven: Yale University Press.

Womack, John, Jr.
1968 *Zapata and the Mexican Revolution.* New York: Random House.

Wylie, Laurence
1964 *Village in the Vaucluse.* New York: Harper Colophon Books.

Zariski, Raphael
1965 "Intra-party Conflict in a Dominant Party: The Experience of Italian Christian Democracy." *Journal of Politics* 27: 3–34.

Ziino, Nunzio
1911 *Latifondo e latifondismo. Studio di economia rurale.* Palermo: Orazio Fiorentina.

Bibliography

Zimmerman, Carle C.
1955   "American Roots in an Italian Village." *Genus* 11: 78–179.
Zincone, Giovanna, ed.
1980   "Il vizio d'origine." *Biblioteca della Libertà* 17 (April–September): 5–216.
Zingarelli, Nicola
1962   *Vocabolario della lingua italiana.* Novissima edizione (VIII). Bologna: Zanichelli.
Zuckerman, Alan S.
1979   *The Politics of Faction: Christian Democratic Rule in Italy.* New Haven: Yale University Press.

Note on Other Principal Sources and Documents

Archival documents, newspaper reports of the time, and villagers were other principal sources for the evidentiary base of the study. Because these papers and people cannot, for obvious reasons, be fully cited or identified, I shall describe them generically and chronologically here.

The largest bits and pieces of documentary evidence for village life under baronial jurisdiction have come from the Archivio di Stato di Palermo. The chief series reviewed there were: (1) Pronotaro del Regno: Processi di investitura; (2) Tribunale Reale Patrimonio; and (3) Deputazione del Regno: Riveli. The files of the Prefettura/Gabinetto (buste 35 and 36, cat. 16 and cat. 25, respectively) also have information about sharecroppers' associations and rural conditions in Camporano and neighboring towns between 1875 and 1876. Descendants of the first Baron of Mogata graciously allowed me to consult their papers, and of these about one hundred original *enfiteusi* contracts drawn up between 1770 and 1789 were especially helpful. The reconstruction of early village life was also helped by bits and pieces of information gleaned from a history of Camporano published in 1900, which utilized baronial papers apparently no longer available. This town history, which I usually found accurate, is mentioned as a source in other parts of the book.

The largest body of documentary evidence about village life in the nineteenth century has come from the Archivio di Stato di "Mozarra." The major series analyzed there were: (1) Prefettura/Sezione Amministrativa; and (2) Pubblica Sicurezza. The Prefettura/Sezione Amministrativa has not only the usual material about the Camporano commune that one can expect about the organization and conduct of communal government in a bureaucratic administration, but also material on: the common property question (*usi civici*) before and after the In-

273

tendancy decision of 1843; *affari speciali* such as the water springs and sheep-walk questions; the wheat bank (*Monte frumentario*); and church-sponsored mutual-aid societies and the like, catalogued under Affari speciali delle Opere Pie. The Pubblica Sicurezza series have information on peace and security in the Camporano countryside, church-sponsored associations monitored by the police, especially between 1894 and 1898, and criminal associations in and around Camporano.

I have drawn significant blocks of information about village life and events before and after the year 1900 from other archival sources as well.

The Archivo Centrale dello Stato in Rome has at least two important documentary sources for Camporano issues. These are the Archivi Parlamentari and the Ministero dell'Interno. The Archivi Parlamentari contain minutes of the 1875–1876 and the 1884–1885 parliamentary commissions, which helped to clarify and reconstruct the Camporano land question in the 1870s and the 1880s and the motives of people involved in it, as well as records of both the Commissariato Civile per la Sicilia 1896–1897 (serie 2) and the Inchiesta parlamentare sulla guerra 1915–1918, which in turn helped to shed light on Camporano communal and agricultural affairs of those years. The principal series reviewed in the Ministero dell'Interno, and found helpful, were: (1) the semiannual electoral reports of the Mozarra prefect between 1883–1888; (2) the files of the Commissariato Civile per la Sicilia 1896–1897 (serie 3) for material on the majority and minority coalitions that dominated Camporano communal politics until the 1890s; and (3) the police and prefectoral reports on public order (Direzione Generale di Pubblica Sicurezza) between 1909 and 1924. These latter reports included accounts of the land invasions and seizures in the Camporano area between 1919 and 1920 which, when I combined with evidence of land dispute and civil law proceedings before the Camporano district judge of those years (Pretura, Sezione Fasc. Cause Civili), proved especially valuable in reconstructing local events, social movements, and the motives of people involved in them. I had access to Pretura documents and proceedings for the entire Fascist period and for the post-1944 land and other civil law questions.

The Camporano church does not have an archive as such, but its documents on the organization and conduct of confraternities during the course of the nineteenth century were a good starting point for the search in state archives of government reports on them, particularly after 1860. The Cancelleria del Tribunale Civile e Penale di "Mozarra" has statutes and annual reports of Camporano voluntary undertakings, ranging from the *Cassa rurale s. Giuseppe* of 1898 to agricultural cooperatives established as late as 1975. All these papers contained useful information and oriented my search for the reasons behind them in and outside of state archives.

Most post-1900 communal papers that are not otherwise available in state ar-

chives are at the Camporano *comune*. I relied on the register of communal deliberations of both the town council and the *giunta* to reconstruct communal issues
and problems and the people behind them between 1906 and 1977. Most of the
local statistical data, including electoral results after 1946, come from the
comune. Cadastral papers there of those entitled to received Mogata lots, and
especially two lists (one dated 20.11.1961, the other 20.6.1964), together with
pretura papers of the period, yielded information about the implementation and
impact of the mafia-sponsored land reform of 1950.

Post-1944 Camporano issues—from the mafia-controlled communal government to the struggle for the control of Mogata, from mayoral philanthropy to the
antimafia war of the 1960s—invariably concerned the regional government and
assembly. The *Gazzetta Ufficiale* and the *Resoconti Parlamentari*, particularly
between 1949 and 1956, and in 1970, contain useful information about
Camporano issues as does the not-so-secret report on Camporano communal authority prepared by two regional inspectors in 1964.

The public documents of the recent Commissione Parlamentare d'Inchiesta
sul Fenomeno della Mafia in Sicilia, together with accessible records of trial
proceedings from 1903 on, papers of the Mori "struggle against the mafia," and
background material prepared by the provincial police (*questura*) for the
antimafia war of the late 1960s, furnished evidence that has helped to piece together biographies of local mafiosi and their activities. Useful though these
sources were, they would be even more incomplete without newspaper accounts
and villagers' recollections.

Newspaper accounts mentioned or referred to, particularly from chapter 6 on,
derive from many sources. Since Sicilian newspapers have been seldom utilized, it may also be of service to others to indicate which newspapers were found
useful. The year or years in bracket denote when they carried local stories. The
Giornale di Sicilia and *L'Ora* carried many accounts almost year by year and for
this reason I am listing them for the entire span of time I combed them:

Il Messaggiere (1871)
L'Unione (1875)
Il Costituzionale (1880)
Il Progresso (1880)
Il Centro (1886)
Il Piccolo Corriere della Provincia (1887)
La Sveglia (1889)
Il Nuovo Giornale della Provincia (1890)
L'Unione (nuova serie) (1891)
Il Dovere (1891)
Giornale del Popolo (1892)
Gazzetta "Mozarrese" (1892–1894)

Vita Nuova (1893)
La Monarchia (1895)
L'Independente (1895)
Il Popolo "Mozarrese" (1896)
La Gallina di Faraone (1898)
L'Aurora (1898–1919)
L'Eco del Popolo (1900)
L'Ora (1900–1970)
Giornale di Sicilia (1901–1978)
Il Rinnovamento (1901)
Il Sole del Mezzogiorno (1901–1903)
La Battaglia (socialista) (1901)

La Bilancia (1901–1902)
La Croce di Costantino (1903)
I Cavallacci (1915)
Il Cittadino (1915)
La Sicilia Centrale (1919)
La Lista Democratica (1919)
Battaglie Popolari (1920–1921)
Il Popolo (1920–1923)
Battaglie Democratiche (1921)
Eccolo Quà (1921)
Il Commercio (1921, 1926)
La Sicilia Fascista (1923–1926)
La Vespa (1924)

La Vittoria (1925–1927)
Battaglie Fasciste (1926–1930)
La Provincia (1926)
La Voce Comunista (1944)
La Voce Socialista (1944)
L'Indipendente (1944)
Il Siciliano Nuovo (1950)
L'Eco della Democrazia (1951)
La Gazzetta del Mattino (1952)
Il Grido di Sicilia (1953–1957)
Catania Espresso (1974)
Il Domani (1977)

Oral trouble cases have been used as evidentiary sources for about seventy years of local development. Who were my informants? What were their social, economic, and political positions? As mentioned in chapter 1, on my first trip to the village I was helped by an unemployed agricultural laborer. As I discovered, he was a staunch Communist with a rich experience in the postwar land struggles. Thus the first impression that villagers had of me as the two of us arrived together was that I was working for some Left cause. This view was further strengthened when, with the help of some other local workers and Socialists, I found lodging in the house of an old sharecropper, a veteran of World War I and a Socialist. But the fortuitous encounter with the Demochristian mayor, who was also of somewhat low peasant origin, in the streets of Palermo helped to mitigate this view. In the end, I came to be accepted, however reluctantly, by people of all social, economic, and political positions. Almost all the villagers cooperated with me or at least agreed to instruct me in their ways, past and present. In fact, accounts of mafia, Demochristian, and Left activities could not have been prepared without the help of many people who took part in them. For all these reasons, I had no particular group of informants for all the trouble cases as is often so in sociological and anthropological research.

How, then, did this evidentiary base enter my analysis? It did so in several ways. First, I used documentary evidence to prepare my own accounts of village events and developments. Second, having gleaned newspapers and archival sources to chart and survey events, I used the list of events (compiled also with the help of the town history written in 1900) to search other public papers for additional information concerning each event on the list. Almost all the events or trouble cases discussed in chapters 3, 4, and 5 emerged by using these two methods. Starting with chapter 6, I used documentary evidence to complement and augment accounts from villagers in two ways. First, I used information gleaned from public papers and newspaper accounts to search and direct inquiry of trouble cases among villagers. Second, having gleaned newspapers and archival sources to chart and survey events, I then turned to this information, whenever possible, to resolve puzzles and minimize inconsistencies in villagers' recollections. Finally, in addition to accounts of trouble cases, local residents were helpful in yet another way—by directing my attention to documentary sources that I did not know or would not otherwise have examined. It was, for example, the communal secretary who suggested, and facilitated access to, the *Pretura* archive, which I had assumed to be restricted and beyond reach. The extent to which I succeeded in systematically studying local events and issues discussed in chapters 6, 7, 8, and 9 owes much to a combination of these strategies of research.

Thus to a question, say, Where did the history of the clergy, the church-sponsored mutual-aid societies, the mafia, the local Christian Democracy, and the Left come from? this Note, together with the relevant items on the list of works cited, suggests the answer.

Index

Administration, 105; baronial, 29, 30, 33–37, 39, 40, 46, 223; decentralized, 28; viceregal, 30–32, 40, 42

Aggression and massacre incident, 151–152, 181

Agrarian associations, 86–88

Agrarian reform, 4

Agricultural activity, 17, 230; baron's control of, 47–48; fascists and, 136–138; land reform and, 178–179; modern economy and, 204–208; national jurisdiction and, 80–82; organization of fief and, 38–39; protection and, 115; Saint Joseph cooperative and, 115–117

Agricultural laborers, 82

Albano, Len, 144, 145

Albano, Salvatore, 166, 169, 180, 194, 195, 199, 200, 201, 212; election of 1952 and, 167; land invasion and, 172; land reform and, 171, 176; as mayor, 218

Aldisio, Salvatore, 157, 186, 187

Alessi, Giuseppe, 186, 187

Allied Military Government (AMGOT), 145, 147. *See also* World War II

Alois, Mansueto, 135–136, 143, 144

Alongi, Giuseppe, 138

Altura, Emanuele, 163–164, 187, 189, 190

Animals: mafia and army, 121–122; tax on (1818), 57

Antimafia campaigns: commission (1963) for, 210–217; in 1874, 10; failure of, 12; of fascists, 135–136, 138; villagers and, 18. *See also* Mafia

Anzalo estate, 129, 136; Ardena and, 130; invasion of, 130–132

Arabs, 28, 37

Ardena family, 141, 154

Ardena, Father Gaetano (brother of Mariano), 23, 163, 190; death of, 191; Demochristian party and, 148; as mayor, 134–135; Popular Party and, 124; Veterans Union and, 128; villagers and, 180

Ardena group: Demochristians and, 162, 164, 190; deputies and, 187; land reform and, 171

Ardena, Mariano, 20, 155, 177, 187, 214; aggression and massacre incident and, 151–152, 181; Allied invasion and, 140, 143–145; Anzalo *gabella* of, 130; army provisions and, 121–122; bandits and, 114; biographical sketch of, 101–102; black market and Vallera and, 146; charges against (1925), 135–136; collective lease and, 116, 128; death of, 190; Demochristians and, 186, 187, 189–190; exempted from war (WWI), 123; family compacts and, 153, 154; independence and, 147; invasion of Anzalo estate and, 131–132; as leader of mafia, 105,

279

Cipolla, Nicola, 216
Circle of the Holy Family confraternity, 92, 98
Clergy. *See* Priests
Clientelism, 209, 235, 237
Climate, 21
Colajanni, Napoleone, 10, 217, 237, 239
Collective action, 4, 13, 15, 84, 226. *See also* Voluntary collective action
Collective inaction, 143–145
Colonization of interior, 35
Combatants Landholding Society, 129, 130, 132, 136–137
Common property: barons and, 50–52; roads and, 58–59; rural development and, 228–231; usufruct rights and, 38–39; water and, 59–61. *See also* Property rights
Commons, John R., 109
Communal activities, 17; common concerns and, 54–55; education and, 61; public officials and, 56–57; roads and, 58–59; taxation and, 57–58; water and, 59–61
Communal deliberations, 54
Communal government; Camporano as smallest unit of, 13; center-periphery relations and, 117–119; election of 1946 and, 159–160; elections from 1950s to 1970s and, 199–201, 217; fascists and, 133–135; mafia and, 117–119, 167–169; structure of, 22, 78–80
Communal officials, 117, 198; appointment of, 55, 56, 57; common property and, 52; communal politics and, 78–80; compensatory laws and, 51; land tax and, 58. *See also* Public officials
Communal papers, 202
Communal services, 167–169, 201–204

Communist (PCI) party, 141, 166, 172, 188, 192, 199, 200, 201, 217; bloc with PSI and, 148–149; election of 1978 and, 218–219; independentists and, 147; mafia and, 209–210. *See also* Popular Front (PCI-PSI bloc)
Community organizations, mafia and, 111, 112, 115–117, 126
Compensation laws, 51–52
Concordia discors, 126–133, 140–141
Confraternities, 87, 97, 98; as mutual-aid societies, 88–92
Congress Movement, 96, 101
Congress of Vienna, 47
Consalvo, Diego, 120, 123, 125, 129, 134, 135
Conscription, 72, 83, 119, 156; draft dodgers and, 62–63; nation-state and, 62; peasants and, 120; rural labor contracts (1861) and, 54; World War I and, 120
Constitution, 42; Anglo-Sicilian, 46; barons and, 45, 47; choice and, 236–237; experiment of 1812 and, 223–224; of fiefs, 33, 34, 35; Mogata fief, 37–40; revolt of 1860 and, 77
Cooperative of War Veterans, 171, 172, 177, 191
Copyhold contracts, 39, 205
Corona, Ciro, 173, 174
Corona family, 67
Cortale, Liborio, 120, 123, 125, 134
Council of chiefs, 107–108
Court of the Royal Patrimony, 30–31, 32, 33, 36
Credit societies, 97. *See also* Saint Joseph cooperative credit union (rural bank)

Land tax, 58
Language: in Camporano, 13, 20; mafia and, 104; of officialdom, 105, 106; peasants and Italian, 61; term mafia and, 9
La Palombara, Joseph, 184, 188
Latin America, 226, 230
Laws, 66; arbitrary, 95; colonization, 170; Falcioni, 131; of inheritance, 35–36, 49; Segni, 170, 171, 173; on usufruct rights, 51; Visocchi, 125, 130
Leasehold contracts, barons and, 36
Leases: baronial estates and, 36, 81; collective, 128; on Mogata after 1860, 52–53; Saint Joseph cooperative and, 115–116, 128
Left: aggression and massacre incident and, 151–152, 181; communal services and, 168; DC coalition with, 161–162; dissident, 153; election of 1946 and, 159–160; election of 1948 and, 165; election of 1952 and, 167; factionalism in, 189; land struggle and, 170–179; mafia and, 209–210, 212; membership policy and, 155; opening to, 197, 199, 200, 206, 209, 217; peasants and literature of, 11; villagers and, 153–154. *See also* Communist (PCI) party; Left dual family compact; Popular Front (PCI-PSI bloc); Socialist (PSI) party
Left dual family compact: aggression and massacre incident and, 151–152, 181; breakdown of consensus and, 153–155; election of 1952 and, 167; election of 1946 and, 159–160; emigration and, 194–196; interpersonal relationships and, 180–181; land struggle and, 169–179; loss of raison d'être

by, 192–194; national and regional politics and, 166–167; villagers and, 155–156, 180–181, 182, 185, 211. *See also* Left
Legal order, 7
Leo XIII, 96, 98, 101, 103
Liberalism, 96, 99, 101
Liberties of Sicily, 41, 43, 45
Lipset, Seymour M., 225
Literacy rate, 61
Llewellyn, K. N., 15, 104
The Logic of Collective Action (Olson), 87
Lombardy, 10
Lo Preato, Joseph, 207
Lozano, Nunzio, 147–148, 164, 187–188, 216

Mafia: aggression and massacre incident and, 151–152, 181; agricultural activities and, 178–179; Allied invasion and, 140, 143–145; army provisional commission and, 121–122; authority pattern and, 104–110; breakdown of consensus about, 122–126; collapse of, 185–186; commission to depose, 210–217; communal government and, 117–119, 167–169; community organizations and, 111, 112, 115–117, 126; cooperative agreements and, 110, 111, 112–119, 126–133; council of chiefs and, 107–108; credit society and, 115–117; Demochristians and, 155, 182, 186–192, 199, 208–217; emigration and, 194–196; ethnic, 232–233; exclusion rule and, 153; fascist war against, 135–136, 138; formation of regime of, 104–110; iron circle and, 110; land invasions and, 172–174; land question and,

Movement for Sicilian Independence (MIS), 146–147, 148, 161
Musical band, 93
Mussolini, Benito, 133, 134–135, 138, 145

National Association of Combatants (ANC), 125–126, 127, 170
National government: agricultural activity and, 80–82; Camporanesi and, 61–63, 75; communal activity and, 78–80; conscription and, 62; impeding of collective action by, 93–94; Left and, 166–167; mafia and, 162–166; regional government and, 184, 185, 186, 187, 196, 197, 210, 238, 239, 240. See also Central government; Regional government.
National Institute of Agricultural Economics (INEA), 174
Nationalism, 123
Neapolitan government, 3; armed reaction to, 68–77; centralized administration and, 5; common property rights and, 51; eighteenth century Sicily and, 29–37; Ferdinand and, 44–47; French political aspects of, 43–45; oppression and, 42; Sicilian fiefs and, 49
Nenni, Pietro, 192
New England, 224
Newspapers, 16, 24; research and, 275
Nicosia, Giacomo, 23, 99
Normans, 28, 33, 37
North, Douglass C., 64
Novara, Franco, 102, 155, 195, 211; Allied invasion and, 143–144; black market and Ardena and, 146; communal functions (1943) and, 145; Demochristian party and,

148–149, 159, 160, 162, 186, 187, 189, 190–191; election of 1947 and, 164; exile and, 213, 214; massacre incident and, 152; Mogata and, 177, 193; Vallera and, 146, 151, 180; villagers and, 180

Officials. See Communal officials; Public officials
Olson, Mancur, 7, 87
Omertà, 114, 153; defined, 107; mafia soldiers and, 108
Organization. See Social organization
Orlando, Vittorio Emanuele, 237
Ostrom, Elinor, 94
Ostrom, Vincent, 7
Our Lady of Sorrows confraternity, 88, 91
Outlaw regime. See Mafia
Outlaw societies, 3–4, 11, 12; mafia in Camporano and, 95–96
Overseer (steward), 80, 137, 150; agrarian associations and, 87; on fief, 39

Pact of the Land, 33, 34, 37
Pafundi, Senator, antimafia commission and, 210
Palermo, 36, 146; revolts and, 72, 73, 74, 76
Pantano, Edoardo, 239
Paraspolari. See Peasants
Parliament, 38, 229; barons and, 32, 33; branches of, 29–30; defining of fiefs and, 49; Ferdinand and barons and, 45–47; reconstructed, 73; revolt of 1848 and, 76; Sicilian abolished (1816), 47, 69; viceregal administration and, 30, 31
Party lists (panachage), 159–160, 167
Paton, W. A., 9

Public officials (*continued*)
regal, 31; voluntary undertakings
and, 8. *See also* Communal officials
Public security, 83–84, 104, 113–
115, 156–158
Public services, 167–169, 201–204
Pyle, Ernie, 142, 143

Rational Peasant (Popkin), 234
Reform, 4; barons and, 42–43; Bourbon officials and, 43–45; church
and social, 96, 97; constitutional
(1813–1814), 46–47. *See also* Land
reform
Regional Association of Agricultural
Cooperatives (ARCA), 171
Regional government, 147; antimafia
campaign and, 213; communal
services and, 168; Demochristians
and, 160–162; Left and, 166–167;
mafia and, 162–166; national government and, 184, 185, 186, 187,
196, 197, 210, 238, 239, 240. *See
also* Central government; National
government
Regional Union of Agricultural
Cooperatives (USCA), 171–172
Religion, 23. *See also* Church; Priests
Rentiers (*gabelloti*), 67, 68, 75, 115,
116, 118; barons and, 35, 36; land
leases and, 53, 81; public security
and, 83; quick profits and, 53
Rents, 137, 149–150, 177; of
Camporano houses, 25; mafia col-
lection of, 150
Rent seeking, 32
Rerum Novarum (encyclical), 96
Research for study, 15–18, 221–222
Restivo, Franco, 186, 187
Revenues, 75; communal taxation
(1818–1885) and, 57–58. *See also*
Taxes

Revolt, 224; background on, 69–71;
of 1820, 50, 71–73; of 1848, 52,
73–76; of 1860, 76–77
Riera, Efisio, 97, 98, 102
Riera, Giuseppe, 91, 92, 97–98,
101, 102, 103, 128
Riera, Isidoro, 124, 128, 143
Riera, Rosalia (Mariano Ardena's
mother), 102
The Rise of the Western World (North
and Thomas), 64
Risorgimento. *See* Unification
Roads, 19, 58–59, 118, 168
Roger, Norman Count, 33
Romeo, Rosario, 230
Rosa, Alberto Asor, 57
Rosselli, John, 45
Rules of conduct (village), 106–107,
114, 127, 1553
Rural Sector, development and,
228–231

Safavia, Paolino, 124, 132, 134
Saint Joseph cooperative credit union
(rural bank), 98–99, 115–117,
120, 127, 136
Sala, Calogero, 202, 203, 217
Salvemini, Gaetano, 134, 135
Savoy rule, 29, 49, 55
Scelba, Mario, 186, 187
Schelling, Thomas C., 128
Schools, 25–26, 61. *See also*
Education
Scott, James C., 234
Security. *See* Public security
Self-government, 63, 97, 110, 231,
238, 239, 240; absence of local,
139; Allied invasion and, 146–149;
mafia as form of, 95–96, 106, 111;
party politics and, 234–238; peas-
ants and artisans and, 7
Self-help, criminal associations and,

Tocqueville, Alexis de, 3, 5, 168, 224, 226
Trading company concept, 141–142, 209, 213; mafia and, 167–169
Tramontana, V., 175
Transportation, 24
Trouble cases, 15, 18, 112, 221, 222

Udo, Antonio (fourth baron of Mogata), 81; in House of Lords, 75; revolt of 1848 and, 52, 76
Udo, Baron Antonio (founder, d.1780), 19, 20, 37, 39
Udo, Epifanio (third baron of Mogata), 50–51, 52, 57, 81; revolt of 1820 and, 72, 73
Udo family, 57, 59, 79
Udo, Filadelfio (second baron of Mogata), 37, 38; agricultural activities and, 39; local taxes and, 40; nonparliamentary taxation and, 45
Udo, Liborio (fifth baron of Mogata), 50; election of 1881 and, 79; land leases and, 52–53; metateria arrangements and, 54; property rights and, 88; sharecroppers and, 81; water and, 60
Under the Axe of Fascism (Salvemini), 112
Unification, 48, 55, 63, 66, 71, 224–225, 229–230, 231, 238
Urban sector, 208, 209, 239
Uria, Rosolino, 143, 191, 212, 213–214
Usufruct rights, 49; agricultural laborers and, 82; common property resources and, 38–39, 229; loss of, 51–52, 70, 89; water and, 59

Valle, Pietro, 23, 191
Vallera, Carlo, 144, 169, 179, 180, 195, 199, 200, 212; aggression and

massacre incident and, 152; communal functions (1943) and, 145; Communist party list and, 201; election of 1947 and, 164; family compacts and, 153; land invasion and, 172, 173–174; land reform and, 150–151, 170, 171, 176, 177; the Left bloc and, 159, 160, 166–167, 190; Left compact and, 192, 193–194, 214; the Left in 1944 and, 148–149, 154; mafiosi and, 155–156; Novara and, 146; parliamentary commission and, 216
Vallera, Ciro, 61, 88
Vallera family, 52, 67, 79, 100, 118, 154; Left and, 141
Vallera, Francesco, 60
Vallera, Nicola, 200, 211, 212
Vallera, Salvatore, 118–119, 122
Vallera, Vincenzo (overseer of Mogata in 1860s), 53, 57, 68, 75, 77, 131
Ventura, Lino, 217–218
Vértiz, Claudio, 226
Veterans Landholding Society, 128, 131, 132, 136, 171
Veterans Union (Unione Reduci), 124, 125, 127, 128
Viceregal administration, 30–32, 40, 42
Victor Emmanuel II, 77
Village charters, 34
Villagers: Allied landing and, 140, 142–145, 146; bandits and, 63; baron and, 39–40; carabinieri and, 62; church sponsored associations and, 89–92, 97, 101; collective efforts and, 84; common property rights and, 50–52; communal government and, 198, 200; criminal associations and, 8; dual political compacts and, 155–156, 180–181,